THE CAMBRIDGE COMPANION TO

BERKELEY

Each volume in this series of companions to major philosophers contains specially commissioned essays by an international team of scholars, together with a substantial bibliography, and will serve as a reference work for students and nonspecialists. One aim of the series is to dispel the intimidation such readers often feel when faced with the work of a difficult and challenging thinker.

George Berkeley is one of the greatest and most influential philosophers of the early modern period. In defending the immaterialism for which he is most famous, he redirected modern thinking about the nature of objectivity and the mind's capacity to come to terms with it. Along the way, he made striking and influential proposals concerning the psychology of the senses, the workings of language, the aim of science, and the foundations of mathematics. In this *Companion* volume, a team of distinguished authors examines not only Berkeley's best-known achievements, but his writings on economics and development, his neglected contributions to moral and political philosophy, and his defense of religious commitment and religious life. The volume places Berkeley in the context of the many social and intellectual traditions – philosophical, scientific, ethical, and religious – to which he fashioned a distinctive response.

OTHER VOLUMES IN THE SERIES OF CAMBRIDGE COMPANIONS:

AQUINAS *Edited by* NORMAN KRETZMANN *and* ELEONORE STUMP
HANNAH ARENDT *Edited by* DANA VILLA
ARISTOTLE *Edited by* JONATHAN BARNES
AUGUSTINE *Edited by* ELEONORE STUMP *and* NORMAN KRETZMANN
BACON *Edited by* MARKKU PELTONEN
DESCARTES *Edited by* JOHN COTTINGHAM
DUNS SCOTUS *Edited by* THOMAS WILLIAMS
EARLY GREEK PHILOSOPHY *Edited by* A. A. LONG
FEMINISM IN PHILOSOPHY *Edited by* MIRANDA FRICKER *and* JENNIFER HORNSBY
FOUCAULT *Edited by* GARY GUTTING
FREUD *Edited by* JEROME NEU
GADAMER *Edited by* ROBERT J. DOSTAL
GALILEO *Edited by* PETER MACHAMER
GERMAN IDEALISM *Edited by* KARL AMERIKS
HABERMAS *Edited by* STEPHEN K. WHITE
HEGEL *Edited by* FREDERICK BEISER
HEIDEGGER *Edited by* CHARLES GUIGNON
HOBBES *Edited by* TOM SORELL
HUME *Edited by* DAVID FATE NORTON
HUSSERL *Edited by* BARRY SMITH *and* DAVID WOODRUFF SMITH
WILLIAM JAMES *Edited by* RUTH ANNA PUTNAM
KANT *Edited by* PAUL GUYER
KIERKEGAARD *Edited by* ALASTAIR HANNAY *and* GORDON MARINO
LEIBNIZ *Edited by* NICHOLAS JOLLEY
LOCKE *Edited by* VERE CHAPPELL
MALEBRANCHE *Edited by* STEVEN NADLER
MARX *Edited by* TERRELL CARVER
MILL *Edited by* JOHN SKORUPSKI
NEWTON *Edited by* I. BERNARD COHEN *and* GEORGE E. SMITH
NIETZSCHE *Edited by* BERND MAGNUS *and* KATHLEEN HIGGINS
OCKHAM *Edited by* PAUL VINCENT SPADE
PLATO *Edited by* RICHARD KRAUT
PLOTINUS *Edited by* LLOYD P. GERSON
ROUSSEAU *Edited by* PATRICK RILEY
SARTRE *Edited by* CHRISTINA HOWELLS
SCHOPENHAUER *Edited by* CHRISTOPHER JANAWAY
SPINOZA *Edited by* DON GARRETT
WITTGENSTEIN *Edited by* KANS SLUGA *and* DAVID STERN

The Cambridge Companion to BERKELEY

Edited by
Kenneth P. Winkler

CAMBRIDGE UNIVERSITY PRESS
Cambridge, New York, Melbourne, Madrid, Cape Town, Singapore, São Paulo

Cambridge University Press
40 West 20th Street, New York, NY 10011-4211, USA

www.cambridge.org
Information on this title: www.cambridge.org/9780521450331

First published 2005

Printed in the United States of America

A catalog record for this publication is available from the British Library.

Library of Congress Cataloging in Publication Data

The Cambridge companion to Berkeley / [edited by] Kenneth P. Winkler.
p. cm. – (Cambridge companions to philosophy)
Includes bibliographical references and indexes.
ISBN-13: 978-0-521-45033-1 (hardback)
ISBN-10: 0-521-45033-0 (hardback)
ISBN-13: 978-0-521-45657-9 (pbk.)
ISBN-10: 0-521-45657-6 (pbk.)
1. Berkeley, George, 1685–1753. I. Winkler, Kenneth, 1950–
II. Title. III. Series.
B1348.C27 2005
192 – dc22 2005012007

ISBN-13 978-0-521-45033-1 hardback
ISBN-10 0-521-45033-0 hardback

ISBN-13 978-0-521-45657-9 paperback
ISBN-10 0-521-45657-6 paperback

CONTENTS

LIST OF FIGURES

CONTRIBUTORS

MARGARET ATHERTON is Professor of Philosophy at the University of Wisconsin, Milwaukee. She is the author of *Berkeley's Revolution in Vision* (1990) and editor of *The Empiricists* (1999), a collection of recent essays on Locke, Berkeley, and Hume, and *Women Philosophers of the Early Modern Period* (1994), an anthology of primary sources.

MICHAEL AYERS is Professor of Philosophy, Emeritus, at Oxford University and a Fellow of Wadham College. He is the author of *Locke: Epistemology and Ontology* (two volumes, 1991) and editor, with Daniel Garber, of *The Cambridge History of Seventeenth-Century Philosophy* (two volumes, 1998). His collection of Berkeley's *Philosophical Works, including the Works on Vision*, was revised and updated in 1993. He is a Fellow of the British Academy.

DAVID BERMAN is Associate Professor of Philosophy and Fellow at Trinity College, Dublin. His books include *Berkeley: Experimental Philosophy* (1997), *George Berkeley: Idealism and the Man* (1994), and *A History of Atheism in Britain* (1988).

STEPHEN R. L. CLARK is Professor of Philosophy at the University of Liverpool. Among his many books are *Biology and Christian Ethics* (2000), *God, Religion and Reality* (1998), *The Moral Status of Animals* (1977), and *Aristotle's Man: Speculations on Aristotelian Anthropology* (1975). His three-volume work *Limits and Renewals*, examining states, selves, and the world from a traditional Christian perspective, includes *Civil Peace and Sacred Order* (1989), *A Parliament of Souls* (1990), and *God's World and the Great Awakening* (1991). He is currently working on Plotinus.

PHILLIP D. CUMMINS is Professor of Philosophy, Emeritus, at the University of Iowa. His many influential articles include studies of Bayle, Berkeley, Hume, Reid, and Kant. He is editor, with Guenter Zoeller, of *Minds, Ideas, and Objects: Essays on the Theory of Representation in Modern Philosophy* (1992).

STEPHEN DARWALL is John Dewey Collegiate Professor of Philosophy at the University of Michigan, Ann Arbor, and a Fellow of the American Academy of Arts and Sciences. He is the author of *Welfare and Rational Care* (2002), *Philosophical Ethics* (1998), *The British Moralists and the Internal 'Ought,' 1640–1740* (1995), and *Impartial Reason* (1983).

LISA DOWNING is Associate Professor of Philosophy at the University of Illinois at Chicago. She has published studies of Boyle, Locke, and Berkeley, and is at work on a book entitled *Empiricism and Newtonianism: Locke, Berkeley, and the Decline of Strict Mechanism.*

A. C. GRAYLING is Reader in Philosophy at Birkbeck College, University of London, and Supernumerary Fellow of St. Anne's College, Oxford. He is the author of *Berkeley: The Central Arguments* (1986). Among his recent books are *The Reason of Things* (2002), *Wittgenstein: A Very Short Introduction* (2001), *Moral Values* (1998), and *An Introduction to Philosophical Logic* (third edition, 1997). His weekly columns for *The Guardian* have been collected in two recent volumes, *Life, Sex, and Ideas: The Good Life without God* (2003) and *Meditations for the Humanist: Ethics for a Seculiar Age* (2002).

DOUGLAS M. JESSEPH is Professor of Philosophy at North Carolina State University. He is the author of *Berkeley's Philosophy of Mathematics* (1993) and editor of Berkeley's *"De Motu" and "The Analyst": A Modern Edition, with Introduction and Commentary* (1992). His most recent book is *Squaring the Circle: The War between Hobbes and Wallis* (2000).

PATRICK KELLY recently retired as Senior Lecturer in Modern History at Trinity College, Dublin, where he also served as Dean of the Faculty of Arts. He has published widely on the history of economics and economic thinking in early modern Ireland. His two-volume edition of Locke's economic writings, *Locke on Money*, in the Clarendon Edition of the Works of John Locke, appeared in 1991.

ROBERT MCKIM is Professor of Religious Studies and of Philosophy at the University of Illinois at Urbana-Champaign. He has published many articles on Berkeley. He is the author of *Religious Ambiguity and Religious Diversity* (2001) and editor, with Jeff McMahan, of *The Morality of Nationalism* (1997), a collection of essays.

KENNETH P. WINKLER is Class of 1919 Professor of Philosophy at Wellesley College. His books include *Berkeley: An Interpretation* (1989) and an abridgment of Locke's *Essay concerning Human Understanding* (1996). From 2000 to 2005 he was editor, with Elizabeth Radcliffe, of the journal *Hume Studies*.

NOTE ON REFERENCES

Except where indicated, passages from Berkeley's writings are quoted from *The Works of George Berkeley, Bishop of Cloyne*, ed. A. A. Luce and T. E. Jessop, 9 vols. (London: Thomas Nelson, 1948–57). Passages are cited by volume and page number; thus "*Works* 6: 148" or "W 6: 148" refers to page 148 in volume 6 of the *Works*.

References to Berkeley's most important writings are provided parenthetically in the text, using the following short titles and letter combinations:

Private notebooks, also known as *Philosophical Commentaries* (1707–8; unpublished until 1871)	Cited as *Notebooks* or N; reference is to entries as numbered by A. A. Luce.
An Essay towards a New Theory of Vision (1709)	Cited as *New Theory* or NTV; reference is to numbered sections.
A Treatise concerning the Principles of Human Knowledge (1710)	Cited as *Principles* or PHK; reference is to numbered sections in Part I (the only part to appear).
Introduction to *A Treatise concerning the Principles of Human Knowledge*	Cited as Introduction or I; reference is to numbered sections.
Three Dialogues between Hylas and Philonous (1713)	Cited as *Three Dialogues, Dialogues,* or DHP; reference is to dialogue, followed by page number in Volume 2 of the *Works*; thus "DHP 3 (246)" refers to the Third Dialogue, at *Works* 2: 246.
Passive Obedience (1714)	Cited as PO; reference is to numbered sections.

De Motu (1721)	Cited as DM; reference is to numbered sections.
Alciphron, or the Minute Philosopher (1732)	Cited as ALC; reference is to dialogue and numbered sections, followed by page number in volume 3 of the *Works*; thus "ALC 7.10 (303)" refers to Section 10 of Dialogue 7, at *Works* 3: 303.
The Theory of Vision or Visual Language . . . Vindicated and Explained (1733)	Cited as *Theory of Vision Vindicated* or TVV; reference is to numbered sections.
The Analyst (1734)	Cited as A; reference is to numbered sections.
A Defence of Free-thinking in Mathematics (1735)	Cited as DFM; reference is to numbered sections.
The Querist (1735–7)	Cited as Q; reference is to numbered query; for the style of references to first edition queries omitted in later editions, see note 1 in Chapter 11.
Siris (1744)	Cited as S; reference is to numbered sections.

KENNETH P. WINKLER

Introduction

The most enduring comment ever made about George Berkeley was conveyed by Samuel Johnson to his friend James Boswell, who records it in the following story:[1]

After we came out of the church, we stood talking for some time together of Bishop Berkeley's ingenious sophistry to prove the non-existence of matter, and that everything in the universe is merely ideal. I observed that though we are satisfied his doctrine is not true, it is impossible to refute it. I never shall forget the alacrity with which Johnson answered, striking his foot with mighty force against a large stone, till he rebounded from it, – 'I refute it thus.' This was a stout exemplification of the first truths ... or ... original principles ... without admitting which we can no more argue in metaphysics, than we can argue in mathematics without axioms. To me it is not conceivable how Berkeley can be answered by pure reasoning.

Johnson portrays Berkeley as a philosopher hopelessly out of touch with human life; one aim of the present *Companion* is to supply a portrait of Berkeley that is more rounded and more just. The Berkeley of the essays that follow is not only an immaterialist philosopher, but a human being engaged – intellectually and often practically – with central issues in psychology, education, natural science, mathematics, economic development, ethics, politics, and religion, many of which are issues of continuing importance. Immaterialism is by no means neglected: Several chapters will help the reader decide whether Johnson was right to suggest that Berkeley's denial of matter is at odds with common sense and everyday experience, or whether Boswell was right to conclude that Berkeley cannot be refuted by reasoning. But Berkeley's immaterialism will, in the *Companion* as a whole, be placed in the context of a richly varied but nonetheless unified life.

If we are unable to do without a summary image of Berkeley, we would be wise to replace the figure of an out-of-touch philosopher with a second image furnished by Johnson, though perhaps not with Berkeley in mind.[2] This is the image of what Johnson calls the "projector": not the violent conqueror or plotting politician, but the private person who hopes to discover "new powers of nature" or to craft "new works of art." Projectors are often ridiculed, as Johnson himself emphasizes, but the folly of a projector is not (or at least not always) the folly of the fool, but rather "the ebullition of a capacious mind, crowded with variety of knowledge, and heated with intenseness of thought." Often, Johnson conjectures, this ebullition or overflowing "proceeds ... from the consciousness of uncommon powers" – from the confidence of someone who, "having already done much," is "easily persuaded [he or she] can do more." The image of a capacious and overflowing activist mind, confident of its powers and burning with ambition for its causes, fits Berkeley remarkably well. Like the projectors described by Johnson, Berkeley "unites ... extent of knowledge and greatness of design." The bold attempts of projectors often "miscarry," as Johnson grants, but often they are our best hope for progress. If projectors are everywhere discouraged, Johnson warns, "art and discovery can make no advance." Projectors "often succeed," after all, "beyond expectation," and when they fail, "even their miscarriages [may] benefit the world."

Johnson's second image is more fitting than the first, in part because it applies to so much more of Berkeley's life. As David Berman explains in the first chapter of this *Companion*, Berkeley's life was dominated not by one but by three great projects or crusades: the defense of immaterialism, which began with the 1710 publication of *A Treatise concerning the Principles of Human Knowledge*; his unsuccessful attempt to found a missionary college on the island of Bermuda, which brought him to America for three years beginning in 1728; and his campaign to promote "tar-water," an infusion of pine tar in water, as a remedy for bodily and possibly even spiritual ills, which commenced with the appearance of *Siris* in 1744. Many smaller projects or crusades, some almost as daring, are touched on by Berman in his sketch of Berkeley's life and examined more closely in later chapters: Berkeley's dramatic reinterpretation of early modern physics (considered by Lisa Downing in Chapter 8); his attack on the foundations of the calculus (discussed by Douglas M. Jesseph in Chapter 9); his attempt to solve the economic problems of his native Ireland (assessed by Patrick Kelly in Chapter 11); and his defense of Christian faith in the dialogue *Alciphron* (recounted by Stephen R. L. Clark in Chapter 12).

Berman begins his chapter with a survey of Berkeley's life and writings, followed by a brief review of the leading biographies of Berkeley published in the eighteenth, nineteenth, and twentieth centuries. He then asks how, in the light of three centuries of still-accumulating evidence, Berkeley should be understood. Was he the bishop with "ev'ry Virtue under Heaven," as his friend the poet Alexander Pope believed?[3] Or was he, at least early in his career, the fierce dissembler unmasked two centuries after his death by the poet W. B. Yeats?[4] Berman's own view lies somewhere in between. He argues that Berkeley was not "transparently honest" (as his biographer A. A. Luce, amplifying Pope, supposed).[5] In Berman's view Berkeley was often, at least as a writer, a deft dissembler. Certainly he was a cunning literary strategist; whether it is fair to call him a dissembler is one of many questions that readers of Berman's chapter are left to ponder.

After Berman places immaterialism in the context of Berkeley's life, Michael Ayers, in Chapter 2, places it against the background of the philosophical tradition. Ayers asks whether Berkeley is a "rationalist" or an "empiricist." These designations for broad tendencies in early modern philosophy were devised by followers of Immanuel Kant, who were taking up hints Kant himself lays down in the closing chapter of the *Critique of Pure Reason* (1781, with a second edition in 1787).[6] By the time the twentieth century began, "rationalist" and "empiricist" had hardened into labels for opposing camps or "schools." When William James, in his 1907 lectures on pragmatism, listed the defining traits of "the two types of mental make-up," one "tender-minded" and the other "tough-minded," the opposition between the rationalist ("going by principles") and the empiricist ("going by 'facts'") headed the list.[7]

According to the prevailing twentieth-century picture, the so-called "British empiricists" – Locke, Berkeley, and Hume – take experience to be the only source of our ideas or conceptions and the only source of justification (in the form of what James calls "facts") for the beliefs those conceptions make possible. The "continental rationalists" – Descartes, Spinoza, and Leibniz – maintain instead that at least some of our conceptions (including those of the greatest philosophical importance) owe nothing to experience, and that the beliefs they make possible (James's "principles") can be justified a priori, independently of experience. In recent years, this picture of early modern philosophy has come in for a fair share of criticism, and Berkeley's place in the picture (or any similar picture) has been the focus of lively controversy.[8]

Ayers begins Chapter 2 by noting that there is no anachronism in asking whether Berkeley is an empiricist or a rationalist, because battle lines very close to those drawn late in the eighteenth century by Kant and his followers had been drawn two thousand years before by Plato. In Plato's dialogue the *Sophist*, a "Stranger" (or, in Nicholas P. White's translation, "Visitor") describes a battle of Gods and Giants.[9] "One party," he says, "is trying to drag everything down to earth out of heaven and the unseen, literally grasping rocks and trees in their hands; for they lay hold upon every stock and stone and strenuously affirm that real existence belongs only to that which can be handled and offers resistance to the touch." According to these so-called Giants, "reality is the same thing as body, and as soon as one of the opposite party asserts that anything without a body is real, they are utterly contemptuous and will not listen to another word." Their adversaries, the Gods, "are very wary in defending their position somewhere in the heights of the unseen, maintaining with all their force that true reality consists in certain intelligible and bodiless Forms. In the clash of argument they shatter and pulverise those bodies which their opponents wield, and what those others allege to be true reality they call, not real being, but a sort of moving process of becoming." The Stranger concludes that "on this issue an interminable battle is always going on between the two camps."

Plato's Giants are materialists – indeed, extreme materialists, because they hold not only that body exists, but that body alone is genuinely real. As Ayers at several points acknowledges, on this point Berkeley sides unreservedly with the Gods. But in other respects – in his emphasis on sensory experience as a genuine source of knowledge, for example – he echoes the Giants. Berkeley puts immaterialism forward, Ayers proposes, as something that combines the insights of both kinds of theory. His "self-consciously synthetic system" is neither neatly rationalist nor neatly empiricist.

One of the most remarkable documents in the history of philosophy is a set of two notebooks Berkeley kept in his early twenties, probably between 1706 and 1708, as a rising scholar at Trinity College, Dublin. Originally published in the nineteenth century as his "Commonplace Book of Occasional Metaphysical Thoughts," the notebooks were renamed "Philosophical Commentaries" by A. A. Luce, who saw them as "commentaries on the arguments for immaterialism which Berkeley had in his mind, and probably on paper also, before he began to make the entries" (*Works* 1: 3. Because there is less-than-powerful evidence for Luce's view, the contributors to this *Companion* usually refer to these manuscripts simply, and more neutrally, as Berkeley's "notebooks"). The notebooks are a unique record of an early modern philosopher just beyond his student days, working out the arguments and rhetorical strategies of what were to become his most seminal books, *An Essay towards a New Theory of Vision* (1709) and the *Principles of Human Knowledge* (1710). In Chapter 3, Robert McKim outlines the contents of the notebooks, offers guidelines for reading them, and interprets Berkeley's developing views on a wide range of themes central to his published works: his arguments for immaterialism; the distinction between primary and secondary qualities; the divisibility of matter; the boundaries between species, sorts, or kinds; the nature of extension; the existence of unperceived objects; and the nature of spirit, mind, or soul.

By the time the *New Theory of Vision* appeared in 1709, Berkeley was already persuaded that bodies have no existence "without the mind" (PHK 44; see also 43). The *New Theory* gives no hint of this, however; making immaterialism public, Berkeley later explained, was "beyond [his] purpose . . . in a discourse concerning *vision*" (PHK 44). Conceived as a contribution to an emerging research tradition in psychology, the *New Theory* instead assumes that bodies exist externally, and that their distance, size, and situation are immediately perceived by touch – and only by touch. Berkeley's aim in the book is to explain how we come to perceive all these things, derivatively, by sight. In Chapter 4, Margaret Atherton offers an account of Berkeley's influential theory of vision and a selective study of its reception from the eighteenth century through the twentieth. She lays particular emphasis on his "heterogeneity thesis," according to which the sensations of sight and touch are altogether different in kind. Because of this heterogeneity, what we see does not represent what we touch in the way a painted image, for example, represents its original. Instead, visual sensations signify distance and other spatial features arbitrarily, in the same way words – arbitrary signs or marks – signify the things they stand for. Berkeley thereby arrives at what Atherton calls a "language model" of vision. We learn to associate visual cues with tangible information, just as we learn to associate words with whatever it is that usage has made them signify. Visual experience does not misrepresent the tangible world, as Atherton explains, but serves as a smoothly running "vehicle for tangible meanings." As her remarks on the reception of the theory indicate, these points have not always been appreciated by Berkeley's readers.

In Chapter 5, my own contribution, I survey Berkeley's "semiotics" or doctrine of signs: his account of the ways in which two kinds of sign – words and ideas – acquire and convey their meaning. Systematic attention to signs – to the source, scope, and limits of their signifying power – is one of Berkeley's most distinctive traits as a philosopher. A central theme in his semiotics was his rejection (in the introduction to the *Principles*) of what he called abstract ideas. His predecessors viewed these ideas as the medium in which thought achieves generalization, and held them to be especially vital to philosophy, where generalization is taken to its limits. Berkeley, though, condemned the belief in abstract general ideas as a chief source of "errors and difficulties in almost all parts of knowledge" (I 6). I argue that Berkeley's doctrine of signs plays an important role in virtually every aspect of his thinking, including his defense of immaterialism, which draws particularly on his condemnation of abstraction.

The defense of immaterialism is A. C. Grayling's subject in Chapter 6. He locates Berkeley's core argument in the opening seven sections of the *Principles*: The things we encounter in perception – houses, mountains, rivers, apples, stones, and trees – are, Berkeley contends there, collections of sensible qualities. Sensible qualities are, however, ideas; and ideas exist only in perceiving minds, on which they depend for their existence. It follows that ordinary things are not substances but ideas: Their *esse* (*to be*) is *percipi* (*to be perceived*). Further, "There is not any other substance than *spirit*, or that which perceives" (PHK 7). As Grayling observes, the remaining sections of the *Principles*, together with the *Three Dialogues between Hylas and Philonous* (1713), elaborate and further fortify this central argument. As an aid in assessing the whole train of Berkeley's argumentation, Grayling identifies three levels at which his thinking operates: the level of ordinary experience, seen as it really is (rather than as ordinary language, for example, suggests that it is); the level of ordinary thought about the world; and a metaphysical level at which the appearances of the first level and the ways of thinking of the second are explained and understood.

When Berkeley's *Principles* was published in 1710, the bulk of the book (following the introduction) was entitled "Part I." Berkeley intended to write at least one further part, concentrating on mind or spirit. He lost the manuscript while traveling in Italy, though, and never found the time (he told a friend) "to do so disagreeable a thing as writing twice on the same subject" (*Works* 2: 282). He has long been criticized for sparing mind or spirit from the vigilant scrutiny he gave to matter. Had he dealt with mind and matter evenhandedly, critics say, he would have rejected mind or (if that seemed too reckless) taken back his rejection of matter. Berkeley anticipates this objection as he does so many others: In the *Principles*, fifty numbered sections are spent in a give-and-take with imagined interlocutors. In the *Three Dialogues*, it is the materialist Hylas who gives voice to it:

> HYLAS. You [Philonous, Berkeley's representative] admit . . . there is spiritual substance, although you have no idea of it; while you deny there can be such a thing as material substance, because you have no notion or idea of it. Is this fair dealing? To act consistently, you must either admit matter or reject spirit. What say you to this? (DHP 3: 232)

Phillip D. Cummins, in Chapter 7, takes up this "parity objection" and other topics in Berkeley's philosophy of mind and agency (genuine agency being, in Berkeley's view, the privilege of mind alone). Despite what Cummins rightly calls the "programmatic and promissory" character of the philosophy of mind Berkeley left us, it remains, as Cummins emphasizes, a suggestive way of thinking. He concludes by observing that the issues that troubled Berkeley most were widely problematic in the eighteenth century and remain problematic even now.

As Lisa Downing points out as she begins Chapter 8, Berkeley's thought was deeply influenced by the rapidly developing natural science of his day. In the *Principles* and the *Dialogues* (as she goes on to explain), immaterialism is advanced as an alternative to the materialist mechanism dominating what was then called "natural philosophy." Nature, as the materialist mechanist portrays it, is populated by mind-independent material particles, too small to be seen or felt, influencing one another primarily, and (in the opinion of some) even solely, by "impulse," pushing or shoving the other particles with which they come in contact. The natural world is a vast impersonal machine. Particles themselves, it was supposed, possess only "primary" qualities – size, shape, number, and motion, together perhaps with other qualities fit for expression in precise mathematical laws. "Secondary" qualities – among them color, taste, and odor – were viewed as powers things possess, as a result of the "texture" or arrangement of the particles within, to cause sensations in perceiving minds – sensations that obscure, rather than disclose, the nature of things as they are in themselves. Berkeley was a declared enemy of this worldview: He denied that particles can be mind-independent; he denied that they can be causes; and he denied that they can be conceived in abstraction from the secondary qualities as we know them in experience (not as powers, but as manifest qualities). He was, however, no enemy of the scientific achievements that this worldview was held (mistakenly, in his view) to support. As he announces on the title page of the *Dialogues*, one of his chief aims was to make the sciences "more easy, useful, and compendious" (*Works* 2: 147). Downing begins her essay with an outline of Berkeley's interpretation of natural philosophy in the *Principles* and the *Dialogues*, highlighting his suggestion that instead of identifying causes, scientific explanations place events in patterns that we can use to anticipate the future. She then shows how, in *De Motu* (1721) – his most sustained examination of natural philosophy – Berkeley is led to an "instrumentalist" conception of forces as devices for calculation and control, and to a revised interpretation of what it is to be a scientific law. In the *Principles*, any true report of an observed pattern or regularity seems to count as a law of nature; in *De Motu*, laws are conceived as general principles from which observed regularities flow. Downing concludes with some remarks on *Siris* (1744), emphasizing its continuities with Berkeley's earlier works.

Berkeley was as closely engaged with mathematics as he was with science. In Chapter 9, on Berkeley's philosophy of mathematics, Douglas M. Jesseph explains why Berkeley departs from the Aristotelian view, still widely influential in the early eighteenth century, that the objects of mathematics are abstractions from ordinary experience. Berkeley instead holds that signs or symbols are the immediate objects of arithmetic (and of algebra as well), and that perceived extension (rather than some abstraction drawn from it) is the object of geometry. Because extension as we perceive it is not infinitely divisible, Berkeley's interpretation of geometry carries with it what Jesseph terms "an element of instrumentalism": When we speak of an inch-long line as if it contains ten thousand parts, for example, we do not mean that it really does, but that it can be used to stand for longer lines that do. If the longer lines for which it stands are, as Berkeley says, "innumerable," it is as if a mere inch can be divided forever (PHK 126). When, in *The Analyst* of 1734, Berkeley turns to the infinitesimal calculus recently developed by Newton and Leibniz, what Jesseph calls his "conception of mathematical rigor" rules out both the nominalist (or formalist) approach he had taken to arithmetic and the instrumentalist approach he had taken to geometry. As Jesseph explains, Berkeley takes the alleged objects of the calculus (quantities less than any positive quantity but greater than zero) to be "entirely incomprehensible." He also makes logical objections to some of Newton's most fundamental demonstrations; these objections, Jesseph tells us in closing, set the agenda for a generation of British mathematicians.

Stephen Darwall begins Chapter 10, on Berkeley's moral and political philosophy, by drawing attention to the ethical motivation of Berkeley's metaphysics. For Berkeley, the defense of immaterialism was not a narrow academic exercise but an urgent moral task. Darwall then outlines Berkeley's "coherent, reasonably comprehensive, and extraordinarily interesting answers" to some of the leading questions in moral philosophy. Berkeley was, among his other achievements, the first to distinguish and defend what is nowadays known as a rule-utilitarian theory of the right. He urges us to live by those rules which, "if universally practised, have, from the nature of things, an essential fitness to procure the well-being of mankind; though in their particular application they are sometimes ... the occasions of great sufferings and misfortunes" (*Passive Obedience*

[1712] 8). These rules are God's commands to us, and they are binding, Berkeley suggests, because of the rewards God has attached to our obedience. This suggestion is in keeping with a British tradition in moral philosophy that Darwall describes as "internalist," because it explicates *what it is we ought to do* in terms of *what we would be moved to do, if we were deliberating rationally* – in full awareness, for example, of even the most distant consequences of our choices. Darwall's essay concludes with a brief discussion of the substantive ethical and political opinions that Berkeley sought, partly by utilitarian means, to defend.

In Chapter 11, Patrick Kelly examines Berkeley's economic writings, particularly *The Querist*, a book consisting wholly of rhetorical questions, released in three installments in 1735, 1736, and 1737. Kelly presents *The Querist* both as an "'improvement' tract" (an early modern genre aimed at advancing the social and economic welfare of a nation) and as an essay in development economics, though at the time it appeared (as Kelly underscores), even the wider field of economics had yet to be clearly defined. After describing economic conditions in early eighteenth-century Ireland, Kelly pursues the themes that made *The Querist* distinctive, among them its innovative conception of money as "a ticket entitling to power" (Q 441) and its morally motivated search for what Kelly calls the "true purpose" – and with it, the proper limits – of economic activity.

The final chapter of the volume, by Stephen R. L. Clark, is a sympathetic study of Berkeley's conception of religious life and his defense of religious commitment. Ranging over almost all of Berkeley's writings, but attending in particular to the seven-part dialogue *Alciphron* (1732), Clark relates Berkeley's views on the authority of tradition, trust, and testimony, the contribution of emotion to religious meaning, the nature of religious truth, the evidence for God's existence, and the bearing of religion on morality.

If we are prepared to embrace the image of Berkeley as projector, Clark's essay teaches us that Berkeley owed the confidence he apparently had in all his projects not just to an awareness of his own powers, but to a rationally articulated faith in God. Whatever we make, in the end, of Johnson's suggestion that the immaterialist is refuted by every stick or stone we push against, Berkeley's work as a whole is resolutely attentive to the concrete circumstances of human life and thought, and to the many "lets and difficulties" (I 4) occasioned by them. His concern for the difficulties was very much of this world, but his hope of overcoming them had its source in what he saw as another.

To complete our picture of Berkeley as a projector and as a writer, I have included as an appendix his "Verses . . . on the prospect of Planting Arts and Learning in America," written in 1726 but first published in his *Miscellany* of 1752.[10]

NOTES

1. In *Boswell's Life of Johnson*, ed. George Birkbeck Hill and L. F. Foster, 6 vols. (Oxford: Clarendon Press, 1934–50), 1: 417.
2. *The Adventurer*, no. 99, in Samuel Johnson, *Selected Writings*, ed. Patrick Cruttwell (Harmondsworth: Penguin, 1968), 191–6; the quotations that follow are all drawn from 194–5. Johnson's essay on projectors can also be found in *The Idler* and *The Adventurer*, ed. W. J. Bate, John M. Bullitt, and L. F. Powell (New Haven: Yale University Press, 1963), 429–35. *Adventurer* 99 first appeared on October 16, 1753, nine months after Berkeley's death in January of the same year. There is no documentary evidence that Johnson was writing with Berkeley's Bermuda project in mind, but Johnson was reflecting on the project and its failure not long after his *Adventurer* essay was published. During a dinner party in Oxford in 1754 (see *Boswell's Life of Johnson*, 1: 270–1, for the dating of Johnson's summer stay at the university), Johnson offended Berkeley's son, then a student there, by "ridiculing Bishop Berkeley's American scheme" (*Poems by the late George-Monck Berkeley, Esq.*, ed. Eliza Berkeley [London: J. Nichols, 1797], ccl; see also ccliii). According to Eliza Berkeley, widow of Berkeley's son, some of Johnson's companions reproved him for his rudeness. "Why, I think the Bishop's scheme no bad one," he replied, "but I abused it, to take down the young gentleman, lest he should be too vain of having had such a father" (*Poems by George-Monck Berkeley*, ccliii).
3. "Epilogue to the Satires. Dialogue II," in Alexander Pope, *Imitations of Horace with An Epistle to Dr. Arbuthnot and The Epilogue to the Satires*, ed. John Butt (London: Methuen, 1939), 317.
4. For Yeats's unusual view of Berkeley, see his introduction to J. M. Hone and M. M. Rossi, *Bishop Berkeley: His Life, Writings, and Philosophy* (London: Faber and Faber, 1931), xv–xxix.
5. A. A. Luce, *Berkeley's Immaterialism* (London: Thomas Nelson, 1945), viii.

6. The final chapter is called "The history of pure reason"; there Kant presents, "in cursory outline," the most significant points of disagreement in the history of philosophy (*Critique of Pure Reason*, ed. Paul Guyer and Allen W. Wood [Cambridge: Cambridge University Press, 1998], 702–4 [A 852 = B 880 through A 855 = B 883]).
7. William James, *Pragmatism* (Cambridge, MA: Harvard University Press, 1975), 13. James's division owes a great deal, I believe, to Ralph Waldo Emerson's separation of humankind as thinkers into "Materialists" and "Idealists" (in his 1842 lecture "Transcendentalism," in *Selected Essays*, ed. Larzer Ziff [Harmondsworth: Penguin, 1982], 239–40). Emerson's separation is itself derived from two Kantian contrasts, extended by Emerson from philosophers in particular to thinking human beings in general: One is between "merely sensual" and "merely intellectual" philosophers (*Critique of Pure Reason*, 702 [A 853 = B 881]); the other is between "empiricists" and "noologists" (703 [A 854 = B 882]).
8. See Louis E. Loeb, *From Descartes to Hume: Continental Metaphysics and the Development of Modern Philosophy* (Ithaca: Cornell University Press, 1981), and Harry M. Bracken, *Berkeley* (London: Macmillan, 1974). Bracken's arresting thesis – that Berkeley is "a philosopher of the Cartesian tradition" (15), "not a British Empiricist" but an "Irish Cartesian" (159) – is not altogether new. At Harvard College in 1876–77, George Herbert Palmer's course on "Cartesianism" dealt with three figures: Descartes, Malebranche, and Berkeley (*The Harvard University Catalogue. 1876–77* [Cambridge, MA: Published for the University, 1876], 55). For Kant's own way of understanding Berkeley, see the *Critique of Pure Reason*, 326 (B 274–5) and 430 (A 377–8), and the *Prolegomena to Any Future Metaphysics*, ed. Gary Hatfield (Cambridge: Cambridge University Press, 2004), 44–5 and 125–7; in the *Prolegomena*, Kant seems to affiliate Berkeley with Plato and the party of the gods. For discussion, see the essays collected in *The Real in the Ideal: Berkeley's Relation to Kant*, ed. Ralph C. S. Walker (New York: Garland, 1989).
9. White's translation appears in Plato, *Complete Works*, ed. John M. Cooper (Indianapolis: Hackett Publishing Company, 1997), 235–93, but I quote from *Sophist* 246 a–c as translated by Francis M. Cornford in his *Plato's Theory of Knowledge: The* Theatetus *and the* Sophist *of Plato* (London: Routledge, 1934), 230. When, in his accompanying commentary, Cornford redescribes the battle of gods and giants as a struggle between "*Idealists and Materialists*" (228), he draws on the same vocabulary used by Emerson in his reworking of Kant.
10. See A. A. Luce, *The Life of George Berkeley, Bishop of Cloyne* (London: Thomas Nelson, 1949), 96.

DAVID BERMAN

1 Berkeley's life and works

I. BERKELEY'S CAREER

George Berkeley was born in County Kilkenny, Ireland, on March 12, 1685, into what now would be called an Anglo-Irish family. He grew up in Dysart Castle, near Thomastown, and attended school at Kilkenny College, which he left in 1700 for Trinity College, Dublin, where he became a scholar and graduated B.A. in 1704. He then remained in college, waiting for a fellowship to fall vacant. It is at this time that his career can be said to have begun. Probably the most helpful way of structuring his career is to see it as falling into three periods – early, middle, and late – each dominated by or centering around a project or crusade. The early period is dominated by Berkeley's immaterialist philosophy, for which he is now best known, a philosophy that was developed around 1707, then published in 1709–13. The second great project was his Bermuda college, conceived circa 1722 and made public in 1724. Berkeley's third and final crusade was about tar-water, a medicine which first attracted his attention around 1741 and which he publicized in 1744.

It was in the years 1705–9 that Berkeley worked out his immaterialist philosophy, a development that to a great extent we can trace in the two notebooks he kept during this period, now called the *Philosophical Commentaries*. This work and the early period itself culminated in Berkeley's three classic books: *An Essay towards a New Theory of Vision* (1709); *A Treatise concerning the Principles of Human Knowledge*, Part 1 (1710); and the *Three Dialogues between Hylas and Philonous* (1713). Within this first period at Trinity College Berkeley also delivered two short papers, one on the cave of Dunmore and the other 'Of Infinites,' which were published posthumously in 1871. He succeeded in winning the coveted fellowship (1707), published his minor mathematical works (1707) – probably to support his candidature to fellowship – as well as his *Passive Obedience, or the Christian Doctrine of Not Resisting the Supreme Power* (1712), his main work of moral or political theory, originally given as three discourses in the College Chapel.

Taking leave from Trinity College, Berkeley left Ireland in 1713, partly with the aim of publishing his *Three Dialogues* in London. Here he became acquainted with many of the leading literary figures of the time – Pope, Addison, Steele, Arbuthnot, and his countryman Swift, whom Berkeley had probably met previously in Ireland. He wrote (or at least published) little between 1713 and his next prolific period of authorship, 1732–5, which rivals that of 1709–13. He did however publish a number of essays in the *Guardian* (1713), edited by Steele, and *Advice to the Tories Who Have Taken the Oath* (1715), which was not identified as one of Berkeley's works until the twentieth century. In 1721 he published *De Motu*, his chief work in the philosophy of science, which had been entered (unsuccessfully) for a prize at the French Academy. During this fallow period Berkeley was travelling on the European continent, mainly in Italy. He probably intended to write some account of his travels. Five volumes containing his travel notes are extant and were first printed in 1871. Berkeley's first-hand account of an eruption of Mt Vesuvius was published in the *Transactions* of the Royal Society in 1717. During this period Berkeley also was working on Part 2 of the *Principles of Human Knowledge*, the manuscript of which (as he informed a correspondent in 1729) was lost in Italy.[1]

Berkeley's interest in his philosophy seems to have waned during this period. There is, for example, virtually no mention of it in his correspondence between 1713 and 1729. Nor could he bring himself to rewrite the work lost in Italy. Indeed he seems to have become generally disenchanted. His pessimism is shown in his *Essay towards Preventing the Ruine of Great Britain*, published in 1721, where he laments the decline in social and religious values.

By 1722, however, Berkeley was inspired by a new cause almost as bold as his immaterialism. Having lost confidence in the Old World, he turned his attention to the New, where he was determined to found in Bermuda a missionary/arts college, which would transform America, he hoped, both morally and spiritually – possibly also becoming part of the Christian world-historical story. His project is outlined in *A Proposal* for *the Better Supplying of Churches in Our Foreign Plantations, and for Converting the Savage Americans to Christianity* (1724). However, the enthusiasm and apocalyptic fervor is probably best captured in the final stanza of his best-known poem, "On the Prospect of Planting Arts and Learning in America," first drafted circa 1726 and published in 1752:[2]

> Westward the Course of Empire takes its Way;
> The four first Acts already past,
> A fifth shall close the Drama with the Day;
> Time's noblest Offspring is the last.

Back in Dublin, Berkeley enlisted considerable backing for his project. Swift supported him, and a number of fellows at Trinity College agreed to become teachers in the projected Bermuda college. Berkeley then went to England, where he enlisted financial backers and obtained a charter for his college (which was to be called St Paul's) and a grant of £20,000 from the British government. In 1724 Berkeley also became Dean of Derry – one of the most lucrative livings in Ireland – mainly in order to facilitate his project. To accelerate payment of the government grant, Berkeley (and his bride, Anne) left England in 1728 for Rhode Island, which was to be the continental base for his college. Here he bought a farm, where he and his wife lived for nearly three years. But the grant was never paid, and the project failed. While in Rhode Island Berkeley wrote his longest book, *Alciphron, or the Minute Philosopher* (1732), a defence of natural religion and Christianity in seven dialogues.

Alciphron was published in London, where Berkeley and his family resided between 1731 and 1734 after their return from America. In this second great period of authorship, he also published these five works: *A Sermon Preached before the Incorporated Society for the Propagation of the Gospel* (1732); *The Theory of Vision Vindicated* (1733) – a defense of the *New Theory of Vision*, which Berkeley had appended to *Alciphron; The Analyst* (1734), which develops Berkeley's defense of religious mystery in *Alciphron*, Dialogue 7, while attacking Newton's theory of fluxions; *A Defence of Free-Thinking in Mathematics* (1735); and *Reasons for Not Replying to Mr Walton's Full Answer* (1735). All five works are, like *Alciphron*, connected in some way with the defense of the Christian religion against freethinking (or the minute philosophy, as Berkeley calls it), which he felt was at least partly responsible for the failure of his Bermuda project.

A new note is introduced with the *Querist* (Part 1, 1735), Berkeley's principal work on economics. Although it was partly written in London, the *Querist* is concerned mainly with the Irish situation – appropriately, as Berkeley's situation had also changed: In January 1734 he had been appointed Bishop of Cloyne. In the summer of that year he moved to his diocese, where he remained almost without interruption until 1752. Although he was an absentee Dean of Derry, he was very much a full-time and conscientious Bishop of Cloyne. His publications in this episcopal period reflect his pastoral and philanthropic concerns. Two further parts of the *Querist* were published in 1736 and 1737, containing observations on the social and economic conditions in Ireland as well as practical proposals, particularly for the setting up of a national bank. A *Discourse to the Magistrates*, which was prompted by rumours of an organized blasphemous society in Dublin, called the Blasters, was issued in 1738. After the *Discourse*, one of Berkeley's least impressive works, there is a publication gap of six years, although Berkeley was still writing, as is evident from his long but private letter to Sir John James on the demerits of Roman Catholicism as against Protestantism.

It was in this second fallow period that Berkeley came upon his third bold idea, which he published in *Siris: a Chain of Philosophical Reflexions and Inquiries concerning the Virtues of Tar-Water* (1744), his last major work. Here he recommends tar-water as a medicine in the context of reflections on chemistry, philosophy of science, ancient philosophy, metaphysics, and theology. Berkeley continued to defend tar-water (which he held, or at least suspected, to be a panacea) in various public letters. Tar-water also was the subject of his last published essay, "Farther Thoughts on Tar-water," which appeared in his *Miscellany, containing Several Tracts on Various Subjects* (1752), which collected a number of his essays, some of an earlier date but most originally published in this period. Among the later works not so far mentioned is *A Word to the Wise*, first published in 1749, which develops his social views on Ireland as set out in the *Querist*, with which it was sometimes printed. In 1752 Berkeley left Cloyne for Oxford, partly in order to supervise the education of his son George. He died in Oxford on January 14, 1753.

II. SCHOLARLY DEVELOPMENTS

Of the four major British philosophers of the early modern period – Hobbes, Locke, Berkeley, and Hume – Berkeley probably has been best served by his biographers, editors, and bibliographers. His first biographer and editor was Joseph Stock, a Fellow of Trinity College, Dublin, and later Bishop of Killala. His *Account of the Life of George Berkeley* was published in 1776, to be followed eight years later by his handsome two-volume edition of Berkeley's *Works*, which also contains a revised version of his *Account* together with the first collection of Berkeley's letters. This was a very creditable first attempt at presenting Berkeley's life and works. Probably the only important published work it omits is Berkeley's *Theory of Vision Vindicated* (1733).

However, Stock's edition (which was reprinted in 1820, 1837, and 1843) makes no attempt at establishing authorized texts, nor are the texts individually introduced or annotated, nor does it draw on manuscript material. This was to be done by the next great Berkeley editor and biographer, A. C. Fraser, a Scotsman, in his four-volume 1871 edition, volume four of which contains Berkeley's *Life and Letters*. Fraser's work represents, in every respect, a vast expansion and improvement on that of Stock. It also made a considerable impact, drawing appreciative reviews from such notable philosophers as J. S. Mill and C. S. Peirce. In 1901 Fraser issued a revised edition, containing a much-scaled-down biography (1: xxiii–lxxxvii) and a neater but less ambitious presentation of Berkeley's texts.

The third great figure in Berkeley scholarship was A. A. Luce, Fellow and Vice Provost of Trinity College, Dublin. His *Life of George Berkeley* appeared in 1949, to be followed by his nine-volume edition, co-edited with T. E. Jessop of Hull, of Berkeley's *Works* (1948–57), the main aim of which, as they note, "was to put out an accurate, scholarly and complete text – for in these respects Fraser's work was uneven."[3] The two men had previously cooperated on a *Bibliography of Berkeley* (1934; revised 2nd edition 1973).

Luce's *Life* and his edition with Jessop of the *Works* was definitive for the twentieth century – as was Stock's work for the eighteenth century and Fraser's for the nineteenth century. (Supposing some sort of progression, one might expect a fourth great scholarly synthesis of Berkeley's life and works in the middle of this century.) In this chapter I will be focussing mainly on the work of Luce and Jessop. Having given a brief survey of Berkeley's life and publications in Section I, I shall now review the main scholarly developments of the past forty years.[4] In a final section I consider our present picture of Berkeley and how it has been (and may be) affected by recent discoveries.

Perhaps the most important document which has come to light since Luce's *Life* is Anne Berkeley's annotated copy of Stock's 1776 *Account of Berkeley*.[5] As Berkeley's wife, Anne's annotations are especially important for the latter part of Berkeley's life, from 1730 to 1753. About fifteen new letters by Berkeley also have been located since Luce's 1956 edition of the letters, in volume eight of the *Works*. Although containing no dramatically new information, these letters throw light on, among others things, his reasons for going to Rhode Island in 1728 and for declining the Bishopric of Clogher in 1745 when it was offered to him by Lord Chesterfield.[6] On the whole, the new factual information fills in detail rather than changing our understanding of Berkeley. Somewhat more consequential are a number of contemporary letters on Berkeley, particularly a letter from Archbishop King on Berkeley's irregular ordination in 1710, one from Duke Tyrrell attacking Berkeley in 1716 as a Jacobite, and one from Elizabeth Montagu on Berkeley's relations with women.[7]

However, the most consequential discovery in the biographical realm was made by Arthur Friedman.[8] This concerns the authorship and early printing of the "Life of George Berkely [sic]," the first substantial memoir of Berkeley, which Luce had singled out as "the source of the general misconception" of Berkeley (*Life*, 2), "a piece of ignorant hack-work without a vestige of authority" (3). Luce argued that because this "caricature" was virtually first in the field, it had a profoundly negative effect on Berkeley's reputation – perhaps encouraging and enforcing the view of Scottish philosophers such as James Beattie that Berkeley's thought was unhinged or crazy, the very opposite of common sense. As much of Luce's philosophical work was aimed at rebutting this view of Berkeley's philosophy, so his *Life of Berkeley* can be seen as a reaction to and an attempt to rectify the early memoir's picture of Berkeley as "a recluse and the butt of college, genius to some, dunce to others, 'the absent-minded philosopher'" (*Life*, 2–3).

However, Luce's dismissal of the early memoir and its picture of Berkeley needs to be reassessed in the light of Friedman's discovery that what Luce and others took to be the first publication of the memoir, in the *British Plutarch* (1762), was in fact its second, and that the original printing in the *Weekly Magazine* (1759/60) contains variants that reveal its author to be Oliver Goldsmith. The important variant is in the memoir's most striking anecdote. It tells how the young Berkeley, after witnessing an execution, became so curious to know the sensations experienced by the malefactor that he arranged with a student friend that they should hang each other. After Berkeley had been "tied up to the ceiling, and the chair taken from under his feet, his companion," Contarine, waited so long to assist him that "as soon as Berkeley was taken down he fell senseless and motionless to the floor. After some trouble however [he] was brought to himself; and observing his band [exclaimed] bless my heart, Contarine . . . you have quite rumpled my band." In the 1759/60 memoir, the writer not only names Berkeley's companion but adds that it was Contarine "from whom I had the story."[9] (There has been only one "Contarine" at Trinity College: the Reverend Thomas Contarine, who entered in 1701, a year after Berkeley, and who was the uncle and patron of Goldsmith.)

Because it is known that Goldsmith was associated with the short-lived *Weekly Magazine*, Friedman concluded that "it is highly improbable that anyone except Goldsmith would have known his uncle, who spent his [entire] life in Ireland" (3: 37). Once we grant – as I think we must – Goldsmith's authorship of the memoir, we can no longer regard it as "a piece of ignorant hack-work without a vestige of authority," as Luce describes it. Not only could Oliver have drawn on his uncle Contarine – at whose house he often stayed – but he also could have gleaned biographical details from another well-placed relative, the Reverend Isaac Goldsmith, who was Dean of Cloyne when Berkeley was Bishop. In short, Goldsmith's wildish picture of Berkeley, conveyed particularly in the hanging episode, cannot be dismissed.

Friedman's discovery has a number of consequences which I shall be examining in the next section, but first I want to note the main bibliographical developments since Luce and Jessop. Probably the most important, philosophically, was the attribution to Berkeley of a long letter to Bishop Peter Browne on religious analogy. Printed anonymously in the Dublin *Literary Journal* in 1745, the letter intitially was sent to Browne soon after the publication of his *Things Divine and Supernatural conceived by Analogy* (1733), which contained an extensive attack on *Alciphron*, Dialogue 4, and, to a lesser extent, Dialogue 7. The letter has been attributed to Berkeley by J.-P. Pittion and the present writer, an attribution accepted by Luce and Jessop and not so far disputed.[10]

Another discovery, made by Stephen Parks, was a contract between Berkeley's friend Richard Steele and the publisher Jacob Tonson which identifies Berkeley as the compiler of the *Ladies Library* (London, 1714), a three-volume educational miscellany, with extracts from the writings of Jeremy Taylor, Locke, and Archbishops Tillotson and Fénelon, among others.[11] A much shorter but philosophically more interesting discovery was made by Bertil Belfrage, who found a three-paragraph summary of Berkeley's metaphysics bound in Samuel Johnson's copy of Berkeley's *De Motu*.[12] Although the manuscript is not in Berkeley's hand, it almost certainly was transcribed by Johnson from one of Berkeley's manuscripts when he visited Berkeley in Rhode Island in the early 1730s.

A bibliographical question about which there has been continuing scholarly debate concerns Berkeley's essays in *The Guardian*. We know that Berkeley wrote for the *Guardian*, because in the publisher's note "To the Reader," he is credited with embellishing the work "with many excellent arguments in Honour of Religion and Virtue." Luce attributed twelve numbers to Berkeley: 27, 35, 39, 49, 55, 62, 70, 77, 83, 88, 89, 126, as well as part of number 9, an attribution largely accepted by J. C. Stephens (the most recent editor of the *Guardian*), who (following E. J. Furlong) attributes no. 58 to Berkeley.[13] A more recent examination by the present writer, based partly on new manuscript evidence, concludes that Berkeley wrote "part of number 9, most of numbers 27, 35, 39, 69, all of 49, 55, 62, 70, 77, 83, 88, 89, 126, and, almost certainly, numbers 81 and 130."[14]

III. A PICTURE OF BERKELEY

What is the picture of Berkeley that has emerged now, in the early twenty-first century? I suggest that it hovers somewhere between the traditional one – of the good bishop with every virtue under heaven (with the possible exception of common sense) – and the portrait in Luce's masterly *Life*: the straightforward Berkeley, "sane, shrewd, and efficient," who if less perfect than the traditional figure, makes up for it by his undeniable possession of common sense. That there is a close connection between Luce's picture of Berkeley's life and his reading of the philosophy comes out most clearly in the Biographical Introduction to his *Berkeley's Immaterialism* (London: Thomas Nelson, 1945) – the embryo of the *Life* – where with admirable candor Luce asserts that "I wish to show [Berkeley] as a normal man of flesh and blood in constant and fruitful touch with the real world" (1). Luce is equally candid in his Preface: "To destroy that pseudo-Berkeley, and to restore to his rightful place the real Berkeley who proved the world no dream are the master aims of this book, as they have been the main motives of my philosophical studies for some years past" (ix).

So the real (as against the pseudo-) Berkeley had his feet planted firmly on the ground – both as a man and as a philosopher. There was nothing wild or dreamy about Berkeley, according to Luce, who here was reacting against W. B. Yeats's picture of "that fierce young man... God-appointed Berkeley," who "proved all things a dream." I have commented elsewhere on the Luce/Yeats disagreement, and my aim here is not to go over the ground already covered, but to build on it.[15]

A natural place to begin is with Luce's claim against Yeats: "There was only one George Berkeley in actual life; he never wore a mask, and he was transparently honest and single-minded" (viii). In my earlier essay I suggested tentatively that Yeats did catch a distant glimpse of a radical Berkeley behind a conventional, accommodating facade.[16] I now think there is even more evidence against Luce's view that Berkeley was "transparently honest" – some of which can be gathered from Luce himself. For the picture that emerges both from Berkeley's private statements and from his practice is of someone who believed in the need for dissembling and had (and recognized that he had) a considerable talent for it. Thus in a key early memorandum Berkeley writes: 'He that would win another over to his opinion must seem to harmonize with him at first and humour him in his own way of talking. From my childhood I had an unaccountable turn of thought that way" (circa 1708–12).[17] Berkeley's ability to harmonize with his opponents comes out in various ways. It is part of his greatness that he was able to see and to express the most formidable arguments and criticisms of his philosophical enemies, as can be seen especially in Sections 34–85 of the *Principles of Human Knowledge* and then in his portrayal of Hylas (in 1713) and later of Alciphron and Lysicles (in 1732) – all of which shows how adept he was at entering into the viewpoints of his opponents.

There is, however, a dark side to this, namely Berkeley's talent for (as he puts it) humouring. This, too, comes out in his works, particularly in the *New Theory of Vision*, which contains at least three important areas of strategic dissembling: on what we immediately see; on the existence of external tangible objects; and in the deliberate omission, in the 1709 editions, of the work's theological conclusion that God is the author of the language of vision.[18]

Berkeley expresses his more general strategic intent in entry 185 of the notebooks or *Philosophical Commentaries*, where he advises himself "to allow existence to colours in the dark ... [for] Tis prudent to correct mens mistakes without altering their language. This makes truth glide into their souls insensibly." In the *Principles*, Section 44, Berkeley himself acknowledges pretty clearly that he had dissembled in the *New Theory of Vision* about external tangible objects: He "supposed [as] true" that which he knew to be an "error." In a private letter to Percival of 1710, Berkeley also discusses his strategy in the *Principles* itself: "Whatever doctrine contradicts vulgar and settled opinion had need be introduced with great caution into the world. For this reason [he says] I omitted all mention of the non-existence of matter in the title-page, dedication, preface and introduction, that so the notion might steal unwares on the reader."[19]

Nor, according to some scholars, is this the only use of strategy in the *Principles*. Luce himself, supported more recently by Michael Ayers, has argued persuasively that there also is humouring in Section 1, where Berkeley suggests that there are ideas "perceived by attending to the passions and operations of the mind," although he does not believe, according to Luce and Ayers, in such Lockean ideas of reflection.[20] If Luce and Ayers are correct, then we have a clear example of deception here, and one made all the more serious by Berkeley's assertions in the preceding section. In the final section of the Introduction, Berkeley entreats his readers to "attain the same train of thoughts in reading, that I had in writing them," so that readers will be "out of danger of being deceived by my words." But what does Berkeley do in the very next section, but deceive his readers by the misleading Lockean suggestion that there are ideas "perceived by attending to the passions and operations of the mind."

Nor was Berkeley's concern with accommodated presentation restricted to the early years. Berkeley was always, I think, prepared to speak with the vulgar and think with the learned. That split came naturally to him. So, too, did the need for gliding the truth imperceptibly into the minds of his opponents. Thus in his Primary Visitation Charge, delivered at Cloyne about 1736, he recommends this latter procedure to his clergy as a helpful technique for bringing Roman Catholics over to Anglicanism: "A subject [he tells his clergy] which if proposed at once might shock, being introduced by degrees might take... What comes as it were by chance is often admitted, while that which looks like design is guarded against."[21] Similarly, Berkeley's wife noted that his "maxim was to nip & not to snatch & thereby lure away mens prejudices."[22]

So if being transparently honest is one of the virtues, then Berkeley did not have every virtue. Yet neither is it clear that for him, being straightforward or open was always a virtue. Berkeley's denunciation of forswearing in *Passive Obedience*, Section 3, has led at least one scholar to conclude that, like Kant, he was opposed to all forms of dissimulation.[23] This is not so, however, for in *Alciphron*, Dialogue 3, Section 16, Berkeley (through Euphranor) opposes the freethinker's principle that one should always be open about the truth; for, he says, "would you undeceive a child that was taking physic? Would you officiously set an enemy right that was making a wrong attack? Would you help an enraged man to his sword?" (*Works* 3: 140).

Berkeley's willingness and flair for dissembling emerges not only in his writings but also in his life. One striking instance is the way he went into the London freethinking clubs disguised as a novice or learner and heard Anthony Collins say that he had found a proof for atheism. It also comes out during the second phase of his career (the Bermuda project) – for example, in his prevarication over the location of his projected college and in his secrecy about coming back to Ireland in 1727.[24] Admittedly, it is not clear to what extent these are instances of dissimulation rather than just muddle. A more clear-cut and striking instance of dissimulation concerns his poem on the westward course of empire. In his letter to Percival of February 1726, in which he includes an early draft of the poem, he says that it was "wrote by a friend of mine with a view to the [Bermuda] scheme."[25]

We know that this is untrue, because Berkeley printed the poem in his *Miscellany* (published four years after Percival's death).

Neither this nor most of the evidence I have presented so far is particularly new, yet I think there has been insufficient appreciation of what it adds up to, in short that Yeats was right and Luce wrong: Berkeley wasn't transparent; he sometimes did mask himself and his views. There was, in other words, a greater than usual split between his appearance and reality. Of course this is not to deny that Berkeley very often was as he appeared. However, in certain crucial matters concerning his highest hopes, he was able and willing to present himself in a strategic way in order to further admirable (as he saw them) long-term aims.

Although it cannot be good news to learn that the philosopher we are trying to understand is willing and able to hide and disguise, revealing himself in a calculating way, we are at any rate learning something important in knowing that he is not transparent or straightforward – although how far or deep this goes still remains to be determined. It also is worth mentioning that Berkeley is by no means the only major philosopher to mask himself. There is a long tradition for this, going back to "the best and most admirable man that the heathen world produced," as Berkeley described Socrates – who, it generally is agreed, could also be significantly covert.[26]

That Berkeley saw himself in this way – accommodating his discourse to his reader or listener – comes out curiously in a rare autobiogaphical remark he once made to Percival: "I know not what it is to fear [Percival records him as saying], but I have a delicate sense of danger."[27] I quoted this in my earlier work but I did not notice then that Berkeley uses the phrase "a delicate sense of danger" in *Alciphron*, Dialogue 5, Section 13, to describe certain cowardly freethinkers or "tame bullies" – as he calls them – who are naturally rude but also restrained, so that although they ridicule defenseless clergymen, they are very cautious in the company of military men who might challenge them to a duel (*Works* 3: 187). In other words, while the tame bullies are naturally aggressive, their aggression comes out only with certain people, in certain situations.

My suggestion is that Berkeley was prompted to see this split in others because he was aware of something similar in himself. Indeed, I should like to go further and claim that Berkeley was able to appreciate the freethinkers' dissimulative strategy because he practised it himself, for there is, as I have argued elsewhere, a remarkable similarity between their strategy – as he perceptively describes it in *Alciphron* and the *Theory of Vision Vindicated* – and his own.[28]

What lay behind Berkeley's "delicate sense of danger" and willingness to dissemble? Where can we find the deep, natural Berkeley, and the source and justification for the dissimulation? Here I do not have anything very new to say. I continue to think that the man behind the mask was the intensely religious Berkeley, the champion of the faith. Yet isn't that what nearly everyone holds – that religiosity was the principal motivation of his life and works? Well, not quite. There is one notable biographer, G. A. Johnston, who denied it.[29] My own suggestion as well is that Berkeley's deep religiosity was more extreme and radical than usually is accepted, and certainly more than would be accepted by Luce. I suggest it was sometimes bordering on the messianic. Of course, if I am right about the religiosity as motivating and lying behind the dissimulation, then it seems natural to suppose that it was extreme. Why else would Berkeley mask it? So just as the freethinkers, such as Collins and John Toland, had to disguise their subversive, antireligious aims and present them cautiously and by degrees, so Berkeley had to disguise his equally subversive religious message, a message that was subversive not only of unbelievers but of the ordinary, limp orthodoxy of the time, of the "demy-atheists" – to use his expression in *Principles* 155 – "who cannot say there is not a God, but neither are they convinced... there is." Berkeley and Collins both were extremists, although with very different ideals, but they shared a willingness to use the same dissimulative and subversive means to realize their antithetical ends: atheism, on the one hand; super-religion, on the other.

That super-religion was the aim of Berkeley's philosophizing comes out, for example, in the final sections of the *Principles*. Of course, it may be objected that his talk of being in "the intimate presence" of God, on whom we have "a most absolute and immediate dependence" is just conventional preacher's talk, which should not be taken too seriously. Yet I don't think that Berkeley's strategic manipulation in the *New Theory of Vision* can be dismissed so lightly. For it is clear from the changes he made in subsequent editions that he wanted to move his readers by stages to a radically theistic view, according to which God literally communicates to us through vision. Originally, in the first two editions of 1709, Berkeley gives little hint that the book has a theological message: He speaks of the "language of nature," which he later changed in the 1732 editions to "the language of the author of nature." Indeed, in the *Theory of Vision Vindicated*, Section 38, he explains that "the conclusion [of the *New Theory* is] that *Vision is the Language of the Author of Nature*." Of course, it might be thought that Berkeley changed his mind, or came to see sometime before 1732 that his new theory of vision had a theological dimension. But that seems extremely unlikely, given what Berkeley says in *Principles* 44 and in his 1710 letter to Percival, where he notes that something is missing from the *New Theory*, "but in time I hope to make what is there laid down subservient to the ends of morality and *religion*."

The extreme religiosity that lay behind Berkeley's dissimulation also emerges – in a different and more personal way – in the deception I mentioned earlier: his lying to Percival about the Bermuda poem. Why was he so anxious not to be known as its author? Because, I suggest, the poem showed probably more than anything else the eschatological character of his project. It showed, in other words, its visionary nature – something Luce, of course, would have disputed.

I can underline my claim in two small but (I think) significant ways. First, note that in its 1726 version the poem's final line was even more pointedly eschatological than in the final version published in the *Miscellany*. There it read, "Time's noblest offspring is the last," whereas in 1726 it was, "The world's great effort is the last."[30] So the Bermuda project was going to bring about a world-historical development of ultimate significance. Yet are we not taking Berkeley's poetry and fancy too seriously? In response to such doubts I think we should consider the words of Berkeley's wife. For in the well-known letter to her son, circa 1760, some of which Luce quotes (with approbation), she says that Berkeley's "scheme for our Colonies and the World in general is not forgot before his eyes for whom it was undertaken."[31] Berkeley's scheme, then, was designed (according to his wife) for "the world in general" and for "the eyes" of God.

Here, in my view, we are getting close to the deep Berkeley who is behind, and requires, the conventional mask. And who else but his wife would see or help us to see this depth? Which of those people who were close to him could provide us with that intimate insight? Well, there was his life-long friend Thomas Prior, but unhappily we have none of Prior's letters and no testimony from him. Then there is Percival, who is undoubtedly an important source, except that Berkeley is guarded with him, to the point of being willing to lie. In short, I think we cannot do any better than Berkeley's wife. Her view of Berkeley has to be taken very seriously, despite recent evidence that she herself may not have been as normal and stable as was formerly supposed.[32] The important document here is her annotated copy of Stock's 1776 *Account of Berkeley*. I already have quoted one of her annotations. Here is another. Berkeley's maxim, she says, "was that nothing very good or very bad could be done until a man entirely got the better of fear of *que dira-ton* [what they say] – but when a man has overcome himself he overcomes the world & then is fitted for his Master's use."[33] Once again we have the world-historical individual, forwarding the aims of God. Because Berkeley believed himself to be without fear, he must also, presumably, have regarded himself as especially well-suited for his Master's use.

This image of Berkeley does not come to the fore, I think, in Luce's *Life*, perhaps because it is too close to Yeats's "God-appointed Berkeley" and too far from the commonsense man, "sane, shrewd and efficient," which Luce was anxious to emphasize in order to bolster his commonsense reading of Berkeley's philosophy.

Perhaps some will feel that I am being too psychological and *ad hominem* – unfair both to Luce and Berkeley. As I noted earlier, though, Luce himself was quite open about his aims. And he also interprets Yeats in a psychological way. Thus in the Preface to *Berkeley's Immaterialism*, Luce says that Yeats came under Berkeley's spell, but "appears to have been perplexed by him." Unable to work out what "manner of man was Berkeley," Yeats "projected his own questionings, it would seem, into the actual experience of the philosopher" (viii). Can we not say the same about Luce, that he projected his own vigorous common sense and straightforwardness into Berkeley? A balanced, normal man was required for the balanced, normal philosophy. This is perhaps one reason why Luce was so angry at the earliest memoir of Berkeley. Particularly in the hanging anecdote, Goldsmith depicts a wildish Berkeley – which for Luce was not acceptable, at least when he published the *Life* in 1949. It is noteworthy that fifteen years earlier, in his *Berkeley and Malebranche* (Oxford: Oxford University Press, 1934), the younger Luce was less inclined to reject the hanging story (7).

Clearly, I cannot here criticize Luce's portrait of Berkeley in any detail. Yet it is worth noting how, in his *Life of Berkeley*, Luce deals with those two extraordinary crusades that largely constitute Berkeley's later career – the Bermuda project and tar-water. Under Luce's careful contextualizing, both turn out to be quite sensible, or only mildly wrong-headed. In fact, I agree with a good deal of Luce's contextualizing. For example, I think that he was right to emphasize that Berkeley's use of tar-water makes sense when one realizes that there were no doctors or hospitals in his diocese.[34] Tar-water was not as crazy as some people – ignorant of Berkeley's work and time – have thought. But I do think that Luce has gone too far in his desire to see the normal Berkeley. Something wild remains in tar-water and Bermuda and perhaps also in immaterialism, something that resists contextualization or rationalization – and that, I would suggest, is the religious, the messianic, the eschatological element.

Among the many admirable features of Luce's *Life* is the way it synthesizes so much from previous biographers, thereby presenting the scholarly state of play in the late 1940s. There are two respects, though – one of commission, the other of omission – where Luce falls short.

First, Luce gives the impression in his *Life* that he is rehabilitating Berkeley from the dire influence of what we now know to be Goldsmith's memoir, from an image of Berkeley as the foolish stage philosopher. I doubt, however, whether this is accurate. Surveying biographical articles from the eighteenth to the twentieth centuries has persuaded me that Berkeley the man has been held almost universally in enormously high esteem, that he was not the figure of fun Luce suggests he was as a result of the early memoir.

The sin of omission relates to Johnston's 1923 book, *The Development of Berkeley's Philosophy*, which as I mentioned above, is unusual, perhaps even unique, in going against the traditional view of Berkeley as a paradigm of virtue and religiosity. Johnston realizes that he is opposing the orthodox view, and that his views "will [as he puts it] no doubt appear startling to those who have been accustomed to picture an angelic Berkeley" (337). Yet despite Johnston's self-confessed iconoclasm concerning Berkeley's character, his views are not canvased by Luce in his *Life*, nor have they been examined seriously, as far as I can tell, by any other writer on Berkeley – although Jessop in his *Bibliography of Berkeley* (1973) describes Johnston's book, which recently has been reprinted, as "one of the ablest books on Berkeley" (see 653). Perhaps one reason that Johnston's heterodox views have not been examined is that they are set out very unmethodically, in long notes or digressions. They also are laced with some pretty extraordinary conjectures – for example, "It has not been noticed... that the most remarkable thing about Berkeley's participation in the deist controversy is just the fact that he did take part in it against the deists" (330). Johnston also suggests that Berkeley's opposition to the freethinkers was motivated in part by pique against Toland for becoming the champion of the freethinkers before Berkeley himself.

I hope it will help the debate if I try to outline Johnston's position in a series of more or less definite propositions with the supporting evidence.

(1) Berkeley was naturally sceptical, distrustful, and critical. In support of this claim Johnston mentions Berkeley's bold critiques of abstract ideas and Newton's fluxions, as well as his autobiographical remark in the *Philosophical Commentaries* 266 that he "was distrustful at 8 years old; and consequently by nature disposed for these new doctrines." Johnston also adverts to "one or two amusing anecdotes of his student years [as, for example, the hanging incident, which] illustrate [Berkeley's] aversion to taking anything on trust" (331).

(2) Berkeley is not, however, sceptical or distrustful of religion in his published works.

(3) This is very odd. Why didn't Berkeley extend his natural freethinking and scepticism, so evident in philosophy and mathematics, to the one area which then was becoming the object of important sceptical criticism? This is the first part of Johnston's argument. His way of resolving the puzzle is as follows:

(4) Berkeley actually was sceptical of religion, but kept his scepticism to himself, letting it out only in his private notebooks, the *Philosophical Commentaries*. Johnston takes entry 720 as the crucial piece of evidence that Berkeley did have serious doubts about the truth of the Christian religion. I will discuss his interpretation of 720 in a moment, but first I should

explain why Johnston thinks that Berkeley was reluctant to express openly his doubts about religion. Briefly, then:

(5) Berkeley was most eager for advancement within the church; and always had his eye on "the main chance." In support of this, Johnston offers a lot of detail about Berkeley's attempts to gain preferment, most of it familiar to readers of Luce's *Life*. Johnston also quotes Berkeley's warning to himself in *Commentaries* 715, "N. B. To use utmost caution not to give the least handle of offence to the Church or Churchmen," and his remark, "I'll never blame a man for acting upon interest. He's a fool that acts upon any other principles" (quoted on 332). Johnston's conclusion is that Berkeley suppressed and dissembled his scepticism about religion to advance himself.

(6) Not only that, but Berkeley compounded his dishonesty by repeatedly attacking the freethinkers, the very people with whom he had so much in common. Berkeley did so, according to Johnston, because (a) that was a recognized way of achieving advancement within the church; (b) Berkeley had a great desire to stand out, to be known; and (c) he was angry at his countryman, John Toland, for beating him to the leadership of the British freethinkers.

Here, then, we have Johnston's unusual perspective on Berkeley – that he was a crypto-sceptic in religion and attacked the freethinkers in bad faith. Needless to say, I do not like this picture. Given my own willingness to see widespread dissimulation in Berkeley's life and works, however, I am hardly in a position to become indignant with Johnston, even though his conclusions go very much against my own. What I should like to point out is that Johnston's argument stands or falls with entry 720; it is this entry which "shows," as he puts it, that Berkeley "did have doubts in religion, and . . . came to the deliberate conclusion that it was necessary to suppress them" (332). But does it? As I (and I think most recent commentators) have interpreted 720, it is aimed against the freethinkers, particularly Toland and Collins, and their attack on mysteries. Indeed, Berkeley here is working out one of his most powerful defences of Christianity, his emotive account of mysteries. Perhaps part of Johnston's difficulty is that he mistakenly thinks that Berkeley is talking of all religion in entry 720. That is not so. It is not natural religion – which would be in the realm of reason and philosophy. Nor is it even all of revealed religion that Berkeley thinks we should give an "humble, implict" assent to, such as the Popish peasant gives to his Latin mass. Berkeley means *only* mysteries in Scripture, such as the Holy Trinity.[35]

Entry 720 is crucial for Johnston's interpretation of Berkeley as dissembling in his Christianity and his attack on the freethinkers. Other parts of Johnston's case also are disputable, as for example his interpretation of entry 715 and the extent to which Berkeley was motivated by the desire for preferment in the church. Luce discusses the latter question and the evidence with considerable care, and it is possible that he had Johnston's claim in mind, although he does not mention him. In any case, the second part of Johnston's argument crumbles with his interpretation of 720. That still leaves the first part, though, namely that there is something psychologically anomalous in the way Berkeley could be iconoclastic and critical in nearly every area but religion. Although I am not entirely sure what to make of this thesis, I don't think that it poses a problem for my interpretation. If anything, it seems to support the picture of Berkeley I have been advancing here, that is the fearless super-Christian, with a delicate sense of danger.[36]

NOTES

1. Letter to Samuel Johnson, November 25, 1729, in *The Works of George Berkeley*, ed. A. A. Luce and T. E. Jessop, 9 vols. (London: Thomas Nelson, 1949–57), 2: 282.
2. *Works* 7: 373. For the complete poem, see the Appendix to this *Companion*.
3. See General Preface in *Works* 1: v. For convenience, I refer to Luce's *Life of Berkeley* (which was reprinted in 1968 with a new preface) as *Life*.
4. For a fuller account, see David Berman, *George Berkelely: Idealism and the Man* (Oxford: Clarendon Press, 1994), referred to as *George Berkeley*. For bibliographical corrections and expansion on Luce and Jessop, see G. Keynes, *A Bibliography of George Berkeley* (Oxford: Clarendon Press, 1976) and the *Berkeley Newsletter*, Dublin, 1977–1998.
5. See D. Berman, "Mrs Berkeley's annotations in her interleaved copy of *An Account of the Life of George Berkeley* (1776)," *Hermathena* 122 (1977): 15–28.
6. See "Mrs Berkeley's annotations," 23–4.

7. See D. Berman, "Berkeley and King," *Notes and Queries* 29 (1982): 528–30, and "The Jacobitism of Berkeley's *Passive Obedience*," *Journal of the History of Ideas* 47 (1986): 309–19; Richard Popkin, *The High Road to Pyrrhonism* (San Diego: Austin Hill Press, 1980), 363–7; and G. N. Cantor, "Two letters relating to Berkeley's social circle," *Berkeley Newsletter* 4 (1980): 2–3.
8. A. Friedman (ed.), *Collected Works of Oliver Goldsmith* (Oxford: Clarendon Press, 1966), Volume 3.
9. See *Collected Works of Goldsmith*, 3: 35. For a facsimile of the memoir, see *George Berkeley: Eighteenth-Century Responses*, ed. David Berman (New York: Garland, 1989), 1: 171–9.
10. See "A new letter by Berkeley to Browne on Divine Analogy," *Mind* 77 (1969): 375–92.
11. "George Berkeley, Sir Richard Steele and the *Ladies Library*," *The Scriblerian* 12 (1980): 1–2; see also E. J. Furlong and D. Berman, "George Berkeley and the *Ladies Library*," *Berkeley Newsletter* 4 (1980): 5–13.
12. See B. Belfrage, "A summary of Berkeley's metaphysics in a hitherto unpublished Berkeleian manuscript," *Berkeley Newsletter* 3 (1979): 1–4.
13. See *The Guardian*, ed. J. C. Stephens (Lexington: University Press of Kentucky, 1982), 27–8; Furlong, "How much of Steele's *Guardian 39* did Berkeley write?" *Hermathena* 89 (1957): 76–88.
14. *George Berkeley*, 73–7.
15. "George Berkeley: pictures by Goldsmith, Yeats and Luce," *Hermathena* 139 (1985): 9–23.
16. "George Berkeley: pictures," 18–21; see also D. Berman, *George Berkeley*, chapter 8.
17. See *Works* 9: 153. From the manuscript it is not clear whether these two sentences should be considered as one or two notes.
18. See D. Berman, *George Berkeley*, 23–5 and 55. Berkeley is dissembling when he suggests that what we immediately see are points on a two-dimensional plane or a flat surface variously coloured; for what we immediately see, according to him, is only diversity of light and colours (*New Theory*, Sections 157–8). His account of the moon illusion (in Sections 67–78) also may be based on dissimulation. In order to have a puzzle to solve Berkeley needs to assume that the visual magnitude of the moon on the horizon is the same as that at the apex of the sky. According to Berkeley, though, there is no sense (strictly speaking) in saying that what we see has any determinate size, which is the reason geometry is about the tangible rather than the visual (see Sections 155–6). I was helped to see these two points in conversations with Dr Bertil Belfrage.

19. *Works* 8: 36.
20. A. A. Luce, "Is there a Berkeleian philosophy?" *Hermathena 25* (1936): 200–1, and *Berkeley: Philosophical Works*, ed. M. R. Ayers (London: Everyman, 1989), 77, note. See also Ayers's discussion of PHK 1 in Chapter 2 of this *Companion*.
21. *Works* 7: 164; also see D. Berman, *George Berkeley*, 189.
22. "Mrs Berkeley's annotations," 21.
23. J. Kupfer, "Universalization in Berkeley's rule utilitarianism," *Revue Internationale de Philosophie* 28 (1974): 511.
24. See *Life*, 106–7. See a forthcoming note by Ian Tipton, who differs from Luce on this episode.
25. *Works* 8: 152.
26. See *Works* 8: 29, and Gregory Vlastos, *Socrates: Ironist and Moral Philosopher* (Cambridge: Cambridge University Press, 1991), 132–3.
27. See A. A. Luce, "More unpublished Berkeley letters and new Berkeleiana," *Hermathena* 48 (1933): 28.
28. *George Berkeley*, 164–6.
29. G. A. Johnston, *The Development of Berkeley's Philosophy* (London: Macmillan, 1923; reprinted New York: Garland, 1988).
30. *Works* 7: 370 and 373.
31. British Museum, Add. Ms. 39, 312, p. 228.
32. This comes out in the Will of her daughter-in-law Eliza, which is now in the Trinity College, Dublin, Library, Ms 3530. Eliza speaks of Anne as a "violent & spirited fretful mother," who "beats maids" and beat her grown son [George, Eliza's husband] in front of his son (f. 37); indeed, according to Eliza, Anne was "esteemed the most violent spirit throughout Ireland" (f. 106).
33. "Mrs Berkeley's annotations," 22. Neither of the two maxims was used in the Addenda and Corrigenda in the *Biographia Brittanica*, 2nd. ed. (London, 1784).
34. See *Life*, especially 197–200.
35. See *George Berkeley*, 13–14, 146–50.
36. I am grateful for the support I have received over the years from the staff of the Trinity College Library, especially the Departments of Older Printed Books and Manuscripts, in my work on Berkeley.

MICHAEL AYERS

2 Was Berkeley an empiricist or a rationalist?

I. INTRODUCTION

The distinction between rationalists and empiricists has become something of a punch-bag in recent decades, and we have been encouraged to pursue supposedly subtler analyses of purposes, influences and allegiances. One line of attack has taken the form of various attempts to divorce the "British Empiricist" Berkeley from either Locke or Hume, or from both Locke and Hume, and to hand him over to the Cartesians. The rationalist-empiricist dichotomy is then dismissed as a construct of nineteenth-century Kantians.[1] My present purpose is to argue, on the contrary, that it is a distinction not only with ancient origins, but with a peculiar relevance to the interpretation of early-modern philosophy, not least that of Berkeley, just because of those origins. On the other hand it needs to be explained how such disagreement over the classification of Berkeley can have arisen.

The distinction was probably first drawn with respect to medical theory, and continued to be so up to modern times, but it was early accorded a wider significance. As Michael Frede has pointed out in his helpful reconstruction of early Greek empiricism, both Plato and Aristotle identified for criticism a type of view, which explains human cognition wholly in terms of sense and memory, and at least some version of which characteristically maintains that all appearances are equally true.[2] Their own theories, on the other hand, and Plato's in particular, ascribe a necessary role to mind or intellect in the achievement of universal knowledge or "science" (*episteme, gnosis*). Intellect is a higher faculty having an affinity with its universal, immutable, immaterial objects, while the senses are similarly akin to what is particular, fleeting and material. A famous passage in *Sophist*,[3] comparing the dispute with the battle between Gods and Giants, makes it clear that empiricism and materialism go together, as do love of the forms and proper recognition of the role of intellect. In another well-known passage, in *Phaedo*,[4] materialist explanations of thought as an operation of the blood or the brain, of air or fire, are linked with an account of knowledge as a kind of stable memory or opinion deriving from sensation. Moreover, the preferred alternative to materialist explanation, when carried to a stage that (as Plato represented him) Socrates found himself unable to reach, will not only recognize thought as a function of the soul, but will be teleological, explaining the universe as ordered throughout by mind in accordance with what is best. The route by which we may move towards such explanation, Plato suggested, is through methodical consideration of the hierarchy of Forms. The top of this hierarchy is variously identified as the Good, Being, and the One, from which the subordinate Forms somehow intelligibly flow. The role of the senses is simply to prompt the intuitive insights of intellect.

Ancient philosophers after Plato are not all so neatly classifiable as either Gods or Giants. Aristotle himself might seem a moderate, seeking a middle road. While retaining universal and intelligible forms in his system as principles of teleological explanation, he brought them down to earth, binding them into the particulars to which he accorded primary reality. In effect he conceded to the empiricist that knowledge is based on material supplied by sense and memory. Yet the inductive leap to the universal is assigned to an intellect which is quasi-Platonic at least to the extent that, whereas the faculties of sense and memory require embodiment in physical organs, the active intellect may exist immaterially, as pure form. Other philosophies create similar problems of classification. Epicureans are clearly Giants, but the Stoic system might seem to span the dichotomy. On the one hand, their world is moved and sustained by a rational power that pervades it as we are pervaded by our soul. On the other hand, there is nothing active which is not a body, including the soul and God, who acts as a form of fire or aether. Stoic epistemology, moreover, is pretty firmly sense-based and nominalist.

Within Hellenistic empiricism there were other important divisions. Epicureans emphasised the dependability of sense-impressions, developing the idea, criticised by Aristotle, that all appearances or impressions are true. They also presented atomism less as certain truth than as the most convincing explanatory hypothesis or speculation. Stoics, on the other hand, recognized some impressions as more dependable than others, and did not rule out systematic demonstrative "science" – indeed they came to hold it necessary for genuine knowledge and certainty even about particulars. The science of the Stoic *sophos* or sage is achieved by building systematically on provisionally accepted clear and evident sense-impressions, employing principles (some borrowed from the Epicureans) which seem to have been regarded as conceptually evident or necessary, such as "If sweat flows through the skin, then there are ducts," or "If there is motion, there is empty space." The possibility of such universal knowledge is not ascribed to forms and the intellect, but to human conceptualization – to abstraction and language. It seems that experience both gives our terms their meanings and ipso facto generates self-evident hypothetical truths that may serve in scientific demonstrations.

Against this background it is not so surprising that the New Philosophers should have fallen at least roughly into two groups, corresponding, indeed, to two possible lines of criticism of Aristotelianism. They were in agreement that forms and teleology should be excluded from physics, that mechanical explanations are paradigms of scientific explanation, and that the only intrinsic attributes of bodies are quantitative, qualities being a matter of the way things appear to perceivers. But were the failings of the Aristotelians due, as Bacon thought, to their being insufficiently attentive to nature as it is open to experience? Were they rationalist spiders spinning their specious teleological and qualitative principles from their own entrails? Or were they, as Descartes seems to suggest in the *Meditations*, blundering empiricists trying vainly to build science from the materials of sense-experience and ignoring the divine gift of mathematics, which is innate and does not draw on experience at all? On the one hand, the new picture of the physical world was deeply indebted to the ancient theory most like it, the atomism of the empiricist Epicurus. On the other hand, it came in with a programme for mathematizing nature, at least some of whose proponents drew their chief philosophical justification from a Platonist view of mathematics as a science prior to experience and brought to the interpretation of experience.

The present proposal, then, is that the question in my title does not rest on anachronistic, presuppositions. There really was a choice facing those seventeenth-century philosophers who drew on ancient models in order to validate and interpret the New Philosophy, a choice reasonably described as being between empiricism and rationalism. The choice was, in effect, whether to go down the Platonist or Augustinian road with such philosophers as Mersenne and Descartes, or to pursue the Epicurean and Stoic path of constructive, antisceptical empiricism, with all its natural and historic affinities with materialism and the hypothesis of atoms and the void. That is not to say that Berkeley, whose purposes were different, fits neatly into either category. There is nothing misguided in asking the question in our title. On the contrary, it is an interesting aspect of Berkeley's argument that he came to present his "immaterialism" as if it combined the best insights of both kinds of theory. There was indeed a division, but Berkeley deliberately operated on both sides of the divide. My strategy in what follows will be to go further into what it was to have been a rationalist or an empiricist in the seventeenth century, and then to show how some of the main doctrines characteristic of each party were adapted and welded together by Berkeley in a self-consciously synthetic system.

II. "RATIONALISM"

One of the first systematic epistemologists of the seventeenth century who deserves to be called a "Rationalist" was Marin Mersenne. As Peter Dear has argued at length, Mersenne's undogmatic antiscepticism was very much motivated and shaped by his desire to enhance the status of mathematics as a tool in natural philosophy.[5] The Aristotelians explained mathematics as concerned with quantity taken abstractly, without respect to real essences or natural change. Consequently, because it was not *scientia per causas* – scientific understanding of things through their causes (unless purely "formal causes") – there was a tendency not to take it seriously. Mersenne conceded that mathematics is not concerned with the essences of things, but held that the eternal truths of mathematics exist as archetypes in the mind of the Creator, employed in the creation of a harmonious universe. Human reason is created in the image of divine reason, allowing us to achieve some understanding of the universal harmony through the "mixed mathematics" of such sciences as optics, astronomy, and mechanics, not to speak of harmonics itself. Like others who had wished to improve the standing of mathematics, such as the sixteenth-century Jesuit, Pedro da Fonseca, Mersenne was calling on the authority of the Christianized Platonism of St Augustine, and indeed on a model that had been widely absorbed into Scholastic Aristotelianism. It is worth pausing to note certain advantages of this theistic version of Platonism.

Plato's epistemology is triangular, a matter of the interrelations between the human mind, universals and particular sensible things. In order to achieve "science," the mind has to apprehend the immutable and eternal Forms, the Triangle itself, Beauty itself and the like, but such sensible things as geometrical diagrams and beautiful people play an important stimulative role, if not an essential one. Moreover, universal science has some relevance to understanding the sensible world: To have knowledge of the forms is in some way to know why sensible things are as they are. Plato left problems with respect to both the relation between mind and forms and the relation between forms and particulars. Such arguments as the "third man" argument of *Parmenides* appear to record self-conscious failure to account for the form-particular relation, while Plato seems not to have decided definitely whether we apprehend the forms in this life or recall their prenatal apprehension. The Augustinian version of the Platonic triangle, however, explains both problematic relations in terms of creation, as well as assigning a mode of existence to universals which avoids setting them up as eternal rivals to God. God creates particular things in accordance with the ideas, essences, eternal truths or archetypes that are the objects of – indeed constitute – divine reason, while human reason is created in the image of divine reason. That explains both why our minds are fitted to apprehend the universal, and why universal knowledge has application to particulars. Just as for Plato, the senses simply prompt the intellect to make such innate knowledge explicit.

Descartes followed Mersenne in basing his epistemology on the Augustinian triangle, but there was a crucial difference. Whereas Mersenne confessed ignorance of the intrinsic essences of things, explaining the usefulness of mathematics by his conception of a divine harmony among God's creatures, Descartes excluded such scepticism simply by abolishing the presumption of unknown essences beyond the eternal truths that are known, thus closing the gap between mathematics and nature. To conceive of material things "in so far as they are the subject matter of pure mathematics"[6] is not to conceive of them merely abstractly, but as they are essentially, as they are capable of concrete existence independent of all but the Creator. By this stroke Descartes assumed the Augustinian model in order to ascribe so much more to mathematics than Plato had done that the kind of teleology characteristic of both Plato's and Aristotle's theory of explanation was driven right out of physics. Yet the attraction of the model lay in more than its power to justify the programme of mathematizing natural philosophy. Whether for their own satisfaction or for the sake of public acceptance, advocates of any form of mechanistic corpuscularianism were faced with the problem of reconciling it with the truths of religion, of showing that it was not, after all, a godless doctrine. In this respect, its incorporation into an Augustinian framework would appear an invaluable line of defence. Descartes certainly seems to have thought so, and continually reminds his reader of his system's theological advantages. The *cogito* itself has an Augustinian origin as an answer to scepticism, but Descartes employed it for the additional purpose of grounding a notion of the soul much like that of Plato's *Timaeus*, an essentially rational being which is liable to be tumbled into error and wrongdoing by the sensations, passions, and false perspectives consequent upon its embodiment.

The Third Meditation also contains strong Platonist overtones, echoing the famous Platonic analogy of the sun much favoured by proponents of the theory of divine, but natural, illumination. The Meditation presents God, as Plato presents the Form the Good, as both the sustainer of the objects of knowledge and the source of the light by which we know them. If we cannot gaze directly at the divine sun in this life,[7] we can at least momentarily perceive it to be the origin of the natural light by which we apprehend truth, a piece of knowledge which, once achieved, permanently validates that light. It is crucial to Descartes' argument that the light in question is the natural light of the intellect. Unsupported, the senses crumple before the onslaught of the sceptic, but the intellect stands firm, validating rather than undermining itself. Certainty extends to the objects of the senses only insofar as their deliverances are subjected to the judgment of reason. Moreover, Descartes' intellect has two traditional functions, both the apprehension of eternal truths and the reflexive knowledge of the mind itself. Indeed, the two functions merge insofar as innate ideas are made explicit precisely through self-reflection. Even the idea of a perfect being is revealed through my reflexive idea of myself as imperfect. Descartes famously goes so far as to say that innate ideas are nothing beyond the mind's faculty of thinking (a doctrine which it seems difficult to extend to the idea of extension).[8]

This is not, perhaps, the place to pursue a controversial interpretation of Descartes, but it does seem relevant to our theme that *Meditations* is both an overtly polemical work and, as such, a sustained attack on empiricism. Commentators tend to assume that Descartes was always targeting Aristotelian epistemology, together with the uncritical, vulgar assumptions on which Aristotelianism was taken by its critics to be based. Yet that cannot entirely explain his emphatic insistence on the limitations of the senses and the imagination, though, or the care with which he draws the distinction, already fully explicit in Aristotelian theory, between imagination and intellect. The form and earlier stages of the First Meditation argument with the sceptic, the notions of a criterion of truth and of clear and distinct perception, and the analysis of judgment which assigns assent to the will, all would have forcibly reminded the philosophical reader of the celebrated debate between Stoics and Academics. The big difference between that debate and Descartes' rerun is that whereas the Stoics settled for a conception of science ultimately based on the clear and evident sense impressions that science comes reciprocally to confirm, the *scientia* with which Descartes returns, in the Sixth Meditation, to certify the deliverances of the senses has independent, innate, purely intellectual foundations. A corollary of that difference is the independence of mind from body. Descartes' motive for this attack on traditional empiricist materialism might simply have been to emphasise to the orthodox that, despite his materialist physics, he was firmly on the side of the Gods. Yet it seems evident that he was already engaged in the battle among the New Philosophers, endeavouring to preempt the kind of arguments immediately brought against him in what were, after all, philosophically by far the most significant of the "Objections" to the *Meditations* – those of Gassendi and Hobbes.

Another feature of Descartes' theory particularly relevant to Berkeley is his "voluntarism," or the role of God in his physics. In the

Third Meditation Descartes set up the metaphysical model according to which God maintains things in being from moment to moment by what is equivalent to a process of constant creation. We learn from *Principles of Philosophy* and elsewhere that, as this model is applied to physical change, the movement of a body is simply a function of the continuous succession of places in which God chooses to recreate it. Consequently, the laws that govern how bodies move and push or knock one another about should not be thought to flow from the intrinsic, geometrical nature of matter, but to be the general rules of the harmony according to which God maintains matter in being. That the rules are as they are flows from the immutable nature of God.[9]

Descartes' motives in thus having God do everything in nature are not entirely clear. It may be, as Gary Hatfield and Daniel Garber say in slightly different ways, that God was brought in to replace the forms and powers ejected from physics together with Aristotelian teleology.[10] Another motive was the thought that, if motions are *modes* of bodies, then it is absurd to suppose that they are transferred between bodies, because a mode (as it were, an abstractly-considered *aspect*) of a substance cannot hop from one substance to another. Rather, "when the motion of one part [of matter] decreases, that of another increases by the same amount."[11] Thus God is kept busy maintaining the constant overall quantity of motion. A yet more fundamental aim, no doubt, was to avoid appearing to postulate a world-machine that could be supposed, once created, to go on working independently of its creator. Descartes' world is rather more austere than Plato's, but after all is one in which, as Plato himself had put it (even if not quite as he had conceived of it), "the ordering mind orders everything and places each thing severally as it is best."

As for other "Rationalists," there are many marks in the systems of Spinoza and Leibniz of the deep influence of Platonism. Moreover, although neither was a voluntarist, their philosophies were shaped deeply by both Cartesian principles and Cartesian problems. Both Spinoza and Leibniz drew strong distinctions equivalent to Descartes' distinction between intellect and imagination, and both focused on the issues raised by the notion of divine ideas, and by what I have called the Augustinian triangle.[12] The rationalist both more overtly Platonist and more closely related to Berkeley than Spinoza and Leibniz are, however, is Malebranche, who rejected innate ideas, embracing the option of direct access to the divine ideas in this life. Malebranche also adopted a rigorous voluntarism. A noteworthy corollary of these famous doctrines is his view that reflexive consciousness does not set an "idea" before us at all, in other words a conception of its object such as God has of it. "*Conscience*" is the mind's immediate reflexive apprehension of itself and its operations. It does not supply the subject matter of science, however, as does intellectual perception of the divine idea of extension.

III. "EMPIRICISM"

I will now consider certain seventeenth-century empiricists who took over Epicurean and Stoic opposition both to transcendent universals and to scepticism. Crucially, they held that there are no universal forms or ideas outside the mind,[13] so that there is no need to postulate a special faculty of reason or intellect with which to apprehend them. Science – if it is not, as some thought, beyond us – is possible only because of the mind's ability to order and abstract the materials received through the senses. Moreover, the senses have an independent authority with respect to the existence of external objects, and their deliverances require no endorsement by reason. On the contrary, reason depends on the senses, so that to doubt the deliverances of the senses is to undermine reason, too.[14]

One aspect of empiricism that underwent considerable development in the seventeenth century was the theory of abstraction. For Gassendi, the great exponent of Epicureanism, a universal concept is a construct achieved either by bundling particulars into a sort of heap to form a class-idea, or by abstracting out a common aspect to form an attribute-idea. Universal propositions owe all their evidence and certainty to induction, that is, to the evidence of particular sensory judgments. Reasoning from universal principles, it seems, is just a way of bringing uniform experience to bear on particulars, whether perceived or unperceived, which are in question.[15]

Hobbes, on the other hand, had a theory designed to explain how rigorous science is possible. Basic knowledge of fact is "nothing else, but Sense and Memory."[16] Thought consists of a stream of sensations and sensory images arising in accordance with principles of association. Thus animal expectation occurs when two things are so linked in experience that one is a natural sign of the other, so that the image of one stimulates the image of the other. The introduction of words into "the train of imaginations" makes it possible, according to Hobbes, to perceive universal truth, and to reason syllogistically. Roughly, he held that general words, as images associated with other images, enable us to universalize the perception of a particular truth – that this triangle has angles equal to two right-angles, for example – by marking the relevant aspects of the particular in a way which makes us think of other particulars – in this example, other triangles.[17] Language thus enables us to analyze the objects of experience and focus on those aspects that matter for the purpose of understanding them geometrically. The same method applies in natural philosophy, at least with respect to its general principles. Sensory knowledge takes things in as wholes, but knowledge of causes requires analysis, since (as Hobbes puts it) "the cause of the whole is compounded from the causes of the parts." Here "parts" are not ingredients but aspects – ways of conceiving of bodies. Eventually analysis will bring us to the most general or simple concepts (the basic concepts of geometry and mechanics), a level at which causal principles become, as Hobbes says, "manifest in themselves."[18] In this way it is possible to arrive at an a priori science of mechanics – a surprising trip, we may feel, for an empiricist to have made, but not so surprising given the Stoic precedent. Bacon himself (who also may have been influenced by Stoic theory) had argued that "science" springs from a properly systematic analysis of experience.

Here, perhaps, it might be worth considering – and moralizing about – the possible claim that the empiricist Hobbes was also a rationalist, in that he was a mechanist who believed that the necessity of the laws of mechanics could become self-evident to us.[19] Does Hobbes's empiricist rationalism show that the dichotomy is, as Louis Loeb puts it, broken-backed? Rather similar arguments have been advanced with respect to Locke. He was picked out as an inconsistent empiricist by Kant,[20] and his intuitionist conception of knowledge together with his mechanist ideal in physics are for Loeb strong grounds for lumping him in with Descartes as a rationalist, and so for dumping the rationalist-empiricist dichotomy altogether.[21]

Loeb, like Richard Aaron before him, proposes that Locke acquired his "rationalist" conception of intuition and demonstration from reading the *Regulae* in the late 1670s.[22] Locke's account of intuition and demonstration, however, like Descartes' superficially similar account, was a response to a thoroughly traditional distinction in logic. In fact, Locke's treatment, although equally antisyllogistic, is very different from Descartes'. Not only is it framed round his conception of the perception of a relation between ideas, but more importantly it assumes that the ideas between which necessary relations may be perceived are ideas of sense and imagination. Indeed Locke offers a long, anti-Cartesian argument in that very chapter for the possibility of demonstrative reasoning concerned with ideas of colors and secondary qualities in general, at least, as he says, "where the difference is so great as to produce in the Mind clearly distinct *Ideas*, whose differences can be properly retained."[23] Locke's sensationist or imagist definition of a clear idea, in another overtly anti-Cartesian passage, runs as follows:

> Our *simple Ideas* are all *clear*, when they are such as the Objects themselves, from whence they were taken, did or might, in a well-ordered Sensation or Perception, present them. Whilst the Memory retains them thus, and can produce them to the Mind, when-ever it has occasion to consider them, they are *clear Ideas*.[24]

For Locke, as for Hobbes, the faculties that supply reasoning with its objects are sense and memory. What makes universalization possible is abstraction, the capacity to pick out significant aspects in the particular case and to employ them to define the relevant classes. Precise abstraction is simply a bit easier in the case of quantitative ideas, and there are no grounds for a distinction between ideas of sense and intellectual ideas. One difference from Hobbes is that Locke did not explain the process in terms of the association of images, and accordingly held general words to be inessential to general thought. Another difference is that Locke did not believe that the methodical analysis of human sense experience will lead us, conveniently, to the necessary principles of physics. Nevertheless, he did accept that mechanical change is intrinsically *more* intelligible to us than qualitative change, and that clockwork does supply us with a glimmering understanding of how bodies necessarily operate on one another.[25] Locke, then, was another empiricist who was a mechanist, if one who believed that a "science of bodies" is for us no more than an ideal possibility.[26]

It seems, then, that it is dangerous to approach the rationalist-empiricist dichotomy with philosophically motivated assumptions as to which doctrines are quintessentially one or the other. History can lay too many surprises for that kind of game, and the consequence will inevitably be that an important division will appear to dissolve in our hands, a division that is not just a convenience of classification but a matter of how philosophers saw themselves in relation to the tradition, or of how they made use of the tradition. Here I would say at least a word for Kant. Admittedly, his criticisms of alleged inconsistency presuppose a philosophical (and hostile) idea of archetypal empiricists and rationalists (not to speak of his actual mistakes about individuals – as when he bizarrely accuses Locke of attempting to prove the immortality of the soul). Yet, despite seeing each "school" as by definition at one erroneous extreme or the other,[27] Kant clearly had a historical understanding of the distinction, which may be why it did not occur to him to doubt that Locke is, after all, on the side of Epicurus and against Plato.

In fact, that is not at all a bad way of reading Locke. What Locke was against in Descartes' philosophy was not just its dogmatism, but the way in which it was imbued with the supernatural, with what Kant called "mysticism." Locke's doctrine of abstract ideas was not just, or primarily, a way of explaining classification – still less an account of our ability to recognize when a general term has application – but was first and foremost a way of explaining away the "eternal truths." His problem was not rule-following – he just assumed that we can remember that there is a precise respect, to be marked by the word "white," in which chalk or snow seen today resembles milk seen yesterday. Locke's problem was with the object of what Kant calls "knowledge through reason." Here is his antimystical, anti-Augustinian solution, much like that of Hobbes:

> Such propositions are therefore called *Eternal Truths*, not because they are Eternal Propositions actually formed, and antecedent to the Understanding, that at any time makes them; nor because they are imprinted on the Mind from any patterns, that are any where of them [*sic*] out of the Mind, and existed before: But because being once made, about abstract *Ideas*, so as to be true, they will, whenever they can be supposed to be made again at any time past or to come, by a Mind having those *Ideas*, always actually be true. For Names being supposed to stand perpetually for the same *Ideas*; and the same *Ideas* having immutably the same Habitudes one to another, Propositions, concerning any abstract *Ideas*, that are once true, must needs be *eternal Verities*.[28]

That he was able to dispense with the eternal truths and divine illumination while maintaining an intuitionist and, for that matter, infallibilist conception of *a priori* knowledge should not mislead us into treating him as any kind of Cartesian. To do that, with respect, is to be insensitive to the way philosophical controversies tend to go. One side may see an intuitive datum or *explicandum*, easily dealt with by their own theory, as the rock on which the opposing theory obviously founders. What tends to happen next is that the other side (perhaps after more or less implausible attempts to reject the intuition) modifies or develops its position in such a way as to generate an explanation. Hobbes and Locke no doubt saw the explicitly intuitionist account of universal knowledge made possible by their development of the empiricist theory of abstraction as a strength, not a qualification of their empiricism. For it enabled them to avoid the implausible inductivism of Gassendi excoriated, for example, in the Port Royal *Logic*. Mathematical truths too, obviously, are not inductive generalizations.[29] Among concessions aimed to disarm criticism we should perhaps see the weakening of the traditional connection between empiricism and materialism. Where Hobbes and the early Gassendi were firmly materialist, late Gassendi and Locke conceded the possibility (even probability) of an immaterial soul. The concession was consonant with their general antidogmatism, but to have judged dualism *probable* seems, given other arguments of theirs, quite likely to have been the deliberate sugaring of an unpopular pill. Locke nevertheless gained considerable notoriety simply by his firm treatment of the issue as an open question of natural fact, undecidable by reason and irrelevant to religion. In general, the constructive empiricists were the philosophical naturalists of the seventeenth century, and deserve our respect as such.

The fundamental naturalism of the empiricists explains what might otherwise seem a somewhat paradoxical feature of seventeenth-century philosophy from a twenty-first-century point of view. The Cartesians, as we have seen, were voluntarists. Geometrically defined matter seemed just the kind of inert stuff as must owe its motion to mind. Plato's dream is thus fulfilled. A minor oddity of this rationalistic voluntarism is its ambivalent attitude towards the mechanist intuition itself. On the one hand, it seemed to Cartesians and many empiricists alike that mechanical processes are intelligible, indeed infallibly predictable.[30] In some form this was an agreed *explicandum* of the New Philosophers' philosophy of physics. The Cartesians, however, were committed to holding that such intuitive reasoning involves implicit reflection on the immutability of the Creator, or on the necessary tendency of a perfect being to produce the richest outcome by the simplest means. Hobbes, on the other hand, could attribute the intelligibility of mechanical change wholly to the perceptible nature of what is happening before our eyes. Locke was more sceptical, yet he too held that if we fully perceived and understood the nature of matter and its mechanical structure, we would be able to predict the outcome of any particular situation "without trial." In other words, there would be no need to bring God into the calculation, since the laws of mechanics are not superimposed by God onto a neutral or inert matter, but flow from the unknown nature of matter itself. In this way, natures are prior to laws.

IV. THE AMBIVALENCE OF BERKELEY'S THEORY

Let us now turn to Berkeley. Why has he been regarded so generally as an empiricist? Two reasons should hit the reader in the eye right at the beginning of the *Principles of Human Knowledge*, and must have been carefully designed to do so. First, of course, comes the heavily nominalist, imagist account of universal knowledge in the Introduction. Whether this theory is essentially Locke's view, as I would argue, is beside the present point.[31] It is indubitably a version of the traditional empiricist doctrine. There is even the characteristic hint that language plays an important role, if not an essential, one.[32] Certainly in his objections to Locke, Berkeley is laying claim to a more rigorous nominalism and imagism than his celebrated predecessor. Equally certainly Berkeley is putting down an unmistakeable marker, whatever later qualifications may emerge. His chosen epistemology is that of the empiricists.

The same goes even more obviously for the opening sentence of *Principles*, Part I, Section 1:

> It is evident to anyone who takes a survey of the objects of human knowledge, that they are either ideas actually imprinted on the senses, or else such as are perceived by attending to the passions and operations of the mind, or

lastly ideas formed by help of memory and imagination, either compounding, dividing, or barely representing those originally perceived in the aforesaid ways.

Notoriously, an apparent implication of this no doubt carefully crafted sentence – that there are ideas of reflection – goes against a Berkeleian principle.[33] That only makes it more certain that at this stage, at least, Berkeley wants his reader to recognize him as a paid-up empiricist, holding a view very like Locke's. The senses and reflection supply the mind with its objects, which are retained in the memory and may be operated on by the imagination. Shortly afterwards we get more Lockean overtones – the term "collections of ideas" is Locke's own. Evidently Berkeley was going out of his way to present himself, at least temporarily, as a kind of Lockean.[34] It soon appears, however, that Berkeley has some distinctly un-Lockean fish to fry. Sections 2 and 3 present us with a new entity, a "perceiving, active being" called "mind, spirit, soul or myself," not to be confused with the ideas that are perceived by it or exist in it. Those "collections of ideas" can exist only in a mind – their *esse* is *percipi*. We are embarked upon Berkeley's metaphysics.

The first question, I suppose, is just how much of the initial appearance of orthodox Lockeanism is going to be retracted? It seems an extreme view that it is going to turn out that Berkeley is not committed to any empiricist epistemology at all, although that is the implication of Loeb's argument (following Bracken) that Berkeley actually held a doctrine of innate ideas. Fortunately, the textual evidence for this view is extremely thin. Entry 645 of Berkeley's notebooks (or *Philosophical Commentaries*) reads: "There are innate Ideas i.e., Ideas created with us."[35] If a soul's *esse* is *percipere*, then at least one idea must be perceived in its first moment of existence. Hardly a thought to conflict with such a round assertion of empiricism as entry 318: "All ideas come from without, they are all particular." Another interesting line of thought ignored by Loeb appears in entries 539 and 547. After the Epicurean reflection, "Foolish in men to despise the senses, if it were not for them the mind could have no knowledge no thought at all", Berkeley criticises as "manifestly absurd" the view that the mind could operate reflexively or by "spiritual acts ... before we had ideas from without by the senses." The somewhat Lockean point is pressed home in entry 547: "We have an intuitive Knowledge of the Existence of other things besides our selves and even praecedaneous to the Knowledge of our own Existence." All this is thoroughly un-Cartesian, if not indeed anti-Cartesian.

Loeb, however, assumes that to think of knowledge as infallibly certain, and as intuitive or demonstrative, is to have an essentially Cartesian or (insofar as he allows the term meaning) "rationalist" conception of knowledge. Hence every entry, such as 547, that mentions certainty, intuition or demonstration automatically becomes "Cartesian." Yet, first, as we have seen, a strong conception of knowledge as evident and secure was the common property of a wide range of philosophers, ancient and modern, rationalist and empiricist. Apart from sceptics who claimed that we do not have such knowledge, ancient constructive empiricists advanced elaborately argued counterclaims that we do have secure criteria of truth, and can indeed have systematic "science" in the strong, traditional sense. Hobbes is only a particularly striking example of a modern philosopher with similar views. Whether a conception of knowledge, however strong, is "rationalist" or "empiricist" depends on the further question whether such knowledge is supposed to be acquired only by means of a faculty of intellect directed towards its special objects, objects explained by some form or other of the metaphysics of "eternal truths," or whether it derives purely by abstraction from what is given in sensation (or in sensation and Lockean "reflection"). The same goes for the distinction between the intuitive apprehension of principles and the demonstration of consequences, the source of both Descartes' and Locke's distinctions between intuition and demonstration. That a philosopher employs this terminology (as Gassendi himself does in the radically empiricist *Institutio Logica*) tells us nothing about their position in relation to the empiricist-rationalist divide, historically conceived.

In fact, from beginning to end Berkeley's notebooks supply strong evidence that if any single philosopher dominated Berkeley's thinking, it was quite overwhelmingly Locke. Even the discussion of human action and morality takes off from, and returns to, such famous (or notorious) Lockean views as that uneasiness determines the will and that morality is capable of demonstration (a theme strangely described by Loeb as "Cartesian"). The optical theory moves well away from Locke, as we might expect, but at its heart is Locke's brief explanation of the perception of depth and his response to Molyneux's Problem – surely the most influential text in the history of optics in proportion to its length.[36] As for Berkeley's attitude towards the senses as a source of knowledge, a key issue between Cartesians and their empiricist opponents, he comes through in both the notebooks and later works as eager to ascribe to them an immediate authority, superior indeed to the authority accorded to them by Locke. That is the point of his claim that our knowledge of sensible things is intuitive. As he says in the Third Dialogue,

> Away then with all that scepticism, all those ridiculous philosophical doubts. What jest is it for a philosopher to question the existence of sensible things, till he hath it proved to him from the veracity of God; or to pretend our knowledge in this point falls short of intuition or demonstration? I might as well doubt of my own being, as the being of those things I actually see and feel. (DHP 3 [230])[37]

Here Locke is rapped over the knuckles for underestimating the independent authority of the senses, and is unjustly assimilated to Descartes, who denied it completely. Berkeley is unmistakably endorsing a crucial empiricist doctrine, if from an idiosyncratic point of view.

Why, then, should we have any doubts about which side Berkeley is on? The answer to that, surely, is that whatever we decide about his technical epistemology, it seems beyond question that Berkeley is at heart on the side of the Gods and against the Giants in a number of fundamental respects. *Siris* expressly alludes to the Platonic battle between "two sorts of philosophers," on the one hand materialists and on the other those who, like Berkeley himself, "making all corporeal things to be dependent upon Soul or Mind, think this to exist in the first place and primary sense, and the being of bodies to be altogether derived from and presuppose that of Mind" (S 253). Moreover, unlike the leading empiricists of his time,[38] Berkeley is a voluntarist. *De Motu* echoes Plato's praise of Anaxagoras as a proto-voluntarist who recognized that mind is the principle of motion of inert, mobile matter. "Of the moderns", it continues, "Descartes has put the same point most forcibly." Thirdly, for Berkeley as for Descartes, the essence of the soul is to think, an operation of which we are immediately, reflexively, nonsensorily aware. Fourthly, God is the immediate source of our knowledge of anything beyond ourselves, directly and by an immediate agency revealing to us the objects of our knowledge – which are, indeed, divine ideas. Finally, in *Siris* at least, Berkeley comes to sound like any rationalist in his apparent denigration of the senses and their corruption of the intellect:

> Thought, reason, intellect introduce us into the knowledge of... causes. Sensible appearances, though of a flowing, unstable, and uncertain nature, yet having first occupied the mind, they do by an early prevention render the aftertask of thought more difficult; and, as they amuse the eyes and ears,... they easily obtain a preference,... sensible and real, to common apprehensions, being the same thing; although it be certain that the principles of science are neither objects of sense nor imagination, and that intellect and reason are alone the sure guides to truth. (S 264; cf. 253 and 303)

This is the passage, no doubt, that inspired Kant's notorious judgment on Berkeley:

> The thesis of all genuine idealists, from the Eleatic School up to Bishop Berkeley, is contained in this formula: "All cognition through the senses and experience is nothing but sheer illusion, and there is truth only in the ideas of pure understanding and reason."[39]

This assertion has led critics to conclude that Kant had little knowledge of Berkeley's philosophy.[40] Should we not perhaps question whether it is, after all, so very wrong?

Much hangs on how we read Berkeley's account of reflection. One line of argument for regarding his theory as essentially Cartesian might run as follows. The intellect is traditionally the faculty by which the mind knows itself and its operations. What Berkeley has done (it might be argued) is to strip intellect of its other traditional role in forming or apprehending the universal notions that were supposed to be the principles of science. As *Notebooks* 735 puts it succinctly: "Qu: what becomes of the eternal truths? Answer: they vanish." But this is simply part and parcel of Berkeley's rejection of matter, and of his thesis that bodies are ideas – things as they are perceived by the senses. The idea of matter and our ability to do mathematics a priori was in any case the only reason for Descartes to distinguish the possession of innate intellectual ideas from the deliverances of reflection. Without matter, the eternal truths can be dropped while the Cartesian self, self-knowledge and knowledge of

God are preserved. Moreover, because ethics has to do with God, action and the will, that too can be included as the object of pure intellect. The laws of nature are explained voluntaristically, as arbitrary constant conjunctions, and the sensible or natural world becomes the object of a domain of thought, inquiry and discourse within which empiricism will serve.

This story has a certain charm, but it cannot be quite right. It underestimates the depth and systematic pervasiveness of Berkeley's differences from Descartes, and it ignores the evidence as to how Berkeley's thought actually did develop. With respect to the former shortcoming, I do not just mean that Descartes without matter is Hamlet without the Prince of Denmark (although we might well ask what is left of Cartesianism if we take away matter as the subject matter of mathematics and put nothing in its place but nominalism and a return to a view of mathematics as largely "trifling"). Consider, for example, Berkeley's conception of an "idea," a term Descartes chose because of its association with divine and therefore purely intellectual thought, but which Berkeley uses for sensations and images. Consider, too, Berkeley's view of the mind, which he himself is on occasion ready to assimilate to that of Descartes. Berkeley's rejection of the substance-mode model itself creates one fundamental difference. Another is that for Descartes the *essential* function of the intellect is purely intellectual thought, while sense and imagination are contingent faculties of the embodied soul.[41] But when Berkeley says that the soul always thinks, or that the mind is an essentially perceiving thing, that means only that we could not exist without ideas of sensation and imagination. As we have seen, Berkeley rejects as absurd the suggestion that reflective contemplation, or any thought at all, could be prior to sensation. In *De Motu* 21, immediately before considering the "two supreme classes of things, body and soul," like any constructive empiricist Berkeley asks "what sense and experience tell us, and reason that rests on them." Just that move cuts him off radically from Descartes.

The truth is that to see Berkeley as a Cartesian is to underestimate his commitment to a general view that we are indebted to experience for *all* our conceptions and knowledge. Reflection or reflexive consciousness was at the time subject to a number of interpretations. There was Descartes' view (shared by Leibniz) that reflection supplies us with intellectual ideas which are thereby innate,

Malebranche's conception of "*conscience*" as immediate awareness without an idea, and Locke's "reflection", which "is very like [sense], and might properly be called internal Sense."[42] Berkeley is struck, in the course of the notebooks, by the impossibility of an idea of reflection, a point which might seem to place him with Malebranche. Yet the excluded possibility is not, as it is for Malebranche, a Cartesian intellectual idea or Platonic universal, but a Lockean quasisensory idea, the product of experience stored up in the memory. What is impossible is that a sensation or image should represent agency. There is therefore something incongruous about entry 230: "Absurd that men should know the soul by idea ideas being inert, thoughtless, Hence Malebranche confuted." For Malebranche's complaint was not that we lack a *sensation* or *sensory image* of the mind, but that we do not have access to the divine idea of it.

Although Berkeley (in contrast to Malebranche) occasionally employed the term "pure intellect", and more frequently the associated term "notions", with respect to knowledge of the mind, he was at the same time explicit that notions are acquired in reflexive "experience" of operations involving sense or imagination. As he wrote,

> I find I can excite ideas in my mind at pleasure.... It is no more than willing, and straightway this or that idea arises in my fancy: and by the same power it is obliterated.... This making and unmaking of ideas doth very properly denominate the mind active. Thus much is certain, and grounded on experience. (PHK 28)

This passage might lead some to suppose that by "experience" Berkeley meant repeated awareness of correlations between volitions and willed outcomes, à la Hume, and it is true that he sometimes did use "experience" in that general sense. In *De Motu*, for example, after writing of "the senses and experience" as "the principles of experimental philosophy", he ascribed to "experience" the power to assure us that the law of inertia is "a primary law of nature" (DM 36 and 51). We might suppose that he meant the same in writing, also in *De Motu*, "[that thinking things have] the power of moving bodies we have learnt by personal experience" (DM 25; cf. 31). What is at issue, however, both here and in the *Principles*, is not the grounding of a universal belief about the correlation of volitions and movements, but the acquisition of our concept of action and power – the way in which words like "active" get their meaning. As he wrote in the Second Dialogue, the question is "whether . . . you can conceive any action besides volition . . . and . . . whether to say something and conceive nothing be not to talk nonsense" (DHP 2 [217]). That is to say, the word "action" gets its meaning from our "daily experience" (DHP 2 [215]) of our own successful willing, a kind of "immediate knowledge" of ourselves DHP 3 [231–3]). This claim, particularly as advanced in the *Principles*, is strongly reminiscent, not so much of Descartes' claim to know indubitably that "I am a thing that thinks: that is, a thing that . . . [among other things] wills"[43] as of Locke's account of our idea of active power, which, he claimed, "we have only from what passes in ourselves, where we find by Experience, that barely by willing it, barely by a thought of the Mind, we can move the parts of our Bodies.[44]

Here, perhaps, it would be appropriate to return to the issue of Berkeley's alleged innatism, as some late passages which have been cited in evidence explicitly concern intellectual notions. In *Alciphron* 1.14 (57–8), Euphranor claims that

> those sublime truths, which are the fruits of mature thought, and have been rationally deduced by men of the best and most improved understandings . . . must be allowed natural to man [as] agreeable to, and growing from, the most excellent and peculiar part of human nature.

This is a passage which seems carefully designed to avoid saying that anything is innate but our capacity to reason. A passage from *Siris* is kind to Plato, but only by implausibly interpreting his "native inbred notions" as the capacity of the mind, once stimulated by sense, to become aware of "her own acts or operations" (S 308–9). Finally, a passage from the Sermon "On the Will of God", supposed by Loeb to "[leave] the matter beyond doubt",[45] is no different from *Alciphron*, unless less clear. The nearest thing to an endorsement of innatism is the statement that we normally arrive at the notion of a superior being as a result of "the natural make of our minds (W 7:131)". Such a claim is entirely compatible with the explanation given in the Third Dialogue between Hylas and Philonous, according to which

> all the notion I have of God is obtained by reflecting on my own soul, heightening its powers, and removing its imperfections. I have therefore, though not an inactive idea, yet in myself some sort of active thinking image of the Deity.

This "extremely inadequate" notion closely resembles the constructed ideas of Gassendi and Locke, and like them stands in contrast to the positive idea of a perfect being to which Descartes is led on by consideration of his own imperfection. It is interesting that another argument in the sermon "On the Will of God," to the effect that our natural inclinations and affections (although presumably not all of them) are indications of how God wishes us to live, also occurs in the fourth of Locke's strongly empiricist *Essays on the Law of Nature*.[46]

The topic of our notion of agency is, of course, very relevant to the question of the place of Berkeley's voluntarism in his philosophy. Loeb provocatively presents Berkeley's metaphysics as a "trivial variant" of Malebranche's, "an occasionalist metaphysics in which God is the sole cause, except that certain volitions of created minds (when directed at their own limbs) are causally efficacious" (229). The suggestion seems to be that Berkeley was at bottom a Malebranchean who had concluded that if God is directly responsible not only for all motions of bodies but also for our perceptions of them, one might as well drop substantial bodies from the system altogether, as having no work to do. Again the picture has some appeal. It is true that Berkeley makes play with the supposed redundancy of matter, at least *ad hominem* in dealing with objections. In *De Motu* he praises the Cartesians for their voluntarism, and alludes approvingly to the principle of constant creation employed by both Descartes and Malebranche:

> For no other cause of the existence of the successive existence of body in different parts of space should be sought, it would seem, than that cause whence is derived the successive existence of the same body in different parts of time. (DM 34)

Yet again one may wonder how a philosopher could be a Malebranchean without intelligible extension, and with divine ideas that are both particular and objects of sense. It is with some reason that Berkeley distances himself from a philosopher who "builds on the most abstract general ideas, which I entirely disclaim" (DHP 2 [214]). Moreover, Berkeley's reasons for voluntarism and his belief in the inertness of bodies overlap those of the Cartesians only at the most general and strategic level. God must be given a direct and continuous role in nature. Otherwise Cartesian grounds for voluntarism lie in just the conception of matter as a substance that Berkeley rejects.

Even Malebranche's theological motive is alien to him. Berkeley approaches God through the notion of a mind whose wisdom, power, and benevolence are manifest in the phenomena, rather than through intellectual ideas of divine perfection, omnipotence, or necessary existence.

To suggest that Berkeley was a voluntarist first and an immaterialist second is surely to get things in the wrong order. Berkeley could not but be a voluntarist just because, if God directly causes ideas of sense, then obviously he has to be directly responsible for the regularities between them. Moreover, the denial of substantial status to bodies, their reduction to things as they appear to the senses, entails the denial of physical agency. In other words, it is just because bodies are mind-dependent that they are "visibly inactive." In Berkeley's words, a "little attention will discover to us that the very being of an idea implies passiveness and inertness in it, in so far as it is impossible for an idea to do anything, or, strictly speaking, to be the cause of anything" (PHK 25). As "experience" gives us the notion of action, so it assures us that sensible things are inactive. None of this, of course, makes Berkeley any the less willing to call on any and every philosopher with voluntaristic tendencies as an ally in his cause, and as having intuitions of a truth that they do not fully understand.

My objection to attempts to see Berkeley as some kind of Cartesian is not that affinities do not exist, or that it is not interesting and revealing to take note of them. What is wrong is to emphasise them over the differences, so that the differences (if not simply denied) appear as no more than the consequences of a Cartesian's or Malebranchian's dispensing with matter. Any such story, I believe, has Berkeley coming from the wrong direction. Here is one example. Loeb cites *Notebooks* 107 as evidence that Berkeley started from a Malebranchean position:

> Strange impotence of men. Man without God. Wretcheder than a stone or tree, he having onely the power to be miserable by his unperformed wills, these having no power at all.

By this point in the notebooks, however, immaterialism is thoroughly set up – as it was, apparently, before the extant notebooks started. We have even been given a version of Berkeley's famous causal argument for God's existence, from which the thought that we cannot affect bodies without God's concurrence directly follows.

Far from introducing a Malebranchean principle for the first time, entry 107 simply draws a consequence from what has gone before. We do not, of course, have direct evidence of Berkeley's earliest philosophical convictions, but the notebooks do provide evidence of where Berkeley was coming from and, as I have already proposed, it strongly suggests that the more noteworthy "Cartesian" elements in his theory were embraced later rather than sooner. That is certainly true of a reflexive pure intellect and the quasi-Cartesian (and yet distinctly *not* Cartesian) conception of the soul, not to speak of graciously "exhibited" divine ideas which do not make their full appearance, perhaps, until the *Three Dialogues between Hylas and Philonous*. At the start of the notebooks the preferred, Lockean term for the subject of thought is "person" rather than "soul".

None of this goes to show that Berkeley's heart was not from the first on the side of the Gods, or that he was not in agreement with Descartes over some fundamental issues. Why otherwise would he be so interested in driving material substance out of the world? The picture that suggests itself is of a philosopher with a new idea that he thinks will once and for all break the traditional link between empiricism and materialism, and will demonstrate that the popular naturalistic epistemology leads directly to main truths of religion. This exegetical hypothesis would help to explain Berkeley's first, hard-nosed insistence on sensory ideas as a condition of knowledge even of the soul, a line of thought that was maintained in the notebooks in one form or another until he became satisfied that the soul can be the object of another kind of experiential knowledge. On such a view of him, Berkeley's first aim was to demonstrate that, after all, a proper understanding of our dependence on sense and imagination for the objects of knowledge will carry us away from materialism, rather than towards it. That purpose appears directly opposed to a famous purpose of Descartes' *Meditations*, to lead the mind away from the senses.

NOTES

1. For criticisms of the dichotomy, see, for example, Louis Loeb, *From Descartes to Hume* (Ithaca: Cornell University Press, 1981); Hidé Ishiguro, "Pre-established Harmony versus Constant Conjunction: A Reconsideration of the Distinction between Rationalism and Empiricism," in

Rationalism, Empiricism, and Idealism: British Academy Lectures on the History of Philosophy, ed. Anthony Kenny (Oxford: Oxford University Press, 1986); H. M. Bracken, *Berkeley* (London: Macmillan, 1974); Stuart Brown, "Leibniz's Break with Cartesian 'Rationalism,'" in *Philosophy, its History and Historiography*, ed. A. J. Holland (Dordrecht: Reidel, 1983). Almost more significant than these frontal attacks are the mandatory disclaimers in prefaces and introductions: R. S. Woolhouse, *The Empiricists* (Oxford: Oxford University Press, 1988), 1–4, and John Cottingham, *The Rationalists* (Oxford: Oxford University Press, 1988), 1–4, are both uneasy with the notion of opposing parties or traditions. Tom Sorell's editorial assertion (in *The Rise of Modern Philosophy*, ed. Tom Sorell [Oxford: Oxford University Press, 1993], 11) that "the ancient/modern distinction cannot be said to be foisted on the period discussed here, in the way that, for example, the rationalist/empiricist distinction has been" expresses a received view about the latter distinction, and my own essay, "Berkeley and Hume: a question of influence," in *Philosophy in History*, ed. Richard Rorty, J. B. Schneewind, and Quentin Skinner (Cambridge: Cambridge University Press, 1984), was for a time fairly lonely in criticism of received argument for that view. Soon after the ancestor of the present paper was presented, however, Thomas Lennon, in *The Battle of the Gods and Giants: The Legacies of Descartes and Gassendi, 1655–1715* (Princeton: Princeton University Press, 1993), advanced a stimulating, if sometimes exegetically daring, argument to the effect that something very like the rationalist/empiricist distinction as I describe it was enormously important in seventeenth-century thought. His argument seemed decisive, but Nicholas Jolley, in his review of Lennon's book (*British Journal for the History of Philosophy* 2 [1994]: 179–81), apparently misled by Lennon's emphasis on Platonism and materialism, sees him as proposing "a new martial model" to *replace* that of the struggle between rationalists and empiricists – as if Kant had never seen the latter in terms of an opposition between Plato and Epicurus (cf. Note 27, here).

2. "An Empiricist View of Knowledge," in *Companions to Ancient Thought*, Volume 1: Epistemology, ed. Stephen Everson (Cambridge: Cambridge University Press, 1990), 225–50
3. *Sophist* 246.
4. *Phaedo* 95–9.
5. P. Dear, *Mersenne and the Learning of the Schools* (Ithaca: Cornell University Press, 1988).
6. Sixth Meditation, in *The Philosophical Writings of Descartes*, 2 vols., trans. John Cottingham, Robert Stoothoff, and Dugald Murdoch (Cambridge: Cambridge University Press, 1984), 2: 50 (AT VII 71).

7. A popular Augustinian theme. Cf. P. Dear, *Mersenne and the Learning of the Schools*, 84f. (which quotes Fonseca), and Antoine Arnauld, *Of True and False Ideas*, trans. Stephen Gaukroger (Manchester: Manchester University Press, 1990), Chapter 13.
8. *Comments on a Certain Broadsheet*, in *Philosophical Writings of Descartes*, 1: 303–4 (AT VIIIB 357–8).
9. Cf. *Principles*, Part Two, sections 36–7 and 42–3, in *Philosophical Writings of Descartes*, 1: 240–1 (AT VIIIA 61–3) and 243–4 (AT VIIIA 66–7).
10. G. Hatfield, "Force (God) in Descartes' Physics," *Studies in the History and Philosophy of Science* 10 (1979): 113–40. Cf. D. Garber, *Descartes' Mathematical Physics* (Chicago: University of Chicago Press, 1992), 305: "Descartes seems less a precursor of later occasionalism than the last of the schoolmen, using God to do what substantial forms did for his teachers." Yet Descartes explicitly reduced all physical force to his first law "that everything tends, so far as lies within itself, to persist in the same state." Because that law was open to treatment as a metaphysical truism, its maintenance hardly seems a serious call on omnipotence.
11. *Principles*, Part Two, Section 36, in *Philosophical Writings of Descartes*, 1: 240 (AT VIIIA 61–2).
12. Spinoza's spectacular ontology solves the epistemological problem by collapsing the triangle into a point. In effect, essences in the divine mind, essences in the human mind and essences in things are all identical.
13. Cf. John Locke, *An Essay concerning Human Understanding*, ed. P. H. Hidditch (Oxford: Clarendon Press, 1975), IV.xii.14, quoted below.
14. Gassendi expounded the Epicurean view that when sensation gives rise to false judgment, the judgment can be corrected by what we may describe as "reason," although this is really correction by the senses themselves. Locke, on the other hand, seems unwilling to treat particular deliverances of the senses as open to correction. Cf. Michael R. Ayers, *Locke*, 2 vols. (London: Routledge, 1991), 1: 166f.
15. Cf. *Institutio Logica*, I.iv, II.xivf., III.xvi, in *Pierre Gassendi's Institutio Logica (1658)*, trans. Howard Jones (Assen: Van Gorcum, 1981).
16. *Leviathan*, ed. Richard Tuck (Cambridge: Cambridge University Press, 1996), Chapter ix, 60.
17. *Leviathan*, chs. iii–v, 20–37; *The Elements of Philosophy, the First Section: concerning Body*, in *The English Works of Thomas Hobbes*, ed. Sir William Molesworth (London: John Bohn, 1839), Volume 1, I.iii.1–8 and iv.
18. *The Elements of Philosophy, the First Section: concerning Body*, I.vi.1–7.
19. Cf. R. S. Woolhouse, *The Empiricists*, 3.

20. *Critique of Pure Reason*, trans. Paul Guyer and Allen W. Wood (Cambridge: Cambridge University Press, 1998), A 94, B 127; A 854f., B 882f.
21. L. Loeb, *Descartes to Hume*, 36–62, which begins, "The principal thesis of the [present] section is that if Descartes is a Rationalist, then so is Locke."
22. In fact, Locke began to move from an inductivist, broadly Gassendist view of universal knowledge to a view more like that of Hobbes (and so, in one respect, that of Descartes) in the course of writing *Draft A* in 1671. Cf. Michael Ayers, "The Structure of Locke's General Philosophy," in *Locke's Philosophy: Content and Context*, ed. G. A. J. Rogers (Oxford: Oxford University Press, 1994), 54–8.
23. *Essay concerning Human Understanding* IV.ii.11–13.
24. *Essay* II.xxix. 2.
25. *Essay* IV.iii.13f and 25; II.viii.11 and 21; II.xxxi.6.
26. For fuller discussion, see Ayers, *Locke*, Chapter 12 in Volume 2.
27. Cf. *Critique* A 853, B 881:

> **With regard to the object** of all of our rational cognitions, some were merely **sensual philosophers**, others merely **intellectual philosophers**. Epicurus can be called the foremost philosopher of sensibility, and Plato that of the intellectual. This difference of schools, however, subtle as it is, had already begun in the earliest times, and has long preserved itself without interruption.

28. Locke, *Essay* IV.xii.14. Suarez had pointed to the mere conditionality of the eternal truths in support of his view that their objective existence in God's understanding did not require an antecedent act of creation – a view notoriously rejected by Descartes. Locke followed ancient empiricism (and Hobbes) in seeing their conditionality as an argument against according them any being at all independent of human thought.
29. Similarly we should not be misled for a moment by Locke's rhetorical insistence that our natural faculties come from God, or even by his description of "reason" as "natural revelation," into supposing that he subscribed to a serious epistemology of divine illumination. Cf. Locke, *Essay* IV. xix.12–13, where the "light from heaven" is firmly opposed to the "light of nature," to the detriment of the former; and Ayers, *Locke*, 1: 122–4 and 143.
30. To take Arnauld's persuasive example, if we see an axle shaped to fit the holes in two mill-stones, one hole round and the other square, we can predict (Arnauld and Nicole say, "infallibly") which one will turn (Antoine Arnauld and Pierre Nicole, *Logic or the Art of Thinking*, trans. Jill Vance Buroker [Cambridge: Cambridge University Press, 1996],

I.i, 28). For Locke, on the other hand, our prediction would presuppose at least the coherence or rigidity of the parts of the machine, a condition we do not understand.

31. That the two philosophers are very close on universality appears from this passage in Berkeley:

> *universality*, so far as I can comprehend, not consisting in the absolute, positive nature of or conception of anything, but in the relation it bears to the particulars signified or represented by it: by virtue whereof it is that things, names, or notions, being in their own nature *particular*, are rendered *universal*. ... [The] particular triangle I consider, whether of this or that sort it matters not, doth equally stand for and represent all rectilinear triangles whatsoever.... (I 16)

For further discussion, see Ayers *Locke*, 1: 248–58. Berkeley may have felt his view to be different just because an ultimate target lay beyond theories of universality in the alleged tendency of philosophers, including Locke, to suppose that we can separate in thought certain items which (Berkeley believed) cannot be so separated, for example, extension from all color or tactile quality.

32. I 16: "There is not the least mention made of them in the proof."
33. Cf. the editors' footnotes *ad loc.* in *Works* 2: 41 and in *Berkeley: Philosophical Works, including the Works on Vision*, ed. M. R. Ayers (London: J. M. Dent & Sons, 1989), 77.
34. The sentence "And as several of these [ideas] are observed to accompany each other, they come to be marked by one name, and so to be reputed one thing" reads as a summary of the famous opening section of Locke's chapter, "Of our Complex Ideas of Substances" (*Essay* II.xxiii.1), but without mentioning the supposed *substratum*. Cf., too, *Essay* II.xxvi.1, carefully noted by Berkeley, in which Locke had written of "the Substance, Wood, which is a certain Collection of simple *Ideas*" (see *Notebooks* 179), and II.xxxi.6: "The complex *Ideas* we have of Substances, are, as it has been shewn, certain Collections of simple *Ideas*. . . . " Both passages omit reference to the idea of substance in general, as an ingredient of ideas of substances.
35. Berkeley is here simply offering a mildly paradoxical gloss on the proposition variously expressed in earlier sections and put just two entries earlier, "Existence not conceivable without perception or volition not distinguished therefrom."
36. *Essay* II.ix.8–10.
37. As he has just said, "When [sensible things] are actually perceived, there can be no doubt of their existence." Cf. Locke, *Essay* IV.xi.2f., IV.ii.14.
38. Boyle certainly can seem to have been a voluntarist, and Newton (even more, some Newtonians) saw direct divine agency as a possible

explanation of gravity. Cf. J. E. McGuire, "Boyle's Conception of Nature," *Journal of the History of Ideas* 33 (1972): 523–42, and, for further references and discussion, Ayers, *Locke*, Volume 2, Chapter 11, and Michael Ayers, "Natures and Laws from Descartes to Hume," in *The Philosophical Canon in the 17th and 18th Centuries*, ed. G. A. J. Rogers and S. Tomaselli (Rochester: University of Rochester Press, 1996).

39. *Prolegomena to Any Future Metaphysics*, trans. Gary Hatfield (Cambridge: Cambridge University Press, 2004), 125 (Ak. 4: 374).
40. For discussion, see Ralph C. S. Walker, *Kant* (London: Routledge, 1989).
41. As he says in the Sixth Meditation (*Philosophical Writings of Descartes*, 2: 51 [AT VII 73]),

    > this power of imagining which is in me, differing as it does from the power of understanding, is not a necessary constituent of my own essence, that is, of the essence of my mind. For if I lacked it, I would undoubtedly remain the same individual as I now am.

42. *Essay* II.i.4.
43. Second Meditation, *Philosophical Writings of Descartes*, 2: 19 (AT VII 28).
44. *Essay* II.xxi.4.
45. Loeb, *From Descartes to Hume*, 69.
46. Locke, *Essays on the Law of Nature*, ed. W. von Leyden (Oxford: Clarendon Press, 1970), 146–59.

ROBERT McKIM

3 Berkeley's notebooks

I. INTRODUCTION

Berkeley graduated from Trinity College, Dublin, in 1704 and continued to live at Trinity in anticipation of becoming a Fellow of the College as soon as a vacancy arose. In 1707, having excelled in the examinations, he became a Junior Fellow. It appears to have been between 1706 and 1708, while he was still only in his early twenties, that Berkeley recorded his developing ideas in the pair of notebooks that are the subject of this chapter. These notebooks, which are now in the British Library, were never intended by Berkeley for publication. In addition to being interesting in their own right, the notebooks are an invaluable tool for understanding Berkeley's philosophy, and especially for understanding its development, for here we can see the genesis of many of the central claims of *The New Theory of Vision* (NTV), *The Principles of Human Knowledge* (PHK), and *Three Dialogues between Hylas and Philonous* (DHP).

The notebooks contain a large number of entries on numerous topics. According to the standard way of numbering them, there are 888 entries. (Although it is not always clear how the entries should be divided up, and hence whether the standard numbering of the entries is correct, I will follow it here.) The best way to convey a sense of the content of the entries is to list some of their topics. The list is a long one. It includes vision (microscopes, magnifying glasses, optics), metaphysics (time, eternity, powers, substance, identity, causation, God, existence, matter, corpuscularian essences, infinity, infinite divisibility), perception (sensation, minima sensibilia, imagination, pleasure and pain), mind (soul, memory, understanding, will), qualities (primary and secondary qualities, extension, number, solidity, figure, motion, color), and ideas (abstract ideas, general ideas, simple ideas). The list also includes body, distance, magnitude, space, geometry, mathematics, abstraction, visible and tangible objects, skepticism, language, morality, common sense, and demonstration. Then there are entries in which Berkeley makes a note about how best to present his views to the world. The list of important thinkers mentioned in the notebooks includes Molyneux, More, Newton, Leibniz, Bayle, Ficino, Bacon, Hobbes, Spinoza, and Epicurus; Locke and Malebranche are mentioned most frequently.

Berkeley's notebooks are not easy reading. Because they contain jottings prepared for his own use and were not intended for public consumption, they lack the grace of style for which the works that he prepared for publication are renowned. Entries on different topics follow one another throughout, and cases in which one theme is pursued continuously across a series of entries are the exception rather than the rule. Sometimes it is unclear what point is being made, or even what issue is being addressed.

My interpretation of the notebooks is based on the assumption that the entries were written more or less in the order in which they are now to be found in the various published editions, with those in what is known as Notebook B being written before those in Notebook A.[1] There is considerable evidence for this, including the fact that much about the evolution of Berkeley's views becomes clear to us if we read the notebooks in this way. In general, Notebook B has an air of discovery about it, whereas Notebook A tends to explore the implications of what already has been discovered. Throughout both notebooks there are, however, some entries that were added later than the entries in their immediate vicinity, including some that have "a" after their number (such as 37a) in the standard editions. For example, N 38 probably was written at about the same time as N 37,[2] but it is hard to tell how much later N 37a was written.

Berkeley also introduced various marginal letters, numbers, and signs into the notebooks, presumably in an attempt to impose some order on the entries, and to prepare for publication. In citing entries, I have preserved these marginal notations, bringing them into the entries for ease of reproduction. (Some of the signs and letters are crossed out, and I have reproduced these corrections too. I also have included corrections in the entries themselves when I think they may be illuminating, and I have maintained the original spelling and most of the punctuation.) Berkeley explains the meaning of the marginal letters at the beginning of Notebook A:

I – Introduction
M – Matter
P – Primary and Secondary Qualities
E – Existence
T – Time
S – Soul – Spirit
G – God
Mo – Moral Philosophy
N – Natural Philosophy

He never explains the meaning of the marginal numbers and signs, however. The two most frequently occurring signs are "X," which seems to signify that the entry is about extension, and "+." There is some disagreement about the meaning of the "+" sign. This is not a trivial matter because it has a bearing on how we ought to read many entries. Recent interpreters generally have taken "+" to mean "delete" or "discard." This view is persistent in spite of the decisive evidence against it.[3]

Berkeley's notebooks have been known variously as the *Commonplace Book* – which is short for *Commonplace Book of Occasional Metaphysical Thoughts*, the name given by A. C. Fraser, who published the first edition of the notebooks in 1871 – and the *Philosophical Commentaries*. Fraser's title suggests that the notebooks contain random thoughts jotted down whenever it was convenient. Luce thought "Philosophical Commentaries" to be the best name because he took the entries to be comments on earlier immaterialist writings he believed Berkeley had written. Although no earlier immaterialist writings have come to light, and we lack any clear indication that they ever existed, Luce may be right that there were some immaterialist writings on which Berkeley drew.[4] Certainly Berkeley was an immaterialist from the time he started the notebooks, as is clear from these entries:

~~MS~~ Extension a sensation, therefore not without the mind. (N 18)

M~~S~~ In ye immaterial hypothesis the wall is white, fire hot & c (N 19)

It would be curious if he had never previously put pen to paper to express his immaterialism. The evidence for there having been an earlier immaterialist work of a developed sort, though, is very slight.[5] I take the absence of any clear references to it in the notebooks to be strong evidence against its existence; thus I shall henceforth use the neutral title "notebooks."

Berkeley is best known for his rejection of matter. Indeed this is the main preoccupation of his philosophy. In this chapter I will concentrate on what we can learn from the notebooks about the evolution of Berkeley's case against matter. His rejection of matter was motivated by many concerns, including some that are epistemological and some that are theological. The most obvious epistemological worry is the skeptical challenge to belief in the material world:

> S M Allowing there be extended solid & c substances without the mind tis impossible the mind should know or perceive them. the mind even according to ye materialists perceiving onely the impressions made upon its brain or rather the ideas attending those impressions. (N 74; see also N 45, 79, 80, 476, 606)

So those who believe that there are external extended substances must allow that we do not know or perceive them. According to materialists, when we perceive an external extended substance all we have immediate perception of is certain impressions or ideas. How can we be sure that we know anything about the alleged external substances?

The theological worries about matter were various. Berkeley alludes to various unfortunate theological implications of the view that there is external matter:

> M S The great danger of making extension exist without the mind. in yt. if it does it must be acknowledg'd infinite immutable eternal & c. wch. will be to make either God extended (wch I think dangerous) or an eternal, immutable, infinite, increate being beside God. (N 290; see also N 17, 298, 391, 799, 824)

He even goes so far as to write that

> M. + Matter once allow'd. I defy any man to prove that God is not matter. (N 625)

II. BERKELEY'S MATURE PHILOSOPHY

If we are going to explore some aspects of how Berkeley's mature views against matter developed, we need to have a grasp of what those mature views were. Consider these remarks in the *Principles*:

> [The] *esse* [of unthinking things] is *percipi*, nor is it possible that they should have any existence, out of the minds or thinking things which perceive them. (PHK 3)

> [What] are . . . houses, mountains, rivers, and in a word all sensible objects . . . but the things we perceive by sense, and what do we perceive besides our own ideas or sensations; and is it not plainly repugnant that any one of these or any combination of them should exist unperceived? (PHK 4)

These remarks express a central principle of Berkeley's mature philosophy, namely that

> (A) for everything other than spirits, to exist is to be perceived.

Sometimes (A) seems to be offered as an account of the meaning of "exists" and its cognates when things other than spirits are said to exist. ("I am persuaded would Men but examine wt they mean by the Word Existence they wou'd agree with me" [N 604; see also N 593 and PHK 3, 24, 81, 89].) However, Berkeley also understands (A) as an account of *what it is* for something other than a spirit to exist: "the existence of our ideas consists in being perceiv'd, imagin'd thought on" (N 472). N 491 combines both ingredients:

> . . . 'tis on the Discovering of the nature & meaning & import of Existence that I chiefly insist. . . .

There are other readings of what exactly Berkeley took to be the new principle at the center of his philosophy. Luce,[6] following G. A. Johnston,[7] thought Berkeley's new principle to be that

> (B) existence is *percipi* or *percipere*.

(B) is of course just the conjunction of (A) with the view that the existence of spirits or minds consists in perceiving. Because *both* those who think that the crucial premise is (A) *and* those who think that it is (B) agree that Berkeley thought the *esse* of spirits to be *percipere*, and also agree that this belief about spirits is central to his system, there is no real disagreement here. In the case of (B) there is also a version that emphasizes meaning: "the meaning and definition of the word Existence . . . is no simple idea distinct from . . . perceiving and being perceiv'd" (N 408).

There are readings that differ considerably from both (A) and (B). Colin Murray Turbayne rejects Luce's account and reads N 379 as the first statement of the central principle of Berkeley's philosophy.[8] At N 379 Berkeley says that there are various ways to demonstrate the principle that

(C) neither . . . our ideas nor anything like our ideas can possibly be in an unperceiving thing.

Berkeley presents (C) at N 379 as the conclusion of a summary of his central case. As Turbayne notes, (C), or one of its variants such as "neither our ideas nor their archetypes can exist in an unperceiving substance," is also advanced by Berkeley in the works he prepared for publication. (See for example, PHK 9, 22, 90, and DHP 1 [206].) Turbayne correctly observes too that at N 279 Berkeley expresses excitement about (C):

1 M S I wonder not at my sagacity in discovering the obvious tho' Amazing truth, I rather wonder at my stupid inadvertency in not finding it out before. 'tis no Witchcraft to see. . . .

The significance of this entry becomes clear when we notice that it continues on into N 280:

Our simple ideas are so many simple thoughts or perceptions, & that a perception . . . cannot exist without a thing to perceive it or any longer than it is perceiv'd, that a thought cannot be in an unthinking thing, that one uniform simple thought can be . . . like . . . to nothing but another uniform simple thought. Complex thoughts or ideas are onely an assemblage of simple ideas and can be the image of nothing or like unto nothing but another assemblage of simple ideas. . . . (N 280)[9]

There can be no doubt about (C)'s importance to Berkeley. Part of its application is as follows. Certain of the things that we immediately perceive – which Berkeley, following Locke and others, calls ideas – are extended. Because nothing can resemble an idea but an idea, nothing that is not an idea can be extended. Otherwise, something that is not an idea would share the quality of being extended with some of our ideas, in which case something that is not an idea would resemble an idea. And that is impossible. Therefore there cannot be anything extended outside of the mind; hence there cannot be extended matter. The claim that nothing can be like an idea but an idea, then, and the further claim that extension is an idea, together entail that extension cannot exist external to the mind.

(C) includes two components, the uncontroversial claim that

(C1) no idea can be in an unperceiving thing

and the very controversial claim that

(C2) nothing like an idea can be in an unperceiving thing.

(C2) seems obviously correct to Berkeley, probably because it is entailed by the conjunction of (C1) and a further claim that also seems to him to be obviously correct, namely that

(C3) nothing can be like an idea but an idea.

(C3) appears to have been accepted by Berkeley when he wrote some of the earliest entries in the notebooks:

M ~~S~~ Qu: wt can be like a sensation but a sensation? (N 46)

~~M S~~ Qu: Did ever any man see any other things besides his own ideas, that he should compare them to these & make these like unto them? (N 47; see also N 51, 299, 378.14, 378.16–378.18.)

Entries such as N 47 provide an argument against someone who denies (C3). To deny (C3) is to assert that something that is not an idea is like an idea, and the point of N 47 is that we could never be justified in making such an assertion. (C3), however, attempts to go one step further than this denial, contending that it is true that nothing is like an idea but an idea.

Berkeley seems to have thought (C3) to be obviously correct. His presentation of it at N 484, where he just asserts that "after all, nothing can be like an idea but an idea" is typical. Why did he think this to be obvious? His reasoning was, I think, as follows. Ideas are observable, and whatever is observable is an idea (N 50). What is observable is so in virtue of having various observable features. And something would resemble what is observable only if it had the same or similar observable features. But then it too would be an idea. Something that is not an idea would lack the phenomenal features or qualities that are necessary in order to resemble an idea.

M. 1 What can an Idea be like, but another Idea, we can compare it with Nothing else, a Sound like a Sound, a Colour like a Colour. (N 861)

M.1 Is it not nonsense to say a Smell is like a thing wch cannot be smelt, a Colour is like a thing which cannot be seen. (N 862)

I do not propose to give a detailed analysis here of this line of thought, which seems obviously flawed.[10] Briefly, one way to see what is flawed about it is to focus on what is meant by "idea." If the term "idea" is introduced as a technical term to refer to whatever is observable, then of course whatever is observable is an idea and whatever is an idea is observable. But that provides us with no reason to believe that ideas, defined in this way, may not exist external to the mind. Nor does the fact that we normally think of ideas as something that can exist only in a mind.

Whatever may be the merits of his case for it, (C) seems not to have given Berkeley the sort of case that he wants. For one thing, it leaves open the possibility of an external substratum that does not resemble the ideas we perceive. Matter is therefore not ruled out tout court, although it would be a pale shadow of matter of the more robust sorts that Berkeley was most eager to oppose, being emptied of all of the qualities with which we are familiar. (If existence is a quality, it would be an exception.) (A), on the other hand, provides a way of *showing* that material things, as conceived of by those whom Berkeley is opposing, are impossible.

I will just mention a final candidate for the role of central principle in Berkeley's philosophy. Michael Ayers takes the new principle to be that

(D) the mind is the substance that supports sensible qualities by perceiving them.[11]

At *Principles* 6 we find these remarks that combine (D) with (A):

[All] the choir of heaven and furniture of the earth, in a word all those bodies which compose the mighty frame of the world, have not any subsistence without a mind, [and]... their being is to be perceived or known;... it [is]... perfectly unintelligible... to attribute to any single part of them an existence independent of spirit. (PHK 6)

It is clear that *each* of the principles (A)–(D) was important to Berkeley in his mature philosophy. Indeed, together these principles serve to summarize much of that philosophy. In what follows I will refer to these principles collectively as the "new principles." Berkeley refers to "the principle" (or sometimes *my* or *this* principle or *my principles* or *my Doctrine*) in many entries in the notebooks, including N 29, 30, 285, 291, 304, 305, 407, 410, and 589, and there is no doubt that during the period in which he wrote the entries in the notebooks he made what he thought to be new and significant discoveries. Unfortunately, much of the time he does not tell us precisely what he has in mind when he refers to "the principle" (etc.), and often there is no way to tell. Sometimes it may be just the denial of matter. Sometimes it probably is one of the new principles (A)–(D), although I see no evidence that any of these new principles was developed prior to N 279, where Berkeley expresses his excitement about "the obvious tho' Amazing truth."

III. "MY FIRST ARGUINGS"

As I have mentioned, it is clear that from the time he wrote the opening entries in the notebooks, Berkeley rejected material substance as it was understood by his various predecessors such as Locke and Descartes. (See, for example, N 18, 19, 71.) From the start of the notebooks he confidently declares that extension is a sensation that could not exist unperceived:

~~M~~ ~~S~~ Extension a sensation, therefore not without the mind (N 18)

+ ~~S~~ Extension so far from being incompatible wth yt 'tis impossible it should exist without thought. (N 33)

M. S. Extension it self or any thing extended cannot think these being mere ideas or sensations whose essence we thoroughly know (N 34)

1 M.~~S~~ Extension to exist in a thoughtless thing is a contradiction. (N 37; see also N 164–5, 249, 270, 287.)

In these entries Berkeley is not merely claiming that we have sensations of extended things or that extension is one of the qualities that we sense. Rather, extension *consists in*, or *amounts to*, the occurrence of certain sensations. It is impossible and "a contradiction" that there should be extension without the mind.

What was the basis of Berkeley's immaterialism prior to his development of his new principles? In an attempt to answer this question I turn in the next section to some early arguments against matter that are distinct from the various new principles already discussed. Once he had developed his new principles, some of these early arguments received less attention, at least as distinct objections to matter, although others appear again either in later entries in the notebooks or in the writings he intended to publish.

Before we turn to the early arguments, however, it is helpful to consider their point. A good place to begin is N 265, where reference is made to some apparent early arguments against matter, arguments that Berkeley evidently understood to be distinct from his new principles, and that he had already decided were unconvincing:

> M P ffrom Malbranch, Locke & my first arguings it cant be prov'd that extension is not in matter ffrom Lockes arguings it can't be prov'd that Colours... are not in Bodies.

The significance of his reference to Malebranche and Locke here may just be that he developed his early arguments while under the influence of Malebranche and Locke. However, as will be clear from what follows, Bayle seems to have had the greatest influence on these early arguments.[12]

N 265 signifies dissatisfaction with some early arguments for immaterialism. When Berkeley says that his early arguments fail to show that extension is not in matter he means that his early arguments fail to show that there is no such thing as matter. This is worth stating because, as already discussed, one *could* think primary qualities such as extension to be in the mind in the sense in which Berkeley's opponents believed secondary qualities to be in the mind, and yet believe in a material substratum of some sort. In pondering this point it is interesting to note that in the *Principles* and *Dialogues* Berkeley uses the term "material substance" in more than one way. He sometimes uses "material substance" to refer to "an inert, senseless, extended, solid, figured, moveable substance existing without the mind" (for example, see PHK 67; DHP 1 [203], 2 [213]). So understood, material substance is something whose essence consists in extension and other primary qualities. An argument to show that extension is not without the mind amounts to an argument against the existence of material substance of *that* sort. Berkeley also, however, uses "material substance" to refer to "an inert, senseless substance, in which extension, figure and motion do actually subsist" (PHK 9; see also PHK 16, 73, 76, 91 and DHP 1 [197ff.]). On this usage, material substance seems to be one thing and the qualities that depend on it, including extension and other primary qualities, another. So construed, matter is something mysterious that is external to us, that causes ideas of both primary and secondary qualities in us, but that in itself has neither primary nor secondary qualities. An argument to show that extension and the other primary qualities that Berkeley's predecessors had thought to be in matter are not without the mind may be insufficient to show that matter, construed in this second way, does not exist. Berkeley mentions this very possibility at N 597, where he also appears to indicate how his new principles enable him to respond to it:

M But perhaps Some man may... [say] an [inert thoughtless] substance may exist tho' not extended, moved & c... but wth other properties whereof we have no Idea. But even this I shall demonstrate to be Impossible wn I come to treat more particularly of Existence.

And in the *Principles* Berkeley considers the possibility that someone might object that although he has shown that there cannot be "an inert, senseless, extended, solid, figured, moveable substance, existing without the mind," there still can be matter of some sort. It would be inert and senseless but yet have a role in the occurrence of our ideas (PHK 67). Berkeley devotes quite a few sections of the *Principles* (most of 68–84) to his response.

However, it seems that Berkeley thought a case against external extension to be a case against matter; it seems that the early lines of argument to which he refers at N 265 were supposed to show that matter does not exist. From the start of the notebooks, much of his effort was devoted to a search for an adequate foundation for the immaterialism that he had already adopted, and for a way to undermine all versions of the belief in matter. The discussion of extension is part of that effort. Moreover, there is clear evidence that early in the notebooks Berkeley had decided that matter could not be something mysterious that is external to us, and that causes ideas of both primary and secondary qualities in us. For he claims as early as N 41 that the powers that produce our ideas, including our ideas of what his opponents classified as primary qualities, are powers in God. In fact, he says that our need to posit such powers provides "a direct and brief demonstration of an active powerful being distinct from us on whom we depend. & c." (See also N 52, 109, 131, 155, 298, 433, 621.) There actually was no room in his scheme of things for a sort of matter that would play a causal role in our experience but that has been emptied of the qualities with which we are familiar. While he does countenance in the *Principles* the possibility that someone might hold out for external matter even though the qualities usually thought to characterize matter have all been shown not to exist external to the mind, and he does set out to refute it, this merely reflects the fact that Berkeley anticipated great difficulty in persuading his opponents. Like Hylas in the *Three Dialogues*, many people are reluctant to give up their belief in matter and will cling to it in one form or other, including this empty one. Berkeley also marks with "M" some early entries that clearly state that extension is not external to the mind – which signifies that he understands himself to be contributing to the case against matter.

It may have been Bayle who first planted in Berkeley's mind the idea that extension is a sensation. In the entry under Zeno of Elea in his *Dictionary*, Bayle considers various arguments Zeno might have relied upon in making a case against the existence of motion. One such argument is simply that since there is no extension, there is no motion. The arguments against extension that Bayle considers, as I will shortly indicate, were of great importance in Berkeley's development. Their conclusion is that "extension exists only in our understanding [and] . . . may very easily be reduced to appearance, just like colors."[13]

It is not clear whether Berkeley thought the blunt assertion that extension is a sensation was one of his early unsuccessful arguments, as distinct from a claim which requires such an argument in its defense. In any case it is merely an assertion. What were the arguments?

IV. PRIMARY AND SECONDARY QUALITIES

One early argument, or rather set of arguments, against matter involves the contention that if secondary qualities such as taste and color are in the mind, then primary qualities such as extension, solidity, figure, and number are also in the mind; primary qualities, in other words, should be understood to have the same sort of existence as secondary qualities. Berkeley refers to some version of this argument at N 20, when he writes that "Primary ideas prov'd not to exist in matter, after the same manner yt secondary ones are provd not to exist therein."

As I have just suggested, there are various versions of this argument. One is that because primary and secondary qualities are inseparable, if secondary qualities are in the mind, then primary qualities, including extension, are also in the mind. (See N 121, 222, 253, 362, 453, 494.) Another is that a certain feature of secondary qualities, on the basis of which they were believed to be in the mind, is also possessed by primary qualities. Thus primary qualities too must be in the mind. Thus Berkeley claims that relativity to the perceiver is a feature of primary qualities just as it is a feature of secondary qualities. This particular feature of secondary qualities, in virtue of which many philosophers and scientists had concluded that secondary qualities are not in external objects, is also a feature of primary qualities. Berkeley seems to follow Bayle's article on Zeno here too: "Since the same bodies are sweet to some men, and bitter to others, one is right in inferring that they are neither sweet nor bitter in themselves and absolutely speaking.... Why should we not say the same thing about extension? If an entity that has no color appears to us, however, with a determinate color with respect to its species, shape, and location, why could not an entity that had no extension be visible to us under an appearance of a determinate, shaped, and located extension of a certain type? And notice carefully that the same body appears to us to be small or large, round or square, according to the place from which it is viewed; and let us have no doubts that a body that seems very small to us appears very large to a fly" (*Historical and Critical Dictionary*, 364–5).

Berkeley's references to his first arguings generally have been understood as a reference to this line of argument.[14] There is some reason to do so: At *Principles* 15, Berkeley says that if anyone will consider "those arguments which are thought manifestly to prove that colours and tastes exist only in the mind, . . . he shall find they may with equal force be brought to prove the same thing of extension, figure, and motion." He goes on to say that "it must be confessed this method of arguing does not so much prove that there is no extension or colour in an outward object, as that we do not know by sense which is the true extension or colour of the object." Thus he indicates that he finds this line of thought unconvincing.[15] He then contrasts "this method of arguing" with "the arguments foregoing [which] plainly show it to be impossible that any colour or extension at all, or other sensible quality whatsoever, should exist in an unthinking subject without the mind, or in truth, that there should be any such thing as an outward object." The "arguments foregoing" rely on the new principles.

V. INFINITE DIVISIBILITY

However, it is clear that *other* arguments and considerations also were important to the early development of Berkeley's immaterialism. There is a case against matter that depends on the assumption that matter, if it were to exist, would be infinitely divisible. Berkeley may have been influenced on this point, too, by Bayle's article on Zeno, where in the course of setting forth the various reasons Zeno may have had for denying that motion exists, it is said that matter, if there were such, would be infinitely divisible, by Locke (for example in *Essay* II.xv.9, II.xvii.12) or by Descartes.

In one entry that bears on the topic of infinite divisibility, Berkeley gives the impression that he recognizes a distinction between extension and our idea of extension:

> 1S M Our ideas we call figure & extension not images of the figure & extension of Matter, these (if such there be) being infinitely divisible, those not so. (N 81)

Because he already has said that extension is a sensation, though, it is hard to know how seriously to take this idea. If extension is a sensation, then presumably it is not infinitely divisible; of course the hard job is to show that extension *is* a sensation. In any case, Berkeley offers arguments against infinitely divisible extension that are independent of the claim that extension is a sensation.

The first of these arguments is that what is infinitely divisible must be infinitely extended:

> 1M. Each [particle] of matter if extended must be infinitely extended. or have an infinite series of extension. (N 67)

> M 1 S Matter tho' allow'd to exist may be no greater than a pin's head. (N 128; see also N 90, 296a, 352, 364, 416. N 88 may also be relevant to this theme.)

The idea, which also found its way into the published works (such as PHK 128), is that what is infinitely divisible must have infinitely many parts. And what has infinitely many parts, each of which is extended to any degree, is infinitely extended. Finally, because the objects around us are not infinitely extended, they are not infinitely divisible. Here again Berkeley follows Bayle's article on Zeno: "We can see at once from a hilltop a vast plain dotted with houses, trees, flocks, and the like. . . . [But if there were infinite divisibility, not] even two of them could find room there. Each requires an infinite space, since it contains an infinity of extended bodies" (*Dictionary*, 363).

The second argument against infinite divisibility is that if extension were infinitely divisible, various states of affairs that we actually know to obtain would not obtain:

> Tis impossible a Material cube should exist, because the edges of a Cube will appear broad to an acute sense. (N 82)

That is, if whatever makes up the edges of a putative cube were infinitely divisible, then what we take to be the edge of a cube would actually be extended, and would in fact not be an edge at all. Hence what appears to us to be a cube would not be a cube. In fact it seems that there would be no such thing as a cube. In general, many things could not have the nature we know them to have. (See also N 45, 322, 877. Bayle had also made suggestions along these lines.)

Third, at N 21 Berkeley says that if extension is infinitely divisible, then there must be "length without breadth wch is absurd." The full entry is: "x Demonstrations of the infinite divisibility of extension suppose length without breadth wch is absurd." At N 21a he modifies N 21, adding the words "or invisible length" before "wch is absurd." Again at N 342 Berkeley initially makes the same point and adds a later modification numbered 342a. N 342 imputes various flaws to the arguments of the mathematicians for infinite divisibility, one of which is that "they suppose that we have an idea of length without breadth.* or that length without breadth does exist." The "*" connects this entry with N 342a: "X or rather that invisible length does exist." So the original (unmodified) point both at N 21 and N 342 was that to believe in infinite divisibility is to believe that there are things that have length but no breadth. The modified point is that to believe in infinite divisibility is to believe that there are invisible lengths.

Why did Berkeley change these entries? Perhaps he concluded that believers in infinite divisibility have no reason to accept that there is length with *no* breadth, and are more likely to say that a length will have some breadth, however small it may be. (He may have been thinking of a length as a geometric line that physically connects two things.) The modified point has more to it: The believers in infinite divisibility presumably *are* committed to there being invisible lengths, because any length that connects two points and has the least breadth that is visible to us, is itself divisible into infinitely many lengths between those same points; any of these divisions will be invisible to us. (Why should there *not* be invisible lengths? If the point is that invisible lengths are out of the question because extension is a sensation, then we need to know on what basis it is said – prior to the discovery of the new principles – that extension is a sensation.)

VI. SORTAL CLAIMS

Of course difficulties that arise in virtue of the infinite divisibility of matter can be evaded by denying that matter is infinitely divisible, and by embracing instead some form of atomism. I turn next to an argument that Berkeley thought to be more sweeping in its implications. It is also the most interesting among his early arguments against external extension. The emphasis is on certain contributions that the mind makes to what we perceive. Consider N 288 and N 289:

> P Malbranch does not prove that the . . . figures & extensions exist nt wn. the are not perceiv'd. Consequently he does not prove nor can it be prov'd on his principles that ye sorts are the work of the mind & onely in the mind. (N 288)

> Tho matter be extended wth an indefinite Extension, yet the mind makes the Sorts, they were not before the mind perceiving them. & [even] now they are not without the mind. Houses trees, &c tho indefinitely extended matter do exist. are not without the mind. (N 289)

Berkeley says that the sorts or concepts (horse, house, tree, etc.) that we use in classifying things are produced by and exist only in our minds. Even if matter were to exist, these sorts still would be imposed by our minds in perception. I refer to these claims as sortal claims. The following early entries also involve or hint at some of the sortal claims:

1M World wthout thought is nec quid nec quantum nec quale [neither what nor how much nor such] &c (N 22)

M 'tis wondrous to contemplate ye. world empty'd of intelligences. (N 23)

1M If the world be granted to consist of matter tis the mind gives it beauty & proportion. (N 68)

X Number not without the mind in any thing, because tis the mind by considering things as one that makes complex ideas of 'em, tis the mind combines into one, wch. by otherwise considering it's ideas might make a score of wt was but one just now. (N 104)

+ Number not in bodies it being the creature of the mind depending entirely on it's consideration & being more or less as the mind pleases. (N 110)[16]

N 22 makes it clear that, in general, the character things have when we perceive them is determined by the mind: Indeed, in the absence of minds the world would be without any nature or qualities or number. Even the advocates of material substance must concede that the physical world is, in large measure, our production and is mind-dependent in certain respects. Later, in *An Essay towards a New Theory of Vision*, Berkeley writes as follows:

[Number] (however some may reckon it amongst the primary qualities) is nothing fixed and settled, really existing in things themselves. It is intirely the creature of the mind, considering either a simple idea by it self, or any combination of simple ideas to which it gives one name, and so makes it pass for a unit.... [It] is evident the unit constantly relates to the particular draughts the mind makes of its ideas, to which it affixes names, and wherein it includes more or less as best suits its own ends and purposes.... [This] naming and combining together of ideas is perfectly arbitrary, and done by the mind in such sort as experience shews it to be most convenient.... (NTV 109)

Some of the remarks I have quoted in this section suggest that it is entirely up to us how large the "draughts" of our ideas are to be. The suggestion seems to be that we can make what we wish of the jumble of unsorted ideas we encounter, combining them together just as we please. It would seem, therefore, that if there were no beings like us around to classify something as a tree, there would be no trees. Indeed, prior to our classifying them in various ways, the things we believe to exist after we have gone through the sorting process may not even be *things*. It is interesting to note that some of the remarks Berkeley makes in this context are strikingly suggestive of (A), the first of the new principles. At N 289 Berkeley concludes his statement of the sortal claims with the remark that "[houses], trees, &c tho indefinitely extended matter do exist. are not without the mind." Compare this with N 427 and 427a where, apparently in a statement of (A), he says that "[we] see the Horse it self, the Church it self... it being an Idea & nothing more.... The Horse it self the Church it self is an Idea i.e. object (immediate object) of thought."

It is clear from N 288 that Berkeley applies this line of thought to extension; this is also clear from the following entries:

> 1M If a piece of matter have extension yt must be determin'd to a particular bigness & figure.... (N 40)

> ~~S~~ + Bigg, little & number are the works of the mind. How therefore can ye extension you suppose in matter be big or little how can it consist of any number of points? (N 325; see also N 271.)

That is, if something is material, it must have a particular extension, which is to say that it must have a particular size, figure, and so on. Consider its length. Because we can decide what the unit of measurement is to be, we can decide what the length is. That it has this length rather than that one is something we determine. Until we do so, there is no such thing as its extension. Further, if it is up to us what "draught" to take, until we do so there is no "it" to have an extension.

At N 874 Berkeley identifies the target at which he is aiming:

> Tis plain the Moderns must by their own Principles own there are no Bodies i.e. no Sort of Bodies without the Mind i.e. unperceived.

Locke is among the moderns he has in mind. According to Locke, "the sorting of [things] under names is the workmanship of the understanding, taking occasion from the similitude it observes among them to make abstract general ideas" (*Essay* III.iii.13). On Locke's view we observe certain similarities among the simple ideas we perceive, and we select some of these similarities when we develop our classificatory scheme. Then we assign a name to each type of thing that we have distinguished. Berkeley adds to the number of characteristics of things he believes to be contributed by the mind. He understands number, size, beauty, figure, and proportion, for example, to be among the sorts imposed by our minds, as well as concepts such as house, horse, or tree.

What are we to make of all this? The claim that we can make what we wish of a jumble of unsorted ideas that we encounter, combining them as we please, is at odds with another Berkeleyan theme, namely that we can infer a great deal about the tangible parts of the world from our visual sensations and, in general, that God speaks to us through the language of nature. If there is a language of nature, then the sensations we receive must come to us already ordered. Otherwise the ideas we perceive would not apprise us of the imminence of others. The divine language requires that there be settled laws of nature that hold between collections of ideas that, as it were, come to us pre-assembled.[17] If there are regularities, and hence if we have any grounds for anticipating that the ideas we have found to be connected in the past will be connected in the same ways in the future, then the ideas we encounter must be related to each other in various ways that we can discover. Further, they must be so related irrespective of how we combine them. Even in the passage quoted from the *New Theory*, Berkeley says that we sort and combine ideas "as best suits [our] ends and purposes [and] experience shows it to be most convenient." If a certain "draught" of ideas is more convenient than some other and better suits our ends and purposes, presumably this must be because it is better adapted to the structure of the world. Berkeley says, to be sure, that there is only a *customary* tie between our ideas, and that "signs are variable, and of human institution" (NTV 144). Such remarks might mistakenly be taken to mean that it is entirely up to us what ideas we combine, in what ways we combine them, and which ideas will serve as signs of which others. Notice, though, that the "customary ties" are said to be *observed*; if we observe them, then they are not arbitrary. And the remark that signs are variable and of human institution is followed by these further remarks:

> ... when we remember that there was a time they were *not* connected in our minds with those things they now so readily suggest; but that their signification was learned by the slow steps of experience: This preserves us from confounding them. (NTV 144)

Of course this worry about the sortal point arises only when the idea of a language of nature has been developed, and it may not have given reason to Berkeley to be dissatisfied with the sortal themes when he first penned the relevant entries in the notebooks.

There are other problems, though, some of which he may have been aware even at that early stage. In particular, as N 288 and 289 explicitly state, the sortal claims seem consistent with the existence of external extension. It could be that there are external extended things *and* that the unit of measurement (and hence the way in which we measure and describe their extension) is determined by us.

Moreover, the sortal claims, at least on one reading, are at odds with what Berkeley says, even from the beginning of the notebooks, about the reality of the physical world. Surely God has created a world with trees, horses, and so forth, which is to say that God has already done a lot of the sorting. Berkeley's sortal claims actually seem to lead him in the direction of doing away with the world of common sense. It would be much better for him to adopt the less radical view that we have to learn to discern certain patterns in what we observe. However well they may fit with other views that Berkeley held, there can be no doubt that the sortal claims were part of his case against external extension in the notebooks.

VII. VISIBLE AND TANGIBLE EXTENSION

Another important early line of argument against external extension, and hence against matter, focuses on the heterogeneity of the objects of sight and touch (for example, see N 114, 206, 226, 227, 246, 256, and NTV throughout), from which Berkeley infers the heterogeneity of visible and tangible extension:

13X Motion, figure & extension perceivable by sight are different from those ideas perceived by touch wch goe by the same name. (N 28)

3X1 Why may I not Say [visible] extension is a continuity of visible points – tangible extension is a continuity of tangible points. (N 78a)

X13 Visible extension cannot be conceiv'd added to tangible extension. Visible & tangible points can't make one sum. therefore these extensions are heterogeneous (N 295; see also N 108, 240.)

Part of his purpose in arguing that visible and tangible extension are not the same thing is to undermine an argument that had been advanced in support of the external existence of extension. Extension,

Berkeley tells us at N 57, was "thought to exist in. [external] matter" because "it was conceiv'd common to 2 senses." It was thought that if an idea is received by more than one sense, it is likely that it is an idea of something that exists externally. If, as Berkeley contends, visible and tangible extension are not the same thing, then at least this reason for thinking extension to be external carries no weight. Berkeley also devotes quite a few entries to considering *why* people have mistakenly thought that the same extension is seen and felt, and have failed to grasp that they are heterogeneous (for example, N 43, 54, 91, 138, 181).

Among the considerations Berkeley offers in support of the heterogeneity of visible and tangible extension is his response to the Molyneux Problem.

> 13X Molyneux's Blind man would not know the sphaere or cube to [be] bodies or extended at first sight. (N 32; see also N 49, 58, 59, 95, 97, 100, 121, 174.)

That is, someone who had been born blind would not, on first being able to see, be able to identify by sight objects such as spheres and cubes that already were known by touch. It follows, Berkeley seems mistakenly to have thought, that what we see and what we touch are not the same thing.

He also appeals to various other features of sight and vision in support of the heterogeneity thesis:

> 2X1 The bigness... of the pictures [in one sense] in the fund is not determin'd, for the nearer a man views them,... [the images of them] (as well as other objects) will... take up the greater room in the fund of his eye. (N 213)

> 3~~S~~ X1 Distinct perception of Visible ideas not so perfect as of tangible, tangible ideas being many at once equally Vivid. Hence heterogeneous... Extension. (N 243)

The point of N 213 may be that tangible size is fixed in a certain way, whereas visible size is relative to a field of vision. (See also N 49, 65, 70, 103.) The point of N 243 appears to be that tangible ideas are more vivid and distinct than visible ideas. The claim in N 78a – namely that visible extension consists of minima visibilia (or the smallest things that are perceivable by vision) whereas tangible extension consists of minima tangibilia (or the smallest things that are perceivable by touch) – is also supportive of heterogeneity, which is a point that Berkeley makes at N 295.

VIII. EXTENSION NOT A SENSATION

A picture of the relationship between tangible extension and other tangible ideas and between visible extension and other visible ideas is presented when Berkeley says, for example, that extension "cannot be conceived distinct from... all tangible or Visible quality" (N 288a), and "is blended wth tangible or visible ideas, & by the mind [is] praescinded therefrom" (N 328). The suggestion is that extension is among the complex set of qualities we immediately perceive. There are passages, though, that present a rather different picture, namely that our perception of extension is mediate, and that we perceive extension via our perception of other qualities. On this account the proper or immediate objects of vision are light and colors; the proper objects of touch are hot and cold, roughness, smoothness, hardness, and so on. On this view not only are the immediate objects of vision and touch heterogeneous, but in addition, extension is not among them. Relevant passages include these:

+S Mem: Quaere whether extension be equally a sensation with colour? (N 111)

M ~~S~~ 1 Qu: wt can we see beside colours, wt can we feel beside, hard, soft, cold warm pleasure pain (N 136)

X+ Extension seems to be perceiv'd by the eye as thoughts by the ear (N 216; also N 215, 220.)

1Xa3 Wt I see is onely variety of colours & light. Wt I feel is hard or soft, hot or cold, rough or smooth, & c.... Wt resemblance have these thoughts wth those? (N 226; also NTV 43, 103, 130, 156; PHK 1.)

1X123 I saw gladness in his looks, I Saw shame in his face so I see figure or Distance (N 231)

The implication is that extension is *not* a sensation, but rather is *known by* sensation. Extension is something we infer from, or that is suggested by, our sensations. Part of the point may be that if extension is something we contribute to what we perceive, rather than something we receive in sense-perception, there is yet more reason to think it to be mind-dependent.

However, there is a respect in which some of these entries are difficult to read. Sometimes Berkeley means by extension just *tangible* extension. (See, for example, N 87, 103, 174, 181, 195–6, 205–6, 220, 297.) His tendency to think of extension as tangible extension may be connected to his thought that tangible extension is fixed, whereas visible extension is relative to the visual field, and to his further thought that the object of geometry is tangible extension (N 101). Moreover, entries that express this view may be part of his preparation for his *Essay towards a New Theory of Vision*, where Berkeley takes the position that visible qualities are in the mind, whereas tangible qualities are external to it. Thus N 216 ("Extension seems to be perceiv'd by the eye as thoughts by the ear") may mean that we never see *tangible* extension. Likewise the latter part of N 215, which says (or at least suggests) that "we think we see extension by meer vision, yet we do not," may have the same meaning. On the other hand, N 226 suggests that neither visible nor tangible extension is a sensation, but rather is mediately perceived by sensation. *Both* views are to be found in the notebooks, and without further clarification the claim that we do not see extension is open to either reading.

To complicate matters further, some entries, including N 226, seem to express a more radical position, namely that what we call extension is actually nothing but a combination of various other ideas. Consider these entries:

1 M Of solidity see L. b2. c4. §1. §5. §6. If any one ask wt solidity is let him put a flint between his hands & he will know. Extension of Body is continuity of solid & C, extension of Space is continuity of unsolid &c. (N 78)

X Extension [or Space] no simple idea, length, breadth &. . solidity being three several ideas (N 105)

+S Extension seems to consist in variety of homogeneal thoughts coexisting without mixture. or rather [visible] Extension seems to be the coexistence of colours in ye mind. (N 164–5; see also N 167.)

Here it seems that talk of extension is actually shorthand for talk of a set of other qualities, qualities that will be different in the two cases of visible and tangible extension. Extension is not something that is inferred from other qualities, then: Rather it consists in them. Furthermore the qualities in which extension of one sort consists are not perceived by the sense or senses that perceive the qualities in which extension of the other sort consists. Thus depth and solidity, which are part of what tangible extension consists in, are not perceivable by sight (N 106). The view that extension is a complex idea with constituent parts in turn bolsters the case for the heterogeneity of visible and tangible extension.

Sometimes Berkeley seems to go even further than this, to say that extension is actually an artificial idea of philosophers:

X The Mob use not the word Extension. tis an abstract term of the Schools. (N 111a)

E.X Existence, Extension &c are abstract i.e. no ideas. they are words unknown and useless to the Vulgar. (N 772; see also N 711.)

Here Berkeley seems to say that extension is *neither* a sensation *nor* something that is known by sensation *nor* something that consists in various sensations; rather there is no such thing as extension at all. Perhaps what he is opposing here is not the existence of extension, but rather the existence of extension separate from other qualities. After all, the vulgar (that is, ordinary people) *do* think that there are extended things.

IX. BODIES AND CONTINUITY

In the remaining sections of this essay I briefly discuss some aspects of what the notebooks tell us about Berkeley's early views concerning physical objects and minds. Throughout the notebooks, and indeed throughout the later published works, Berkeley is insistent that to do away with matter is not at all to do away with physical objects.[18] N 79 makes the point well:

M Mem. that I take notice that I do not fall in wth Sceptics Fardella &c, in yt I make bodies to exist... certainly, wch they doubt of.

We find, too, that from the outset a radically immaterialist entry such as N 18 ("~~MS~~ Extension a sensation, therefore not without the mind.") is followed by an expression of a firmly realist position concerning the external world at N 19 ("M~~S~~ In ye immaterial hypothesis the wall is white; fire hot & c.").

If everything other than minds exists only as a set of sensations, though, and hence exists only if and when it is perceived, do physical objects come into and go out of existence in accordance with whether someone is perceiving them? In the notebooks, Berkeley addresses this issue on a number of occasions. He presents the idea, which also occurs in the major works (for instance, PHK 3, DHP 3 [251]), that objects we do not currently perceive exist in that we would perceive them if we were correctly situated:

M. The Trees are in the Park, that is, whether I will or no whether I imagine any thing about them or no, let me but go thither & open my Eyes by day & I shall not avoid seeing them. (N 98)

Other reactions to the continuity question that show up in the notebooks include the thought that we are incapable of thinking of something that exists but is unperceived, because if we think of any such thing it *is* perceived (N 472). These reactions also include an appeal to powers in God:

~~M~~ + Bodies & c do exist even wn not perceiv'd they being powers in the active Being. (N 52)

Berkeley does not tell us much about the powers he has in mind, but because he appeals to them in attempting to account for the continuity of physical objects, they cannot amount merely to abilities or capacities. God, being omnipotent, has the ability or capacity to produce things that never exist. The powers in question thus must involve something like an *inclination* or *disposition* on God's part to produce certain ideas rather than others.[19]

There seems to have been a phase in his development during which Berkeley was prepared to allow unperceived objects only a second-class existence:

M. P. Mem: to allow existence to colours in the dark, persons not thinking &c but not an absolute actual existence.... (N 185)

At this stage he seems to have thought that being perceived actually is necessary for existence, at least for first-class existence. (Curiously, he says he is in agreement with common sense on this point; thus at N 473 he says that "existence is vulgarly restrain'd to actuall perception." See also, for instance, N 408.) N 293a adds that existence as powers is also second-class existence:

+ Bodies taken for Powers do exist wn. not perceived but this existence is not actual. wn I say a power exists no more is meant than that if in ye light I open my eyes & look that way [I] shall see it i.e. [ye body] & c

In the second sentence Berkeley says that the appeal to powers amounts to nothing more than the idea, familiar from N 98, that currently unperceived objects exist in that one *would* perceive them if one were suitably placed. The first sentence seems to say, though, that insofar as objects exist as powers, they lack actual existence. Actually, N 293a appears both to identify the view that unperceived objects exist as powers in God's mind with the view that unperceived objects exist in that if we were suitably located we would perceive them, *and* to say that the existence involved in all of this is *not* actual existence.

In an entry that appears to have been added later than N 293a, the full-blooded existence of unperceived objects is restored:

M.P Colours in ye dark do exist really i.e. were there light or as soon as light comes we shall see them provided we open our eyes. & that whether we will or no. (N 185a)

Here Berkeley says that the existence of unperceived objects actually is perfectly secure, and the fact that we would perceive them if we were properly situated is what guarantees their existence. As this view continued to be expressed in the later published writings, I infer that 185a is the later entry and that N 293a represents an abandoned phase in Berkeley's development. N 802 confirms he had decided that unperceived objects have, after all, first-class existence:

M. P. Not to mention the Combinations of Powers but to say the things the effects themselves to really exist even wn. not actually . . . perceiv'd but still with relation to perception. (N 802)

X. MINDS OR SOULS

Finally, a word on the views of the mind that are to be found in the notebooks. Especially in Notebook A, the second notebook, there is a good deal of attention to the nature of the mind or soul. ("Mind" and "soul" are used interchangeably.) On this issue, too, Berkeley goes through a number of phases in his thinking.[20] His view in the *Principles* and *Dialogues* (and hence, as one would expect, at the end of Notebook A) is that the mind is an active entity, and is active in perceiving as well as in willing:

S Understanding is in some sort an Action. (N 821)

S. Substance of a Spirit is that it acts, causes, wills, operates, or if you please (to avoid the quibble yt may be made on ye word it) to act, cause, will, operate. . . . (N 829)

Again at N 848 Berkeley says that "[by spirit]...I mean all that is active." (See also N 854.) On this view the mind is an active entity, consisting of a combination of an active will and an active understanding.

A number of other positions are represented in the notebooks, though, and the course of Berkeley's progress through these positions is not altogether clear. At times he seems to *identify* the mind and the will, leaving out the understanding:

S We cannot possibly conceive any active power but the Will (N 155)

M P Qu: whether I had [not] better allow Colours to exist without the Mind taking the Mind for the Active thing wch I call I, my self. yt seems to be distinct from ye Understanding (362a)

S The soul is the will properly speaking & as it is distinct from Ideas. (478a; see also N 194a, 712, 814, 829, 847.)

Perhaps the idea that we are in various respects passive in sense-perception contributed to the occurrence of this phase. Passages in which perception is said to be passive include the following:

M1 ~~S~~ Whatsoever has any of our ideas in it must perceive, it being that very having, that passive reception of ideas that denominates the mind perceiving...[that] being the very essence of perception, or that wherein perception [consists]. (N 301)

the bare passive reception or having of ideas is call'd perception (N 378.10; see also N 286, 645.)

The idea that the understanding is passive whereas the will is active also may contribute to explaining the occurrence of the view that the mind consists of a will and an understanding, which are said to be two distinct beings (N 708; this explanation is suggested by N 643; see also N 659).

Berkeley also toys with a more extreme Humean view that the understanding, and even sometimes the mind, is nothing but a set of ideas.

+ The very existence of Ideas constitutes the soul. (N 577)

+ Consult, ransack yr Understanding wt find you there besides several perceptions or thoughts.... (N 579)

+ Mind is a congeries of Perceptions. Take away Perceptions & you take away the Mind...put the Perceptions & you put the mind. (N 580)

+ Say you the Mind is not the Perceptions. but that thing wch perceives. I answer you are abused by the words that & thing these are vague empty words without a meaning. (N 581. See also N 587, 637, 643.)

The view that the understanding is just a set of ideas is sometimes accompanied by the thought that the will is nothing but a set of volitions:

S Doctrine of Identity best explain'd by Taking the Will for Volitions, the Understanding for Ideas.... (N 681)

In any case, by the end of the notebooks, after having considered various possibilities, Berkeley seems to have concluded that perception also involves activity, and he embraces the idea of a unified active mind. N 429 and 429a are particularly revealing in that N 429 says that "Existere is percipi or percipere" and to this N 429a adds: "or velle i.e. agere."

XI. CONCLUSION

From the time he wrote the earliest entries in the notebooks, Berkeley denied matter and held that physical objects and all of their properties, including extension, are immaterial. I have explored a series of maneuvers to which Berkeley had recourse in an attempt to make extension dependent on the mind. I doubt that it is possible to give a full account of how precisely the new principles emerged from these early maneuvers, but it seems clear that Berkeley concluded that his new principles get to the heart of what he had been arguing for, and provide an effective and economical way to articulate and to defend immaterialism.[21]

NOTES

1. For discussion, see George Thomas's introduction to George Berkeley, *Philosophical Commentaries*, ed. George H. Thomas (Alliance, OH: Mt. Union College, 1976); Bertil Belfrage, "Dating Berkeley's Notebook B," *Berkeley Newsletter* 7 (1984): 7–13, "The Order and Dating of Berkeley's Notebooks," *Revue Internationale de Philosophie* 1985 fasc. 3, "The Clash on Semantics in Berkeley's Notebook A," *Hermathena* 139 (1985): 117–26, reprinted in *George Berkeley: Essays and Replies*, ed. David Berman (Dublin: Irish Academic Press, 1986), 117–26, "A New Approach

to Berkeley's *Philosophical Notebooks*," in *Essays on the Philosophy of George Berkeley*, ed. Ernest Sosa (Dordrecht: Reidel, 1987), 217–30; and M. A. Stewart, "Add. MS. 39315," *Berkeley Newsletter* 9 (1986): 6–11.

2. "N" stands for the notebooks. "N" is followed by the number of the entry to which I am referring. In presenting the entries I follow George Berkeley, *Philosophical Commentaries*, ed. George H. Thomas, which I believe to be the edition that is most faithful to the original, reproducing even deletions when they are legible. Thomas makes many corrections to the text of the notebooks prepared by A. A. Luce for Volume 1 of *The Works of George Berkeley, Bishop of Cloyne*, ed. A. A. Luce and T. E. Jessop, 9 vols. (London: Thomas Nelson, 1948–57), but he preserves Luce's numbering. Thomas's more significant corrections are incorporated into the notebooks as they appear in George Berkeley, *Philosophical Works*, ed. Michael R. Ayers (London: J. M. Dent, 1975), in printings released in 1989 and later years.
3. Luce may have been the first to advance this reading. In his diplomatic edition of Berkeley's notebooks, which he entitled *Philosophical Commentaries* (London: Nelson, 1944), he proposed this reading, although not without reservations. However, by the time he came to write a later essay, "Another Look at Berkeley's Notebooks," *Hermathena* 110 [1970]: 5–23, Luce had decided (correctly in my view) that there is little to be said for the standard reading. Bertil Belfrage convincingly points out some of its defects in "A New Approach to Berkeley's *Philosophical Notebooks*."
4. See, for example, A. A. Luce, *The Life of George Berkeley* (London: Thomas Nelson, 1949), 37ff.
5. Some relevant evidence is discussed by George Thomas in the introduction to his edition, *Philosophical Commentaries*, iv. Actually a glance at the original manuscript in the British Library is enough to see that Berkeley sometimes recorded a number of entries on a variety of topics at one time. We can tell this merely by observing the points at which he refreshed his ink. He probably had a practice of jotting down his thoughts elsewhere as they occurred to him and then transcribing them into his notebooks, a few at a time, when occasion arose.
6. A. A. Luce, *The Dialectic of Immaterialism* (London: Hodder and Stoughton, 1963), 92ff.
7. G. A. Johnston, *The Development of Berkeley's Philosophy* (London: Macmillan, 1923), 19–32.
8. C. M. Turbayne, "The Influence of Berkeley's Science on His Metaphysics." *Philosophy and Phenomenological Research* 16 (1956): 476–87, 480.

9. In reading entry 280 as a continuation of entry 279 I follow a suggestion made by Bertil Belfrage in conversation. (This reading is also proposed by A. C. Grayling in *Berkeley: The Central Arguments* (London: Duckworth, 1986), 48.) Turbayne reads N 279 as announcing a discovery which is not actually stated until 100 entries later, and which Berkeley there refers to as "the Principle":

   > neither . . . our Ideas nor any thing like our ideas can possibly be in an unperceiving thing. (N 379)

   I do not see, though, that N 379 adds anything to N 280. At N 280 Berkeley says that ideas exist only when they are perceived, that they therefore cannot exist in "unthinking things," and that anything which resembles an idea is an idea. It follows that nothing which resembles an idea can exist external to minds.
10. For discussion see George Pitcher, *Berkeley* (London: Routledge and Kegan Paul, 1977), 115–24; also Kenneth P. Winkler, *Berkeley: An Interpretation* (Oxford: Clarendon Press, 1989), 141ff.
11. M. R. Ayers, "Substance, Reality, and the Great Dead Philosophers," *American Philosophical Quarterly* 7 (1970), 49. Incidentally, (A)–(D) are not the only readings of Berkeley's new principle that have been suggested. For instance, Grayling (*Berkeley: The Central Arguments*, 48) proposes that the new principle actually is a combination of (B) and (D).
12. For discussion of Bayle's influence on Berkeley see Richard H. Popkin, "Berkeley and Pyrrhonism," in *The Skeptical Tradition*, ed. Myles Burnyeat (Berkeley: University of California Press, 1983), 377–96. Popkin's essay originally appeared in *The Review of Metaphysics* 5 (1951–52): 223–46.
13. Pierre Bayle, *Historical and Critical Dictionary: Selections*, ed. Richard H. Popkin (Indianapolis: Hackett, 1991), 366, 373.
14. See, for example, I. C. Tipton, *Berkeley: The Philosophy of Immaterialism* (London: Methuen, 1974), 39; A. A. Luce, *The Dialectic of Immaterialism*, ch. 5; C. M. Turbayne, "The Influence of Berkeley's Science," 477.
15. On the other hand, as various commentators have noted, in the *Dialogues* the case for primary and secondary qualities being treated in the same way seems to be presented as a convincing argument (for example at DHP1 [188ff.]). Perhaps the explanation is that not everything said by Philonous, the character who usually presents Berkeley's view, should be imputed to Berkeley. Incidentally, there is an important reason why this entire line of argument was doomed to failure, although I do not think that Berkeley ever recognized it. The view of Locke, who was one of Berkeley's main targets on this issue, was not that secondary qualities

are in the mind; rather, secondary qualities are actually in external objects. They are combinations of the primary qualities of the minute parts of those objects which suffice to cause in us certain ideas, which Locke thought of as ideas of secondary qualities. See John Locke, *An Essay concerning Human Understanding*, ed. P. H. Hidditch (Oxford: Clarendon Press, 1975), II.viii. 7–10, 13–14.

16. The remark that number is "more or less as the mind pleases" does not mean that to some considerable extent number is as the mind pleases, but rather that number is entirely the product of the mind, and hence that how many things of a certain type there are is a product of the mind.
17. For some discussion of relevant issues see Bertil Belfrage, "The Constructivism of Berkeley's New Theory of Vision," in *Minds, Ideas, and Objects: Essays on the Theory of Representation in Modern Philosophy*, Volume 2 of North American Kant Society Studies in the History of Philosophy, ed. Phillip D. Cummins and Guenter Zoeller (Atascadero, CA: Ridgeview Press, 1992).
18. Luce thought there to be an early stage in the development of Berkeley's immaterialism in which he denied the existence of the physical world. There is some evidence for this view, including N 24: "+ Nothing properly but persons . . . i.e. conscious things do exist, all other things are not so much existences as manners of ye existence of persons." I give my reasons for disagreeing with Luce in "Luce's Account of the Development of Berkeley's Immaterialism," *Journal of the History of Ideas* 48 (1987): 649–69.
19. Charles J. McCracken, "What Does Berkeley's God See in the Quad?" *Archiv für Geschichte der Philosophie* 61 (1979): 280–92, takes the powers to be abilities; hence he sees this view as one that generates more problems than it solves, and as one that Berkeley quickly abandoned.
20. For a more detailed account of the development of Berkeley's mind in the notebooks see Charles J. McCracken,"Berkeley's Notion of Spirit," *History of European Ideas* 7 (1986): 597–602; see also chapters 3 and 6 of Robert G. Muehlmann, *Berkeley's Ontology* (Indianapolis: Hackett, 1992).
21. Some of the research on which this paper is based was supported by a Research Fellowship at the Institute for Irish Studies at the Queen's University of Belfast. I am grateful to the Institute for Irish Studies for this support. I am also grateful to Bertil Belfrage, Matt Davidson, Charles McCracken, David Raynor, and Ken Winkler for comments on earlier drafts.

MARGARET ATHERTON

4 Berkeley's theory of vision and its reception

Berkeley's *New Theory of Vision* has had an excellent press. In the introduction to his edition, A. A. Luce presents it as a book that, from early on, received wide acclaim; a number of other authors have reinforced that impression. In the second part of his *Dissertation* (first published in 1821) Dugald Stewart makes this report:

> The solid additions, however, made by Berkeley to the stock of human knowledge were important and brilliant. Among these, the first place is unquestionably due to his *New Theory of Vision*; a work abounding with ideas so different from those commonly received, and, at the same time, so true, so profound and refined, that it was regarded by all but a few accustomed to deep metaphysical reflection, rather in the light of a philosophical romance than of a sober inquiry after truth. Such, however, has been since the progress and diffusion of this sort of knowledge, that the leading and most abstracted doctrines contained in it, form now an essential part of every elementary treatise of optics, and are adopted by the most superficial smatterers in science as fundamental articles of their faith.[1]

Samuel Bailey introduces his book on Berkeley's theory of vision, published in 1842, by saying:

> The doctrine contained in "An Essay towards a new Theory of Vision," which was first published in 1709 by the celebrated Bishop of Cloyne, seems to have become the established creed of philosophers almost from the moment of its appearance. In the last century, Hartley, Reid, Adam Smith, Condillac, Voltaire, Dugald Stewart (not to mention less eminent authors), all in succession adopted, extolled and enforced it; and a further proof of its extensive prevalence is furnished by the sanction more or less explicit, which it met with from such writers as Diderot, Buffon, and D' Alembert.[2]

In general we are given the impression of a highly successful theory that was adopted almost immediately and almost without reservation.

These reports of the success of Berkeley's *New Theory* exist by stark contrast to the reputation of the works he published only a few years later, the *Principles of Human Knowledge* and *Three Dialogues between Hylas and Philonous*. In the case of these volumes, we know Berkeley had a hard time even getting them a reading, that his friend Percival reported to him from London that without opening his book, men were calling him mad; and everyone has heard how Dr. Johnson refuted Berkeley with a kick. Harry Bracken has amply demonstrated that early on and within Berkeley's lifetime, Berkeley's metaphysics was being treated highly negatively, as the ravings of one who would turn everything into a dream.[3] The most flattering kind of reaction Berkeley's words received echoes Hume's famous judgment: "That they admit of no answer and produce no conviction."[4] It is interesting, therefore, to wonder why it is that the reputation of these different aspects of Berkeley's work took such different paths, the one so universally acclaimed, the other so widely derided.

Not surprisingly, perhaps, a closer examination of the facts about the reception of Berkeley's *theory* of vision shows things are actually more complicated. When we ask what it is about Berkeley's theory that was so generally accepted, we find that the area given approval was considerably narrower than the theory Berkeley put forward. It also becomes clear that the account of Berkeley's theory as silencing all opposition must be tempered by recognizing the considerable reservations expressed about the theory. Finally, the view that Berkeley's work achieved two opposing reputations also must be reexamined. It is possible to identify a strain of Berkeley commentary that not only takes a broader look at the theory of vision, but, in so doing, provides grounds for a generally positive response to Berkeley's overall theory.

I do not have space here to give a complete history of the reception of Berkeley's *New Theory*. What I intend to do first is give an account of Berkeley's theory of vision, in order to make plain both the richness of Berkeley's actual theory and to explain something of what Berkeley hoped to accomplish. Second, I will give a flavor of the complexity of the response to the *New Theory* by dipping into the history of its reception at a number of different points. Instead of mentioning all responses to Berkeley, I have selected a representative sample to discuss in some detail. In making my selection, I have tried to choose episodes that either have been important in shaping the history of Berkeley scholarship, or that will reveal something of the gamut of responses available. I intend my history, although selective, to provide the underpinnings for a more accurate understanding of a complex event in the history of philosophy, the reception of Berkeley's *New Theory of Vision*, and to show something of what goes into the reading of such a text.

I. AN ACCOUNT OF BERKELEY'S THEORY OF VISION[5]

Berkeley begins the *New Theory* quite baldly, with an introductory paragraph telling his readers what the book is about: "My design is to shew the manner wherein we perceive by sight the distance, magnitude, and situation of objects. Also to consider the difference there is betwixt the ideas of sight and touch and whether there be any idea common to both senses" (NTV 1). What this paragraph does not tell us is why Berkeley considered this investigation into space perception worth doing, and in particular why Berkeley thought a consideration of the difference between the ideas of sight and touch was peculiarly relevant.

These deficiencies, however, are amply made up in Berkeley's later summary of his theory, *Theory of Vision Vindicated and Explained*. In that work, Berkeley tells us that instead of following the synthetical method of the *New Theory*, "wherein, from false and popular suppositions, men do often arrive at truth" (TVV 38), he will now follow the reverse order: Starting from the conclusion of the *New Theory* he will deduce from it the truth it supports. In *Theory of Vision Vindicated*, then, we find an unequivocal statement of what Berkeley set out to prove through his investigation of vision in the *New Theory*: It is that *"Vision is the Language of the Author of Nature"* (TVV 8). Berkeley undertook his investigation of distance, size, and situation perception in order to demonstrate the truth of the conclusions he draws in *New Theory* 147:

> Upon the whole, I think we may fairly conclude that the proper objects of vision constitute an universal language of the Author of nature, whereby we are instructed how to regulate our actions in order to attain those things that

are necessary to the preservation and well-being of our bodies, as also to avoid whatever may be hurtful and destructive of them. It is by their information that we are principally guided in all the transactions and concerns of life. And the manner wherein they signify and mark unto us the objects which are at a distance is the same with that of languages and signs of human appointment, which do not suggest the things signified by any likeness or identity of nature, but only by an habitual connexion that experience has made us to observe between them.

If vision is a language, our visual ideas work as signs suggesting to us the various tangible and other meanings that come to be associated with them in our experience.

The importance of the heterogeneity thesis – the claim that ideas of sight are of a different kind than ideas of touch – also is spelled out clearly in *Theory of Vision Vindicated*. Language is a kind of symbol system in which there is a purely arbitrary connection between the signs and what they signify. Language thus provides a model whereby we can understand how visual signs can suggest, and hence call to mind, information supplied by touch. As in a language, visual signs can lead the mind to their meanings through what Berkeley calls "suggestion." Vision need not resemble the nonvisual for it to inform us of what it stands for, nor need there be a necessary connection between what we see and what it signifies so that we can reason our way from one to the other.

Berkeley spends considerable amounts of time establishing the truth of the heterogeneity thesis. His basic claim is that if we pay attention to the nature of the objects of our various senses, we are forced to conclude that the proper objects of each sense are different one from another, that by sight we apprehend light and colors but not solidity, by touch we apprehend solidity, distance, and so forth, but not sounds, by hearing we are aware of sounds but not smells, and so on. Not only is it the case that by sight we are aware of a different range of qualities than we are by touch, but in fact visual qualities have nothing in common with tangible qualities, so there is no way the experience of a visual quality can be connected with the experience of a tangible quality, except arbitrarily. This amounts to a denial that we can abstract from the experience of a colored patch any information that could also be abstracted from the experience of a solid tangible surface, or that in our visual experience of a colored patch there is anything resembling what we experience when we touch a solid surface. Berkeley repeatedly hammers home this claim by means of a thought-experiment: He asks us to imagine what a man born blind, but thoroughly informed about the tangible qualities of things, would be able to recognize if he were given sight. Berkeley thinks this thought-experiment will get us to recognize the disparate nature of the ideas of sight and touch, because he supposes attention will make clear that the formerly blind man's knowledge of tangible qualities will not help him understand the colors he now sees.

The argument of *Theory of Vision Vindicated*, then, suggests that in the *New Theory*, Berkeley takes himself to be showing that because the ideas of sight and touch are heterogeneous, vision represents in the way a language does. Ideas of sight come to mean entirely unrelated ideas of touch. We also know from *Theory of Vision Vindicated* that Berkeley considered the heterogeneity thesis the cornerstone of his argument; he describes it there as the "main part and pillar" of his theory (TVV 41). Berkeley identifies the theories against which he is arguing as being committed to a homogeneity thesis, the claim that ideas of sight look like or are conceptually connected to what they signify. Both Berkeley and the theories of which he is critical assume we see only visual qualities. The theories Berkeley rejects, however, take seeing to be successful only to the extent that what we see resembles or can be connected conceptually with what it stands for. Because what we see often is not very much like what it stands for (as when the apparent moon we see, for example, is very much smaller than the real moon), vision is held to be frequently unsuccessful in providing information.

It is a feature of the geometric theories of vision, such as those of Descartes and Malebranche, that they contended vision is an unsatisfactory means of learning about the world. Malebranche, for example, took it to be one of his purposes to demonstrate "that our eyes generally deceive us in everything they represent to us: in the size of bodies, in their figure and motion, and in light and colors, which are the only things we see."[6] Malebranche contends that what we see is always relative to the sort of sense organ we have and to the situation of the object perceived relative to that sense organ. Seeing red, for example, is the result of the way our corporeal organs are stimulated. But while we could not see unless the appropriate organs (such as the retina) are stimulated, what we see is not precisely what is represented on the retina. If it were, then, for example, we would perceive the objects coming closer to us as growing larger, because the retinal stimulation is of an increasing size. For Malebranche, then, vision is a two-stage process in which we construct a visual representation on the basis of our immediate stimulation. (This is where geometry comes in.) Our vision misleads us because we take mind-dependent visual constructions, many of whose features are due to the nature of the sensory system, to be accurate depictions of the mind-independent world the visual construction represents. Berkeley's account of vision as a language combats the view that vision misrepresents. As the signs of a language are connected only arbitrarily to what they signify, Berkeley can claim that vision suggests to us not something it misrepresents, but the tangible and other qualities of things.

An important result of Berkeley's language model of vision is the demonstration that visual cues successfully work to suggest to us tangible meanings. The nature of Berkeley's argument in this section is again clarified by the way he proceeds in *Theory of Vision Vindicated*. Berkeley intends to reverse the argument of the *New Theory* in order to proceed analytically in *Theory of Vision Vindicated*, so it can be no accident that in *Theory of Vision Vindicated* Berkeley discusses the various problems of space perception in reverse order from that found in the *New Theory*. In *Theory of Vision Vindicated* he first takes up situation, then size, and finally distance. In neither work is Berkeley making the same point about space perception in three different ways. Instead, in the *New Theory* the argument about situation perception must provide the culmination of an argument for which the discussion about distance perception provides the preliminary evidence.

In all three cases, Berkeley is arguing that we have to learn how to perceive situation, size, and distance by sight, and that this learning consists in associating visual cues with tangible meanings. In *Theory of Vision Vindicated*, however, Berkeley moves to a discussion of situation perception directly from a discussion of the difference between the ideas of sight and touch. The connecting link is this:

> More and less, greater and smaller, extent, proportion, interval are all found in time as in space; but it will not therefore follow that these are homogeneous quantities. No more will it follow, from the attribution of common

names, that visible ideas are homogeneous with those of feeling. It is true that terms denoting tangible extension, figure, location, motion, and the like, are also applied to denote the quantity, relation, and order of the proper visible objects or ideas of sight. But this proceeds only from experience and analogy. There is a *higher* and *lower* in the notes of music. Men speak in a high or a low key. And this, it is plain, is no more than metaphor or analogy. So likewise, to express the order of visible ideas, the words, *situation, high* and *low, up* and *down*, are made use of, and their sense, when so applied, is analogical. (TVV 46)

According to the *Theory of Vision Vindicated*, Berkeley's solution to the problem of situation perception follows from the fact that ideas of sight are entirely unrelated to ideas of touch. Thus, in the *New Theory*, Berkeley must take this fact to be supported by his account of situation perception, and this is indeed the case. In the *New Theory*, Berkeley argues that a man born blind would understand terms like "up" and "down" through his tangible experience. Such a man would not be able to link his tangible understanding to sight, until he is able to correlate what he sees with what he touches. In spelling out the consequences of this claim, Berkeley makes it plain that the visual field for the newly sighted man born blind would lack not only spatial organization, but would in fact lack any organization whatsoever. The newly sighted man not only would be unable to recognize whether a man he is now seeing has his head up or down, but would also be unable to recognize anything he is seeing as a head. Nor could he tell a head from a foot, or even know whether there was one head and two feet. Until he had learned to correlate the visual properties of the head and the feet with the tangible properties with which he was familiar, there would be no reason for him to bundle the various colors he sees into head and feet bundles at all. By the end of the discussion of situation perception in the *New Theory*, then, Berkeley has destroyed the supposition on which a theory like Malebranche's is based, that the visual system alone provides an organized picture or representation. Berkeley in fact has pulled apart the meaningful visual world of our ordinary experience into those elements that are due to vision alone – light and colors. If the order of argument in the *New Theory* is deconstructive, then presumably the order in *Theory of Vision Vindicated* is reconstructive: Berkeley will start with meaningless light and color and then show how, as these visual ideas come to mean first situation, then size, and then distance, we arrive at a fully meaningful visual world.

The discussion of size perception in *Theory of Vision Vindicated* reveals the extent to which Berkeley thinks our ability to make judgments about size depends upon our ability to make judgments about situation. His account of size perception requires that our visual field be sufficiently stabilized that we can perceive different colors at different locations. We see that some patches of light and color take up greater amounts of the visual field, and that some are higher and some lower in the visual field, as well as being either fainter or what Berkeley calls "livelier." These features provide the cues to tangible size. Visible size alone clearly is insufficient, because the same tangible object can be correlated with visual extents of any size at all. We also must take into account that color patches higher in the visual field and fainter come to mean greater tangible size than those that are lower and more lively.

Although they come to suggest greater or lesser tangible size, cues like faintness and position in the visual field are connected only arbitrarily with size, and therefore, Berkeley argues, are as available to suggest distance as they are to suggest size. There is no need to suppose that our visual system first calculates size and then works out distance, or that it first identifies a distance and then figures out the size. A consequence of understanding that vision is a language is that we no longer are required to provide reasoning chains between the cues and what they represent, and therefore can appreciate that the same cues can indifferently represent both size and distance. Berkeley proposes that cues like faintness and height in the visual field also come to mean greater distances. We see things as taking a great deal of time to reach. Because considerable associative work has been done before we turn to distance perception, it makes sense to speak (as Berkeley does in the *New Theory*) of judging the distance not of color patches, but of sensible objects like trees or people.

Reading Berkeley's theory of vision through the lens of *Theory of Vision Vindicated* highlights the extent to which Berkeley's theory of distance, size, and situation perception is in the service of a wider project, a project that also is important to the *New Theory*. He provides an account of distance, size, and situation perception showing that we learn to see them all by associating visual cues with tangible information. On the basis of this account, he argues for a particular understanding of the nature of visual representation. It is not the goal of the visual system to produce a representation that stands for a world it either resembles or fails to resemble. Rather, the job of the visual system is just to perceive visual qualities, which represent by suggesting tangible and other sensible qualities. When we take vision to function as a language, we will understand it does not misrepresent the world it stands for, but is a successful vehicle for tangible meanings. This wider project, however, which I have tried to show is central to Berkeley's theory of vision, has by no means always been the primary focus of his readers.

II. THE RECEPTION OF THE *NEW THEORY*

Episode one: some early readers

Robert Smith's *A Compleat System of Optics*[7] at first appears to support the judgment that Berkeley's theory almost immediately met with universal approval. Smith's treatise, published only twenty-nine years after the *New Theory* first appeared and six years after it was republished with *Alciphron*, specifically refers to Berkeley's *New Theory* and seems to give a Berkeleyan account of how we learn to see. Smith cites an actual account of the restoration of sight to a man born blind, the Cheseldon case previously mentioned by Berkeley himself, and uses this example as a thought-experiment to construct a picture of what learning to see is like. Smith sums it up as follows:

> From what has been said it appears that our perception of things by sight is no more than this: by memory of former perceptions by sight and other senses compared together, we collect in an instant that the thing we now perceive by sight only will affect our other senses, upon trial, as it formerly used to do. I say in an instant, which will less surprise us, when we consider how quick the characters or sounds of words, whose signification we could hardly remember at first, do excite in our minds the ideas of things they are constantly used to signify: so great is the force of habits in bringing our ideas together. And so it appears at last, that the manner, wherein external objects are signified to us, by the sensations of light and colours, is the same with that of languages and signs of human appointment: which do not suggest the things signified by any likeness or identity of nature, but only by an habitual connection that constant experience has made us observe between them. (*Compleat System*, 45)

Smith very properly footnotes this passage to Berkeley's *New Theory*. He wants to hold with Berkeley that learning to see is a matter of making habitual connections, as we do in learning a language.

While Smith's debt to Berkeley is obvious, it is equally obvious this debt is extremely limited. Smith is prepared to agree with Berkeley that problems in space perception are to be solved by looking for cues regularly associated with such experiences as feeling the body moving toward objects at a distance, and in consequence he rejects the sort of distance cues, like divergence of rays, used by the geometric writers. Smith's focus, though, is on the solution to such perceptual problems as how do we learn to perceive distance by sight? Smith's use of Berkeley's language analogy is strictly to make the point that space perception is a matter of association, and he shows no interest in Berkeley's further claim that we are equipped via our senses to acquire knowledge of the natural world through reading perceptual signs.

The same impression of a rather reduced interest in the details of Berkeley's theory is gained from reading David Hartley's *Observations on Man*.[8] Hartley's work was published in 1749, some four years before Berkeley's death, and is often cited as a work that adopted Berkeley's theory of vision. However, Hartley is interested in Berkeley to the extent Berkeley is in agreement with Hartley's own doctrine of association. Hartley's actual discussion of space perception does not mention Berkeley, although he does refer to Smith. His discussion is considerably less detailed than Berkeley's and is Berkeleyan only to the extent that it is a theory that employs association. For example, Hartley does not make use of Berkeley's list of cues; unlike Berkeley, Hartley thinks distance is a cue to size, and like Smith he shows no interest in any of Berkeley's metaphysical or epistemological conclusions.

Another writer on optics, William Porterfield, who published in 1759 (not long after Berkeley's death), did take an interest in Berkeley's metaphysics, but only to condemn it.[9] Porterfield is credited by A. A. Luce with helping to make the *New Theory* famous, but in fact he gives an account of vision that owes more to Malebranche than to Berkeley and mentions Berkeley only to refute him. Porterfield's position is that we judge the spatial location of external objects by sight by means of an "original, connate immutable law" that allows us to trace back the light rays from the point at which they hit the retina to the object from which they originate. That is, he puts forward the kind of geometric theory Berkeley had set out to refute. In addition, Porterfield adopts many of the implications of such a theory that were important to Malebranche. He mentions that our visual perception of distance is uncertain, and that we never perceive absolute size but only size relative to our bodies. He rejects Berkeley's account because he thinks sensations of touch are no more suitable than sensations of sight to inform us about the external world, both being, as he says, equally "present to the mind." He is committed to the picture that we are aware of mind-dependent sensations and that, from them, we have to calculate knowledge of a mind-independent world. Porterfield understands Berkeley to be denying the existence of the external world, and hence levels at him the charge of skepticism. "In fine," he says, "this is not to solve the Problem, whether it be from Custom and Experience, or by virtue of an original connate Law, that, by Sight, we come to judge of the Situation of external Things, but, by exterminating all Things external, to make the problem itself absurd and ridiculous" (*Treatise on the Eye*, 308). Porterfield is taking Berkeley's metaphysics very seriously, but because he interprets it as requiring a disbelief in an external world, he sees this as a reason for rejecting Berkeley's theory of vision.

These examples of the way Berkeley's theory was discussed in the accounts of optics closest to him in time do not support the picture of a theory that met with instant success. Not only do we find examples like Porterfield, who read the *Theory* as a work of skepticism-inducing idealism, and who otherwise put forward the theory Berkeley hoped to refute, but those who found Berkeley's theory more commendable were interested strictly in his associationist solutions to problems in space perception, and ignored his wider theory entirely. This latter is a pattern that recurs among those who put forward a "Berkeleyan" theory, particularly those whose interests are primarily psychological in nature: Their theory is Berkeleyan only to the extent that they adopt the associationist outline of his solution to the problem of distance perception.[10]

Episode two: Thomas Reid

Thomas Reid contributes a very important episode in the story of the reception of Berkeley's ideas, even though the conclusions of Reid's theory are conceived in explicit opposition to Berkeley. Reid chose to cast his own theory in historical terms, as the inevitable solution to the problems of his predecessors concerning the theory of ideas. In telling this historical story, Reid gives Berkeley a pivotal role: Berkeley is the person who realized that the theory of ideas led to a denial of the existence of an external, material world. Reid gave the Bishop of Cloyne a pivotal role, and kept a version of Berkeleyanism in the forefront of philosophical discussion, albeit as a theory in need of refutation.

Berkeley's importance to Reid, however, is equally due to the large area of agreement Reid shared with Berkeley. Reid tells us that at one time he accepted Berkeley's system in its entirety until, disturbed by its consequences, he began to question the claim that our knowledge is of our ideas.[11] Reid continued to maintain important aspects of Berkeley's theory. In particular, Reid tells us he took his account of sensation from Berkeley.[12] Reid disagrees with Berkeley, however, that we can have knowledge only of our sensations. This disagreement is reflected in the second important element Reid took from Berkeley, the view that our sensations can serve as natural signs suggesting ideas to which they lack any necessary or resembling connection. Reid thought knowledge is not limited to sensations; he extended the idea of natural signs, and claimed sensations could also suggest that which is nonsensory. For Reid, sensations of touch could suggest nonsensible extension, figure, and motion (*Inquiry*, 111). Such suggestions are not, as was the case for Berkeley, based on habit, but instead are a function of our constitution.

These areas of agreement and disagreement shape Reid's response to the *New Theory*. Reid certainly is one of those who consistently spoke well of the *New Theory*, saying it "contains very important discoveries, and marks of great genius" (*Essays*, 281). Despite Reid's praise of the *New Theory*, though, he adopts it far from wholeheartedly. Reid's restricted focus is apparent in his lengthy discussion of seeing in the *Inquiry*. Reid's account of distance perception in section 23 is very Berkeleyan in nature, and he refers admiringly to Berkeley (*Inquiry*, 193). An earlier discussion in the *Inquiry* is equally Berkeleyan: "There are certain things in the visible appearance, which are signs of distance from the eye, and from which, as we shall afterwards shew, we learn from experience to judge of that distance within certain limits; but it seems beyond doubt, that a man born blind, and suddenly made to see, could form no judgment at first the distance of the objects which he saw" (136). In this section, Reid goes on to speak of the experience of the man born blind when made to see in terms reminiscent of Berkeley (137). Reid takes Berkeley's account of distance perception to be an example of the theory of natural signs, which he admired and appears to have adopted without reservation.

In later sections, however, Reid deviates dramatically from Berkeley's position. In Section 7, he says there is a mathematical connection between the visible figure and what he calls the "real figure." A blind man would be able to work out, for example, the circumstances in which a circle would be seen as an ellipse, and hence to have some understanding, even while blind, of the notion of visible figure. For Reid to be able to make this claim, he has to differ from Berkeley in two important respects: He must hold that we can have a notion of visible figure abstractable from color; and he must hold that this visible figure is of the same kind as the real figure.

Because he disagrees with Berkeley in these areas, Reid puts forward an entirely different account of size perception: "The distance of the whole object makes me likewise perceive the real magnitude; for, being accustomed to observe how an inch or a foot of length affects the eye at that distance, I plainly perceive by my eye the linear dimensions of the globe, and can affirm with certainty that its diameter is about one foot and three inches" (193). Reid ignores Berkeley's argument that, because the cues suggesting distance lack any conceptual connection with distance, they are equally suited to suggest size. He reverts instead to the geometrical model, in which distance information is used to calculate the size of the object. Reid similarly rejects Berkeley's claim that situation is perceived immediately only by touch, and proposes that visual sensations themselves suggest location (145). Finally, while Reid adopts Berkeley's distinction between visible and tangible extension, he does not agree there is a difference in kind between the two. Instead, he writes: "I take them to be different conceptions of the same thing; the one very partial, and the other more complete; but both distinct and just, as far as they reach" (325).

It should be clear Reid's enthusiasm for Berkeley's *New Theory of Vision* did not lead him to adopt, or perhaps even to appreciate, the theory in its entirety. He was not interested in those aspects of Berkeley's account where Berkeley spelled out the way his view differed from those of the geometric theory. To Reid, the real dangers of skepticism are represented by Hume and not by Malebranche. Reid is not willing to follow Berkeley into the heterogeneity thesis because for Reid, this would cut off a sensory world from the "real" world. Reid's reading of the *New Theory* is significantly colored by his fears of immaterialism. He retains only that portion of the *New Theory* – the account of distance – that presents the least obvious threat to a realist ontology.

Episode three: Bailey and Ferrier

Toward the middle of the nineteenth century, a work appeared aimed explicitly to refute Berkeley's *New Theory of Vision*. Samuel Bailey, in his *A Review of Berkeley's Theory of Vision*, published in 1842,[13] set himself to break what he took to be a hitherto unbroken chain of praise for Berkeley's theory. Bailey's account of Berkeley was influential immediately,[14] and has been subsequently admired,[15] but almost instantly it was the subject of a rebuttal by the Scottish philosopher J. F. Ferrier. Ferrier's response is especially interesting, not only because it is able and sympathetic, but because of the pains Ferrier takes to locate Berkeley's theory of vision within Berkeley's broader theory, which Ferrier calls idealism.[16]

His attack on Berkeley reveals that Bailey prefers a very different approach to the theory of vision. Bailey is convinced an appeal to consciousness plainly shows that what we perceive by sight are external, spatially organized objects. His position is that physiological facts about retinas, optic nerves, or anything else are irrelevant to determining the nature of the deliverances of consciousness. It is perfectly obvious that we do indeed see external, solid objects. If information about our physiology does not explain this, then the most we are entitled to conclude is that we don't know how it is done. Bailey's position is that we have no need of tactual information in order to see objects in space. Indeed, our tactual information in general is inferior to that provided by vision.

Because Bailey thinks we just see objects in space, he is quite unable to accept the belief about distance perception Berkeley said was agreed to by all, "that distance of itself and immediately, cannot be seen" (NTV 2). In fact, Bailey makes heavy weather of the argument

Berkeley took over from Molyneux and used to motivate the claim that distance is not immediately perceived by sight: "For distance being a line directed end-wise to the eye, it projects only one point in the fund of the eye, which point remains invariably the same, whether the distance be longer or shorter" (NTV 2). Berkeley's point is there is no way to account physiologically for visual perception of distance, but to Bailey, Berkeley seems to be saying we perceive light rays, or perhaps the ends of light rays, and to Bailey this is clearly false, because we perceive objects.[17] Bailey does not find the successful perception of distance to be problematic.

Because Bailey thinks it is obvious we just see distance, he also has no use for Berkeley's distinction between mediate and immediate perception, or for Reid's similar distinction between sensation and perception. (Bailey tends to use these expressions interchangeably.) Berkeley's enterprise – to show how it is we mediately perceive distance by sight on the basis of the light and colors we immediately perceive – makes no sense to Bailey. Instead, he conceives Berkeley's project in much more skeptical terms: "It is impossible, according to him, to see the real relative position of lines and surfaces, and their true ratio respectively to each other; in other words, we cannot see either real magnitude or solid figure, or even plane figure; all which positions, as we have seen, are exactly the reverse of the truth" (147). Bailey sets himself to refute an account of vision having these skeptical consequences.

Bailey divides his account of Berkeley's theory into four parts: outness or externality; distance; real magnitude; and real figure. He ignores what Berkeley says about situation perception and about heterogeneity. Additionally, Bailey gives great prominence to the issue of externality or outness, drawing upon Berkeley's remark in *New Theory* 41 about the man born blind, that "[t]he objects intromitted by sight would seem to him (as in truth they are) no other than a new set of thoughts or sensations, each whereof is as near to him as the perceptions of pain or pleasure, or the most inward passions of the soul." Bailey takes this to mean Berkeley holds that our visual ideas of light and color are originally what Bailey calls "internal sensations" rendered external through association with the "external sensations" of touch. Bailey supposes Berkeley is claiming we first experience "internal" color sensations, which, because they are frequently accompanied by "external" tangible sensations, come (as a result of this association) to be experienced themselves as external. Bailey takes it to be a feature of Berkeley's theory that what we see itself changes in character as a result of being associated with the tangible. Not surprisingly, Bailey finds this process to be impossible. As a result of association, he says, one sensation might call to mind another, but it can never do what Berkeley's theory requires, namely, convert one sensation into another.

This theme, that sensations cannot be transmuted in character, runs through Bailey's account of distance perception as well. He takes Berkeley to be arguing that originally we see a multicolored plane, which through association with tangible sensations is altered so that things now look three-dimensional. But how, Bailey asks, can ideas of touch, through association, make any difference to ideas of sight? In raising a question of this sort, Bailey is taking Berkeley's concept of suggestion to be the same as association, as a process in which one idea calls to mind a second, as salt suggests pepper, but that further has the mysterious effect of actually altering the nature of what is associated. Not surprisingly, Bailey does not find any evidence in consciousness for the existence of such a process.

Throughout Bailey's account of Berkeley, there is an undercurrent of amazement that anyone could have taken seriously such peculiar claims. Indeed, Bailey's reading of Berkeley produces some very peculiar claims indeed. Bailey shares with Reid the view that Berkeley's thrust is inherently skeptical, so that accepting what Berkeley is saying amounts to denying the existence of the real world. Bailey, however, has a view of perception as being much more successfully direct than does Reid. Therefore, unlike Reid, Bailey has no use for a concept like Berkeley's notion of suggestion, and so cannot join Reid even in adopting Berkeley's account of distance perception. In any case, Bailey follows Hartley in taking Berkeley's account of space perception to be straightforwardly associationistic. This means he is denying Berkeley the resources of the language analogy, under which signs, without changing their own nature, can acquire meanings. The assimilation of Berkeley's theory to associationism may have contributed to the theory's longevity, but it does not always permit Berkeley's claims to be fully intelligible.

Bailey's account removes Berkeley entirely from the intellectual context from which Berkeley took his original problem about distance perception. J. F. Ferrier, in his reply to Bailey,[18] begins by setting

Berkeley's theory in an historical context. It is not his theory of vision that is thus contextualized, but his broader idealism, "to which" Ferrier says, "his speculations on the eye were but the tentative herald or preliminary stepping-stone" (813). Berkeley's idealism, according to Ferrier, is a response to those philosophers who grounded their theories in an account of matter, understood as inaccessible to the senses, but standing as a real world behind the sensory world and imperfectly represented by it. In combatting this view, Berkeley set himself *against* skepticism: "He saw that philosophy, in giving up the reality immediately within her grasp, in favour of a reality supposed to be less delusive, which lay beyond the limits of experience, resembled the dog in the fable, who, carrying a piece of meat across a river, let the substance slip from his jaws, while, with foolish greed, he snatched at its shadow in the stream. The dog lost his dinner, and philosophy let go her secure hold upon the truth" (814). Ferrier positions Berkeley as one whose rejection of matter is in the defense of common sense.

Berkeley's title as a defender of common sense derives from his identification of ideas and things, or, as Ferrier puts it, "the inviolable identity of objects and the appearance of objects" (816). Ferrier's Berkeley is a realist for whom the things we see, touch, and smell are the real things. Ferrier, recognizes, though, that ordinarily it is not thought commonsensical to claim the being of things lies in their being perceived. This is because, Ferrier thinks, we fail to appreciate the force of Berkeley's antiabstractionism and, instead, think we can intelligibly annihilate the perceiver and retain a world to be perceived. On the contrary, Berkeley has shown us, according to Ferrier, that "Nature herself, we may say, has so *beaten up together* sight and colour, that man's faculty of abstraction is utterly powerless to dissolve the charmed union. The two (supposed) elements are not two, but only one, for they *cannot be* separated in thought even by the craft of the subtlest analysis. It is God's synthesis, and man cannot analyze it" (817). Ferrier suggests we should even extend Berkeley's point in order to recognize that just as we cannot conceive a world with all perceivers annihilated, so we cannot conceive a not-world either, the one as much as the other depending upon our mind-dependent conceptions.

Ferrier thinks what Bailey has missed about Berkeley's theory of vision is that in it he is putting forward an "idealism of the eye, and of the eye alone" (823). Berkeley was striving, according to Ferrier, to give an account of vision that must be unintelligible to the blind, because it tried "leaving all geometrical and anatomical considerations out of the question, to apprehend the proper and peculiar facts of *sight* – the facts, the whole facts, and *nothing but* the facts, of that particular and isolated sense" (823). Of course this is, in some sense, what Bailey also intended to do, but he erred, according to Ferrier, by not properly distinguishing the deliverances of sight from those of touch. Bailey makes a mistake when he assumes that according to Berkeley, outness is merely not *initially* acquired by sight; in fact, says Ferrier, not only do we initially see only colored appearances, we never see anything *but* colored appearances. Bailey is quite mistaken in supposing we ever are held by Berkeley to undergo a process of transmuting a visual sensation into something having "outness." "The 'outness' which he here declares Berkeley to hold *as suggested*," Ferrier writes, "he evidently imagines to be *visible* outness: whereas Berkeley distinctly holds that visible outness is never *suggested* by sight at all, or by any 'visible ideas or sensations attending vision,' and that it is only *tangible* outness which is so suggested" (826). The sort of outness suggested by vision is itself not visible because it is tangible. Indeed, Ferrier points out, it is only through touch, when we touch or cover up an eye, that we come to have a notion of an organ out of which our visible sensations arise. Otherwise, Ferrier writes, "The conclusion, therefore, is irresistible, that, in mere vision, the sight and its objects cling together in a union of synthesis, which no function of that sense, and no knowledge imparted to us by it, (and, according to the supposition, we have, as yet, no other knowledge,) can enable us to discriminate or dissolve. Where the seeing is, there is the thing seen, and where the thing seen is, there is the seeing of it" ("Mr. Bailey's Reply," 767). Bailey's prime mistake, according to Ferrier, was to assume that seeing itself could include, as part of the act of seeing, an awareness of the independence from the eye of the object seen.

It is interesting to find, in one and the same year, two such different responses to Berkeley's ideas. In Bailey, we find someone quite outside Berkeley's frame of reference. He is unable to perceive the virtue in Berkeley's belief in the inescapably mind-dependent nature of vision. In his own approach, Bailey ignores the subjectivity of vision almost entirely, or regards the apparent, such as apparent size, as readily correctable by the real. Because Bailey takes the perception of the real to be unproblematic, he reads Berkeley as threatening Bailey's own commonsense trust in his senses by suggesting the real is not what we see. Ferrier, on the other hand, is entirely in sympathy with Berkeley's view that we cannot abstract the perception from the perceiver. Ferrier gives us a realist Berkeley, for whom the world of the senses is the only world there is. Bailey's Berkeley, who thinks we perceive only our ideas and invites skepticism about a world outside ideas, is a very familiar reading of Berkeley. Ferrier's realist Berkeley, who rejects the use of the word "only" on the grounds that it suggests the possibility of something more to be perceived, while less familiar than Bailey's, nevertheless embodies a reading that others have found appealing.

Episode four: Elsie Graham, with some remarks about F. J. E. Woodbridge

In 1929, Elsie C. Graham published, *Optics and Vision: The Background of the Metaphysics of Berkeley*, which seems to have been her dissertation for a Ph.D. at Columbia University. In it she argues Berkeley successfully dissolves the theory of vision that had been based on a confusion of vision with optics. In her eyes, however, still confused by some of the mistakes of the old optical theory, Berkeley did not go far enough in the development of his own theory. "That he found in idealism the only means of saving realism," she writes, "is a paradox due to his incomplete emancipation from the very habits of thought whose consequences he was attacking."[19] Graham is in complete agreement with Ferrier that the right way to understand Berkeley is to place him in an historical context in which he is seen as addressing the weakness of a materialism that divorces the real world, described mathematically, from the world of experience. Although Graham offers an account of Berkeley's context that is somewhat similar to Ferrier's, she derives from that contextualizing a considerably less positive account of Berkeley's achievements.

Graham rather surprisingly takes this historical context completely for granted. She claims that "[e]ven the most superficial student of *philosophy* links in his memory, and many historians of philosophy in one sentence, two pieces of information about Berkeley: that he was the first formidable opponent of the so-called Newtonian cosmology, and that he launched his attack upon it by an *Essay towards a New Theory of Vision*" (7). In taking these facts to be so generally recognized, Graham is perhaps exaggerating the influence of her thesis advisor, F. J. E. Woodbridge. In a paper called "Berkeley's Realism,"[20] Woodbridge had argued Berkeley ought not properly to be seen as a follower of Locke, but rather as an opponent of that metaphysics based on mathematical principles for which Woodbridge takes Newton to be the chief spokesperson. Woodbridge thinks it is important to realize the *New Theory* is not just an account of space perception, but is primarily an attack on mathematical optics. The question Graham proposes to take up is why did Berkeley choose to begin by attacking optics?

Graham's answer is Berkeley took materialism to be supported by and to be the creature of a theory of optics that rested on serious confusions about the nature of vision or perception. As Graham reconstructs the series of events that led to Berkeley's problem, the most important step was the discovery of the inverted image on the retina. A misplaced belief in the importance of this discovery encouraged a confusion of the physical conditions of vision with the psychological process, and led theorists to suppose that facts about the organ of vision can account for the object of vision. What we see was identified with the retinal image or taken to be a construction based upon it. As Graham puts it: "The eye delivers the data, the mind performs the construction and views its own conclusions" (40). On this account we do not see the real world, but are merely connected to it by means of geometry. What turns out to be real is not what we see, but rather a geometrical projection of what we see. The only real or trustworthy properties of what we see are spatial properties. Such a theory, Graham believes, gives rise to the sort of skepticism embodied in what she takes to be Lockean representationalism, by encouraging the question, how can we know the nature of the things themselves, if all we know are our own ideas?

According to Graham, Berkeley's success lies in discrediting this confusion of vision and optics, psychology and physiology. She credits him with an argument that points out all knowledge of the physiological facts, in the first place, is derived entirely from perception. How could we have known, for example, there is even an inverted image on the retina, if we had not seen it? It is therefore irrational,

Graham has Berkeley argue, to conclude on the basis of visual facts that the world is completely other than it is seen to be. "Their result" she says, "is unintelligible because their procedure is vicious. They have sawn off the limb they were sitting on. If our knowledge is of things seen, Berkeley points out, it must be of things *as they are seen*, not as they inconceivably might be if we could not see them. Starting with the perceived, there being no other way to start, science has gravely demonstrated, by arguments chiefly drawn from the mechanism of sight, that reality is unperceivable, and has put philosophy in the absurd position of having to explain knowledge" (99). Graham takes Berkeley to have successfully exploded the optical basis for materialism.

Graham, however, believes Berkeley to be considerably less successful when it comes to putting forward his own theory. Graham has Berkeley reasoning that if the unseen world is not real, then ideas are. For Graham, Berkeley's realism consists in an assertion that only ideas are real. She thinks he found himself in this position because although he recognized that objects of sight could not represent the unseeable, he did not realize it was necessary to give up the characterization of ideas as existing only in the mind. Instead, Graham thinks Berkeley, in the *New Theory*, took it as his project to defend the mind-dependence of ideas by arguing there is no external space for ideas to exist in, so perforce they have nowhere to exist but in the mind. Graham takes it to be Berkeley's purpose to argue that distance cannot be immediately perceived by sight. She claims this demonstration fails utterly, because it rests illegitimately on an assumption that we see things as flat. This accusation of Graham's, that Berkeley's procedure is circular, would have merit if Berkeley rested his case that we do not perceive an external world out there on an unexamined claim that what we perceive is flat. But in the *New Theory* Berkeley does not attempt to demonstrate that we do not perceive an external world. He takes it for granted distance cannot be immediately perceived by sight, and he argues it can be immediately perceived by touch.[21]

While Graham is in agreement with Ferrier that Berkeley's theory of vision should be understood as motivated by a desire to expose the inconsistencies and dangers of mathematical materialism, her understanding of the theory Berkeley puts forward as an alternative is not as sympathetic as Ferrier's. Less attracted than Ferrier to an account of the natural world as mind-dependent, she misses what Ferrier exploits, the way in which Berkeley's antiabstractionism can be understood to provide a justification for the otherwise puzzling claim that *esse* is *percipi*. Graham takes Berkeley to be claiming that reality consists in ideas shorn from their extramental backing, and she reads the *New Theory* as motivated by a desire to establish such an idealistic account of reality.

It is interesting that both Graham and Ferrier take Berkeley's account of reality to be entirely encapsulated in the *esse* is *percipi* doctrine. They take Berkeley's claim about reality to be limited to the view that what is real are ideas and minds that have them. They each ignore the possibilities of the language analogy. In particular, they overlook Berkeley's idea that what is real can be understood in terms of the regularities discerned when some ideas stand for other ideas. In overlooking this element in Berkeley's thought, Graham appears to be equally overlooking an important element in Woodbridge's account of Berkeley's theory. Woodbridge highlights the importance of Berkeley's conclusion that the thought-experiment of the man born blind indicates that ideas of sight and touch do not stand for a single mathematically describable object. The point of this example for Berkeley, Woodbridge says, is

> confirmation of his own conclusion that the proper objects of vision constitute the universal language of nature. We should read his whole theory of vision and particularly his emphatic insistence that visible extension is different from tangible extension in the light of this conclusion and not in the light of the associationist psychology. That is, our ideas of visible and tangible extension are not associated or combined by experience into an idea of extension itself. They do not unite to give us the idea of an object which they represent. Berkeley's doctrine is radically different. Visible and tangible extension are precisely what we see and feel directly and immediately. He calls them "ideas", but they are not "ideas of" anything. They are real components of nature and not components of the mind. They enter into the composition and framework of nature and not into the composition and framework of the mind. They are things we immediately perceive and these things are held together not in some embracing space, but in a system of mutual representation and symbolism. They are not held together in the mind by psychological laws of association, but they are perceived by the mind and the way they are connected is learned by the mind through experience of their actual symbolism. (201–2)

Woodbridge shares Ferrier's understanding of the way in which visible and tangible extension are both real and ideal for Berkeley, but he embeds this insight in an appreciation of the resources of the language analogy. Graham is enthusiastic about Berkeley's language analogy as an alternative to Locke's epistemology, but she does not see Berkeley's characterization of vision as the universal language of nature, in the way Woodbridge clearly does, as the element unifing his claims. Graham, unlike Bailey, works hard to situate Berkeley in his historical context, but she nevertheless shares with Bailey a view of Berkeley as a skepticism-provoking idealist.

Episode five: Armstrong and Turbayne

In 1956, D. M. Armstrong published a discussion note[22] commenting on a paper of C. M. Turbayne's, "Berkeley and Molyneux on Retinal Images."[23] While this note is the only point of contact between the two, the issues raised in it are symptomatic of the much wider differences to be found in their more extended treatments of the *New Theory* – Armstrong's *Berkeley's Theory of Vision*[24] and Turbayne's *Myth of Metaphor* and his editor's commentary on Berkeley's *Works on Vision.*[25] These works illustrate, each in an admirably clear manner, elements of the different approaches we have seen taken toward Berkeley's theory of vision. For Armstrong, on the one hand, Berkeley is most centrally an idealist, while Turbayne, on the other, stresses the importance of the language analogy for a realist reading of Berkeley.

While Armstrong makes several points in his note, the one most clearly expressing the contrast between himself and Turbayne concerns their differing views about the goals of the *New Theory.* Armstrong criticizes Turbayne for endorsing Berkeley's own account of the relationship between the *New Theory* and the *Principles* as a halfway house to immaterialism. Turbayne claims the account of vision worked out in the *New Theory* provided Berkeley with an important principle enabling him to establish the immaterialism of whose truth Berkeley was already convinced. For Turbayne, the importance of the *New Theory* is it allowed Berkeley to demonstrate that the proper objects of sight are not "images of external things," as Berkeley puts it in *Principles* 44. Armstrong thinks Berkeley and hence Turbayne are just deluding themselves about the importance of the claims established in the *New Theory* for the immaterialism of the *Principles*. In fact, according to Armstrong, the central claims of the *New Theory* stand in the relationship of logical indifference to immaterialism. According to Armstrong, the most important of these is that distance cannot be seen immediately. Armstrong takes Berkeley to be saying distance cannot be immediately perceived because by sight we perceive a two-dimensional manifold, which is other than the three-dimensional objects of touch.[26] But, says Armstrong, there is no reason why a two-dimensional manifold shouldn't be "out there" rather than "in the mind." Thus Armstrong thinks Berkeley has just tricked himself into thinking that what is not at a distance from the mind must be in the mind. Because this last conclusion (that the visual field is in the mind) is in fact unsupported by any evidence about distance perception, Armstrong concludes Berkeley is just mistaken in thinking that the subject matter of the *New Theory* has anything to do with the *Principles*.

One thing that emerges very clearly is that Armstrong and Turbayne actually have very different understandings of what the *New Theory* is all about. In the Introduction to his *Berkeley's Theory of Vision*, Armstrong reiterates the view he put forth in his note. The important conclusions of the *New Theory* are, "firstly, that whatever is immediately seen has no existence outside the mind; and secondly, that visible and tangible objects have no manner of spatial connection" (xi). According to Armstrong, these conclusions are thought by Berkeley to follow from the central claim of the *New Theory*, that distance is not immediately seen. Armstrong sees Berkeley as seeking to establish the mind-dependence of visual objects through the claim that distance is not immediately perceived. Turbayne, on the other hand, subjects this approach to explicit criticism. In "Berkeley and Molyneux on Retinal Images," for example, he points out that the view that distance is not immediately perceived is one Berkeley took over from the geometric theories he was criticizing, and hence cannot be regarded as an important discovery of his. Moreover, Turbayne says, Berkeley was not in fact denying that distance is perceived by sight, but merely trying to analyze the process into its component parts. Turbayne takes the goal of the *New Theory* to be to establish that vision ought properly to be regarded as a language, in which visual ideas serve as signs or cues to tangible meanings. Turbayne presents Berkeley's project as one of undermining the materialist thesis that visual ideas serve as representatives of the external world that causes them. For Turbayne, it is important to establish that ideas can stand only for other ideas, because it is this premise that supports Berkeley's language model against the representative theory of the materialists, which takes visual ideas to stand for their nonideational causes.

In developing their different accounts of the nature of the *New Theory*, Armstrong and Turbayne stress different portions of the argument. For Armstrong, what is most important is Berkeley's account of distance perception, and it is to this portion of the *Essay* he devotes most of his attention because, he says, "the last three parts are of much less importance than the first, and really only serve to amplify and apply the argument of the first" (38).[27] Once it has been demonstrated that visual objects exist only in the mind, via the argument from distance perception, the rest of the *New Theory* can do little more than provide additional reasons for the mind-dependence of visual objects. Turbayne, however, takes the argument of the *New Theory* to be cumulative, building to the claim that vision is a language, and his account tends to stress the discussion of situation perception. This is because Turbayne takes this account to be important in driving home the distinction between what he calls the primary and secondary objects of sight – that is, the distinction between the lights and colors we strictly speaking or immediately see, and the tangible objects serving as their meanings. For Turbayne, the important lesson of the puzzle of the inverted image on the retina is that we can only compare visual ideas – as the visual ideas we imagine we could receive when looking at someone's else's retina – with other visual ideas – those of our own visual field. We are not, in the way the materialist theory supposes, in a position to compare other people's visual fields, represented by their retinal images, with the external objects causing the images these images are then thought to copy.

Finally, it should be clear that Armstrong and Turbayne not only have different versions of the point of the *New Theory*, they also have different versions of the immaterialism they take to be Berkeley's ultimate aim to establish. For Armstrong, the *New Theory* would have been a halfway house to immaterialism if Berkeley had been able to demonstrate the mind-dependence of visual objects. Thus, a full-blown immaterialism presumably seeks to establish the mind-dependence of all sensible objects. Immaterialism is a view that says things exist "in the mind" and not "out there." Turbayne, on the other hand, ties immaterialism to a rejection of claims of seventeenth-century materialists, in particular, that our ideas can stand for or represent mind-independent matter. Turbayne sees Berkeley as developing an alternative theory of how ideas represent.

Although Armstrong's assessment of Berkeley's accomplishments in the *New Theory* is less positive than Reid's, he shares with Reid the tendency to see Berkeley's idealism as all-important to his theory. Armstrong and Reid have something else in common as well. Armstrong uses the following quotation from Reid's *Essays on the Intellectual Powers of Man* as an epigraph for his *Berkeley's New Theory of Vision*: "But we ought to consider that the more closely and ingeniously men reason from false principles, the more absurdities they will be led into; and when such absurdities help to bring to light the false principles from which they are drawn, they may be the more easily forgiven." Both Reid and Armstrong take the point of discussing an historical text like the *New Theory* to be to expose the false principles lying behind its absurdities. Here too there is a sharp contrast with Turbayne. Turbayne's most extended treatment of Berkeley's theory of vision occurs in his *Myth of Metaphor*, which is not a commentary on Berkeley's texts at all. In that work, Turbayne presents a reworking of the material of the *New Theory* and *Theory of Vision Vindicated* in order to spell out a lesson from these works that he thinks has contemporary application: The psychology of vision is better understood if it is treated metaphorically as a language than if it is treated as a geometric machine. Turbayne hopes through this lesson to help break the grip of the machine metaphor on current thought. He writes not to expose Berkeley but to employ him.

III. SOME CONCLUDING REMARKS

Given the episodic nature of the account I have provided, it clearly would be inappropriate to give a sweeping diagnosis of trends, or to try to link favorable or negative treatments of Berkeley to events in one historical period or another. Even from the evidence I have made available, it is not clear such a story would be appropriate. Each response to the *New Theory* is to some extent *sui generis*, the product in part of the predilections encouraged by the general intellectual context in which each author worked, but equally by each one's own preferences and intellectual gifts. In fact, it is especially striking that the same time period has seen very different interpretations and assessments of the text.

It does seem possible, at the very least, to cast doubt on some previous generalizations. The first is that the *New Theory* has not been the outstanding success it has sometimes been represented as being.[28] While it certainly is true that the theory against which Berkeley argued, the geometric theory, did not find many supporters in the years following Berkeley's *New Theory*, it is also true Berkeley's own theory can at best be regarded as a limited success. Even though theories subsequent to Berkeley's frequently endorsed the general position that space perception requires learning, they very rarely adopted Berkeley's language model as a learning theory, but instead made use of some general account based on association. Very few of the details of Berkeley's theory survived, and of the various issues he took up, only his account of distance perception received much support, while even professed admirers of Berkeley's theory of vision, such as Reid, adopted different accounts of size and situation perception. Finally, an admiration for Berkeley's theory of space perception in no sense implied an admiration for or even an interest in the epistemological or metaphysical consequences that supplied Berkeley's own motivation for writing the *New Theory*. Much of the success the *New Theory* enjoyed was in a severely truncated and somewhat distorted form.

If Berkeley's theory of vision was not as successful as sometimes claimed, the variety of critical responses to it show that an appreciation of Berkeley's theory of vision on occasion has been part and parcel of a general appreciation of his approach. While there have been some, such as Bailey and Armstrong, who wrote of the *New Theory* primarily to criticize it, we can also find those who wrote more positively. Among those who attempt a defense of the *New Theory*, such as Ferrier, Woodbridge, or Turbayne, moreover, the defense is often couched in terms of the contribution the *New Theory* makes to Berkeley's overall theory, to his idealism or immaterialism. Berkeley has certainly had readers who did not see him in negative terms, as one who by his rejection of matter reduced everything to a dream. Instead, although their interpretations vary, there are those who see the *New Theory* as helping to establish a positive account of Berkeley's enterprise.

Readers who provide a positive interpretation of Berkeley differ from those whose assessment is more negative in a number of interpretive strategies. The first is simply that they are inclined to accept Berkeley's problems about space perception, especially the problem of distance perception, as real problems. Those who think we just do see objects existing at a distance in space and that there is no reason to look for an explanation for how we do this are less likely to find Berkeley's enterprise intelligible. It has been very easy to follow Berkeley this far, though, and to accept his solutions to these problems only in the broadest outline. A second barrier standing in the way of a positive interpretation of Berkeley has been the difficulty of dealing with his idealism. Those who, like Ferrier, find a way of making sense of Berkeley's claim that our ontology is restricted to ideas and minds, have an easier time appreciating his position than those who, like Reid or Graham, see idealism as an inherently skeptical doctrine. Finally, interpretations have been less likely to see Berkeley as leading to skepticism to the extent that they emphasize the importance of Berkeley's language analogy. This is a strategy that has been employed particularly effectively by Turbayne, but is also present in Woodbridge.

In sum, the alleged success of Berkeley's theory of vision must be seen as the success of a severely truncated version of his theory. Only his account of distance perception attained widespread currency, and then only as the claim that distance perception is learned. By and large, though, those who have been critical of his theory have also dealt only with a partial account. They too focus on his account of distance and ignore the importance of the claim Berkeley said his work was written to establish, which is that vision is a language. It is also useful to recognize that the history of Berkeley's reception is not limited to these partial and negative accounts. When Harry Bracken wrote his story of the earliest years of Berkeley's reception, he was motivated, he tells us, by a desire to understand why readers of Berkeley had to wait for Luce and Jessop to show them that Berkeley was a man of common sense (*The Early Reception of Berkeley's Immaterialism*, 82). There has always been more than one kind of reader of Berkeley, however, and a complete account of the history of the reception of Berkeley's philosophy will include those who see Berkeley in a fuller and more positive light.[29]

NOTES

1. *Dissertation: Exhibiting the Progress of Metaphysical, Ethical and Political Philosophy, since the Revival of Letters in Europe*, ed. Sir William Hamilton (Edinburgh: Thomas Constable, 1854), 340.
2. *A Review of Berkeley's Theory of Vision* (London: James Ridgeway, 1842), 1.
3. Harry M. Bracken, *The Early Reception of Berkeley's Immaterialism, 1710–1733*, revised edition (The Hague: Martinus Nijhoff, 1965).
4. David Hume, *An Enquiry concerning Human Understanding* 3rd ed. Tom L. Beauchamp (Oxford: Oxford University Press, 1999), 12.15. Reid had almost the same reaction, saying of Berkeley "that he hath proved by unanswerable arguments what no man in his senses can believe" (*Inquiry into the Human Mind*, 101). All references to Reid are to Thomas Reid, *Philosophical Works*, 2 vols., ed. Sir William Hamilton (Edinburgh, 1895, reprinted Hildesheim: George Olms, 1967). In the text, *Inquiry into the Human Mind* will be referred to as *Inquiry*, and *Essays on the Intellectual Powers of Man* will be referred to as *Essays*.
5. The account I give here is derived in part from Atherton, *Berkeley's Revolution in Vision* (Ithaca: Cornell University Press, 1990). I want to acknowledge again my debt to C. M. Turbayne in the development of my views. I have developed the account of TVV in "Apprendre à voir: les enseignements de la *Défense* de la théorie de la vision," in *Berkeley: langage de la perception et art de voir*, ed. Dominique Berlioz (Paris: Presses Universitaires de France, 2003), 135–57.
6. Nicolas Malebranche, *The Search after Truth*, translated by Thomas M. Lennon and Paul J. Olscamp (Columbus: Ohio State University Press, 1980), Book I, chapter 6, p. 25.
7. (Cambridge: Cornelius Crownsfield, 1738).
8. *Observations on Man, His Frame, His Duty, and His Expectations* (London, 1749; reprinted Delmar, NY: Scholars' Facsimiles and Reprints, 1976).
9. William Porterfield, *A Treatise on the Eye, The Manner and Phaenomena of Vision* (London and Edinburgh: A. Miller, G. Hamilton, and J. Balfour, 1759).
10. This is not to say that there were not, in Berkeley's lifetime, interested and careful readers of the *New Theory*. An exchange in the *Gentleman's*

Magazine in 1752 (reprinted in *George Berkeley: Eighteenth Century Responses*, Volume 1, ed. David Berman (New York: Garland, 1989), shows this is not the case. The objections raised by Anti-Berkeley are serious and not doctrinaire, while W. W.'s responses reveal a thorough understanding of Berkeley's text.

11. The reference to Berkeley's influence on Reid is from *Essays*, 283.
12. *Essays*, 289. See Phillip Cummins, "Berkeley's Ideas of Sense," *Nous* 9 (1975): 55–72, for the resemblance between Reid's and Berkeley's views on sensations.
13. Samuel Bailey, *A Review of Berkeley's Theory of Vision, Designed to Show the Unsoundness of That Celebrated Speculation* (London: James Ridgway, 1842), reprinted in *Berkeley on Vision: A Nineteenth Century Debate*, ed. George Pitcher (New York: Garland Publishing Company, 1988).
14. Bailey's arguments were extremely important to T. K. Abbott's *Sight and Touch: An Attempt to Disprove the Received (or Berkeleian) Theory of Vision* (London: Longman, Roberts and Green, 1864). I have discussed Abbott in "Mr Abbott and Prof. Fraser: A Nineteenth Century Debate about Berkeley's Theory of Vision," *Archiv für Geschichte der Philosophie* 85 (2003): 21–50.
15. Pitcher, for example, in the introduction to his edition of Bailey, says that Bailey's arguments are "quite justifiable." Nicholas Pastore writes recently favorably of Bailey in *Selective History of Theories of Visual Perception 1650–1950* (New York: Oxford University Press, 1971), and in "Samuel Bailey's critique of Berkeley's theory of vision," *Journal of the History of Behavioral Sciences* 1 (1965): 321–37.
16. Bailey's attack on Berkeley was also the subject of an equally able and sympathetic defense by John Stuart Mill, "Bailey on Berkeley's Theory of Vision," *Westminster Review* 38 (1842): 318–36, and "Rejoinder to Mr Bailey's Reply," *Westminster Review* 39 (1843): 491–4, both reprinted in Pitcher's *Berkeley on Vision: A Nineteenth Century Debate*. Mill, unlike Ferrier, is not interested in defending the wider implications of Berkeley's theory, but simply in showing the viability of a Berkeleyan theory of vision.
17. Mill struggled manfully to make this issue clear, pointing out in his rejoinder to Bailey's reply that "We can *see* nothing except in so far as it is represented on our retina; and things which are represented on our retina exactly alike will be seen alike" ("Rejoinder to Mr Bailey's Reply," 492). The futility of making this sort of argument to one who is convinced that the phenomenological facts are otherwise is clear from Pastore. Pastore quotes this passage from Mill, but says Bailey successfully raised doubts about the distance premise.

18. *Blackwood's Magazine* (June, 1842): 812–30, reprinted in Pitcher, *Berkeley on Vision: a Nineteenth Century Debate.* See also J. F. Ferrier, "Mr Bailey's Reply to an Article in Blackwood's Magazine," *Blackwood's Magazine* (June, 1843): 762–70, also reprinted in Pitcher.
19. Elsie C. Graham, *Optics and Vision: The Background of the Metaphysics of Berkeley* (New York: Columbia University Press, 1929), 9.
20. *Studies in the History of Ideas*, Volume 1, ed. the Department of Philosophy of Columbia University (New York: Columbia University Press, 1918).
21. Berkeley also, so far from assuming that what we immediately perceive is flat, asserts in NTV 158 that "plains are no more the immediate objects of sight than solids."
22. D. M. Armstrong, "Discussion: Berkeley's New Theory of Vision," *Journal of the History of Ideas* 17 (1956): 127–9.
23. *Journal of the History of Ideas* 16 (1955): 339–55.
24. D. M. Armstrong, *Berkeley's Theory of Vision: A Critical Examination of Bishop Berkeley's Essay Towards a New Theory of Vision* (Melbourne: Melbourne University Press, 1960).
25. C. M. Turbayne, *The Myth of Metaphor*, revised edition (Columbia: University of South Carolina Press, 1970), and "Editor's Commentary," in George Berkeley, *Works on Vision*, ed. C. M. Turbayne (Indianapolis: Bobbs-Merrill, 1963).
26. Armstrong recognizes, as Graham did not, that Berkeley explicitly denies that we can immediately perceive flatness, but Armstrong contends that a two-dimensional manifold, that is, a visual array lacking depth or distance, is not the same as a flat surface.
27. I have argued against this claim in my account of the argument of the *New Theory* given above.
28. I should point out that I have been among those who made this claim about the successful nature of Berkeley's theory of vision, in *Berkeley's Revolution in Vision.*
29. I would like to thank Robert Schwartz for his great help in writing this paper.

KENNETH P. WINKLER

5 Berkeley and the doctrine of signs

In the final chapter of his *Essay concerning Human Understanding*, Locke divides all of human knowledge into three parts: the knowledge of things as they are; the skill of achieving what is good and useful; and the knowledge of signs.[1] Locke calls the third part "logic," "semiotics," or "the doctrine of signs." The present chapter is a survey and assessment of Berkeley's main contributions to this "great Province" (as Locke called it) of the early modern intellectual world.[2] It was a province to which Berkeley attached particular importance and promise. In the seventh dialogue of *Alciphron*, his spokesperson Euphranor announces that he is "inclined to think the doctrine of signs a point of great importance and general extent, which, if duly considered, would cast no small light upon things, and afford a just and genuine solution of many difficulties" (ALC 7.13 [307]).[3]

The doctrine of signs as Locke and Berkeley understood it included not only what we now call the philosophy of language, but a great deal more, and Berkeley was not alone in attaching importance and promise to it. For Locke and the eighteenth-century philosophers he influenced, signs were the very vehicles of thought. To understand how signs signify their objects was therefore to understand how thoughts of those objects were possible. To discover the limits of signification was to discover the limits of thought. And to identify the ways in which signs might mislead or confuse us was to identify some of the core ways in which our thought might fail. Berkeley was convinced that in drawing us toward what he called "materialism" – the belief that objects have an existence, "natural or real," apart from their being perceived by the understanding (PHK 4) – human thought had failed. He thought that an improved understanding of signification could persuade us of the failure, disclose its sources, and afford us hope of correcting it.

I begin this chapter by presenting, in Section I, Berkeley's ways of classifying signs, paying particular attention to the differences between two kinds of sign Berkeley followed Locke in recognizing: words (whether spoken or written); and ideas. In Section II, I briefly explain how, in Berkeley's theory of vision, ideas of sense constitute a language, a topic discussed at greater length by Margaret Atherton in Chapter 4 of this volume. In the third section I turn to Berkeley's influential attack on "abstraction" – the doctrine that we think about a group of things by forming a special idea that, by virtue of its abbreviation or incompleteness, represents all and only the features that members of the group have in common. Berkeley's repudiation of abstract ideas led him to a novel conception of the aims of language. I outline this conception in Section IV, where I explain why Berkeley disputes Locke's declaration that every significant word stands for an idea.[4] In the closing sections of the chapter I discuss the methodological and metaphysical implications of Berkeley's doctrine of signs (Section V), and briefly examine some of his remarks on analogical speech, a topic at the center of his philosophy of religion (Section VI). Wide-ranging as this survey is, it falls short of the full extent of Berkeley's doctrine. I say nothing, for example, about his economic writings, in which money is interpreted as a sign – as a "ticket," "counter," or "token" – recording and conveying wealth or power (Q 23, 35, 475). This topic is addressed by Patrick Kelly in Chapter 11.

I. WORDS AND IDEAS

Although Euphranor speaks at one point of "the general nature of sign" (3: 157), Berkeley never actually presents a general account of what a sign is. He does, however, provide what amounts to a general account of the kind of sign I propose to call a "mark."[5] In the present section, we will confine our attention to simple signs of this kind.

A mark is a sign that stands for one particular object as opposed to another. The "standing for" relation is, at least initially, best clarified by example. In a particular conversational context, a proper name (such as "Aristotle") stands for a particular person. In a different context, the same person might be picked out by a stick figure in a diagram or by a circle in an organizational flow chart. The name, the stick figure, and the circle all *stand for* Aristotle. They serve to represent him. This makes them marks in the sense I am trying to elucidate.

The *standing for* relation holds between marks on the one hand and persons, places, and things in the world on the other, but in Berkeley's view this is a surface relation, supported by a pair of relations that are deeper and more fundamental. The first of these more fundamental relations, holding between marks and ideas in the mind, is what Berkeley calls *suggestion* (at PHK 43 and DHP 1 [174], for example): A mark stands for something in the world insofar as it gives rise, or tends to give rise, to ideas of the object in the minds of the mark's intended audience. Suggestion can take many different forms. A mark may move the mind simply to conceive of its object (as one might conceive of Aristotle upon mention of his name); it may move the mind to expect its object (as one might anticipate Aristotle's arrival, upon hearing his name announced); or it may move the mind to seek its object out (as one might look for Aristotle, upon hearing his name in an anxious and imploring voice). Often, as these examples suggest, a mark triggers – and licenses or legitimates – an inference.[6]

When, by means of a mark, a speaker aims to communicate a thought, that is presumably because the mark suggests to the speaker the very ideas the speaker hopes they will suggest to listeners. As Berkeley writes in the Draft Introduction to the *Principles*,

> . . . the ideas that in every man's mind ly hidden & cannot of themselves be brought into the view of another. It was therefore necessary for discourse & communication, that men should institute sounds to be signs of their ideas, which being raised in the mind of the hearer shall bring along with them into his understanding such ideas, as in the propriety of any language were annexed to them. (*Works* 2: 128)

In emphasizing both the privacy of our thoughts and our reliance on linguistic signs to make them public, this passage closely resembles the following passage from Locke's *Essay*:

> [Thoughts] are all within [Man's] own Breast, invisible, and hidden from others, nor can of themselves be made appear. The Comfort, and Advantage of Society, not being to be had without Communication of Thoughts, it was necessary, that Man should find out some external sensible Signs, whereby those invisible *Ideas*, which his thoughts are made up of, might be made known to others. (*Essay* III.ii.1)

Though Locke may not have agreed, the verbal signification of things in the world (as Berkeley understands it) arises out of the verbal suggestion of ideas. It is, in Berkeley's view, only because a mark suggests an idea that it can stand for something in the world.

I spoke of a pair of relations underlying a mark's relation to its object in the world. The first relation in the pair – the suggestion relation – holds, as we have seen, between words and ideas. The second relation holds between ideas and things themselves, and to understand it fully we need to look closely at the difference between ideas and words.

It is easy enough to say what words are: They are either inscriptions (if written) or noises (if vocalized) – modifications of light or sound (see TVV 40 and 44). But what are ideas? This is a question Berkeley does not face squarely, at least not in his published works,[7] and readers and critics have found distinct and sometimes competing answers implicit in his writings. According to one of those answers, an idea is simply a particular act or episode of thinking, or what philosophers call an *occurrent thought*: a whole occurrent thought, corresponding to a grammatically complete sentence. This is, perhaps, what Berkeley has in mind in the Introduction to the *Principles*, when he assures us that our "naked, undisguised ideas" will not mislead us:

> Whoever... designs to read the following sheets, I entreat him to make my words the occasion of his own thinking, and endeavour to attain the same train of thoughts in reading, that I had in writing them. By this means it will be easy for him to discover the truth or falsity of what I say. He will be out of all danger of being deceived by my words, and I do not see how he can be led into error by considering his own naked, undisguised ideas. (I 25)

Here, perhaps, the "naked, undisguised ideas" Berkeley mentions are the thoughts he hopes we will, after studying his book, come to share – thoughts that, as components of Berkeley's argument, presumably correspond to complete sentences. But even here there is a hint of a second understanding of "idea": an idea as an *object* of thought, as something toward which acts of thought are directed.

In my view, it is the second understanding that dominates Berkeley's thinking. He generally characterizes ideas not as acts of thinking but as objects of thought, for example in the following passages:

Note that when I speak of tangible ideas, I take the word idea for any the immediate object of sense or understanding, in which large signification it is commonly used by the moderns. (NTV 45)[8]

One idea *or object of thought* cannot produce, or make any alteration in another. (PHK 25, emphasis mine; see also PHK 139.)

The contrast between a *thought*, considered as an act or operation of thinking, and an *idea*, considered as an object or "Subject" of thought ("Subject" in the sense of *subject matter* or *concern*, as at entry 808 of the notebooks), is prominent throughout Berkeley's writings. In Section 21 of the Introduction to the *Principles*, for example, he resolves to take ideas "bare and naked into my view, keeping out of my thoughts, so far as I am able, those names which long and constant use hath so strictly united with them." Turning in the following section to the advantages he may expect from this, he explains that "so long as I confine my thoughts to my own ideas divested of words, I do not see how I can easily be mistaken. The objects I consider, I clearly and adequately know.... To discern the agreements or disagreements there are between my ideas, to see what ideas are included in any compound idea, and what not, there is nothing more requisite, than an attentive perception of what passes in my own understanding." These passages are typical of Berkeley's writings in distinguishing between, on the one hand, an act of thought, and, on the other, an object standing before it, to be viewed, considered, assessed, dissected, and known. Philonous exemplifies the same way of thinking in the *Three Dialogues*. "How often must I repeat," he asks Hylas, "that I know or am conscious of my own being; and that I myself am not my ideas, but somewhat else, a thinking active principle that perceives, knows, wills, and operates about ideas" (DHP 3 [233]).

Ideas as objects include ideas of particular things: of the book I left back in my office; of my dog Luisa; or of my Fairbanks by Vega Imperial Electric Banjo, serial number 30220. Unlike ideas considered as whole thoughts, which correspond to grammatically complete sentences, ideas of the things listed correspond to single words or expressions that Berkeley and his contemporaries called "names." These ideas qualify as marks in the sense I have identified, because they stand for particular things. The corresponding names are also marks in that sense, but according to Berkeley in the Draft Introduction, the two kinds of mark point beyond themselves in "different manners" (2: 129). "There is," he explains there,

> ...no similitude or resemblance betwixt words & the ideas that are marked by them. Any name may be used indifferently for the sign of any idea, or any number of ideas, it not being determin'd by any likeness to represent one more than another. But it is not so with ideas in respect of things, of which they are suppos'd to be the copies & images. They are not thought to represent them any otherwise, than as they resemble them. Whence it follows, that an idea is not capable of representing indifferently any thing or number of things it being limited by the likeness it beares to some particular existence, to represent it rather than any other.

We are now in a position to see how the relation between linguistic marks and things in the world takes rise from the pair of relations I have identified. "Aristotle" marks a particular man because it suggests, or tends to suggest, an idea of that man, an idea that is "of" that man because it resembles him.

In the Draft Introduction, Berkeley says a name is not determined by any *likeness* to represent one object more than another, but his actual view seems to be that *nothing* about a name determines it to represent what it does. That is why he says that a name "may be used indifferently," meaning *indiscriminately*, for any idea: There is nothing intrinsic to the name – nothing in its own nature – that makes it the mark of one thing rather than another. How then does it acquire its distinctive signifying role? Berkeley's answer is that the role is assigned by us: Names, he says, signify by arbitrary appointment, institution, or convention. It was "necessary for discourse & communication," as he explains in the Draft Introduction, "that men should institute sounds to be the signs of their ideas, which being raised in the mind of the hearer shall bring along with them into his understanding such ideas, as in the propriety of any language were annexed to them" (2: 128). Berkeley often draws attention to the arbitrariness of words:

> Languages and signs of human appointment...do not suggest the things signified by any likeness or identity of nature, but only by an habitual connexion that experience has made us to observe between them. (NTV 62)

> A great number of arbitrary signs, various and apposite, do constitute a language. (TVV 40)

PHILONOUS. Words are of arbitrary imposition. (DHP 3 [247])

HYLAS.... [I]t were absurd to think *God* or *Virtue* sensible things, though they may be signified and suggested to the mind by sensible marks, with which they have an arbitrary connexion. (DHP 1 [174])

In these passages, Berkeley is expounding what he rightly saw as a widely held view. It is conspicuous in Locke, among many others. At *Essay* III.iii.1, for example, Locke writes that words signify ideas "not by any natural connexion," but by "a voluntary Imposition, whereby such a Word is made arbitrarily the Mark of such an *Idea*." Words, Locke believes, are the instituted or conventional signs of ideas, which signify *their* objects – the realities that fill the world beyond ideas – quite apart from any act of institution or annexation. A Lockean idea might fairly be described as a "natural" idea of its object, because the very nature of the idea determines what it signifies. Berkeley, though, reserves the word "natural" for another purpose. Instead of opposing the arbitrary to the natural, he proposes a contrast between signs that signify their objects "in virtue of an arbitrary connexion" and those that do so in virtue of a connection he calls "necessary" (TVV 43). He uses the word "natural," as we will see in a moment, for arbitrary connections forged by God. Berkeley says very little about signs necessarily connected to what they signify; his standard examples are ideas of imagination, which he takes to be faint or languid copies of more vivid ideas of sense.[9] He says much more about signs that are connected arbitrarily to their objects. An arbitrary connection between sign and signified can be established, he thinks, by as little as co-presence, as he explains at *Theory of Vision Vindicated* 39:

As sounds suggest other things, so characters suggest those sounds; and, in general, all signs suggest the things signified, there being no idea which may not offer to the mind another idea which hath been frequently joined with it. In certain cases a sign may suggest its correlate as an image, in others as an effect, in others as a cause. But where there is no such relation of similitude or causality, nor any necessary connexion whatsoever, two things, by their mere coexistence, or two ideas, merely by being perceived together, may suggest or signify one the other, their connexion being all the while arbitrary; for it is the connexion only, as such, that causeth this effect.

Arbitrary connections can be established even when object and sign occur apart. Intelligent agents can literally attach inscriptions to objects (by painting a name on a boat's prow, for example), but they can assign names just as securely and with less effort simply by announcement. ("That rowboat will be called 'Titanic,' but for good luck's sake we'll leave the hull blank, and never mention the name in the boat's presence.") Strictly speaking, neither attachment nor announcement is enough all by itself; once it is attached to its object or its role is announced, we must go on to use the sign in the manner suggested (or at the very least we must intend to). By contrast, what might be called "compulsory" signs – nonarbitrary signs with a necessary connection to what they signify – in no way depend on our actions or intentions. Berkeley seems to view them as a prerequisite of intelligence (or of the application of intelligence to the world), rather than as something that might be owed, like arbitrary signs, to its exercise.

We can summarize our results so far in the following table, a preliminary catalogue of marks as Berkeley understood them:

MARKS (signs of particular things)	
ARBITRARY or CONVENTIONAL	NONARBITRARY or COMPULSORY
names	ideas of imagination

Though this table does not reveal it, we have also learned that the marking of particular things by arbitrary or conventional signs arises out of the marking of those things by nonarbitrary or compulsory signs (that is, by ideas). The *standing for* relation that holds between names and things, though it may seem at first to be a brute or unmediated relation between words and their counterparts in the world, actually rests on relations more basic. These relations (between words and ideas, and between ideas and things) run through us, because the ideas that intervene between words and things are ideas that exist in our own minds.

The examples I have provided up to now may suggest that arbitrary connections can only be established deliberately, thanks to some sort of stipulation or ceremony, but there is no reason to suppose this is Berkeley's view. The imposition or appointment of signs may be unconscious, the associated conventions tacit or implicit. As David Hume observes, "two men, who pull the oars of a boat, do it by an agreement or convention, tho' they have never given promises to each other."[10] In much the same way, a group of us might come to call our favorite picnic spot "the hill" – *agreeing*, in effect, to make "the hill" its mark – without an explicit christening.

To clarify further the notion of institution, annexation, or convention, and with it the notion of a nonarbitrary or compulsory sign, we can consider a thought-experiment of "contrary signification" devised by Berkeley in his *New Theory of Vision*. He imagines a speaker of English who meets a non-English speaker using English words "in a direct contrary signification" (NTV 32). The English speaker, Berkeley predicts, "would not fail to make a wrong judgment of the ideas annexed to those sounds in the mind of him that used them." Unlike a word, a thought cannot come to have a contrary signification – at least not for the person who has the thought – without ceasing to be the thought it is. If another person were able to read my mind, *perhaps* we could arrange for my thought of one thing to serve as code for my thought of something else. In that case, the thought would come to signify something other than what it signified at first. It would continue to signify the thing it originally signified, though, even if that aspect of its signification played no role in the strange parlor game we might be playing.

We have already noted that appointment or annexation is not the only way in which something can become a sign. "One idea [can be] qualified to suggest another," and thereby become a sign of the other, "merely by being often perceived with it" (TVV 68, provided of course that their co-presence gives rise to a custom or intention). This is one reason why, as Euphranor observes, "all signs are not language." As he explains, "not even all significant sounds, such as the natural cries of animals, or the inarticulate sounds and interjections of men," count as language. "It is the articulation, combination, variety, copiousness, extensive use and easy application of signs . . . that constitute the true nature of language" (ALC 4.12 [157]).

The nonarbitrary signs I have called "compulsory" are, by their very nature, determined to mark one thing rather than another. Hence, unlike arbitrary signs, their meanings need not be learned. Berkeley's leading examples are, as I have already remarked, ideas of imagination. These he takes to be faint copies of sensations, or novel combinations of copies of sensations (in which case they could have been copied from sense directly, had the constituent ideas appeared in the required combinations). "The ideas imprinted on the senses," Berkeley writes,

> ... are called *real things*: and those excited in the imagination being less regular, vivid and constant, are more properly termed *ideas*, or *images of things*, which they copy and represent. (PHK 33)

When I recollect an earlier pain or pleasure, for example, the recollected idea (an idea of imagination) marks or refers to the earlier idea (the idea of sense that is the pain or pleasure itself) by its very nature. When I recall the setting of the summer sun, or the smell of fresh mud in spring, the ideas I form cannot help but signify the ideas of sense that are their objects. Imagination, which Berkeley often links with representation, functions, in effect, as a faculty of *re*-presentation: as a power that returns to the mind ideas already exhibited there.[11] The opening section of the body of the *Principles* is especially revealing in this connection. There Berkeley speaks of the imagination's "compounding, dividing, or *barely* representing [ideas or objects] originally perceived by sense or reflection" (emphasis mine). The word "barely" is meant to indicate that representing is the rock-bottom function of the imagination. It is a function the imagination can carry out, of course, only because its ideas are likenesses or resemblances of their sensed originals. An idea of imagination *re*-presents an earlier idea nonarbitrarily, apart from institution or convention, only because it resembles it.

Berkeley is unwavering in viewing ideas as images or likenesses of their objects, and he assumes that other philosophers – in particular, his materialist opponents – view them in the same way. In the first set of passages quoted below, Berkeley is recounting the views of the materialists, represented by an imaginary interlocutor (addressed as "you") in the *Principles* and by Hylas in the *Three Dialogues*:

> But say you, though ... ideas themselves do not exist without the mind, yet there may be things like them whereof they are copies or resemblances, which things exist without the mind, in an unthinking substance. (PHK 8)

> HYLAS. To speak the truth, Philonous, I think there are two kinds of objects, the one perceived immediately, which are likewise called *ideas*; the other are real things or external objects perceived by the mediation of ideas, which are their images and representations. (DHP 1 [203])

PHILONOUS. If I understand you rightly, you say our ideas do not exist without the mind; but that they are copies, images, or representations of certain originals that do. (DHP 1 [205])

PHILONOUS. It is your opinion, the ideas we perceive by our sense are not real things, but images, or copies of them. Our knowledge therefore is no farther real, than as our ideas are the true representations of those originals. (DHP 3 [246]

In a second set of passages, he sets forth the same view as his own, or takes it for granted in unfolding his own arguments:

All ideas whatever, being passive and inert, ... cannot represent unto us, by way of image or likeness, that which acts. (PHK 27)

As we conceive the ideas that are in the minds of other spirits by means of our own, which we suppose to be resemblances of them: so we know other spirits by means of our own soul, which in that sense is the image or idea of them, it having a like respect to other spirits, that blueness or heat by me perceived hath to those ideas perceived by another. (PHK 140)

Now for an important complication. Arbitrary signs, Berkeley holds, are of two notably different kinds: those instituted by human beings; and those instituted by God, the "author of nature." The word "Aristotle," for example, is a humanly appointed sign of an idea (and of the philosopher signified by that idea). An idea of smoke, on the other hand, is a divinely appointed sign of fire. God's arbitrary appointments constitute what Berkeley calls a "language of Nature" (NTV 140; see also PHK 108 in the first edition [*Works* 2: 89]). This language "doth not vary in different ages or nations, hence it is that in all times and places visible figures are call'd by the same names as the respective tangible figures suggested by them, and not because they are alike or of the same sort with them" (NTV 140; see also NTV 147). The signs of this language are ideas of sense, and they mark or refer to other ideas of sense. The faint appearance of a distant object, for example, is a sign of the object's distance, communicating information about the bodily movements (themselves detectable by touch or kinesthesia) required to reach it. (The communication of distance by visual ideas and sensations attending vision is more fully described in the following section, and in Chapter 4 of this volume.)

Because their signifying role is an aspect of the course of nature as God has ordained it, Berkeley describes the signs instituted by

God as "natural," even though they are arbitrary.[12] "A connexion established by the Author of nature, in the ordinary course of things," he writes, "may surely be called natural; as that made by men will be named artificial. And yet this doth not hinder but the one may be as arbitrary as the other. And, in fact, there is no more likeness to exhibit, or necessity to infer, things tangible from the modifications of light, than there is in language to collect the meaning from the sound" (TVV 40). Because a language is "a great number of arbitrary signs, various, and apposite" (TVV 40), languages, as we have seen, can be either artificial or natural.[13] "If such arbitrary connexion be instituted by men," Berkeley writes, "it is an artificial language; if by the Author of nature, it is a natural language."[14]

Our taxonomy of marks as Berkeley views them now becomes more complicated:

MARKS (signs of particular things)

ARBITRARY or CONVENTIONAL		NONARBITRARY or COMPULSORY
APPOINTED BY US	APPOINTED BY GOD	ideas of imagination
artificial (and if part of an eligible system of signs, an artificial language)	natural (and if part of an eligible system of signs, a natural language)	
words	ideas of sense	

We now know a great deal about ideas as Berkeley understood them, at least as they compare to words: They are objects of thought; they make it possible for words to mark things; they are, as ideas of imagination, compulsory signs of ideas of sense, and as ideas of sense, they are arbitrary signs in a language of nature. But we do not yet know their "metaphysical status" – what they are in themselves. To repeat some questions Locke raised about ideas as they were understood by his contemporary, the French philosopher Nicolas Malebranche (another important influence on Berkeley): Are ideas substances – that is, independently existing things – or are they modifications – that is, qualities or states that exist only *in* the substances they modify, and on which they depend for their existence?[15]

My own view is that Berkeleyan ideas are not either of these things: They are not substances, because they depend for their existence on the mind; yet they are not modifications – at least not as modifications were understood traditionally – because they cannot be *predicated of* the mind. In order for *F* to be predicated (truly) of the subject *x*, the subject-predicate sentence "*x* is *F*" must be true. If I am imagining yellow, for example, although *imagining yellow* can be predicated of me – imagining yellow is truly an act or operation of my mind – *yellow* itself, the object of that act, cannot be. Ideas are neither substances nor modifications, but actual objects that exist in mind and depend on the mind for their existence: "private presences," as Simon Blackburn aptly calls them.[16] This has recently become a controversial interpretation of Berkeley, but I think it is fair to say that it is also traditional. It was codified by Thomas Reid in the late eighteenth century.[17] According to a competing interpretation – originating with A. A. Luce early in the twentieth century and elaborated later in the century by John W. Yolton – a Berkeleyan idea, if it is not simply an act of thought (or an ordinary object, conceived in an essentially sense-based fashion), is instead the subject-matter of a thought.[18] When I remember to run home to feed my dog Luisa, for example, Luisa becomes the subject-matter of my thought and in that sense its "object." This is nothing more than a philosophical way of saying that I am thinking of Luisa. I may think at one moment of my dog who, waiting hungrily but loyally by the door, happens to exist, but a moment later I may imagine another pet (my tame cassowary) who does not exist. That nonexistent pet will be an "object" of my thought in the relevant sense, even though it is not an actually existing thing. If a Berkeleyan idea is an object only in this sense – an *intentional* object, as philosophers sometimes say – then it is not a private presence. It is not an actual entity, and it is incapable of explaining why our thought has the content that it has. It is simply the content of my thought (or an aspect of the content) itself.

I will not argue here for the traditional view – interested readers can instead consult Reid and his critics – except to observe that in his positive account of general thinking, which I take up in Section III, Berkeley in effect *distinguishes* between idea and content. A distinction between idea and content is likewise implicit in his remarks on notions, which will be discussed in Section IV. These are obstacles in the way of revisionist interpretations that are, at least in my opinion, very difficult to overcome.

I turn now to Berkeley's *New Theory of Vision*, in which visual experience is depicted in all strictness as a language addressed to us by our creator. Although this natural language is wider in extent than any human language and more vital to our welfare, it is made up entirely of marks,[19] and is therefore, as we will discover, substantially simpler than human languages as Berkeley came in the end to understand them.

II. BERKELEY'S THEORY OF VISION AND THE LANGUAGE OF NATURE

The aim of Berkeley's theory of vision is to explain how we perceive by sight the distance, size, and situation of objects. It is, as we will see, a semiotic theory. According to the theory, it is because ideas of sight are signs, strongly analogous to words, that they succeed in conveying information.

Berkeley assumes (with his contemporaries) that distance is not immediately perceived by sight. How then is it visually detected? Berkeley proposes that distance is "suggested to our thoughts, by certain visible ideas and sensations attending vision, which in their own nature have no manner of similitude or relation, either with distance, or things placed at a distance" (PHK 43). The ideas and sensations by which distance is suggested are, in other words, arbitrary signs. "By a connexion taught us by experience," rather than by a necessary connection discernible by pure reason, "they come to signify and suggest them to us, after the same manner that words of any language suggest the ideas they are made to stand for." Hence "visible ideas are the language whereby the governing spirit, on whom we depend, informs us what tangible ideas he is about to imprint upon us, in case we excite this or that motion in our own bodies" (PHK 44).

It is, for example, "certain by experience that when we look at a near object with both eyes, according as it approaches or recedes from us, we alter the disposition [or direction] of our eyes, by lessening or widening the interval between the pupils" (NTV 16). As soon as experience has taught us this, the sensation attending the altered "turn" or disposition of the eyes suggests ideas of lesser or greater distance (§ 16). Nearer objects also impart a more confused impression (§ 20), and the strain we experience when we try to keep them in focus is yet a third sign of distance variation (§ 27). Once these associations are learned, and only once they are learned, visible ideas acquire what Margaret Atherton has aptly called a "distance meaning."[20]

In the *New Theory of Vision*, the signs connected arbitrarily with the world's spatial features are ideas of sight, or sensations that accompany sight. The language comprising them is therefore exclusively visual. In *A Treatise concerning the Principles of Human Knowledge*, where all ideas of sense are portrayed as "marks or signs for our information" (PHK 66), what was at first a language of vision becomes a language of experience.[21] Because careful inspection reveals that ideas of sense have no causal power (PHK 25), "the connexion of ideas does not imply the relation of cause and effect, but only of a mark or sign with the thing signified" (PHK 65). Berkeley's examples in the *Principles* include not only the visible idea of fire – which is not the cause of the pain I suffer on approaching it but merely "the mark that forewarns me of it" – but also the noise of colliding bodies, which is not the effect of the collision but the sign that draws it to our attention. The scientist's task is to discover the laws of nature. These laws, however, do not pick out causes and their effects; they are, instead, the grammatical rules of the language in which God speaks to us for the sake of our well-being. "It is the searching after, and endeavoring to understand those signs instituted by the Author of Nature, that ought to be the employment of the natural philosopher," Berkeley advises, "not the pretending to explain things by natural causes" (PHK 66). Berkeley's conception of the task of natural science is discussed further by Lisa Downing in Chapter 8.

In *Alciphron* (which was bound, in each of its three editions, with the essay on vision), Berkeley argues (though his spokesperson Euphranor) that visual experience, conceived as a language, provides us with as forceful a reason to believe in the existence of God as we have to believe in the existence of other minds like our own. An "individual thinking thing" is, as Euphranor points out, strictly invisible. All that sight makes available are "such visible signs and tokens as suggest and infer the being of that invisible thinking principle or soul" (ALC 4.5 [147]). "In the self-same manner," he then says, "though I cannot with eyes of flesh behold the invisible God, yet I do in the strictest sense behold and perceive by my senses such signs and tokens, such effects and operations, as suggest, indicate, and demonstrate an invisible God" (4.5 [147]). This is, so far, a standard theistic argument "a posteriori," from observed effects to their hypothesized cause. That the effects are described as signs is the only real semiotic twist – and it is a modest twist at that, because earlier defenders could comfortably describe the effects to which they pointed as "signs," in the sense of *indications*, of their divine cause.[22] Berkeley had already offered this kind of argument in the *Principles* (see PHK 145 and 148). But when he elaborates the argument in *Alciphron*, it becomes more boldly semiotic: It becomes, in fact, explicitly linguistic. The skeptical freethinker Alciphron has challenged Berkeley's hero, Euphranor, by observing that the only real proof of another living soul is full-fledged speech. "Nothing so much convinces me of the existence of another person," he says, "as his speaking to me" (ALC 4.6 [148]). Euphranor then surprises Alciphron by replying that God actually speaks to all of us:

> If it shall appear plainly that God speaks to me by the intervention and use of arbitrary, outward, sensible signs, having no resemblance or necessary connexion with the things they stand for and suggest; if it shall appear that, by innumerable combinations of these signs, an endless variety of things is discovered and made known to us; and that we are thereby instructed or informed in their different natures; that we are taught and admonished what to shun, and what to pursue; and are directed how to regulate our motions, and how to act with respect to things distant from us, as well in time as place: will this content you? (4.7 [149]; for another version of the same argument see *Siris* 254.)

Here the argument retains its original form as an argument from effects or signs to causes, but when the signs are portrayed as a language, it is arguably more compelling. A mechanical explanation of a sign, even an array of signs, is one thing; a mechanical explanation of language (see ALC 4.14 [159]) is something else.

In developing his theory of vision, Berkeley calls attention to an important phenomenon in the psychology of signs: the tendency of signs to become transparent.[23] "No sooner do we hear the words of a familiar language pronounced in our ears," Berkeley explains,

> but the ideas corresponding thereto present themselves to our minds: in the very same instant the sound and the meaning enter the understanding: so closely are they united that it is not in our power to keep out the one,

except we exclude the other also. We even act in all respects as if we heard the very thoughts themselves. So likewise the secondary objects; or those which are only suggested by sight, do often more strongly affect us, and are more regarded than the proper objects of that sense; along with which they enter into the mind, and with which they have a far more strict connexion, than ideas have with words. (NTV 51)

Like the bilingual speaker who remembers what was said but not the language used to say it, we are inclined not to notice signs as we perceive through them, attending only to the objects they signify. It takes effort to consider ideas of sense as they are in themselves – to "disinterpret" our experience so that we contemplate only what the signs contain, and not what they have come to signify. "So swift and sudden and unperceived is the transition from visible to tangible ideas," Berkeley writes, "that we can scarce forbear thinking them equally the immediate object of vision" (NTV 145; see also NTV 144, TVV 52, and ALC 4.12 [156]). The transparency of signs explains why ordinary people are inclined to think, contrary to what the early modern science of vision suggests, that they perceive distance immediately by sight. It also explains why we are inclined to believe in "common sensibles," qualities immediately perceived by more than one sense (NTV 59 and 140) – a belief portrayed, at least in Berkeley's notebooks (N 57), as upholding materialism. Novice artists are often instructed by their teachers to draw what they actually see, rather than what they know or assume to be there. When he goes on to defend immaterialism, Berkeley will be calling for an equally demanding feat of disinterpretation. He will be urging us to see our ideas as they are in themselves, to hold them apart from what experience has made them signify.

III. ABSTRACT IDEAS

The signs we have examined up to now have all been particular signs: signs of particular things. But in thinking and speaking we do not simply refer to particular objects; we characterize them in ways that are inherently general, because we ascribe to them features that could be exemplified by other things, even if they happen not to be. A simple sentence of the subject-predicate form, for example, most often attributes a general feature, expressed by the predicate, to the particular that is marked out by the subject. And we often want to speak not of particulars, but of classes, kinds, or shareable features themselves.

To account for general thinking, Locke had appealed in the *Essay* to what he called "abstract ideas"; Berkeley vigorously opposed the account he took Locke to be offering. Locke is the only target Berkeley names in his attack on abstract ideas, but he is taking aim at what he sees as a long tradition. "Abstract general ideas," he tells a friend, "was a notion that Mr. Locke held in common with . . . I think all other philosophers" (*Works* 2: 293). Berkeley's target is any view that invests an idea or object of thought with inherent generality. He believes that objects of thought are inescapably particular, and that general thinking is a matter of attending selectively to features that are, in the object, inseparably joined to others that we happen at that moment to ignore.

Berkeley actually targets two kinds of abstract idea: ideas in which particular qualities are isolated from other particular qualities with which they must occur (an idea of color without extension, for example); and ideas in which general qualities are isolated from the more specific qualities falling under them (for example, an idea of color in general). "It is agreed on all hands," Berkeley writes in Introduction 7, "that the qualities or modes of things do never really exist each of them apart by it self, and separated from all other qualities, but are mixed, as it were, and blended together, several in the same object. But we are told, the mind being able to consider each quality singly, or abstracted from those other qualities with which it is united, does by that means frame to it self abstract ideas." For example, the mind is said to be able to resolve the idea of a colored object in motion into ideas of extension, color, and motion in isolation. "Not that it is possible for colour or motion to exist without extension: but only that the mind can frame to it self by abstraction the idea of colour exclusive of extension, and of motion exclusive of both colour and extension." The ideas of color exclusive of extension, and motion exclusive of color and extension, are abstract ideas of the first kind.

Berkeley moves on to abstract ideas of the second kind in Introduction 8. The mind, he writes, "having observed that in the particular extensions perceived by sense, there is something common and alike in all, and some other things peculiar, as this or that figure or magnitude, which distinguish them one from another," singles out what is common, "making thereof a most abstract idea of extension" – "most abstract" because it is isolated not only from qualities of other kinds with which extension must occur, but from particular determinations of extension. In the same way, the mind frames abstract ideas of "the more compounded beings, which include several coexistent qualities" (I 9). This "precision or mental separation" results in abstract ideas of, among other things, man, animal, and body.

Berkeley's main complaint against abstraction is that its alleged products are simply impossible. Viewing abstraction as a kind of mental separation or detachment, he argues that ideas can be separated only when their corresponding objects can be separated. "To be plain," he writes in Introduction 10, "I own my self able to abstract in one sense, as when I consider some particular parts or qualities separated from others, with which though they are united in some object, yet, it is possible they may really exist without them. But I deny that I can abstract one from another, or conceive separately, those qualities *which it is impossible should exist so separated* [emphasis mine]; or that I can frame a general notion by abstracting from particulars in the manner aforesaid. Which two last are the proper acceptations of abstraction." The argument is more explicit in the Draft Introduction to the *Principles*.

> It is, I think, a receiv'd axiom that an impossibility cannot be conceiv'd. For what created intelligence will pretend to conceive, that which God cannot cause to be? Now it is on all hands agreed, that nothing abstract or general can be made really to exist, whence it should seem to follow, that it cannot have so much as an ideal existence in the understanding.

Although no exact counterpart of this passage appears in the published introduction, the same line of reasoning, without the reference to God, is pursued in the body of the *Principles*:[24]

> I [can] imagine the trunk of a human body without the limbs, or conceive the smell of a rose without thinking on the rose itself. So far I will not deny I can abstract, if that may properly be called *abstraction*, which extends only to the conceiving separately such objects, as it is possible may really exist or be actually perceived asunder. But my conceiving or imagining power does not extend beyond the possibility of real existence or perception. (PHK 5)

What do its defenders have to say on behalf of abstraction? Their evidence for abstract ideas is that we use general words, but as Berkeley points out, this is good evidence only if "the making use of [general] words, implies the having" of abstract ideas. Berkeley denies this. An idea is made general simply "by being made to represent or stand for all other particular ideas of the same sort" (I 12). The idea itself does not change; the mind takes it as it is, and makes it stand for other ideas, by attending selectively to some features and ignoring others. "We may consider Peter so far forth as man, or so far forth as animal," Berkeley explains, "without framing the forementioned abstract idea, either of man or of animal, in as much as all that is perceived is not considered" (I 16). In the same way, we may consider a particular triangle – one that is, in itself, either equilateral, isosceles, or scalene – merely as a triangle (I 15). Although the idea perceived is "in it self...particular," such partial consideration renders it, "*with regard to its signification* general, since as it is there used" – for example, in a geometrical proof – "it represents all particular[s]...whatsoever" of a given kind (I 12, my emphasis). Hence a proof that seems centered on a particular – a particular diagram, say – can nonetheless be general: The individuating features of the diagram are not at all "concerned in the demonstration." (Berkeley's antiabstractionist treatment of mathematical proof is discussed further by Douglas M. Jesseph in Chapter 9.) General words derive their generality from "the same cause, namely, the various particular[s]" they indifferently denote. Universality does not consist "in the absolute, positive nature or conception of any thing, but in the relation it bears to the particulars signified or represented by it" (I 15).

It is in Berkeley's appeal to selective attention that idea and content, as I suggested in Section I, come apart. One person confronts the idea of Peter and thinks only of him. Another confronts the same idea and thinks of human beings in general – or of boys unaccountably good at chess. Our interpreting minds make their own contributions to content, a contribution that ideas themselves do not fix. When we fail to notice that the work of selection or generalization is our own, something like transparency seems to be at work: In rushing interpretively toward the general, we suppress vivid awareness of the particular.

Why is Berkeley so troubled by the doctrine of abstract ideas – troubled enough to devote the introduction to his first defense of immaterialism to an unraveling of the "fine and subtle net" (I 22) it has created? He grants, after all, that we can attend selectively to our ideas, and in the end, as several scholars have contended, this may be all that Locke himself sought to emphasize. Berkeley's official answer is that the doctrine has "occasioned innumerable errors and difficulties in almost all parts of knowledge" (I 6), but the Introduction itself does not specify them. The body of the *Principles* reveals that a specific error – materialism – was of particular concern, but before I turn to it, I want to identify a wider error that may account for Berkeley's general anxiety. It is an error of which materialism is arguably a special case.

In Section I of this chapter, I emphasized the "likeness" that ideas bear to their objects. Now I want to suggest that the same likeness relation between ideas and objects accounts, at least in part, for Berkeley's refusal to countenance abstraction. If idea *x* can represent object *y* only by resembling it, it is by no means far-fetched to conclude that if *x* represents *y*, *x*'s relations to other ideas must mirror *y*'s relations to the objects of the same ideas. Consider, for example, relations of separability. If *x* resembles *y* closely enough to represent it, and if *y* (motion, let us say) is inseparable from extension, should not *x*, as the idea of motion, be equally inseparable from the idea of extension? If it were not, would that not compromise its claim to resemble motion? It seems that the *separability of ideas has metaphysical significance*. If two ideas can be separated, it seems reasonable to suppose that their objects can be separated. What is conceivable, it seems, must be possible too.

That "my conceiving or imagining power does not extend beyond the possibility of real existence or perception" (PHK 5) is, of course, Berkeley's argument against abstraction. My point so far has been that Berkeley takes our conceiving power to have metaphysical bearing, and does so because he takes ideas to be likenesses of objects. If this is on the right track, then Berkeley should take the separability of words, which are merely arbitrary signs of their objects, to be metaphysically *in*significant. And it turns out that he does. Returning in the *Defence of Free-thinking in Mathematics* (published in 1735) to his earlier polemic against abstraction, Berkeley points out that "nothing is easier than to define in terms or words that which is incomprehensible in idea, forasmuch as any words can be either separated or joined as you please, but ideas always cannot." It is, for example, "as easy to say a round square as an oblong square, though the former be inconceivable" (DFM 48). It is, for the same reason, easy to detach the words "motion" and "extension," though motion without extension is both inconceivable and impossible.

Though Berkeley does not always make it clear, he takes the doctrine of abstraction to apply to every general term. Thus he traces the doctrine to the thought that "*every* name [my emphasis] hath, or ought to have, one only precise and settled signification, which inclines men to think there are certain *abstract, determinate ideas* [Berkeley's emphasis], which constitute the true and only signification of *each* general name [my emphasis again]" (I 18). He restates the assumption at *Principles* 116: "We are apt to think every noun substantive stands for a distinct idea, that may be separated from all others" (see also ALC 7.5 [293]). If the scope of the doctrine is absolutely general, it follows that every general word stands for an idea separable from every other idea, and if this consequence has the metaphysical bearing Berkeley thinks it has, it will follow that every general idea stands for something separable from every other thing. Necessary connections among things will be abrogated: Motion will be possible without extension, extension will be possible without shape, and shape in general will be possible without any shape in particular.

It is, I think, the anticipated metaphysical consequences of the doctrine of abstraction that move Berkeley to make his case against it. The separability of words does not worry him, because it has by itself no metaphysical significance. The "separation" achieved by selective attention does not worry him either, because it, too, carries no metaphysical weight. What troubles him is the separation of ideas – ideas whose separation entails the separability of the things they represent.

We can now make some sense, I think, of Berkeley's initially perplexing observation that materialism "will, perhaps, be found at bottom to depend on the doctrine of *abstract ideas*" (PHK 5), and of the rhetorical question he goes on to pose there: Can there be "a nicer strain of abstraction than to distinguish the existence of sensible objects from their being perceived, so as to conceive them existing unperceived?" To conceive of the unperceived existence of sensible objects is to separate (sensible) existence from perception. According to the doctrine of abstraction as Berkeley understands it, their separability by the mind entails their separability in the world. Hence if the doctrine of abstraction is true, materialism is both conceivable and possible. Locke himself implies, in a passage well-known to Berkeley, that sensible existence is a distinct idea (*Essay* II.vii.7, alluded to by Berkeley at N 746 and PHK 13). In view of the system of Berkeleyan assumptions I have identified (assumptions not always shared, it should be said, by Locke), it makes sense for Berkeley to suppose that Lockean materialism draws support from the doctrine of abstract ideas. If Locke's doctrine of abstract ideas is correct, sensible existence without perception is both conceivable and possible.

The doctrine of abstraction has, according to Berkeley, suspect sources as well as unfortunate consequences. It is those sources to which we now turn.

IV. THE ENDS OF LANGUAGE; IDEAS AND NOTIONS

Berkeley traces the doctrine of abstraction to language – specifically, to two widespread assumptions about language and its aims: the first, that language has "no other end but the communicating our ideas"; the second, "that every significant name stands for an idea" (I 19).[25] He questions each of these prevailing commitments.

The communicating of ideas is not, he contends, "the chief and only end of language, as is commonly supposed" (I 20). Other ends include "the raising of some passion, the exciting to, or deterring from an action, the putting the mind in some particular disposition" (20). The communicating of ideas is often subservient to such ends, and it is sometimes bypassed altogether. Berkeley entreats the reader "to reflect with himself, and see if it doth not often happen either in hearing or reading a discourse, that the passions of fear, love, hatred, admiration, disdain, and the like arise, immediately in his mind upon the perception of certain words, without any ideas coming between" (I 20). At first, he admits, the words might have occasioned ideas that themselves produced the requisite emotions. But "when language is once grown familiar," words are often "immediately attended with those passions, which at first were wont to be produced by the intervention of ideas, that are now quite omitted." A promise of a good thing can put me in a happy mood, even if I form no idea of the promised reward. (I conceive neither of a particular reward, nor of an abstract reward-in-general.) "Is not the being threatened with danger sufficient to excite a dread, though we think not of any particular evil likely to befall us, nor yet frame to our selves an idea of danger in abstract?" (20). The psychological mechanism at work in such examples is akin to what I earlier called the transparency of ideas, but there is a crucial difference: When an idea becomes "transparent," it continues to be perceived even though we no longer attend to it. When the emotional weight of an idea is transmitted to a word, the idea may, in contrast, drop out of mind altogether. In the first case an idea that remains on hand simply goes unnoticed, which suggests that it may continue to play a causal role; in the second, causal power originally vested in an idea is actually transferred to a word, so the idea itself becomes causally dispensable.[26]

As for the assumption that every significant name stands for an idea, it is not always honored, Berkeley claims, even in "the strictest reasonings" (I 19). For the most part, he suggests, names are used "as letters are in *algebra*, in which though a particular quantity be marked by each letter, yet to proceed right it is not requisite that in every step each letter suggest to your thoughts, that particular quantity it was appointed to stand for" (I 19).

To this it may be objected that even if a significant name does not always suggest an idea, it must have done so originally. Had it not, there could be nothing for which it was "appointed" to stand. As the *Principles* continues, Berkeley departs more radically from the assumption that every significant name stands for an idea, arguing that there are many words that never stand for or signify ideas.

As we learned in Section I, Berkeley believes that ideas are likenesses of what they represent. He also believes, on the basis of what he takes to be thorough and bias-free inspection, that ideas are entirely passive and inert (PHK 25). Mind or spirit, by contrast, is essentially active. He therefore concludes that "there can be no idea formed of a soul or spirit, for all ideas whatever, being passive and inert, ... cannot represent unto us, by way of image or likeness, that which acts" (PHK 27). Hence "the words *will*, *soul*, *spirit*, do not stand for different ideas, or in truth, for any idea at all" (PHK 27).[27]

The *Principles* was first published in 1710. In the second edition, published twenty-four years later, Berkeley added the following words to the ones just quoted: "It must be owned at the same time, that we have some *notion* of soul, [or] spirit . . . inasmuch as we know or understand the meaning of those words" (PHK 27, emphasis mine). In early modern philosophical English, the word "notion" sometimes served simply as a substitute for "idea," but at other times notions and ideas were distinguished. The difference, roughly put, is that notions were regarded as objects more of intellect than of sense, and as objects whose conception requires active intellectual effort, as opposed to passive reception. Berkeley's second-edition uses of "notion" recall that contrast. In the second edition he says not only that we have notions rather than ideas of the mind itself, but that we have notions rather than ideas of its acts or operations (PHK 142, in the second edition; see also PHK 27, 89, and 140 in the second edition, and DHP 3 [232–4] in its second edition). He is willing to speak of words for the mind and its actions as "meaning," "signifying," or "denoting" their objects (PHK 139), but they do so without the intervention of ideas.

Berkeley's departure from the assumption that words always signify ideas continues with his treatment of words for relations (such as *larger than* or *lighter than*). His line of thought here is obscure, but it seems to rest on the observation that relations are "distinct from the ideas or things related, inasmuch as the latter may be perceived by us without our perceiving the former" (PHK 89, in the second edition only). From this he apparently inferred that "all relations [include] an act of the mind" (PHK 142, in the second edition only), his thought perhaps being that relations are superimposed on things by mental acts of juxtaposition and comparison. If juxtaposition and comparison are acts, perhaps the relations they sustain are also acts. If it is Berkeley's view that relations can persist through time only so long as the mental acts sustaining them are renewed – if the existence of relations, in other words, calls for constant re-creation – relations begin to look very much like facets of the mind's activity.

In denying that words for spirits, acts, and relations signify ideas, Berkeley, in the body of the *Principles*, departs more radically from received views than he had in the Introduction. Although the Introduction drew attention to words that do not always suggest ideas, it saw them as deriving their significance from a past (and perhaps persisting, even if no longer activated) power to suggest ideas. The significance of words for spirits, acts, and relations has an entirely different basis, of which Berkeley offers only the merest sketch. That basis lies, he suggests, in the immediate acquaintance I have with my own self. As Philonous assures Hylas, "I know what I mean by the terms *I* and *myself*; and I know this immediately, or intuitively, though I do not perceive it as I perceive a triangle, a colour, or a sound" (DHP 3 [231]). "My own mind," he says later, "I have an immediate knowledge of" (DHP 3 [232]). From the knowledge of what "I" or "self" means, it is apparently Berkeley's view that I can advance to a knowledge of the meaning of *spirit*, *soul*, or *substance* as applied to others, even God (see PHK 139–40 and DHP 3 [232]).[28] (A similar account can presumably be given of the meaning of words signifying mental acts or operations, and through them, perhaps, of words signifying relations.) As Philonous explains, "I have ... in my self some sort of active thinking image of the Deity. And though I perceive Him not by sense, yet I have a notion of Him, or know him by reflexion and reasoning" (DHP 3 [232]).[29]

In works published after the *Principles*, particularly in *Alciphron* (1732), Berkeley grew even more doubtful of the assumption that meaningful words signify ideas. In *Alciphron*, the freethinker after whom the dialogue is named objects to religious faith on the ground that the vocabulary of that faith does not excite ideas. "There can be no assent where there are no ideas: and where there is no assent there can be no faith: and what cannot be, that no man is obliged to. This is as clear as anything in Euclid!" (7.4 [291]). For this reason, he alleges, the word "grace" (for example) is perfect nonsense. Berkeley's hero Euphranor replies that "we shall find it as difficult to form an idea of force as of grace" (7.6 [295]), and yet the word *force* is nonetheless perfectly meaningful:

> There are very evident propositions or theorems relating to force, which contain useful truths.... And if, by considering this doctrine of force, men arrive at the knowledge of many inventions in Mechanics, and are taught to frame engines, by means of which things difficult and otherwise impossible may be performed; and if the same doctrine which is so beneficial here below serveth also as a key to discover the nature of the celestial motions; shall we deny that it is of use, either in practice or speculation, because we have no distinct idea of force? (ALC 7.7 [295–6])

Euphranor further illustrates his point with mathematical examples (7.5 [293], 7.12 [304–5]), and then applies its lessons to faith:[30]

It seems ... that a man may believe in the doctrine of the Trinity, if he finds it revealed in Holy Scripture that the Father, the Son, and the Holy Ghost, are God, and that there is but one God, although he doth not frame in his mind any abstract or distinct ideas of trinity, substance, or personality; provided that this doctrine of a Creator, Redeemer, and Sanctifier makes proper impressions on his mind, producing therein love, hope, gratitude, and obedience, and thereby becomes a lively operative principle, influencing his life and actions, agreeably to that notion of saving faith which is required in a Christian. (7.8 [297])

Although the details are sketchy, Berkeley's basic point is clear: A sign may be significant not because it marks an idea, or even because it can be traced to something with which we are immediately acquainted, but because it is a working part of a system of signs that makes a genuine difference to our lives – to our thoughts, actions, and emotions. We have moved from what might be called an *acquaintance* model of meaning to what William James, early in the twentieth century, called a *pragmatic* one. "The pragmatic method," James wrote,[31]

is to try to interpret each notion by tracing its respective practical consequences.... If no practical difference whatever can be traced, then the alternatives mean practically the same thing, and all dispute is idle. Whenever a dispute is serious, we ought to be able to show some practical difference that must follow from one side or the other side's being right.

There is, as James goes on to acknowledge, "absolutely nothing new in the pragmatic method." In fact he credits Berkeley with "momentous achievements" by means of it.

V. THE STATEMENT AND DEFENSE OF IMMATERIALISM; SPEAKING WITH THE VULGAR AND THINKING WITH THE LEARNED

Berkeley takes his most momentous achievement to be defeat of materialism, which he condemns in terms provided by the doctrine of signs. Materialism, as he argues, is either contradictory or meaningless:

When I consider the two parts or branches which make the signification of the words *material substance* [namely, the idea of being in general, and the notion of its supporting accidents], I am convinced that there is no distinct meaning annexed to them. But why should we trouble ourselves any farther, in discussing this material *substratum* or support of figure and motion, and other sensible qualities? Does it not suppose they have an existence without the mind? And is not this a direct repugnancy, and altogether inconceivable? (PHK 17)

It is very obvious, upon the least inquiry into our own thoughts, to know whether it to be possible for us to understand what is meant, by the *absolute existence of sensible objects in themselves, or without the mind.* To me it is evident those words mark out either a direct contradiction, or else nothing at all.... It is on this that I insist, to wit, that the absolute existence of unthinking things are words without a meaning, or which include a contradiction. This is what I repeat and inculcate, and earnestly recommend to the attentive thoughts of the reader. (PHK 24)

All the themes I have so far emphasized – the difference between words and ideas, Berkeley's reinterpretation of vision, his repudiation of abstract ideas, his enlarged conception of the ends of language, his pragmatic test of meaning – are brought together in his elaboration and defense of immaterialism. Berkeley's central immaterialist argument is examined closely by A. C. Grayling in Chapter 6. Here I can do no more than call attention to the presence of semiotic doctrines and concerns in core arguments of the *Principles* and the *Three Dialogues*.

Immaterialism itself can be stated in semiotic form. According to materialist philosophers as Berkeley portrays them, ideas of sense are nonarbitrary, mind-dependent signs of external, mind-independent objects. Immaterialism is then, in part, the view that ideas of sense are, by nature, not mind-dependent signs, but mind-dependent *objects* of signs. Although they are, by divine appointment, arbitrary signs of other ideas of sense – "words," as it were, in a God-given language of nature – they are not compulsory signs of anything. They are, instead, the inevitable *objects* of corresponding ideas of imagination.

Berkeley argues partly in semiotic terms against the materialist's contention that ideas of sense represent external objects in the same way ideas of imagination represent ideas of sense (PHK 8):

But say you, though the ideas themselves do not exist without the mind, yet there may be things like them whereof they are copies or resemblances, which things exist without the mind, in an unthinking substance. I answer, an idea can be like nothing but an idea; a colour or figure can be like nothing but another colour or figure. If we look but ever so little into our thoughts, we shall find it impossible for us to conceive a likeness except only between our ideas. Against, I ask whether these supposed originals or external things, of which our ideas are the pictures or representations, be themselves perceivable or no? If they are, then they are ideas, as we have gained our point; but if you say they are not, I appeal to anyone whether it be sense, to assert a colour is like something which is invisible; hard or soft, like something which is intangible; and so of the rest.

The semiotic language of "representation" and "original" recurs in the *Dialogues*, where Philonous explains that he takes Hylas to be saying that although ideas "do not exist without the mind," they are "copies, images, or representations of certain originals that do" (DHP 1 [205]). "You take me right," Hylas answers, provoking the following questions from Philonous:

How . . . is it possible, that things perpetually fleeting and variable as our ideas, should be copies or images of any thing fixed and constant? Or in other words, since . . . our ideas are continually changing . . . ; how can any determinate material objects be properly represented or painted forth by several distinct things, each of which is so different from and unlike the rest? Or if you say it resembles some one only of our ideas, how shall we be able to distinguish the true copy from all the false ones? (DHP 1 [205–6])[32]

Berkeley's doctrine of signs shapes not only his objections to materialism, but the positive case for his immaterialist alternative. What do we mean, for example, when we say that a sensible thing exists? A simple but illuminating answer, friendly to immaterialism, is furnished by the pragmatic method:

The table I write on, I say, exists, that is, I see and feel it; and if I were out of my study I should say it existed, meaning thereby that if I was in my study I might perceive it, or that some other spirit actually does perceive it. There was an odour, that is, it was smelled; there was a sound, that is to say, it was heard; a colour or figure, and it was perceived by sight or touch. That is all that I can understand by these and the like expressions. For as to what is said of the absolute existence of unthinking things without any relation to their being perceived, that seems perfectly unintelligible. Their *esse* is *percipi*, nor is it possible they should have any existence, out of the minds or thinking things which perceive them. (PHK 3)

Berkeley uses the same method to clarify what we mean when we speak of something sensed as real. We do not use the word "real" to pick out an idea distinct from all others, he tells us, but to speak compendiously of the steadiness, strength, and liveliness of our ideas, and of their coherence with other ideas like themselves (PHK 30–3).

"To employ a term and conceive nothing by it is unworthy of a philosopher," Berkeley writes at *De Motu* 29. Despite his insistence that words do not always signify particular ideas, Berkeley never abandons the view that the "proper use of words, is the marking our conceptions, or things only as they are known and perceived by us" (PHK 83). Philosophically central terms still call for clarification; debatable conceptions still need spelling out. But the spelling out need not take the one-size-fits-all form suggested by the prevailing view: the display of a distinct idea signified by the word. The result is a dramatic widening of the clarifactory strategies available to philosophy. Liberated from the requirement that a separately conceivable idea be supplied for every meaningful word, Berkeley can acknowledge the significance of a controversial or difficult expression without having to enumerate the parts of the complex idea corresponding to it. He can set out to analyze larger units of discourse – whole sentences or ways of speaking – and offer in their place more perspicuous discursive units of similar (or even larger) size. He is, as a result, cautious about the conclusions that can safely be drawn from the successful use of a single expression. It cannot be assumed that a fruitful expression signifies an idea or stands for a particular thing. Berkeley is, however, in a delicate position here, because his main complaint against materialism is that it cannot be adequately clarified. The flexible strategies that enlarge his power to clarify could interfere with his work as a hard-edged critic of conceptions.

His caution in drawing conclusions from the surface appearance of language gives Berkeley a way of protecting immaterialism from the objection that it diverges from ordinary ways of speaking. In such cases, he suggests, we can think "with the learned" – that is, with the immaterialists – though we speak "with the vulgar":

> It will . . . be demanded whether it does not seem absurd to take away natural causes, and ascribe everything to the immediate operation of spirits? We must no longer say upon these principles that figure heats, or water cools, but that a spirit heats, and so forth. Would not a man be deservedly laughed at, who should take after this manner? I answer, he would so; in such things we ought to *think with the learned, and speak with the vulgar*. They who to demonstration are convinced of the truth of the *Copernican* system, do nevertheless say the sun rises, the sun sets, or comes to the meridian; and

if they affected a contrary style in common talk, it would without doubt appear very ridiculous. A little reflection on what is here said will make it manifest, that the common use of language would receive no manner of alteration or disturbance from the admission of our tenets. (PHK 51)

This is part of what it means to "draw the curtain of words," as Berkeley urges us to do in the Introduction to the *Principles* (I 5).

VI. FIGURATIVE LANGUAGE AND THE PERFECTION OF CONCEPTIONS

So far we have considered only literal signs, or literal uses of signs. As the chapter draws to a close, I would like to guide us through some of Berkeley's thoughts about figurative language. An obvious starting point is his bold announcement, in *De Motu*, that "a philosopher should abstain from metaphor" (DM 3). Berkeley does not consistently practice what he preaches here, but this blanket prohibition, simple as it seems, is actually a fair indication of the standard he aspired to meet when making his core philosophical claims.

The early modern world owed its definition of metaphor to Aristotle, who writes in his *Poetics* that "metaphor consists in giving the thing a name that belongs to something else" (1457b). Aristotle describes metaphor as the "transference" of a name from one thing to another (1457b). Metaphors, he warns, must be "fitting." They must correspond "fairly" to the new thing they are made to signify (*Rhetoric* 1405a). He condemns the use of metaphor in scientific argument (*Posterior Analytics* 97b), making him one potential source of the disparaging attitude toward metaphor (widespread among early modern philosophers) that Berkeley voices in *De Motu*. Aristotle also observes that skill in making metaphors cannot be taught. Berkeley himself had a knack for them. In the Introduction to the *Principles*, to take just one example, Berkeley uses a memorable metaphor to say that philosophers are to blame for the difficulties blocking their progress: "we have first raised a dust, and then complain, we cannot see" (I 3).

This memorable metaphor is peripheral to Berkeley's core philosophical claims, so it need not compromise his warning in *De Motu*. (Perhaps this metaphor also could be paraphrased away.) Consider, instead, a philosophically central passage in the *Three Dialogues*, where Hylas charges that in saying that objects exist in the mind, Philonous is guilty of "some abuse of language" (DHP 3 [250]). "I would not be understood in the gross literal sense," Philonous replies, "as when bodies are said to exist in a place, or a seal to make an impression upon wax. My meaning is only that the mind comprehends or perceives them; and that it is affected from without, or by some being distinct from itself." There is nothing here, he says, "but what is conformable to the general analogy of language: most part of the mental operations being signified by words borrowed from sensible things; as is plain in the terms *comprehend*, *reflect*, *discourse*, *etc.*, which, being applied to the mind, must not be taken in their gross, original sense."[33]

It may seem that Philonous is openly resorting here to ineliminable metaphor, thereby offending against the rule Berkeley lays down in *De Motu*, but the actual situation is more complicated. In disavowing the "gross literal sense" that might be assigned to his words, Philonous is deliberately echoing words Hylas had introduced in the First Dialogue. Under pressure from Philonous to explain what it means to say that extension, like other modes of body, is supported by a "material substratum" spread beneath it, Hylas says, "I do not mean that matter is *spread* in a gross literal sense under extension. The word *substratum* is used only to express in general the same thing with *substance*" (DHP 1 [198]). When Philonous disavows the "gross literal" interpretation of his words, the interpretation he is asking for is not other than literal, but other than "gross" or *corporeal*. Substratum is, etymologically or originally, "that which is spread under"; substance is "that which stands beneath." Minds cannot extend or stand as bodies can. Nor can they be spatially beneath something else. Philonous admits that *words* for the mind are borrowed from bodies, but their application to mind is, he thinks, nonetheless perfectly literal. It is just that the literal meaning they have in the case of body differs from the literal meaning they have in the case of mind. It is literally true, for example, that I comprehend Newton's laws. I do not comprehend them in the gross or physical sense in which my arms "comprehend" my daughter when I comfort her. Yet I comprehend them in a perfectly literal sense, brought home to me by reflection on my mind and its operations. A word is borrowed, but there is no transference or substitution of conceptions.

Berkeley believes that materialists are regularly misled by corporeal metaphors. At entry 822 in the notebooks, for example, Hobbes is condemned for speaking of the will as if it were motion, "wth wch it has," Berkeley cautions, "no likeness." The theme is developed more fully at *Principles* 144: "Nothing seems more to have contributed towards engaging men in controversies and mistakes, with regard to the nature and operations of the mind," he writes, "than the being used to speak of those things, in terms borrowed from sensible ideas." Berkeley's view is that in spite of the borrowing, we have non-sense-based notions of the nature and operations of the mind; even though the words expressing these notions were originally associated with sense, they come to express non-sense-derived conceptions.[34] Notwithstanding Philonous's disavowal of a "gross literal sense" of his words, then, Berkeley's view is that immaterialism can be nonmetaphorically conceived. The immaterialist's corporeal metaphors can be redeemed, in the hard currency of immediate reflection. The core claims of immaterialism are literally true, though metaphorically clothed.

Words such as *knowledge, wisdom,* and *goodness,* as applied to God, raise a more serious difficulty. In *Alciphron,* Lysicles makes the plausible suggestion that because of the vast difference between God and finite creatures, such words "must be understood in a quite different sense from what they signify in the vulgar acceptation" (4.17 [163–4]). He then goes on to add, "or from anything that we can form a notion of or conceive." Crito condemns this suggestion as a "method of growing in expression and dwindling in notion" (4.19 [167]), realizing that if the notion of God dwindles down too far, the content of belief in God will dwindle with it.[35]

Crito therefore proposes a different account. He agrees that words such as *knowledge, wisdom,* and *goodness* are, when assigned to God, "borrowed" from "perfection[s]" found in "creatures." He cites with approval St. Thomas's observation that "our intellect gets its notions of all sorts of perfections from ... creatures, and that as it apprehends those perfections so it signifies them by names" (4.20 [168]). When we assign these names to God, then, "we are to consider two things": first, the perfections themselves; and second, "the manner which is peculiar to the creature, and cannot, strictly and properly speaking, be said to agree to the Creator" (4.20 [168]). On this basis he denies that "knowledge, in its proper sense, may not be attributed to God" (4.20 [168–9]). The perfection itself is attributed to God, even if it does not exist in God in the imperfect manner in which it exists in us.

If Crito is correct, the fact that we speak analogically of God does not mean that we cannot frame "a true and proper notion of attributes applied by analogy" (4.21 [169]). We have, for example, a "true and proper notion" of knowledge, one we can detach from our notion of the manner in which knowledge exists in us. But if our only route to such a notion is through the creaturely or imperfect, how do we find our way to it? Crito distinguishes between two kinds of analogy, metaphorical and proper (4.21 [169–70]). (The distinction between the metaphorical and the proper again goes back to Aristotle, *Rhetoric* 1404b.) When God is said to have an ear, for example, the analogy is metaphorical. It means that God knows of something we have voiced, or even kept to ourselves – our most profound concerns, for example. Here the metaphor can be paraphrased: that is, defeated and replaced. "But the case is different when wisdom and knowledge are attributed to God" (ALC 4.21 [170)]. In knowledge simply or as such there is, Crito explains, no defect. So although attributes "which in themselves simply, and as such, denote perfection," can safely be applied to God, they must be applied "proportionably" (4.21 [170]), meaning for example that because God is infinitely above ourselves, his knowledge is infinitely greater than our own. They are applied proportionately, but Berkeley's view seems to be that they are still applied properly or literally.

But how, exactly, is this "proportional" understanding achieved? Berkeley condemns misguided friends of religion who infer from the doctrine of analogy "that we cannot frame any direct and proper notion, though never so [that is, ever so] inadequate, of knowledge or wisdom, as they are in the Deity" (ALC 4.21 [170]). In the *Three Dialogues*, we are said to form a conception of God's knowledge by a process disturbingly akin to abstraction, removing imperfections from the knowledge we find in our own selves (DHP 3 [231–2]). But can we remove the imperfections from knowledge as we know it in our own case? And if we can, how do we render perfect that which remains? This is the kind of question raised by Plato in the *Phaedo* and by Descartes in the Third Meditation. In their different ways, they appeal to something that does not seem available to Berkeley (a recollected conception in Plato's case, and a divinely given innate idea in Descartes'). Berkeley's conception must be borrowed from sensation and reflection, but then something like abstraction is required: We must, it seems, abstract from notions, even though we cannot abstract from ideas. And once we have abstracted some core of knowlege, common to God and our own selves – a core distinct from the "manner" in which knowledge is realized in us – it is unclear how we manage to heighten or perfect it. There is a serious tension here among three doctrines Berkeley affirms: his belief that our conception of God has its source in reflection on our own selves; his antiabstractionism; and his literalism regarding the divine attributes.

Berkeley shows signs of struggling with these issues, however obscurely, in the closing sections of his late work *Siris* (see in particular articles 343, 360, 363–8). Many readers have noticed the Platonism of *Siris*; the book is most authentically Platonic, I think, in seeking out perfected conceptions of mind and the good, but how such perfected conceptions can be achieved is never clearly articulated.

VII. EUPHRANOR'S SUMMING UP

Earlier I observed that Berkeley gives no fully general account of the nature of signs, but he does offer, through Euphranor, the following broad summary of his account of verbal signs. It can serve as a summary of much (though not all) of this chapter.

> Thus much, upon the whole, may be said of all signs: – that they do not always suggest ideas signified to the mind: that when they suggest ideas, they are not general abstract ideas: that they have other uses besides barely standing for and exhibiting ideas, such as raising proper emotions, producing certain dispositions or habits of mind, and directing our actions in pursuit of that happiness which is the ultimate end and design, the primary spring and motive, that sets rational agents at work: that signs may imply or suggest the relations of things; which relations, habitudes, or proportions, as they cannot be by us understood but by the help of signs, so being thereby expressed and confuted, they direct and enable us to act with regard to things: that the true end of speech, reason, science, faith, assent, in all its different degrees, is not merely, or principally, or always, the imparting or acquiring of ideas, but rather something of an active operative nature, tending to a conceived good: which may sometimes be obtained, not only although the ideas marked are not offered to the mind, but even although there should be no possibility of offering or exhibiting any such idea to the mind: for instance, the algebraic

mark, which denotes the root of a negative square, hath its use in logistic operations, although it be impossible to form an idea of any such quantity. And what is true of algebraic signs is also true of words or language, modern algebra being in fact a more short, apposite, and artificial sort of language. (ALC 7.14 [307])

Berkeley's doctrine of signs is not the key that unlocks all his thinking: There is no such key. But I hope this chapter has established that the doctrine of signs runs through, and to some extent unifies, almost everything Berkeley wrote. It shapes his account of vision; it is of direct concern in his attack on abstraction; it figures in his defense of immaterialism; it supplies him with new strategies for assessing and clarifying meaning; and it incorporates a view of language that has important consequences for the defense of religion and for the interpretation and practice of science and mathematics.

NOTES

1. *Essay concerning Human Understanding*, ed. P. H. Nidditch (Oxford: Clarendon Press, 1975), IV.xxi.1–4. This tripartite division did not originate with the *Essay*, as Locke's use of Greek labels for each of the three parts is probably meant to indicate. According to an ancient tradition, the division (or the gathering of three scattered investigations into one whole) originates with Plato and the Academy. See Alcinous, *The Handbook of Platonism*, ed. John Dillon (Oxford: Clarendon Press, 1995), 4, and Dillon's commentary, xxvii and 57.
2. *Essay* IV.xxi.5.
3. William H. McGowan was, I think, the first commentator on Berkeley to speak, as Berkeley does, of the "doctrine of signs." I follow McGowan not only in this, and but in opening my discussion by setting *Alciphron* 7.13 in the context of Book IV, chapter xii of Locke's *Essay*. For McGowan's illuminating comparison of Berkeley and Locke, see his "Berkeley's Doctrine of Signs," in *Berkeley: Critical and Interpretive Essays*, ed. C. M. Turbayne (Minneapolis: University of Minnesota Press, 1982), 231–46.
4. Locke actually recognizes some exceptions: particles (*Essay* III.vii); and "negative Names" (II.viii.5, III. i. 4). Berkeley takes note of the exception for particles at entries 661, 661a, and 667 of the notebooks.
5. See for example NTV 140, where words are described as "marks" of the things they signify. At I 20 Berkeley again describes words as marks, but of ideas rather than of things themselves. At PHK 1 he writes that as

several ideas "are observed to accompany each other, they come to be marked by one name, and so to be reputed as one thing," and at PHK 44 he observes that ideas do not "suggest or mark out to us things actually existing at a distance." Later (PHK 147 and 148) he speaks of ideas or sensations that "mark out unto us the existence of finite and created spirits like ourselves." God and virtue are not sensible things, Hylas says at DHP 1 [174], "though they may be signified and suggested to the mind by sensible marks, with which they have an arbitrary connexion." Although Berkeley sometimes uses "mark" in the way I am using it here, it sometimes serves him as a substitute for "sign."

6. On signs as inference tickets, see DHP 2 (223) and 2 (233). Inference, however, is not to be identified with suggestion, a fact that became progressively clearer to Berkeley over time. For a clear statement of the difference in a late work see *Theory of Vision Vindicated* 42: "To be suggested is one thing, and to be inferred another." Berkeley explains that "things are suggested and perceived by sense. We make judgments and inferences by the understanding." The contrast between passive sense and active understanding is a major theme in *Siris*, where knowing what a sign signifies, as opposed to being sensitive to its suggestions, is placed on the active side of the dichotomy. "We know a thing when we understand it," Berkeley writes there, "and we understand it when we can interpret or tell what it signifies. Strictly, the sense knows nothing" (S 253).
7. Berkeley's notebooks record his intention to address the question, apparently in the Introduction to the *Principles*:

   I Mem. to Premise a Definition of Idea. (N 507)

   In the notebooks themselves, Berkeley comes closest to a definition in entries 775 and 808.
8. "The moderns" include Locke, who, after apologizing for his frequent use of the word "idea" in the *Essay*, says it is the term that "serves best to stand for whatsoever is the Object of the Understanding when a Man thinks." He has used it broadly, he then explains, "to express whatever is meant by *Phantasm, Notion, Species,* or whatever it is, which the Mind can be employ'd about in thinking" (I.i.8; as *Notebooks* 685 reveals, Berkeley had at one time considered offering the same apology). Later in the *Essay*, Locke calls an idea "whatsoever the Mind perceives in it self, or is the immediate object of Perception, Thought, or Understanding" (II.viii.8).
9. Whether there are other examples of signs necessarily connected to their objects depends in part on whether Berkeley views causation as necessary connection.

10. *A Treatise of Human Nature,* ed. David Fate Norton and Mary J. Norton (Oxford: Oxford University Press, 2000), 3.2.2.10.
11. See I 10, PHK 1, PHK 33, and DHP 1 [194] ("represented by the imagination"). Strictly speaking, imagination returns to the mind not the very ideas already exhibited there, but accurate copies: new instances or "tokens" of earlier "types."
12. These signs presumably include the cries of animals. Because animals are not genuine agents, the signifying power of these cries depends not on their will, but on the will of their creator. Berkeley briefly discusses such signs in *Alciphron* 4.12.
13. How can a sign be both arbitrary and "apposite" (TVV 40)? One way, Berkeley plausibly answers, is by co-variation with the thing signified. If one idea "increaseth either directly or inversely as the other," for example, "various degrees of the former" will conveniently signify "various degrees of the latter" (TVV 68; see also see NTV 46 and 142–3, as well as TVV 53 and 57). Thunder, for example, is an arbitrary sign of lightning, but it is also an apposite sign, because the louder the pounding of the thunder, the closer (or the more dramatic) the flash of the lightning.
14. TVV 40. In *Alciphron,* Euphranor seems at one point to contrast the artificial – or, at least, more artificial – language of algebra with languages such as English or Latin (see ALC 7.14 [307]).
15. See Locke, *An Examination of P. Malebranche's Opinion of Seeing All Things in God,* in *The Works of John Locke,* 10 vols. (London: Thomas Tegg, 1823), 9: 224.
16. *The Oxford Dictionary of Philosophy* (Oxford: Oxford University Press, 1994), 183. On ideas as modifications see *Principles* 49.
17. See Reid's *Essays on the Intellectual Powers of Man,* Essay 2, chapters 10 and 11, in *The Works of Thomas Reid,* ed. Sir William Hamilton, 6th edition (Edinburgh: MacLachlan and Stewart, 1863), vol. 2.
18. For Luce see "Berkeley's Existence in the Mind," *Mind* 50 (1941): 258–67, reprinted in *Locke and Berkeley,* ed. C. B. Martin and D. M. Armstrong (Garden City, NY: Doubleday, 1968), 284–95, and *Berkeley's Immaterialism* (London: Nelson, 1945), 55. For Yolton see *Perceptual Acquaintance from Descartes to Reid* (Minneapolis: University of Minnesota Press, 1984), 134–7, 209–10. For further discussion see Kenneth P. Winkler, *Berkeley: An Interpretation* (Oxford: Clarendon Press, 1989), 3–14, 46–8, 74–5, and 298–309.
19. This is perhaps too simple, because a particular idea of sense will resemble an abstract idea in signifying indifferently a great many ideas of the same type. A particular wisp of smoke, for example, often signifies fire, rather than some fire in particular. But it remains true that the

language of nature includes nothing analogous to "force" and "grace," as described in Section IV.

20. Margaret Atherton, *Berkeley's Revolution in Vision* (Ithaca: Cornell University Press, 1990), 106. See also Chapter 4 of this volume.
21. This is, at any rate, the usual view, as sketched for example by A. A. Luce at *Works* 1: 231. Luce distinguishes there between "the divine visual language of the Essay [on vision]," in which ideas of vision are alone symbolic, and "the divine sensible language of the *Principles*," in which "tangible data and tangible things also form a universal language, and so do the data and things of the other senses." But in *Alciphron*, Euphranor seems to deny that nonvisual ideas can form a language; see ALC 4.12 (157).
22. On signs as indications, and on the role of this conception in Locke's doctrine of signs, see Walter R. Ott, "Locke and Signification," *Journal of Philosophical Research* 27 (2002): 449–73, and his book *Locke's Philosophy of Language* (Cambridge: Cambridge University Press, 2004), 7–33. Ott discusses Berkeley briefly in his article (471) and more extensively in his book (117–29).
23. Locke also calls attention to this phenomenon. See *Essay* III.ii.6. Neither Locke nor Berkeley uses the word "transparency" in this connection, though. I believe the term was first used in connection with Berkeley by Richard J. Brook, "Berkeley's Theory of Vision: Transparency and Signification," *British Journal for the History of Philosophy* 11 (2003): 691–9.
24. Another statement of the argument appears in the *Defence of Free-thinking in Mathematics* 45 and 46. See also *De Motu* 47, where abstraction is called "the division of things truly inseparable."
25. Berkeley sometimes targets the assumption that every word has one precise and settled signification, but he finds this assumption objectionable, I think, only when it leads to the conclusion that every significant word stands for a distinct idea. If a word's signification is carried by what Berkeley at Introduction 18 calls its *definition* (as opposed to an idea for which it stands), he seems to agree that every word (or, to make room for ambiguity, every use of every word) has a precise and settled signification. As he observes, "'Tis one thing for to keep a name constantly to the same definition, and another to make it stand every where for the same idea: the one is necessary, the other useless and impracticable" (I 18).
26. I speak here as if ideas are causal agents, as Berkeley does when he says that they suggest other ideas. Later in the *Principles*, he will argue that ideas are entirely passive and inert (PHK 25). His final view of claims of the sort I make here is that they can be reinterpreted in a way that empties them of causal meaning (PHK 51, 65). Whether Berkeley is justified in his confidence is an interesting question: If knowing what

signification comes to depends on knowing what suggestion is, then analyzing suggestion noncausally, in terms of signification (along the lines suggested in PHK 65) would perhaps be circular.

27. For other statements of the exception, see PHK 2, 89, 135–40, and 142. The exception is endorsed by Philonous in DHP 3 [231–2]).
28. The way in which we attach significance to "God" closely resembles the way in which we attach significance to what Berkeley calls, even in the first edition of the *Principles*, "relative notions" or "relative ideas." (For "relative notion," see PHK 80; for "relative idea," see PHK 16 and DHP 1 [199]. At PHK 17 and 68, "relative notion" seems to mean *notion of relation.*) These are not the essentially non-sense-based conceptions of the second-edition revisions, but conceptions that depend on active inferential effort. Philonous provides helpful accounts of their formation in the *Dialogues*: In two different places (DHP 1 [197] and 2 [223]) he compares them to the kind of "direct and positive" notions that only acquaintance can provide. To form a relative notion of a thing (and to attach significance to the associated word) is to conceive of it in relation to something of which we already have some conception. To get the process started, we of course need nonrelative or "positive" notions: notions derived from immediate acquaintance, either with ideas or with the mind and its operations. I take it Berkeley assumes that when the process comes to an end, we have on hand a compact verbal formula that captures the newly achieved conception. My companion, for example, might be "the person who is causing the articulate sounds I am now hearing."
29. In Berkeley's second-edition uses of "notion," as in his positive account of abstract thinking, content and idea come apart. I take this to be further evidence in favor of the traditional understanding of Berkeleyan ideas that I put forward at the end of Section I.
30. Berkeley had put forward simpler versions of these claims in *De Motu*, and they are echoed briefly in *The Analyst*. Of the word *force*, for example, he writes in *De Motu* that it is often used "as if it meant a known quality, and one distinct from motion, figure, and every other sensible thing and also from every affection of the living thing" (5). Force so understood is an "occult quality." Properly understood, it is a mathematical hypothesis, a device for making predictions about the behavior of observed bodies. In Chapter 8, Lisa Downing examines the role of this conception of force in Berkeley's philosophy of science.
31. *Pragmatism: A New Name for Some Old Ways of Thinking* (Cambridge, MA: Harvard University Press, 1975), 28; further quotations are from 30.
32. The concluding question, insinuating that materialism encourages skepticism, already had been asked in the *Principles*, where it was also

cast in semiotic terms (PHK 20, culminating a line of argument that commences with PHK 18).

33. This is another Berkeleyan theme anticipated by Locke, for example at *Essay* III.i.1: "we should find, in all Languages, the names, which stand for Things that fall not under our Senses, to have had their first rise from sensible *Ideas*."
34. In *Alciphron*, the transference or substitution of signs is described at length. "As the mind is better acquainted with some sort of objects" than with others, because objects of the first sort are "earlier offered to it," for example, or because they "strike it more sensibly," or are easier to comprehend, "it seems naturally led to substitute those objects for such as are more subtle, fleeting, or difficult to conceive.... Hence figures, metaphors, and types. We illustrate spiritual things by corporeal, we substitute sounds for thoughts, and written letters for sounds; emblems, symbols, and hieroglyphics, for things too obscure to strike, and too various or too fleeting to be retained. We substitute things imaginable for things intelligible, sensible things for imaginable, smaller things for those that are too great to comprehend easily, and greater things for such as are too small to be discerned distinctly, present things for absent, permanent for perishing, and visible for invisible. Hence the use of models and diagrams" (7.13 [306]). Thus we speak of spirits "in a figurative style, expressing the operations of the mind by allusions and terms borrowed from sensible things, such as *apprehend, conceive, reflect, discourse*, and such-like." Here again, Berkeley's point is that we can speak figuratively while thinking literally.
35. The notion of God has already been drained of much of its content by this point in the discussion: God is a mind observing everything, but stolidly indifferent to it. As Lysicles points out (ALC 4.18 [164–5]), from so intellectualist a conception of the deity, nothing can be inferred about conscience, worship, or religion.

A. C. GRAYLING

6 Berkeley's argument for immaterialism

Berkeley's philosophical view is often described as an argument for "immaterialism", by which is meant a denial of the existence of matter (or more precisely, *material substance*). But he also, famously, argued in support of three further theses. He argued for idealism, the thesis that mind constitutes the ultimate reality. He argued that the existence of sensible things consists in their being perceived. And he argued that the mind which is the substance of the world is a single infinite mind – in short, God. These are four different theses, but they are intimately connected in Berkeley's presentation of them, the arguments for the first three sharing most of their premisses and steps. My chief purpose in what follows is to give an account of these arguments, their interactions, and the assumptions and methods underlying them. Doing so makes their strengths and weaknesses both conspicuous and perspicuous.

Berkeley's philosophical aim in arguing for these theses is to refute two kinds of skepticism. One is epistemological skepticism, which says that we cannot know the true nature of things because (familiarly) certain perceptual relativities and psychological contingencies oblige us to distinguish appearance from reality in such a way that knowledge of the latter is at least problematic and at worst impossible. The other is theological skepticism, which Berkeley calls "atheism", and which in his view includes not only views that deny the existence of a deity outright, but also deism, for which the universe subsists without a deity's continual creative activity. In opposing the first skepticism Berkeley took himself to be defending common sense and eradicating "causes of error and difficulty in the sciences." In opposing the second he took himself to be defending religion.

The attack on theological skepticism is effected on a metaphysical rather than doctrinal level in *A Treatise concerning the Principles of Human Knowledge* and *Three Dialogues between Hylas and Philonous*. Doctrinal questions receive more attention in such later writings as *Alciphron*. But in one important respect Berkeley saw his views as a fundamental contribution to natural theology, in that he thought they constitute a powerful new proof of the existence of a God.

Berkeley takes the root of skepticism to be the opening of a gap between experience and the world, forced by theories of ideas, like Locke's, which involve "supposing a twofold existence of the objects of sense, the one *intelligible*, or in the mind, the other real and without the mind" (PHK 86). Skepticism arises because "for so long as men thought that *real* things subsisted without the mind, and that their knowledge was only so far forth *real* as it was conformable to *real things*, it follows, they could not be certain they had any real knowledge at all. For how can it be known, that the things which are perceived, are conformable to those which are not perceived, or exist without the mind?" (PHK 86) The nub of the problem is that if we are acquainted only with our own perceptions, and never with the things which are supposed to lie beyond them, how can we hope for knowledge of those things, or even be justified in asserting their existence?

Berkeley's predecessors talked of *qualities* inhering in *matter* and causing ideas in us which *represent* or even *resemble* those qualities. *Matter* or *material substance* is a technical concept in metaphysics, denoting a supposed corporeal basis underlying the qualities of things. Berkeley was especially troubled by the un-empiricist character of this view. If we are to be consistent in our empiricist principles, he asked, how can we tolerate the concept of something which by definition is empirically undetectable, lying hidden behind the perceptible qualities of things as their supposed basis or support? If the concept of matter cannot be defended, we must find a different account of experience and knowledge. Berkeley summarises his diagnosis of the source of skepticism, and signals the positive theory he has in response to it, in a pregnant remark in his notebooks (also known as the *Philosophical Commentaries*): "The supposition that things are distinct from Ideas takes away all real Truth, & consequently brings in a Universal Skepticism, since all our knowledge is confin'd barely to our own Ideas" (N 606).

A point that requires immediate emphasis is that Berkeley's denial of the existence of matter is not a denial of the existence of the external world and the physical objects it contains, such as tables and chairs, mountains and trees. Nor does Berkeley hold that the world exists only because it is thought of by any one or more finite minds. In one sense of the term "realist", indeed, Berkeley is a realist, in holding that the existence of the physical world is independent of finite minds, individually or collectively. What he argues instead is that its existence is not independent of Mind.

I. BERKELEY'S "NEW PRINCIPLE"

Berkeley's answer to skepticism, therefore, is to deny that there is a gap between experience and the world – in his and Locke's terminology; between ideas and things – by asserting that things *are* ideas. The argument is stated with admirable concision in *Principles* 1–6, its conclusion being the first sentence of *Principles* 7: "From what has been said, it follows, that there is not any other substance than *spirit*, or that which perceives." All the rest of the *Principles*, the *Three Dialogues*, and parts of his later writings consist in expansion, clarification, and defense of this thesis. The argument is as follows.

Berkeley begins in Lockean fashion by offering an inventory: The "objects of human knowledge" are "either ideas actually imprinted on the senses, or such as are perceived by attending to the passions and operations of the mind, or lastly ideas formed by help of memory and imagination, either compounding, dividing, or barely representing those originally perceived in the aforesaid ways" (PHK 1). Ideas of sense – colors, shapes, and the rest – are "observed to accompany each other" in certain ways; "collections" of them "come to be marked by one name, and so to be reputed one thing", for example an apple or tree (PHK 1).

Besides these ideas there is "something which knows or perceives them"; this "perceiving, active being is what I call *mind, spirit, soul* or *myself*,"and it is "entirely distinct" from the ideas it perceives (PHK 2).

It is, says Berkeley, universally allowed that our thoughts, passions, and ideas of imagination do not "exist without the mind." But it is "no less evident that the various sensations or ideas imprinted on the sense, however blended or combined together (that is, whatever objects they compose) cannot exist otherwise than in a mind perceiving them" (PHK 3).

From these claims it follows that the gap between things and ideas vanishes. If things are collections of qualities, and qualities are sensible ideas, and sensible ideas exist only in mind, then what it is for a thing to exist is for it to be perceived – in Berkeley's phrase, to be is to be perceived: *esse* is *percipi*. "For what is said of the absolute [that is, mind-independent] existence of unthinking things [ideas or collections of ideas] without any relation to their being perceived, that seems perfectly unintelligible. Their *esse* is *percipi*, nor is it possible that they should have any existence, out of the minds or thinking things which perceive them" (PHK 3).

Berkeley knows that this claim is surprising, so he remarks that although people think that sensible objects like mountains and houses have an "absolute", that is, perception-independent, existence, reflection on the points just made show that this is a contradiction. "For what," he asks, "are the aforementioned objects but the things we perceive by sense, and what do we perceive besides our own ideas or sensations; and is it not plainly repugnant [illogical, contradictory] that any of these or any combination of them should exist unperceived?" (PHK 4)

The source of the belief that things can exist apart from perception of them is the doctrine of "abstract ideas", which Berkeley attacks in his Introduction to the *Principles*. Abstraction consists in separating things which can be separated only in thought but not in reality (for example the colour and the extension of a surface), or in noting a feature common to many different things, and attending only to that feature and not its particular instantiations. In this way we arrive at the "abstract idea" of, say, redness, apart from any particular red object (I 6–17). Abstraction is a falsifying move; what prompts the "common opinion" about houses and mountains is that we abstract existence from perception, and so come to believe that things can exist unperceived. But because things are ideas, and because ideas exist only if perceived by minds, the notion of "absolute existence without the mind" (in other words, without reference to mind) is a contradiction (PHK 5).

So, says Berkeley, to say that things exist is to say that they are perceived, and therefore "so long as they are not perceived by me, or do not exist in my mind or that of any created spirit, they must either have no existence at all, or else subsist in the mind of some eternal spirit" (PHK 6). And from this it follows that "there is not any other substance than *spirit*, or that which perceives" (PHK 7).

In sum, the argument is this: The things we encounter in episodes of perceptual experience – apples, stones, trees – are collections of "ideas". Ideas are the immediate objects of awareness. To exist they must be perceived; they cannot exist "without the mind". Therefore mind is the substance of the world.

Berkeley's defence of this argument from *Principles* 7 onwards reveals the machinery that drives it, consisting of the interplay between three crucial commitments and the application of an analytic method which requires us to recognise three different levels of explanation – whose own interrelations, in turn, are pivotal to his case.[1]

II. THE MACHINERY OF BERKELEY'S ARGUMENT

Let us take the question of the three levels first. Berkeley distinguishes between "strict", "speculative", or "philosophical" ways of understanding matters, and ordinary or "vulgar" ways of doing so. When we "think with the wise" we find it necessary to give explanations at what I shall label "level 1" and "level 3." When we "talk with the vulgar" we do so at "level 2" (see, for example, PHK 34–40, esp. PHK 37; 45–8, DHP 3 [234–5], N 274).

Level 1 concerns the *phenomenology* of experience, consisting of the data of sensory awareness in the form of minima of colour, sound, and so for the other senses. Level 2 concerns the *phenomena* of experience – the tables, trees, and so forth, that we see and touch in the normal course of perception. The phenomenological level (call it level 1) is apparent to us only on a "strict and speculative" examination of experience. Level 2 phenomena are constituted by level 1 data – not reductively, but mediated in a way revealed by a third, metaphysical, level of explanation (level 3), which describes the causal-intentional activity of mind (ultimately, of an infinite mind) in producing the level 1 data and the level 2 world constituted for us by the organization, coherence, and character of the level 1 data (PHK 25–9, 51–2, DHP 2 [216]).

The analysis can be illustrated by Berkeley's account of causality, which is fundamental to his thesis (PHK 25–9, 51–2, DHP 2 [216]). At level 3 the world is described as consisting of spirits (minds) and their ideas. Spirits are active, ideas inert. What we take at level 2 to be a case of natural causality – the heat of a fire causing water in a kettle to boil – is, strictly, a succession of individual ideas (composed of level 1 data) caused in us by God (level 3) in such a way that the regularity and consistency of their relations establishes in us a custom of thinking in the familiar level 2 way. This application of the distinction of levels provides, moreover, the basis of the proto-positivistic philosophy of science sketched by Berkeley later in the *Principles* (86–117).

It is a common mistake among commentators to describe Berkeley as a phenomenalist. The distinction of levels shows why they are wrong. Briefly, classical phenomenalism is the view that physical objects are ("logical") constructions out of actual and possible sense-data. The modal adjectives in that sentence serve to explain how the desk in my study exists when not currently being perceived, by showing that we take as true a counterfactual conditional stating that the desk could be perceived if any perceiver were suitably placed. That indeed defines what, on the phenomenalist view, it is for such objects to exist – namely, as at least enduring possibilities of perception. An essential commitment of phenomenalism, therefore, is that certain counterfactuals are to be taken as barely (that is, nonreductively) true; which says, in material mode, that the world contains irreducible possibilia.

Berkeley's view is completely different. The *esse* is *percipi* principle requires that a thing must be perceived – actually perceived – in order to exist. The perceivability of my desk when it is not currently being perceived (by a finite mind) is therefore cashed in terms of its actually being perceived (by an infinite mind). In phenomenalism there are only levels 1 and 2. It is a familiar problem for phenomenalism that level 2 cannot be reduced to level 1 without remainder, and that therefore level 1 can be sufficient for level 2 only if suitably supplemented. The supplement is acceptance of the bare truth of appropriate counterfactuals (and thus an ontology of possibilia). This exacts a high price for the explanatory shortfall. But for Berkeley there is no such shortfall; his third level of explanation shows how level 1 constitutes level 2, and simultaneously gives us a simple account of counterfactuals by having their truth-conditions fully statable in indicative terms: "If I were in my study I would see my desk" is true just in case "My desk is perceived by the infinite mind" is true (= "the desk exists"). So on Berkeley's view possibility is relative to finite minds only – for the infinite mind, whatever is, is actual. (Whether any of it is also necessary is of course a different and further matter.)[2]

Many of the difficulties standardly alleged in Berkeley's argument vanish when understood in light of the three-level analysis. Illustrations of this occur in due place further on.

As noted, three crucial commitments interact with the distinction-of-levels thesis to underwrite Berkeley's argument. They are commitments to empiricism, to the epistemic character of modality, and, as we have already seen, to the vacuity of the notion of abstract ideas. It might be more accurate to describe the first two as commitments and the third as the conclusion of an argument; but because the first two are premisses of that argument, and because all three powerfully combine in the process of refuting skepticism and establishing spirit as the only possible substance, it is convenient to take them together.

Berkeley is a rigorous empiricist; we are not entitled to assert, believe, or regard as meaningful, anything not justified by experience.[3] The constraint is applied austerely: Level 2 is exhaustively explained by level 1 under government of the level 3 causal-intentional story (see for example PHK 38). It might appear that Berkeley is less rigorous in his empiricism than Hume because he introduces the notion of "notions"[4] to explain our knowledge of spirit (other minds and God), which expressly seems to involve a nonsensuous epistemic source, and therefore to conflict with his notebook commitment to the strong principle *nihil est in intellectu quod non prius fuit in sensu* [nothing is in the intellect that is not first in sense] (N 779). But we should allow Berkeley at least as much latitude as Locke claims in countenancing intellectual sources of experience. In this sense notions are the counterpart of "ideas" in Berkeley's sense (mental contents) in the experience of encountering minds through a certain class of their effects. Of course, the ideas that constitute the world are the effects of God's causal influence on our sensory modalities, and are therefore encountered as level 2 physical objects in the standard way. But Berkeley argues that from the character of these ideas and their relations we grasp something further, which is that a particular sort of mind wills them. (This is part of his argument that the world's substance is a deity somewhat of the personal type offered in revealed religion.)[5] Parallel reasoning applies to finite spirits. In *De Motu* Berkeley discusses the kind of experience that has self-awareness as its object; he calls it "reflexion" (DM 40). But at *Principles* 27 and elsewhere we learn that we have knowledge of spirit by its effects, and infer therefore that notions, too, are the objects of awareness – a second-order awareness, so to speak, consisting in grasp of the significance of ideas acquired in the standard sensory way. The signal point is that without experience *as such* we do not come by notions; so Berkeley's empiricism is unequivocal (PHK 22, DHP 1 [200]).[6]

The second and third commitments – that possibility is an epistemic concept, viz. *conceivability*; and that there are no abstract ideas – arise from the first (I 9 et seq., PHK 4, DHP 1 [177], 3 [194]).[7] His chief form of argument is indeed a conceivability argument: We cannot conceive colour apart from extension, ideas apart from mind, existence apart from perception (PHK 4, 7; I 8, 9). In both cases the dependence on the empirical commitment is direct. Concepts lack content unless they are empirically derived; the thesis is forcefully stated in the *New Theory of Vision* where Berkeley asks whether it is possible for anyone "to frame in his mind a distinct abstract idea of visible extension or figure exclusive of all colour: and on the other hand, whether he can conceive colour without visible extension?" and replies, "For my own part, I must confess I am not able to attain so great a nicety of abstraction: in a strict sense, I see nothing but light and colours, with their several shades and variations" (NTV 130). To "frame in the mind" is to conceive; the "strict sense" is the level 1 or phenomenological sense; concepts of extension and figure therefore derive their content wholly from their experiential source, namely, visual minima of "light and colour".

There is an important point to be noted at this juncture, anticipated in the presentation given above of Berkeley's argument in the opening sections of the *Principles*. It is that where Berkeley uses his habitual locution "without the mind," we do better to use "without reference to mind". The point of this recommendation is illustrated by what is at stake in contemporary debates about "realism" and "antirealism". In this connection realism is the claim that the entities in a given domain exist independently of knowledge or experience of them. The antirealist denies this. One way of sketching why he denies it is offered by the idiom of relations. Thus recast, realism is the view that the relation between thought or experience and their objects is contingent or external, in the sense that description of neither relatum essentially involves reference to the other. On the antirealist's view, to take the thought-object relation as external is a mistake at least for the direction object-to-thought, because any account of the content of thoughts about things, and in particular the individuation of thoughts about things, essentially involves reference to the things thought about. This is the force of the least that can be said in favor of notions of broad content. Thus realism appears to offer a peculiarly hybrid relation: external in the direction thought-to-things; internal in the direction things-to-thought. It is a short step for the antirealist to argue that thought about (perception of, theories of) things is always and inescapably present in, and therefore conditions, any full account of the things thought about. The poorly-worded "Master Argument" in Berkeley, aimed at showing that one cannot conceive of an unconceived thing, is aimed at making just that elementary point (PHK 23, DHP 1 [200]).[8] The best example of such a view is afforded by the Copenhagen interpretation of quantum theory, in which descriptions of quantum phenomena are taken *essentially* to involve reference to observers and conditions of observation. Such a view does not constitute a claim that the phenomena are caused by observations of them; no more does antirealism claim this in respect of the subject-matters in which it argues its case, for it is not a metaphysical but an epistemological thesis. This is why antirealism is not idealism, for idealism is a metaphysical thesis about the constitution of reality (namely, that reality is mental), not, as antirealism is, an epistemological thesis about the relation of thought or experience to that reality.[9] In expressing his view, the antirealist therefore does best to say, "Anti-realism is the thesis that, with respect to a given domain, any full description of the objects of thought or experience in that domain has to make essential reference to the thinker or experiencer and the conditions under which the thinking or experience occurs."

And this is the least that Berkeley means by "within the mind". Of course, it is clear that Berkeley is not only an antirealist but also an idealist, and that the latter, metaphysical, thesis depends crucially on his argument for the former, epistemological, thesis. The fact that antirealism and idealism are independent theses (one can be committed to either without being committed to the other) is masked in Berkeley's case by the fact that his "in the mind" idiom does duty both for "with essential reference to mind" and "made of mind-stuff". It is not hard to know, however, which reading is intended at any point in his exposition.

III. THE ARGUMENT RESTATED

Equipped with this account of Berkeley's commitments and method, we can restate his argument as follows. If we examine the phenomenology of consciousness (level 1) we see that it consists of sensory data, notions, and compounds of either or both of these. Experience is generally orderly, giving rise to the familiar phenomena of level 2 – apples and trees, stones and books (PHK 1). We are also intimately acquainted with ourselves as the subjects of this experience, and not merely as passive recipients of it but causally active participants who imagine, will, and remember (PHK 2). Nothing of level 1 can be conceived without reference to the minds for which they exist as the contents of consciousness. But because the phenomena of level 2 are constituted by data of level 1, neither can the phenomena of level 2 be conceived independently of the minds for which they are phenomena (PHK 3). It is commonly held that sensible objects exist independently of mind, but this, on the foregoing, is a contradiction which rests on the mistaken doctrine of abstraction (PHK 4, 5). It follows that the only substance there can be is mind or spirit (PHK 6, 7).

The argument has made no explicit mention of material substance; the first full-dress appearance of matter, as the focus of "received opinion" in this debate, has to wait a further ten paragraphs (PHK 16–17). The denial of its possibility has already been registered, though, for if things are ideas, and ideas are essentially mental, then nothing other than mind can substantiate them. The doctrine that there is "unthinking stuff," which is the substance of things *qua* collections of ideas is accordingly an obvious "repugnancy" (contradiction): for how can an unthinking thing have ideas? (PHK 7).

A crucial consideration for Berkeley in rejecting the concept of material substance is that there are no empirical grounds for it; its philosophical supporters (he has Locke in mind) "acknowledge they have no other meaning annexed to those sounds, but the idea of being in general, together with the relative notion of its supporting accidents" (PHK 17). Berkeley finds the concept of "being in general" the most "abstract and incomprehensible" he has ever encountered, and he has no time for the metaphor of "support" invoked to explain the relation between matter and its accidents. But more importantly still, the only thing which we are entitled to say is causally efficacious is spirit or mind (PHK 26–7); ideas are the effects of the causal activity of mind, whether our own or that of an infinite spirit (PHK 28–33).

In the course of unfolding his argument Berkeley tells us that although there is a distinction between primary and secondary qualities, they are the same in one crucial respect: They are both *sensible* properties, and therefore cannot exist otherwise than as ideas, and therefore again cannot exist otherwise than in relation to mind (PHK 9–15). He also points out that because nothing but an idea can be like an idea, the seductive thought that ideas are resemblances or copies which represent nonideas makes no sense. Can we, he asks, "assert that a colour is like something which is invisible; hard or soft, like something which is intangible; and so of the rest"? (PHK 8).

IV. IDEAS, PERCEPTION, AND MIND

A key concept in the foregoing is that of ideas. Berkeley uses "idea" to mean "any immediate object of sense or understanding", but as already noted he is careful to distinguish this from what, in the second paragraph of the *Principles*, he had described as "such as are perceived by attending to the passions and operations of the mind", which he later calls *notions*. The distinction is as follows. Ideas are always *sensory*; they are either the content of states of sensory awareness, or the copies of these in memory and imagination. *Notions* on the other hand are concepts of spirit – of self, mind, and God – and have a more complex origin. As regards self-knowledge, notions originate in immediate intuition; as regards other minds, in interpretation; and as regards God, in "reflexion and reasoning" (PHK 42, 140–2, DHP 3 [232]).

Two features of ideas are crucial for Berkeley: their *inertness*; and their *mind-dependence*. They are the latter simply in virtue of being ideas. Their being the former is a more intricate matter. Anticipating Hume, Berkeley argues that there are no necessary connections between ideas; they are individual entities "with no power or agency included in them. So that one idea or object of thought cannot produce or make an alteration in another" (PHK 25). We verify this by introspecting, which reveals, says Berkeley, that "there is nothing in [ideas] but what we perceive", and we perceive no power or activity in them (PHK 25). We have a "continual succession" of ideas, some arising and others disappearing; but because they are causally inert, they are not themselves responsible for these changes, so there must be some other cause of them (PHK 26). The only candidate remaining for this role is spirit or mind. Because my mind is causally responsible for very few ideas and their changes, there must be "some other spirit that produces them" (PHK 29).

Berkeley gives the name *perception* to any way of having ideas and notions before the mind, in sensing, conceiving, imagining, remembering, reasoning, and the rest. It is accordingly a generic term, and is not restricted to sensory perception alone. "Perceiving" involves a causal relation: Minds perceive ideas either by causing them (as when finite minds imagine or dream, and as when the infinite mind wills the existence of the universe) or by being causally affected by them (as when finite minds receive the ideas caused by God = encounter the physical world).

Any inference to the nature of the spirit that is causally responsible for ideas and their changes must start from the nature of those ideas and their changes. "The ideas of sense", says Berkeley, again anticipating Hume, "are more strong, lively, and distinct than those of imagination; they have likewise a steadiness, order, and coherence, and are not excited at random, as those which are the effects of human wills often are, but in a regular train or series" (PHK 30). These "set rules or methods" we call "*Laws of Nature*; and these we learn by experience, which teaches us that such and such ideas are attended with such and such other ideas, in the ordinary course of things" (PHK 30). From this Berkeley concludes that God, the "Author of Nature," is the ultimate source of ideas and their connections.

From this, in turn, it follows that although everything that exists is mind-dependent, it is not dependent on particular or finite minds, but has an objective source and structure, namely, the eternal, ubiquitous and law-like perceiving of an infinite mind. This is the sense in which Berkeley is a realist: the world exists independently of the thought and experience of finite minds (DHP 2 [210–11]). This explains what he means by claiming to defend common sense, because common sense holds that grass is green and the sky is blue whether or not any of us happen to be looking at either, whereas Locke and the corpuscularians held otherwise – that grass has powers to make us see green, but it is not itself green. Indeed, on the Lockean view as Berkeley understands it, the world is colourless, odorless, and silent until perceived, and then it produces in the perceiver visual, olfactory, and auditory experiences. For Berkeley, though, the world is just as we perceive it to be even when we are not perceiving it, because it is always and everywhere perceived by the infinite mind of a deity.

The deity perceives the universe by thinking it, that is, causing it to exist by conceiving it. In a letter to the American Dr Samuel Johnson, Berkeley remarks that his view differs only verbally from the theological doctrine that God maintains the universe in existence by an act of continual creation.[10] So the ideas which constitute the world are caused by the deity, and appear in our consciousnesses as the effects of his causal activity: this is the *metaphysical* way (level 3) of describing what, in ordinary terminology, we describe as seeing trees, tasting ice cream, and so forth. The latter way of describing the facts is not incorrect; Berkeley's argument is that the ordinary and the metaphysical ways of describing reality are alternative descriptions of the same thing.

A significant feature of this account is its view of causality. Locke had argued that the empirical basis for our concept of causality comes from our own felt powers as agents, able to initiate and intervene in trains of events in the world. This sense of our own efficacy we "project" onto the world to explain chains of events in it, imputing to events we describe as "causes" an agency or power on analogy with our own. For Berkeley, the projective move is empirically ungrounded. We indeed have experience of causal agency as spirits, which are the only active things we know. But although it is a convenience to impute causal agency to things (ideas) in our ordinary way of talking, they are inert, and apparent causal connections between them are ultimately owed to the regular, consistent, law-like causal activity of God.

V. THE ARGUMENT'S RESILIENCE TO OBJECTIONS

It is obvious that Berkeley's theory rests upon a vital and very debatable assumption, borrowed unquestioningly from Locke who equally unquestioningly borrowed it from the Cartesians – namely that the place to begin philosophical inquiry is among the private data of individual consciousness, that is, among the ideas constituting an individual's experience. If one accepts this Cartesian super-premiss (a large "if"), the early part of Berkeley's argument appears persuasive, as may be seen by considering a proposed objection to it, namely, that it commits the elementary error of identifying sensible qualities and sensory ideas; for – says the objection – there is a large difference between "the table is brown" and "the table looks brown to me", because the truth-conditions of the two statements differ. The table could be brown without it seeming so to me, and vice versa; so Berkeley's argument collapses.

But this argument begs the question against Berkeley by assuming that claims about what qualities an object possesses are independent of claims about how they can be known to possess them, which amounts to the claim that there are observation-independent facts about the qualities of objects which can be stated without any reference to experience of them. But this claim is exactly what Berkeley rejects, on the grounds that any characterization of a sensible quality has to make essential reference to how it appears to some actual or possible perceiver. How, he asks, does one explain redness, smoothness, and other sensible qualities independently of how they appear? The objection fails by premissing a seems/is distinction which is precisely what Berkeley opposes on the grounds that it leads to skepticism.

To deny that there is a seems/is distinction is just another way of asserting that sensible objects (things in the world) are collections of sensible qualities, and hence of ideas. So Berkeley takes the contrast he wishes to resist to be one between (a) sensible objects, which as collections of sensible qualities are what is immediately perceived, and (b) objects existing independently of perception but causing it. This is not the same contrast as between (c) sense data in the sense of uninterpreted contents of sensory states, and (a) sensible objects. It is important to note this, because for Berkeley what is immediately present in experience is the sensible object, not some mediating representation (or collection of representations) different from the object. We do not, he says, infer from colour patches and other sensory data to the existence, in a world beyond them, of books and trees; what we see (and touch, and so forth) are, immediately, books and trees.

This, however, prompts another objection, this time that Berkeley is having things both ways: He says that we immediately perceive such familiar objects of sense-experience as books and trees, while at the same time saying that what we immediately perceive are colours and textures. To see what is involved here, consider an argument advanced in more recent philosophy, which says that books and trees are interpretations of, or inferences from, the sensory data of experience. In speaking of books rather than colour-patches, we are going beyond what talk of colour patches strictly licenses. This is because we take physical objects to exist independently of particular perceivings of them, to be publicly available to more than one perceiver at a time, and so on – none of which is true of the sensory ideas from which they are inferred. So we have to keep (a) and (c) strictly separate.

Berkeley can be defended against this objection by appealing to the distinction of levels. At level 1 we immediately perceive colours and textures, while at level 2 we immediately perceive books and trees. The latter consist wholly of the former, and it is only if one disregards the distinction of levels that one might fall into the mistake of thinking that when one perceives a smooth red book, one perceives redness and smoothness *and* a book, as if the book were something additional to the sensible qualities constituting it. Just such a view is forced by the materialist view, in which something inaccessible to sensory awareness constitutes the underlying causal origin of the sensible qualities we perceive.

Some critics object that having thus argued that all perception is immediate, Berkeley promptly proceeds to admit a species of *mediate* perception by inference or "suggestion". The passage cited is the one where Berkeley says, "When I hear a coach drive along the streets, immediately I perceive only the sound; but from the experience I have had that such a sound is connected with a coach, I am said to hear the coach" (DHP 1 [204]). This might count as a case of mediate perception if Berkeley did not immediately add, "It is nevertheless evident, that in truth and strictness, nothing can be *heard* but *sound*: and the coach is not then properly perceived by sense, but suggested from experience." The same applies to our practice of saying elliptically that one sees that the poker is hot; again, one does not see heat, one sees *that* something is hot; one infers on the basis of experience that when something looks like that, it will feel a certain way if you touch it. These are not cases of mediate perception, but of experience-based inference, to which Berkeley gives the name "suggestion": the ideas of one sense *suggest* the ideas of another.

The foregoing shows that as long as certain of Berkeley's premisses are accepted, and as long as discussion of the main plank of his views (the notion of God and his metaphysical activity) is deferred, his views are resilient to objection. If we reject the Cartesian superpremiss – that the place to start is the data of individual experience – his views are not so resilient.[11]

These remarks touch upon one set of objections to Berkeley's views. Others, more threatening to his position, concern its underpinning, namely the infinite mind to which a central metaphysical role is allotted. This is discussed below.

VI. MATTER AND MATERIALISM

The concept of matter is redundant, Berkeley's argument purports to demonstrate, because everything required to explain the world and experience of it is available in recognizing that minds and ideas are all there can be. Nevertheless Berkeley adds to this argument-by-exclusion a set of positive antimaterialist considerations.

An important argument for materialism is that use of a concept of matter explains much in science. Berkeley summarises the view thus: "There have been a great many things explained by matter and motion: take away these, and you destroy the whole corpuscular philosophy, and undermine those mechanical principles which have been applied with such success to account for the phenomena. In short, whatever advances have been made... in the study of nature, do all proceed on the supposition that corporeal substance or matter doth really exist" (PHK 50). Berkeley's reply is that science's explanatory power and practical utility neither entail the truth of, nor depend upon, the materialist hypothesis, for these can equally (if not better, because more economically) be explained in instrumentalist terms. Instrumentalism is the view that scientific theories are tools, and as such are not candidates for assessment as true or false, but rather as more or less useful. One does not ask whether a gardening utensil such as a spade is true, but whether it does its intended job effectively – and not merely effectively, but, as required by Ockham's Razor, as simply and economically as possible.

Berkeley expressed his early version of instrumentalism as a "doctrine of signs", in which the regularity and order among our ideas reflect the steady will of God, which is so reliable that we can represent the connections thus observed as laws. He writes, "the steady, consistent methods of Nature, may not unfitly be styled the *language* of its Author, whereby he . . . directs us how to act for the convenience and felicity of life" (PHK 109). Science is thus a convenient summary, for sublunary purposes, of what at the metaphysical level of explanation would be described in terms of the activity of infinite spirit.

This is a rejoinder to an attempted "appeal to the best explanation" on behalf of the materialist hypothesis. It is at the same time a rejoinder to a closely allied argument, an "appeal to the simplest explanation". This says that postulating the existence of matter simplifies the account we give of the world. The rejoinder consists in the same slash of Ockham's Razor; it is that because experience could be exactly as it is without matter existing independently of it, the materialist hypothesis is not the simplest explanation after all.

But the key point for Berkeley is that whatever else matter is, by definition: (a) it is nonmental, and as such cannot be the support of qualities, because qualities are ideas, and ideas can only exist in a thinking substance; and (b) it is inert, that is, causally inactive, and so cannot produce change, motion, or ideas.

For Locke and others among Berkeley's predecessors the concept of primary qualities was important because, they held, experience of them puts us most closely in touch with independent reality. Berkeley rejects their view on the ground already mentioned, that "nothing can be like an idea but an idea" (PHK 8). Materialists hold that primary qualities are "resemblances" of "things which exist without the mind" (PHK 9); but because primary qualities are ideas, and only ideas can resemble ideas, it follows that "neither they nor their archetypes can be in an unperceiving substance" (PHK 9). Moreover, as also already noted, the primary-secondary quality distinction, understood in terms of a supposed difference between the way each kind of quality relates to mind, involves a specious abstraction of one kind from the other; for, since one cannot conceive such primary qualities as motion or number apart from such secondary qualities as colour, both are on a par in the way they relate to mind, viz. by being essentially dependent upon mind for their existence as ideas.

Some of Berkeley's critics think he failed to separate the question of material substance from that of the primary-secondary quality distinction, because one can reject materialism while retaining the distinction. But this in fact is what Berkeley does, for he does not deny that there is a distinction between primary and secondary qualities – he recognises that the former are available to more than one sense at a time, the latter to one sense only; the former are measurable, the latter not (or not so straightforwardly); and so on. He points out that in the *crucial* respect of their relation to mind, however, they are on a par in both being *sensible* and hence mind-dependent.

VII. THE MIND-IDEA RELATION

One charge levelled at Berkeley is that his account of the crucial relation between minds and ideas is contradictory or at very least confused. At *Principles* 2 he says that the mind "is a thing *entirely distinct* from [ideas], *wherein they exist*, or, which is the same thing, whereby they are perceived" (my emphases). At *Principles* 5 he adds that it is not possible to conceive "any sensible thing or object *distinct from* the sensation or perception of it," and in the same paragraph he remarks, "is it possible to separate, even in thought, my ideas from perception? For my part, I might as easily divide a thing from itself." These assertions appear to commit him to three principles which together are inconsistent, each of which plays an important part in his argument.[12]

The three principles have been called the *Distinction Principle*, asserting that minds and ideas are distinct from one another (PHK 2, 27, 80, 142), the *Inherence Principle*, asserting that ideas exist only in the mind (PHK 2, 3, and throughout), and the *Identity Principle*, asserting that ideas are not distinct from perceivings of them

(PHK 5, DHP 1 [195 ff]). The second and third are consistent; the first and third appear to contradict each other; and the relation between the first two at the very least demands explanation.

Most critics think that the best solution is to abandon the Distinction Principle. One reason is that it appears to commit Berkeley to an *act-object* analysis of perception, whereas the Identity Principle commits him to an *adverbial* analysis. The first describes perceiving as an act of mind directed upon an object, rather as the beam of a torch is directed upon something we wish to illuminate; the object is independent of the act, which can be repeated with different objects (the act of looking, like the beam of the torch, can have as its successive objects a book, a cat, a desk). The adverbial analysis has it that perception is a modification of the mind, so that, for example, to see a cat is to have one's mind shaped or modified into a "catly-perceiving state". Here there is one event – the modification of one's mental states in a certain way – whereas on the act-object analysis there is the mental act and something independent of it, that is, its object. Because this analysis demands the *independence* of the objects of perception, which on Berkeley's theory are ideas and hence incapable of independence from mind, the Distinction Principle seems to be the obvious candidate for rejection.

The principle is however crucial to Berkeley; the very plan of the *Principles* depends on it: "Human knowledge [reduces] to two heads, that of *ideas* and that of *spirits*" (PHK 86). And this is no surprise, because if the principle were rejected, minds would be identical with their ideas, but this cannot be, for Berkeley insists on the differences: minds are active, ideas inert; ideas are dependent entities, minds substantial. In the *Three Dialogues* Berkeley considered and rejected the notion (yet again anticipating Hume) that minds are just bundles of ideas, on the good ground that "a colour cannot perceive a sound, nor a sound a colour . . . therefore I am one individual principle, distinct from colour and sound; and, for the same reason, from all other sensible things and inert ideas" (DHP 3 [234]).

The Distinction Principle, therefore, cannot be abandoned. But neither can the others; the Inherence Principle, after all, is simply a version of *esse* is *percipi*, and the Identity Principle follows from the attack on abstraction, which tells us that we cannot abstract ideas from perception of them. Is there a solution?

There is; and it is to be found in recognising that the expressions "Inherence" and "Identity" are misleading. Berkeley does not hold that ideas "inhere" in the mind, as attributes are said to inhere in substance, nor that ideas and perception of them are identical. I take each point in turn.

The "Inherence" Principle states that "ideas exist in the mind". The formula "in the mind", as already noted, is to be understood as "with essential reference to mind", in the sense that the existence of an idea is dependent upon its being perceived – *actually*, not just *possibly*, perceived: recall that in Berkeley's theory everything that exists is actual. The sense of "dependence" here is that in which (to adapt an obstetric example of Plato's) an embryo is dependent on a womb: it exists in it, and cannot exist without it, but it is nevertheless distinct from it. "Inherence" is an adverbial notion, whereas Berkeley holds that ideas and minds stand in the internal causal relation denoted by the generic concept of perception: "There can be no substratum of... qualities but spirit, in which they exist, not by way of mode or property, but as a thing perceived in that which perceives it" (DHP 3 [237]).

As for the "Identity" Principle, it is a straightforward mistake to construe Berkeley's antiabstractionist view – namely, that any account of ideas cannot be abstracted from an account of perception – as amounting to an assertion of the identity of ideas with perception of them. The assertion that one cannot "conceive apart" any "sensible thing or object distinct from the perception of it" (PHK 5) is not a claim that these are numerically the same thing. Consider an example: bread and the process by which it is baked are internally related; there cannot be one without the other; but bread is not numerically identical with the baking of it. The same kind of internality characterises the relation of minds and ideas. As one would expect, that merely iterates the point made about the "Inherence" Principle.

The question of the mind-idea relation is important because it is the only major threat to the *internal* coherence of Berkeley's theory. These comments show that there is not after all such a threat. As before, it remains that the Cartesian basis of the project, and its linchpin metaphysical thesis that an infinite mind perceives everything always, are the two real problems with Berkeley's theory. It is time to consider the second of these.

VIII. SPIRIT AS SUBSTANCE

Berkeley took his arguments to amount to a new and powerful argument for the existence of a God. As such, they are a contribution to natural theology; nothing turns on revelation or traditional conceptions of deity, beyond that such a being has to be infinite and omnipotent. Indeed, Berkeley's arguments require no more than a metaphysical god thus conceived. Whether such a being is a single person, or whether it is interested in what it has created, for example, is neither here nor there, so long as it fulfils its function of making the universe exist.

The nub of Berkeley's argument for God is that because everything that exists is either mind or ideas, and because finite minds, even in concert, could not perceive all the ideas that constitute the universe, there must be an infinite mind which perceives everything always and thereby keeps it in being.

The classic statement of the argument occurs in the second of the *Three Dialogues* (DHP 2 [212–4]). From the proposition "that sensible things cannot exist otherwise than in a mind or spirit", Berkeley concludes "not that they have no real existence, but that seeing they depend not on my thought, and have an existence distinct from being perceived by me, *there must be some other mind wherein they exist.*" This conclusion is a weaker one than that there is a single infinite mind which perceives everything always; it establishes no more than that there is "some other mind" – who might for all we know be the next door neighbor. But in the very next sentence Berkeley adds, "As sure therefore as the sensible world really exists, so sure is there an infinite omnipresent spirit who contains and supports it." This is quite a leap. The missing step is provided later (DHP 2 [215]): "I perceive numberless ideas; and by an act of my Will can form a great variety of them, and raise them up in my imagination: though it must be confessed, these creatures of the fancy are not altogether so distinct, so strong, vivid, permanent, as those perceived by my senses, which latter are called *real things*. From all which I conclude, *there is a mind which affects me every moment with all the sensible impressions I perceive*. And from the variety, order and manner of these, I conclude the Author of them to be *wise, powerful, and good beyond comprehension.*" This "Author" Berkeley a few lines later describes as "God the Supreme and Universal Cause of all things". The missing step is, accordingly, a version of the teleological argument for the existence of a God.

The argument in fact has two stages. The first argues that things are causally dependent on mind for their existence, and therefore, because I cannot think of everything always, there must be mental activity elsewhere carrying out the task. The second stage says that one can infer the character of that mind by inspecting the nature of its ideas: because the universe is so huge, beautiful, intricate, and so on, it must be a "*wise, powerful*", and so on, mind.

The first thing to note is the inadequacy of the teleological argument here co-opted as the second stage. The appearance of design, purpose, or beauty in the universe does not entail that it was designed; and even if it did entail this, it does not thereby entail that it was designed by a single mind, or an infinite mind, or a good mind. (What if – regarding this last point – we reflected on the cruelty in nature, and the disease, waste, pain, and other evils abundant there? What picture of a creating mind would this suggest?) In any case there are more economical ways to explain the teleological appearance of the universe, the best being evolutionary theory.

What of the first stage? The most it establishes is the conclusion that what exists can do so only in relation to mind. The relation in question needs to be explained; Berkeley is committed to saying that it is a *causal* relation, but it is exactly this which pushes him to the unpersuasive second stage of the argument for an infinite mind. An alternative resource might be to say that there is no account to be given of the world which does not make essential reference to facts about thought or experience of it, and this might furnish the starting point for views like Kant's or those of certain contemporary "antirealists".

Although Berkeley does not need the God of traditional theology but only a metaphysical being causally competent for its task, his employment of teleological considerations mixes tradition with metaphysics to the injury of the latter. There is certainly no shadow of an argument why the mental activity to which the existence of the whole universe is referred has to be a single mind or an infinite one. A committee of finite minds might seem an even less palatable option, but nothing in the argument excludes it.

Upon inspection, accordingly, the argument for the metaphysical linchpin of Berkeley's theory does not work. If this does not entail the collapse of the project, it will be because there is some other way of substantiating the idea that what exists stands in an internal relation to thought or experience of it. On that score, philosophy is not without resources.

IX. CONCLUDING REMARKS

Other points in Berkeley's views repay further examination, for example his concept of conceivability, the character of his idealism, his views of time, and – as just suggested – the metaphysical implications of his arguments considered independently of their theistic basis. But enough has been said to suggest reasons for his influence on later thinkers, not least among them the phenomenalists and the logical positivists. It is in particular both interesting and philosophically important to understand why phenomenalism, as a version of Berkeley's theory in which the bare concept of "possibilities of perception" ("possibilia") has been substituted for the concept of a deity, is arguably less cogent than the original. From the point of view of acceptability there is little to choose between a metaphysics of possibilia and a theological basis for the universe, neither of which is especially attractive. At least in Berkeley's thesis, everything that exists is actual.

NOTES

1. I deal with the commitments and the three-level analysis in A. C. Grayling, *Berkeley: The Central Arguments* (London: Duckworth, 1986); see especially 22–49, but throughout for their application.
2. Grayling, *Berkeley*, 95–117.
3. The nuance to the effect that no belief or concept is contentful unless *either* acquired by *or* applicable to experience describes a form of empiricism that Berkeley doubtless would accept, but this is not his way of putting things.
4. Named as such only in the second edition of the *Principles*, but importantly present from the outset: See the first sentence of PHK 1 where "ideas of reflection" occur second on the list.
5. The argument is deeply flawed: I discuss it at length in Grayling, *Berkeley*, 183–203.
6. In *Berkeley* (28) I had characterized Berkeley as less thoroughgoing in his empiricism than Hume because of the apparently ambivalent status of notions. This marks a development of view.

7. Also see Grayling, *Berkeley*, 28–40. I shall not rehearse the detailed considerations that show Berkeley's epistemic rendering of possibility to be persuasive – it is a commitment shared widely by his contemporaries – but I should mention that "conceivability" and "imaginability" are to be sharply distinguished, the former being controlled strictly by empirical constraints on content, the latter consisting in something like the free play of fancy.
8. See Grayling, *Berkeley*, 113–7.
9. I argue this at greater length in *An Introduction to Philosophical Logic* (Oxford: Blackwell, 1998), 310–12, and *The Question of Realism* (Oxford: Oxford University Press, forthcoming).
10. *Works* 2: 281.
11. It must be said, in relation to this strategy, that in adopting such an approach one is well advised to keep sight of the subjective perspective, for any account of the nature of experience and its relation to knowledge has to be sensitive to the fact – for fact it is – that each subject of experience is to some degree in the solipsistic and finitary predicament which the Cartesian tradition emphasises. This remains so even if we argue, as we doubtless should, that assumptions about shared language and therefore a shared world, on we which we have a participant rather than a merely passive perspective, provide material for a better account.
12. This question has additional importance in that resolving it in the way I here propose contributes to settling a debate which has much exercised Berkeley scholars in recent decades: Edwin B. Allaire's "inherence pattern" argument, proposing that Berkeley's view is that because mind is the substance of the world, the relation that ideas bear to mind is that of inherence, and that "perceives" is explicated by "inheres in" ("Berkeley's Idealism," *Theoria* 29 [1963]: 229–44). See Robert G. Muehlmann, *Berkeley's Metaphysics: Structural, Interpretive, and Critical Essays* (University Park: Pennsylvania State University Press, 1995), especially the introduction and essays in Part I.

PHILLIP D. CUMMINS

7 Berkeley on minds and agency

I. THE SCARCITY OF BERKELEY'S PHILOSOPHY OF MIND

To demand a comprehensive, detailed, and fully documented account of the part of Berkeley's philosophy that pertains to the mind and its states is to demand the impossible. Unlike some prominent philosophers, Berkeley says too little, not too much. In his published writings he was completely silent on many central issues in the philosophy of mind. An example is animal minds. Neither the question do nonhuman animals[1] have consciousness, nor the question are they capable of reasoning, is addressed in *An Essay towards a New Theory of Vision, A Treatise concerning the Principles of Human Knowledge*, or *Three Dialogues between Hylas and Philonous*, the three early books on which Berkeley's present-day reputation for philosophical acumen is founded. On the rare occasions when Berkeley did address topics in the philosophy of mind, all too often they received only cursory treatment. An example is causation. Berkeley vigorously challenged the practice of positing material causes. He affirmed volitional causation by minds, yet he never offered a systematic characterization of his alternative. He answered several objections to his denial of nonmental causes, but ignored numerous questions raised by his positive thesis. Berkeley's account of causation is thus programmatic and promissory, as is his philosophy of mind in general.

Berkeley's projects in the three early works, especially the *Principles* – the central work – yield an explanation of why he said so little about mind despite its centrality for his philosophy. Consider the Introduction to the *Principles*. There he identifies those who deny human knowledge as the enemies of sound philosophy. It is they who "have first raised a dust, and then complain, we cannot see" (I 3). To combat these would-be skeptics and their dupes, Berkeley announced his intention "to try if I can discover what those principles are, which have introduced all that doubtfulness and uncertainty. . . ." [I 4]. The two chief principles that allegedly lead to skepticism, as well as irreligion and paradox, are, first, that humans can form and employ abstract general idea to secure general knowledge, and second, that sensible objects can have a real existence distinct from their being perceived. Berkeley attacked both principles, challenging the doctrine of abstract ideas in the Introduction and the principle of perception-independence of sensibles in many of the 156 numbered paragraphs that follow it. This latter material, as its label – Part I – implies, was intended to be only the first of several major divisions of the work. At least one subsequent part was to have provided a systematic account of mind and its activities. With those other parts unwritten or unavailable, we are left with Part I, a text devoted to denying the unperceived existence of sensible things, answering objections to that denial, and establishing the fruitfulness of its consequences.

Mind is discussed in the *Principles*, but chiefly in ways that reflect the overall goals of the book and the structure of the main text. Part I is best divided into three blocks. There is the initial presentation of immaterialism in Sections 1 through 33. In Sections 34 through 84 Berkeley states and answers objections to immaterialism. The final block of text, Sections 85 through 156, concerns consequences. Only the final sub-block (Sections 135 through 156) concerns minds. Not surprisingly for a book whose Preface targets as its audience those who want "a demonstration of the existence and immateriality of God, or the natural immortality of the soul," the *Principles* ends on those themes of primary importance to one claiming that sound philosophy can lead his readers to theism in general and Christianity in particular. The material that precedes the metaphysical/religious finale, Sections 135 through 145, considers chiefly the consequences of the sharp contrast between minds and ideas, which was introduced in Section 2 and expanded in Section 27. It is a sustained attempt to combat the skeptical inference that minds are beyond human knowledge because we lack ideas of them. Berkeley, of course, embraces and defends anew its minor premise that minds cannot be known by way of ideas. An idea is a mind-dependent sensible or a mind-dependent likeness of a sensible. Minds are not sensibles and cannot be represented by them or their images, because the only thing like an idea is an idea, and the two are utterly unlike. He rejects, however, the implied major premise that the only knowledge is knowledge of or through ideas. Though not by way of ideas, minds can be known. They even can be known to be immaterial and thus capable of nonbodily existence. Such is Berkeley's triumphant conclusion.

Detailed treatment of Berkeley's defense of knowledge of minds will come later. For now it is enough to call attention to the way this last sub-block fits with the other groups of text devoted to various types of knowledge, and the way in which the defense of knowledge (which dominates Berkeley's treatment of the consequences of immaterialism) fits the originally announced project of securing human knowledge against those who would portray us as perpetually lost in ignorance or confusion. In the *Principles* Berkeley may not have presented a detailed and comprehensive philosophy of mind, but without question he defended our cognitive access to minds – our own and others – and did so as part of his overall project of defending human knowledge.

As he made very clear from the outset, one of Berkeley's main goals in the *Three Dialogues* was establishing that immaterialism is neither skepticism in disguise nor a grand paradox designed solely to embarrass the new philosophy.[2] The chief philosophical claim about mind in the *Principles* (mind can be known, but not by way of ideas) is addressed again in the *Dialogues*, but is fitted into the project of showing that immaterialism can eliminate material substance without subverting either itself or commonsense knowledge. As I will show, this question of whether Berkeley has defended or subverted human knowledge greatly affects his treatment of mind in the *Dialogues*.

II. BERKELEY'S MAIN POSITIONS ON MINDS

It is not unreasonable to expect Berkeley's presentation of his philosophy of mind, narrowly circumscribed and epistemologically oriented though it is, to exhibit his main metaphysical positions clearly and straightforwardly on the weight of vigorously stated arguments. This expectation is at least partially met, provided one sticks with those few passages that explicitly state Berkeley's main positions about mind and its role in nature. Puzzles emerge, however, when one proceeds more comprehensively, analyzing arguments in depth and considering the implications for minds and their activities of arguments formulated on other topics. I shall first specify the primary positions, then examine the problems, especially those relating to the *Principles*.

There are minds wholly distinct from sensible objects

Not surprisingly, Berkeley's first commitment about minds is that there *are* minds. The first two sections of Part I of the *Principles* contrast ideas and minds while affirming the existence of both. Minds perceive ideas; ideas are perceived by minds. At this stage it is not made clear whether "idea" is equivalent to "object of knowledge" or is restricted in denotation to objects of sense and images employed in imagination to represent actual or possible objects of sense. In Section 2 Berkeley says of "mind," "spirit," "soul," and "my self" that these words "do not denote any one of my ideas, but a thing entirely distinct from them, wherein they exist, or, which is the same thing, whereby they are perceived; for the existence of an idea consists in being perceived." In the next four sections Berkeley develops arguments to support this final provocative thesis about ideas, leaving behind the question of the force and implications of "or, which is the same thing" in the passage above. More specifically, these questions linger: whether a purported relation, *existing in*, is being reduced to the relation, *being perceived by*; whether, instead, *being perceived by* is being reduced to *existing in*; or whether, finally, neither is being reduced to the other.

According to Berkeley, a mind is entirely distinct from any idea it perceives. This claim deserves more attention than it usually receives. One could claim with confidence that perceiving presupposes two relata, that which is perceived and that which perceives. This difference in relata is really a difference in roles. Perceiving requires something that perceives and something that is perceived. These two roles clearly are different, but this difference in role does not in itself imply numerical difference in the items that fills the roles. It only means that if there is something that is perceived, then there is also something that perceives, and conversely. To say that something moved implies a mover, and conversely that a mover implies something moved, is to leave open the question for any given case whether that which moves is self-moving or is moved by something else. Similarly, that perceiving presupposes both a perceived and a perceiver leaves open the question whether the perceiver perceives itself. If a mind is defined as that which perceives, and a sensible is defined as that which is or can be perceived – that is, if minds and sensibles are defined functionally – the difference between mind and sensible is clear enough. Indeed, sensibles could be said to imply minds and minds sensibles. Nonetheless, no issues regarding the numerical identity or diversity of minds and sensibles have been settled. One could so define mind and still consistently claim that on some occasions a perceiver can perceive itself, assigning perception to a body and claiming that in suitable circumstances it can perceive itself. To say otherwise requires additional arguments.

Berkeley's thesis that a mind is entirely distinct (wholly different) from any of its ideas – that is, from any item it perceives – must therefore be recognized as a substantive philosophical claim that goes beyond the truism that perceiving requires both a perceived and a perceiver, a sensible and a mind. It rests upon the unstated premise that no item capable of being perceived is itself capable of perceiving. The incapacity being asserted is presumably grounded in what kind of thing is capable of doing something like perceiving. Because numerical difference and difference in kind cut both ways, the ideas perceived, for their part, are also wholly different in number and kind from the minds that perceive them. Nonetheless, according to Berkeley, their existence or being is to be perceived. They have no "existence independent of spirit" (PHK 6). Berkeley's use of "spirit," which unlike "perceiver" and "mind" does not easily take a functional interpretation, is his way of indicating that mind – that which perceives – differs both in number and kind from any and all sensibles. It is a very important claim.

Minds and only minds are substances

The dependence of ideas for their existence upon their perceivers, a radical noncausal dependence, seems to be the overt ground for Berkeley's second main claim about minds. At the beginning of *Principles* 7 he asserts, "From what has been said, it follows, there is not any other substance than *spirit* or that which perceives." Berkeley does not here retract the distinction between two fundamental kinds of entity – sensible objects and minds; on the contrary, he reinforces it by placing them in contrasting ontological categories. Minds (spirits) are substances. Nonminds are not substances. Neither here nor elsewhere in the *Principles* does he define "substance." This encourages his reader to take it in a routine sense. In one routine sense (that is, in a sense long recognized by philosophers), to be a substance is to be an enduring individual to which various states and activities are ascribed by asserting predicate expressions of it. On this approach, a standard example is that Socrates is a substance; his baldness, walking, and wit are not. Two additional criteria often imposed were independence and autonomy. The thought behind the former is that some entities depend for their existence on what is done by or through some relationship they bear to a different entity. They are thus dependent entities and so cannot be substances. The thought behind the autonomy criterion is that something is a substance only if a universe consisting of it alone is possible or intelligible. Most substance theorists would not consider a smile to be a substance, even though it has a duration and can have predicates applied to it. Why not? Because it cannot exist by itself; it exists as a state or feature of the being whose face exhibits the smile. The same might be said of faces. What about heads? As these examples illustrate, the line between independence and autonomy is not always unblurred. Dependence precludes autonomy; what is not obvious is whether independence implies autonomy.

Berkeley's position, again, is that only minds can correctly be placed in the category of substance. This claim has a positive component (minds are substances) and a negative component (no nonminds are substances). Surprisingly, in the *Principles* Berkeley explicitly argues only for the latter. Notice, though, that in introducing in *Principles* 7 his thesis that only minds are substances, he presents it as an obvious consequence of what already has been maintained. The connection is left for the reader's discovery. It may turn on *esse* is *percipi*. Berkeley already had argued that the being of a sensible object is its being perceived, so his point apparently is that the existence of a sensible object presupposes a perceiver, understood to be a distinct thing. Consequently, a sensible depends for its existence on a perceptual act or process carried out by another entity, a mind.

A sensible, therefore, cannot be a substance. This argument might also support the claim that minds are substances, given an additional premise: that which (noncausally) grounds the existence of a dependent entity is a substance. So much for the implicit argument of *Principles* 7. The explicit argument follows:

> But for a fuller proof of this point, let it be considered, the sensible qualities are colour, figure, motion, smell, taste, and such like, that is, the ideas perceived by sense. Now for an idea to exist in an unperceiving thing, is a manifest contradiction; for to have an idea is all one as to perceive: that therefore wherein colour, figure, and the like qualities exist, must perceive them; hence it is clear there can be no unthinking substance or *substratum* of those ideas.

Detailed analysis of this argument comes later, when problems are considered. Here it is enough to note that, neither alone nor together can the explicit and implicit arguments establish Berkeley's claim that no nonminds are substances. The implicit argument concerns only sensible objects; the explicit concerns only things in which the qualities sensible objects are composed of are said to exist. Neither argument has sufficient scope to apply to all nonminds that might be posited or considered; neither speaks, for example, to the status of imperceptible unperceiving things that are not thought to support or have sensible qualities. One way to interpret the next ten sections (PHK 8–17), is as a sustained attempt to deny the existence of imperceptible material substances, purported entities that are not sensible objects and are not thought to have sensible qualities, yet are related to sensible objects causally, by partial or full resemblance, or yet some other relation.

Minds and only minds are causes

Not only are minds and only minds substances, they and only they are causes, or so Berkeley argued in Sections 25 and 26 of the *Principles*. This parallel thesis is defended more fully than the substance thesis. The argument of Section 25 for the negative component (no nonminds are causes) is followed in Section 26 by an argument for the positive component (minds are causes). Berkeley may hold that all minds are causes, but his argument is not intended to prove that generalization. Instead, it prepares the ground for an account of the different causal roles played by finite minds and God. In Sections 28 through 30 he argues that each human perceiver can know from experience that he or she actually causes certain ideas. These idea-effects do not, however, include sensible objects – ideas of sense. Other minds or another mind must cause them. By reflecting upon sensory experience and its patterns, humans can acquire conclusive inferential evidence that there is a single cause of all or the vast majority of the ideas of sense. The requirements for such a single cause of our actual sensory experience show that the single cause is God. Such is Berkeley's stance. Despite the importance, both philosophical and cultural, of these further developments of his theory of agency for the project of securing an orthodox theistic account of God and Divine Providence, we shall concentrate here on the main argument that (a) no nonminds are causes, but (b) at least some minds are causes.

Berkeley's argumentative strategy is relatively uncomplicated. We perceive change. Change requires a cause or causes. Some thing or things, either the ideas perceived, nonideas that resemble ideas, or minds, are the candidates for the role of causes of the various changes. No idea nor anything like an idea can cause anything, though. Consequently, minds alone cause those changes. Eliminating ideas and their replicas as causes comes first in the actual working out of this proof pattern. Besides implicitly embracing the causal maxim that whatever exists or occurs has a cause, Berkeley sets an implicit – hence unexplained and unargued – requirement for causes: Only active beings can be causes. The first explicit part of Berkeley's argument is that none of the things we perceive by sense meet the activity requirement. Section 25 begins,

> All our ideas, sensations, or the things which we perceive, by whatsoever names they may be distinguished, are visibly inactive, there is nothing of power or agency included in them. So that one idea or object of thought cannot produce, or make any alteration in another.

Many readers might feel that Berkeley's inactivity claim is refuted by everyday sensory experience – for example, by seeing a fire scorch a piece of wood. He nevertheless continues his argument as follows:

> To be satisfied of the truth of this, there is nothing else requisite but a bare observation of our ideas. For since they and every part of them exist only

> in the mind, it follows that there is nothing in them but what is perceived. But whoever shall attend to his ideas, whether of sense or reflexion, will not perceive in them any power or activity; there is therefore no such thing contained in them.

When one attends to one's immediate objects of sensory awareness and imagination (Berkeley says reflexion, but surely does not mean by it inner awareness of one's own mental states, for example acts of will), one is aware of no activity. For this to be at all plausible, Berkeley must sharply distinguish activity from alteration. The flames of the perceived fire undergo constant change or alteration, but these sensed changes and motions are not to be characterized as activity. Even granting this, one is likely to insist that the sensed changes signify unsensed activity in the object perceived. The truly challenging part of Berkeley's argument is now invoked to block this alternative. His blocking proposition, which I have labeled the Manifest Qualities Thesis (MQT), is that there is nothing in a perceived object but what is perceived. An image – what is imagined – has only those qualities it reveals when imagined; a sensed object has only those qualities discovered when it is sensed. Berkeley offers an enthymematic argument for MQT. He says of ideas (what is sensed or imagined), "Since they and every part of them exist only in the mind, it follows there is nothing in them but what is perceived." If this is accepted, one cannot infer activity in a perceived fire from its sensed alterations, when these are properly distinguished from activity, because the sensed fire exists only in mind and so is only what it is perceived to be. It is not sensed as active, therefore it is inactive.

To accept this characterization of objects of sense as perceiver-dependent, and the implication that they are only what they are perceived to be, is indeed to concede that objects of sense, so understood, are inactive. However, it is not yet to commit oneself to Berkeley's conclusion that no nonminds are causes. If forced to agree that what one sees when one sees a fire exists only as seen, so that it is only what it is seen to be, one is likely to insist that: first, one must then distinguish between the seen fire, the visual object, and the real fire; second, the inactivity of the former in no way implies the inactivity of the latter; and third, genuine causal processes occur at the level of real material objects and, in fact, account for the occurrences of seen fires and the like. Berkeley counters this in the remainder of Section 25, invoking his principle from Section 8 that "an idea can be like nothing but an idea" and insisting that no idea can be the resemblance or pattern of any active being.[3]

Satisfied, rightly or wrongly, that he has nailed down his conclusion regarding the causal impotence of nonminds, Berkeley proceeds to the rest of his argument, writing,

> We perceive a continual succession of ideas, some are anew excited, others are changed or totally disappear. There is therefore some cause of these ideas whereon they depend, and which produces and changes them. That this cause cannot be any quality or idea or combination of ideas, is clear from the preceding section. It must therefore be a substance; but it has been shewn that there is no corporeal or material substance: it remains therefore that the cause of ideas is an incorporeal active substance or spirit. (PHK 26)

Relying implicitly on the causal maxim, Berkeley insists that the items occurring in sensory experience, here labeled ideas, must be caused. Because in the preceding section he had first argued that ideas cannot be causes, then inferred that neither can unsensed extended, figured, moving things (thus covering all the nonminds to which he would grant intelligibility), one might expect Berkeley to move directly from "no nonminds are causes" to "minds are causes" by a simple disjunctive syllogism. Instead, after stating that earlier result, he infers that the sought-after cause must be a substance. Recalling his earlier denial of material substances, he reaches his ultimate conclusion that ideas are caused by minds, mental or spiritual substances. Neither here nor elsewhere does Berkeley explain the excursion concerning substance. With or without it, his argument easily can be expanded to cover all effects, and so can be considered a sweeping argument for the general thesis that minds and only minds are causes.

Whatever its complications, Berkeley's argument has affirmed unequivocally that minds, understood to be unextended active perceiving beings, are the only causes. No doubt with a grander end in view, he subsequently answers the unstated but pressing objection that he has not yet shown minds are active, and so has not yet shown that they meet the activity requirement that was invoked in Section 25 to deny ideas are causes. In Section 28 he claims familiarity with his power over his own ideas of imagination. His ability to will such ideas is taken to demonstrate his activity. At this juncture Berkeley reveals his indifference to what might seem the important but purely philosophical task of spelling out exactly what his volitional theory of causes comprises. He proceeds, instead, to an argument for the existence of God and an account of the distinction between the real and the imaginary. In Section 29 one's lack of power over one's own ideas of sense is affirmed and taken as evidence for the existence of another mind or minds, which alone or together cause those ideas. In Section 30 the character of the pattern of ideas of sense is used to argue that there is but a single cause of that sequence, one possessing power and wisdom sufficient for the task, and therefore sufficient to merit the name "God." Finally, in Section 33 Berkeley claims ideas of sense are regarded as real things, whereas those of imagination, being less "regular, vivid, and constant," are more properly termed "ideas, or images of things." Objections to Berkeley's denial of material causes and questions about the compatibility of his account with the new science were to follow, but the constructive account of volitional causation, such as it is, is over. The absence of a detailed account reflects Berkeley's priorities in Part I of the *Principles*. In the *Three Dialogues* the situation is, if anything, worse, because there is no positive account of mental causation at all.[4]

Minds of several kinds are known

The minds or spirits, knowledge of which is in question, can be placed into four groups: first the self; second, God; third, other minds fundamentally like one's own (that is, human and humanlike minds); and fourth, alien minds (minds that cannot be conceived with reference to one's own mental operations). Of these, for Berkeley only the last fully evade human knowledge. As in the case of sensible objects (things that are or can be sensed) his position on knowledge of alien minds is built on a distinction between objects of acquaintance (things that are fully known in experience) and objects that lie beyond direct observation, either fully or in part, either temporarily or permanently, either contingently or by nature and in principle. His general position is that an object of acquaintance, that which is fully present to a knower, is known to exist with complete certainty. Things that are not objects of acquaintance must be inferred, and one must be able to conceive them and know what they are before discovering that they are. One needs to know how the available evidence implicates them, and this requires knowing what they are supposed to be and do.

In the case of minds, all knowledge begins with self-knowledge. Self-awareness not only secures knowledge of the existence of the self as mind, it also permits other minds to be conceived and inferred. If we use m_1 to signify a particular mind, we can say that Berkeley's position begins with his doctrine that m_1, as a conscious being, is aware of both m_1 and various activities in which it engages, reporting "I am aware I am feeling anger," or "I am aware that I am choosing to imagine a full moon," and so on. This, he claims, permits it to conceive of beings partially or fully similar to itself. Thus one conceives of the human mind as a kind or sort. This conception enables one, with suitable evidence, to infer that other human minds exist. God is conceived analogically with reference to mental operations humans discover in themselves. Our conceptions of those operations yield conceptions of strengthened or perfected operations, and thus a conception of a perfect agent – a supreme spirit. According to Berkeley, God, so conceived, can be proven to exist. The inventory of spirits is not yet finished. According to Berkeley, we can conceive of at least one group of minds that are neither human nor divine. We can conceive of angels as beings capable of performing, more effectively and with greater scope but still imperfectly, the very operations we discover in ourselves. Berkeley probably believed in the existence of angels, but did not claim knowledge of their existence. The case is much different in the case of God.

That God exists and that humans can attain indisputable knowledge that God exists are positions of great importance to Berkeley, clearly capturing his emotions as well as his intelligence. One need only read *Alciphron, or the Minute Philosopher*, his stylish yet impassioned defense of Christianity against his freethinking contemporaries, to realize this. One can know that God exists, according to Berkeley, but not with intuitive certainty. Negatively, this means God is not an object of acquaintance, either sensory or reflexive. Awareness of self is not accompanied by awareness of God. The interesting question concerns the degree of certainty Berkeley attributed to his proof or proofs of God. It is a complex question because many, including Berkeley, held knowledge of God's existence to be demonstrative, then disagreed on what it was for an argument to provide a demonstration. It is highly unlikely, but not impossible, that Berkeley believed knowledge of God's existence attains demonstrative certainty, in the strict Lockean sense, even though Locke had made such a claim.[5]

In the *Dialogues* are passages that have been cited as evidence that Berkeley there added a new argument for the existence of God. As these passages are commonly interpreted, the role assigned to God is that of sustaining perceiver of the objects of sense, rather than their sustaining cause. Near the beginning of the Second Dialogue, attempting to explain why he is free from the skepticism in which Hylas, by his own admission, is ensnared, Philonous invokes *esse* is *percipi* to tie the existence of a sensible to its perception by a mind. Then he states:

> To me it is evident, for the reasons you allow of, that sensible things cannot exist otherwise than in a mind or spirit. Whence I conclude, not that they have no real existence, but that seeing they depend not on my thought, and have an existence distinct from being perceived by me, there must be some other mind wherein they exist. As sure therefore as the sensible world really exists, so sure is there an infinite omnipresent spirit who contains and supports them. (DHP 2 [212])

Philonous claims a distinctive point of view, adding, "Men commonly believe that all things are known or perceived by God, because they believe the being of a God, whereas I on the other side, immediately and necessarily conclude the being of a God, because all sensible things must be perceived by him" (DHP 2 [212]). According to the most common interpretation of these passages, Berkeley argues for God's existence but completely ignores volition and causation. Instead, he argues from the continued existence of the sensible world to the existence of God as its sustaining perceiver. An example might reveal how the continuity argument works. I am presently looking at a sensible object, for example my coffee cup. I rest my eyes by closing them for three or four seconds. I reopen them and once again see my coffee cup. Close attention must be paid to what is being claimed. It is not that what I see on the second occasion exactly resembles what I saw on the first; it is, rather, that one and the same object is seen on both occasions. On this strict sense of numerical sameness, had the object seen on the first occasion ceased to exist when it ceased to be sensed, it could not have been the object seen on the second. Identity through a period of time requires continuous existence throughout the period. Consequently, because it is the same sensible that is seen on both occasions, it continued to exist during the interval when my eyes were closed. Now, by hypothesis, the cup was not perceived continuously by me. If sensibles can exist only when perceived, as Berkeley claims, a pair of conclusions follow. First, the cup does not depend for its existence upon being perceived by me. Consequently, secondly, there must be a different mind whose perception of the cup sustains its existence.

Readers with a special interest in arguments for God's existence or the development of Berkeley's thought outside the *Principles* and *Dialogues* would do well to shift their attention to Berkeley's "linguistic" argument, as suggested in *New Theory of Vision* and stated in *Alciphron*. Berkeley held that although no visual object is either numerically or qualitatively the same as any tangible object, and although no mathematical or causal principles can be used to deduce features or relationships of the latter from features and relationships of the former, we infer tangibles from visuals. How? By their concomitance with one another in experience. Humans learn that experiences of colored objects follow or are followed by experiences of tangible objects, including kinesthetic sensations. After a sufficiently long train of experiences, one can anticipate tactile experiences on the basis of visual experiences. Berkeley characterized such suggestive visual objects as signs, and held that with time we carelessly conflate these signs with what they signify, thus thinking we see objects, qualities, and relationships that in truth are proper objects of touch only.

What was mere metaphor in the first two editions of the *New Theory* became an element in a relatively complex argument for God's existence in *Alciphron*. The argument is noteworthy for another reason – Berkeley's insight concerning the shared logical structure of inferences to God and inferences to other human minds. First, Euphranor, Berkeley's representative, gets Alciphron, representing the freethinkers (the so-called minute philosophers), to agree that inferring a nonobservable entity – for instance another mind – from observable signs – bodily behavior – is not unacceptable in principle. Then he argues from various general features of the observed parts of nature to a power and wisdom that "must be supposed in one and the same Agent, Spirit, or Mind," so that "we have at least as clear, full, and immediate certainty of the being of this infinitely wise and powerful Spirit, as of any one human soul whatsoever besides our own" (ALC 4.5 [147]). An epistemological twist occurs in the last clause of this passage. It provokes Alciphron to exclaim, "What! Do you pretend you can have the same assurance of the being of a God that you can have of mine, whom you actually see stand before you and talk to you?" Euphranor replies, "The very same, if not greater."

In the *Principles*, which culminates with an account of our knowledge of God and the practical implications of that knowledge, Berkeley did not explicitly link or subordinate knowledge of other human minds to knowledge of God. There is, to be sure, a cursory account of the former in Section 145, where the nonimmediacy of such knowledge is emphasized as follows:

> From what hath been said, it is plain that we cannot know the existence of other spirits, otherwise than by their operations, or the ideas by them excited in us. I perceive several motions, changes, and combinations of ideas, that inform me there are certain particular agents like myself, which accompany them, and concur in their production. Hence the knowledge I have of other spirits is not immediate, as is the knowledge of my ideas; but depending upon the intervention of ideas, by me referred to agents or spirits distinct from myself, as effects or concomitant signs.

Berkeley's treatment of knowledge of other human minds is given a more positive tone in the *Dialogues*, where he answered the objection that immaterialism inconsistently affirmed minds, which cannot be known, while denying material substances on the ground they cannot be known. Even there, however, the probable evidence for the existence of other finite spirits was contrasted to both immediate evidence and demonstrative knowledge.[6]

III. PROBLEMS: MINDS AS OBJECTS OF KNOWLEDGE

I shall proceed now to investigate three types of problem relating to Berkeley's account of minds and agency, beginning with issues relating to minds as objects of experience and thought. Any account of this topic should begin with the first two sections of Part I of the *Principles*, where, interestingly, one finds signs of problems to come. Section 1 purports to be an inventory of the objects of human knowledge. They are "either ideas imprinted on the senses, or else such as are perceived by attending to the passions and operations of the mind, or lastly ideas formed by help of memory and imagination, either compounding, dividing, or barely representing those originally perceived in the aforesaid ways." The first sentence of Section 2 reads, "But besides all that endless variety of ideas or objects of knowledge, there is likewise something which knows or perceives them, and exercises divers operations, as willing, imagining, remembering about them." Here the perceiving mind is being contrasted to ideas; the latter seemingly have been equated with objects of knowledge. The two sentences thus suggest a dualism. On the one side are known objects that are themselves incapable of cognition and, on the other side, knowers who are not themselves known. Another reading compatible with the text is that Section 1 concerns what can be directly known; on this account minds are known, but only inferentially, not directly. These early passages are hardly enough to establish either alternative.

In Section 27, where more detail is provided about minds, Berkeley writes so as to suggest that minds cannot be directly or immediately known. He insists, first, that no mind is an idea, and second, that there can be no idea of a mind. He then writes, "Such is the nature of spirit or that which acts, that it cannot be of itself perceived, but only by the effects which it produceth." Does "perceived" mean "perceived by sense" or "directly observed"? One might well take Berkeley to mean the latter, especially because the passions and operations of the mind were included among the objects of knowledge in Section 1. His position there thus seems to be that humans have immediate sensory awareness of colors, sounds, odors, and so on, and combinations of such qualities, but also have immediate inner awareness of the mind's states, its passions and operations. Both types of immediate objects can be represented in thought (memory and imagination) by likenesses of them. Mind, however, as distinct from its passions and operations, is not itself an immediate object of experience. It is to be inferred from its operations, or rather the effects of those operations.

This would be perfectly innocuous, but for how it fits or fails to fit with the project of denying the existence of material substances. Berkeley, it will be recalled, did not simply doubt their existence on the basis of arguments that they cannot be known to exist. His primary line of argument is that material substance is impossible. Such an argument proceeds on conceptual grounds. Because sensibles are not themselves substances, material substance is not itself immediately known. It is thus conceptualized either via likeness to sensibles or through some other relationship it is supposed to have to sensibles. Berkeley argued that every relationship proposed, including likeness, leads to an inconsistent conception of material substance. The term material substance is thus either self-contradictory or meaningless. Even if material substance were possible, contrary to Berkeley's argument, there could be no idea of it and no knowledge of it. How do these results relate to mind? Were Berkeley to hold that mind is itself never an immediate object of experience, he would be required to provide a relational conception of mind. The one outcome he must avoid is admitting "mind" and its cognate terms are either self-contradictory or meaningless. While this goal does not seem beyond reach, and Berkeley took several steps toward it by characterizing minds as perceivers and causes, one can understand why he might have had second thoughts about denying that mind is not accessible to immediate experience. The rhetorical risk of denying unobservable material substances while embracing unobservable mental substances might have seemed too great. By Section 135 he seems to have had those second thoughts.

Without mentioning names or titles Berkeley strongly suggests in Section 135 that some philosophers have denied humans have knowledge of mind on the ground that we lack an idea of mind.[7] He responds, "But surely it ought not to be looked on as a defect in a human understanding, that it does not perceive the idea of spirit, if it is manifestly impossible there should be any such idea." Berkeley proceeds in Sections 136 through 138 to expand on an argument first given in Section 27, which was intended to prove that an idea of a mind is truly impossible. This expanded argument will be considered shortly. Whatever else it shows, the argument reveals that Berkeley stood firm in claiming minds are completely dissimilar to ideas and cannot be represented by them. Next, in Section 139, comes the crucial point. Berkeley writes, "But it will be objected, that if there is no idea signified by the terms soul, spirit, and substance, they are wholly insignificant, or have no meaning in them." Berkeley's reply is swift and unequivocal. "I answer, those words do mean or signify a real thing, which is neither an idea nor like an idea, but that which perceives ideas, and wills, and reasons about them. What I am myself, that which I denote by the term I, is the same with what is meant by soul or spiritual substance." He proceeds to reject emphatically the suggestion that this is just a verbal dispute, concluding, "It is therefore necessary, in order to prevent equivocation and confounding natures perfectly disagreeing and unlike, that we distinguish between spirit and idea." Berkeley was committed to the meaningfulness of "spirit," "mental substance," and related terms and understood them with reference to the self, "that which I denote by the term I." The pressing questions are what exactly is denoted by "I," and what conception of it can and do I have, given that it neither is nor can be represented by an idea? Before considering Berkeley's answer or answers, let us consider the arguments used to establish that there can be no idea of a mind.

Section 27 is devoted to Berkeley's denial of ideas of minds. It begins by emphasizing the activity of minds and passivity of ideas.

> A spirit is one simple, undivided, active being: as it perceives ideas, it is called the understanding, and as it produces or otherwise operates about them, it is called the will. Hence, there can be no idea formed of a soul or spirit: for all ideas whatever, being passive and inert, *vide* Sect. 25, they cannot represent unto us, by way of image or likeness, that which acts. A little attention will make it plain to anyone, that to have an idea which shall be like that active principle of motion and change of ideas, is absolutely impossible.

In Section 2, Berkeley insisted that a mind differs from any idea it perceives. In the present passage he emphasizes how minds differ from ideas. They are active; ideas are inert. He infers no idea can represent (be of) a mind. The underlying assumption is that ideas represent by similarity. Being similar to another thing, an idea reflects, as it were, that other thing. Without knowing the details of how representation by likeness works and the type or degree of resemblance it requires, one can summarize Berkeley's argument as follows. An idea represents by likeness (similarity), hence what an idea represents resembles the idea doing the representing. Minds, however, are unlike ideas. Hence, no idea can represent a mind. If to be an object of thought is to be represented by an idea, this argument leads to the further undesirable conclusion that minds cannot be objects of thought. The argument of Section 139 establishes that Berkeley rejected this conclusion and instead held that minds can be conceived even though they cannot be represented by ideas.[8] The pressing question is: How? Did Berkeley have any alternative account of conceiving things? If so, what is it? There is evidence from the *Principles* that he considered two alternatives and without explicitly repudiating one, settled on the other, at least in the second edition.

In Section 27 Berkeley seems to lay the foundation for the claim that minds are thought by means of relative notions. Let a notion be any thought that represents, but is neither a sensible nor like a sensible. What is a relative notion? Berkeley provides a clue. After insisting that to have an idea of a spirit is absolutely impossible, he writes, "Such is the nature of spirit or that which acts, that it cannot be of itself perceived, but only by the effects which it produceth." A negative claim – mind cannot itself be perceived – is joined to a positive claim – mind can be perceived by its effects. How? To perceive something by the effects it produces, it seems, is to know it as the cause of those effects. How is a cause conceived? By combining a notion of the relation of causing (which requires two relata – an effect and a cause) and some idea (the effect) one could form a notion of the cause of that idea, without having an idea of that cause. Appealing to a relative notion permits one to explain how one can think of an otherwise unknown relata of some known effect. The problem with an appeal to a relative notion is that the object so conceived is unknown, whereas Berkeley claims to know what a mind is and that minds cause ideas. At any rate, Berkeley seems to have decided after the first edition of the *Principles* was published that the passages we have been examining come perilously close to denying that minds can be conceived or known. In the second edition the following concluding sentence was added to Section 27: "Though it must be owned at the same time, that we have some notion of soul, spirit, and the operations of the mind, such as willing, loving, hating, inasmuch as we know or understand the meaning of those words." Having dropped his earlier position that all significant words stand for ideas, Berkeley could consistently claim to have this kind of meaningful word; what seems unexplained, however, is his inference from understanding the meaning of the appropriate words to having notions. One can understand the claim that, after hearing a sound, someone can form a likeness of the sound heard, which permits the person to think about it in its absence. But what is it to have a notion? What experiences, if any, are required to have notions? Must all notions be founded on relations as relative notions are supposed to be?

All these questions spring to mind when notions are introduced. They go unanswered, at least in Section 27. One must turn to later sections of the *Principles* for partial enlightenment.

Section 140 was a late addition to the manuscript that became the *Principles*. It begins with the thesis that mental words can be understood (which does not get us very far) but quickly advances to a new explanation of how mind can be conceived. The text, as it appeared in the second edition,[9] begins as follows: "In a large sense indeed, we may be said to have an idea, or rather a notion of spirit, that is, we understand the meaning of the word, otherwise we could not affirm or deny anything of it."[10] True, if we can make meaningful assertions about mind, "mind" must have meaning. Why does it have meaning for us, though? The answer is provided in the continuation:

> Moreover, as we conceive the ideas that are in the minds of other spirits by means of our own, which we suppose to be resemblances of them: so we know other spirits by means of our own soul, which in that sense is the image or idea of them, it having a like respect to other spirits, that blueness or heat by me perceived hath to those ideas perceived by another.

Note the analogy. One's own soul, the I, is to other minds (spirits) as my ideas are to the ideas in other minds that are represented by them. In both cases representation is founded on likeness. In both cases, too, it presupposes awareness of the entity that represents. What can be thought is a function of what is experienced. Berkeley's statement strongly suggests that awareness of self provides a ground for conceiving minds in general and thus other particular minds. This is not having a relative conception. Instead, it parallels the way in which sensory or imaginative awareness of an instance of heat provides, through likeness, a ground for representing other instances of heat and, further, heat in general. In both the *Dialogues* and the second edition of the *Principles*, awareness of self is insisted upon, and in the former it is again appealed to in the explanation of how one conceives minds other than one's own.[11]

IV. PROBLEMS: SUBSTANCE IN BERKELEY'S PHILOSOPHY

The topic of substance provides an important second example of difficulties Berkeley encountered in articulating an adequate account of mind. I begin by rehearsing a criticism of my earlier brief summary of his denial of material substance and affirmation of mental substance. One might claim that by not attending to genuine problems or at least obvious peculiarities in Berkeley's treatment of substance, I have encouraged unwary readers to take his pronouncements about immaterial substance at face value, that is, as resting upon a well-established and orthodox conception of substance, when the truth is he has revised or repudiated that conception. Before responding to this criticism by discussing some passages that have generated questions about Berkeley's commitment to substance, I want to distinguish three positions one might take on this point. One charges Berkeley with inconsistency. Here is the argument. Berkeley based his rejection of material substance on the repudiation of the philosophical theory of substance. To repudiate substance, even implicitly, is to invalidate any endorsement of mental substance. Because Berkeley affirmed mental substance in numerous places, he was inconsistent. Within this position there are two main ways to portray the inconsistency: Either Berkeley was aware of it or not. On the former, there are again two alternatives. On the less charitable interpretation, Berkeley at some point recognized his inconsistency in denying substance in order to deny material substance and affirming it in order to save immaterial substance. So trapped, he tried vainly to conceal the inconsistency. A more charitable reading would regard him as openly and intentionally inconsistent, artfully leading others to the conclusion, too dangerous to draw explicitly himself, that because the arguments that tell against material substance apply equally to mental substance, both are to be denied by a consistent reasoner. The difference is between a desperate Berkeley and an artful, even cunning one.

Whichever variant one endorses, for two reasons this first approach is bold indeed. The more obvious reason is that Berkeley is accused of inconsistency. The less obvious is that the charge of inconsistency is founded on the highly controversial claim that Berkeley's rejection of material substance is founded on the denial of substance or on principles that preclude substances. A more measured approach does not tie the rejection of material substance to the rejection of substance; it merely holds that Berkeley abandoned the substance doctrine inasmuch as behind his use of the expression "immaterial substance," there was no distinctive and well-defined position at all.

On this account the concept of substance plays no genuine role in his philosophy, so that the language of "substance" plays only a rhetorical role. This judgment is accompanied by the speculation that to satisfy the religious philosophical community on which he had to rely for advancement, Berkeley affirmed that minds are immaterial substances – the orthodox position – but assigned no specific doctrinal meaning to that claim. No traditional substance function is carried out by Berkeleyan minds, despite the substance label assigned them.[12]

A third position sees Berkeley as a revisionist, whose critical atttitude toward abstract philosophical terms is applied to the term substance as well. He required that its meaningfulness be established with reference to actual objects, objects of experience. The resulting position is that one can comprehend what is meant by "minds are substances" and grasp its truth, whereas attempts to assign meaning to "material substance" fail completely. On this view, Berkeley retained enough of the established connotation to be entitled to use the term "substance," yet could find precise concrete meaning only in the case of minds, perceiving substances. On this view, the case of substance parallels that of causation. In both cases, to give precise meaning to these terms is to discover that they apply only to minds.

Defenders of all three positions must acknowledge that Berkeley was far from a constant and complacent defender of mental substance, and at times had doubts about the doctrine of substance itself. In his notebooks Berkeley struggled to find an account of mind he could accept and defend; in several places he dismissed outright the doctrine of substance.[13] It must be acknowledged equally that the doubts and difficulties about substance expressed in the notebooks were absent from the printed texts of the *Principles* and the *Dialogues.* In them Berkeley definitely asserted mental substances while denying material substances. The key questions are do his various pronouncements yield inconsistency and, if not, do they add up to a coherent and substantive conception of substance? Before answering them, we should try to sharpen our picture of the doctrine of substance being considered.

From the prephilosophical or commonsense point of view, there are in nature innumerable discrete things that have their own identity at a time – that is, are numerically different from other things – and sustain that identity over time – that is, persist or endure. On one philosophical use of the term "substance" these items are substances. There is an abundance of examples: dogs, trees, rocks, and tables are substances. Some are artifacts; others are not. Some are living; some are not. All are substances. This vast array of individual things exhibits similarities and differences; two individuals, for example, may differ or agree in color. They may also differ or agree in kind. Philosophers have introduced the term "quality" to signify whatever in the object is the ground or basis for the application of some adjective or predicate expression to it, terms that mark those similarities and differences. On this approach, adjectives signify qualities and can be applied correctly to objects having those qualities. So states the theory.

Philosophers have tried to give an account of what it is for an object to have a quality. Among the questions addressed are these: Is a quality a component or constituent of an object, so that apart from all other senses in which, say, a baseball is a composite, it is a logical or ontological composite consisting entirely or partially of its qualities? Does the ball stand to each of its qualities as whole to part? Or, rather, is each quality possessed or instantiated by the object, which is distinct from any and all of its qualities. On the second alternative, it is a serious mistake to think of the object's qualities as its proper parts.

A second and more technical sense of the term "substance" is associated with the view just introduced that ordinary enduring individuals are not composites of their qualities. Accordingly, a substance is an entity distinct from each and every quality; it instantiates or exemplifies a set or sequence of qualities. It is an individuator, that is, it provides ultimate difference, unity, and identity over time. Each substance has or instantiates at every moment of its existence a set of qualities. A substance may change over time by losing or gaining qualities, but identity is preserved because it is one and the same substance that gains or loses the qualities. An apple, on this doctrine, continues to be the same thing even if it changes from green to red. This is intelligible, if it is intelligible, just because the individual object is not merely a combination of qualities or over time a series of such combinations. It requires a substance, the persisting bearer of those qualities.

Berkeley begins his consideration of sensible objects in Part I of the *Principles* by specifying various sensible qualities as the proper and immediate objects of each of five sensory modalities – seeing, hearing, smelling, touching, and tasting. The names of ordinary sensible objects are given meaning with reference to combinations of the qualities so introduced. Here is a passage from Section 1.

And as several of these are observed to accompany each other, they come to be marked by one name, and so to be reputed as one thing. Thus, for example, a certain colour, taste, smell, figure and consistence having been observed to go together, are accounted one distinct thing, signified by the name *apple.*

If taken to be an account of what is experienced, Berkeley's Section 1 characterization of sensible objects, though not perhaps his accompanying comment on names such as "apple," is fully compatible with a doctrine of bodily substances along the lines just sketched.

Beginning with Section 2 of the *Principles*, Berkeley insisted that the being of a sensible object consists in being perceived. An unsensed sensible object is impossible. Beginning with Section 8 he introduced and critiqued an account of material things that conceded his claim about sensible objects, then overrode it by distinguishing between such objects, as actually sensed, and the unsensed and unperceiving things that resemble, support, or cause them. On each variant account of the second kind of object a relation was invoked in order to make the hypothesis of unsensed material things intelligible. As our present concern is with substance, we shall ignore Berkeley's arguments that neither the relations of resemblance or causation can be used to conceptualize and defend unsensed unperceiving things.[14] Instead, the arguments of Sections 16 and 17 will be examined. The former states what is at issue:

It is said extension is a mode or accident of matter, and that matter is the *substratum* that supports it. Now I desire that you would explain what is meant by matter's *supporting* extension: say you, I have no idea of matter, and therefore cannot explain it. I answer, though you have no positive, yet if you have any meaning at all, you must at least have a relative idea of matter; though you know not what it is, yet you must be supposed to know what relation it bears to accidents, and what is meant by its supporting them.

It will not do, Berkeley continues, to take *support* literally, "as when we say that pillars support a building." He then asks, "In what sense therefore must it be taken?"

Section 17, wherein the supposed answer is to be discredited, is one of the two main published texts that can be used to support the claim that part of Berkeley's arsenal against material substance is a repudiation of the doctrine of substance. The nominal argument is for the conclusion that even for its proponents, "material substance" is meaningless. The interpretive point is that the definition that is lambasted in order to reach that conclusion is a definition of substance, not material substance. Here are Berkeley's words:

> If we inquire into what the most accurate philosophers declare themselves to mean by *material substance*; we shall find them acknowledge, they have no other meaning annexed to those sounds, but the idea of being in general, together with the relative notion of its supporting accidents. The general idea of being appeareth to me the most abstract and incomprehensible of all other; and as for its supporting accidents, this, as we have just now observed, cannot be understood in the common sense of those words; it must therefore be taken in some other sense, but what that is they do not explain. So that when I consider the two parts or branches which make the signification of the words *material substance*, I am convinced there is no distinct meaning annexed to them.[15]

"The idea of being in general, together with the relative notion of its supporting accidents" makes no mention of whether the accidents are material or mental; it therefore is a purported definition of "substance" rather than "material substance." (Recall Section 27's attack on the supposed idea of mental substance, characterized as the idea of "being in general, with a relative notion of its supporting or being the subject of the aforesaid powers.") These considerations lead some to claim that Berkeley in Section 17 argues that material substance is incomprehensible, because substance is so, and to conclude that, a fortiori, so is immaterial or mental substance.

If this reading is accepted, those who hold that Berkeley inconsistently both affirmed and denied substance need only direct their attention from Section 17 back to Section 7, where he wrote, "From what has been said, it follows, there is no other substance than *spirit*, or that which perceives," or forward to Section 26, where he asserts of whatever causes sensible ideas, "It must therefore be a substance; but it has been shewn that there is no corporeal or material substance; it remains therefore that the cause of ideas is an incorporeal active substance or spirit." The former passage, however, provides a good reason to resist reading Section 17 as an attack on substance. If we recall Berkeley's well-known antipathy to abstract general ideas, we can reach an interpretation of the overall argument of Sections 7, 16, and 17 that can be summarized as follows. First, as regards ideas and minds, the vague abstract terms "having" and "supporting" can be made intelligible with reference to perceiving. "Minds have ideas" means "minds perceive ideas," and "minds support ideas" means "because ideas must be perceived to exist, minds by perceiving them sustain their existence." Second, as it regards sensible objects, especially extended solid things such as tables and chairs, supporting means holding up. Finally, as for the supposed abstract common meaning of support, which some invoke to define substance as a category common to sensible objects and minds, there is none.

More can and should be said about Berkeley's puzzling comments about substance as support in the *Principles*. We, however, must turn instead to Section 49 of the *Principles*, the other passage where Berkeley is thought to have fully revealed his rejection of the doctrine of substance. He writes there,

> It may be objected, that if extension and figure exist only in the mind, it follows that the mind is extended and figured; since extension is a mode or attribute, which (to speak with the Schools) is predicated of the subject in which it exists.

A sensible object is not in the mind as one body can be contained in another, so it might seem that "in the mind" means inheres in the mind as a quality inheres in a substance. On the traditional doctrine of substance, a quality's name is or can be predicated of any substance in which it inheres. Thus the objection portrays Berkeley as holding the qualities that make up sensible objects inhere in the mind that perceives them, in which case their names are to be predicated of that mind. This result would commit Berkeley to extension, figure, and motion being predicated of the mind, a very embarrassing result for a philosopher who insists again and again that the mind is unextended and who is anxious to secure the natural immortality of the soul on the basis of its unextendedness.[16]

The key interpretive question is whether in repelling the objection, Berkeley discards or renounces the doctrine of substance. It can be conceded that if he does, then he cannot elsewhere affirm spiritual substance without inconsistency. The issue is did he? His initial response to the objection does not support an affirmative answer. Berkeley merely proclaims that he does not use "in the mind" to mean inhere in the mind as a quality in a substance. To be in the mind merely is to be perceived by the mind. In his words:

> I answer, those qualities are in the mind only as they are perceived by it, that is, not by way of mode or attribute, but only by way of idea; and it no more follows, that the soul or mind is extended because extension exists in it alone, than it does that it is red or blue, because those colours are on all hands acknowledged to exist in it, and no where else.

The crucial words are "qualities are in the mind only as they are perceived by it." This response would be patently ineffective, not to say disingenuous, were "being perceived" itself understood to mean inhering in. Consequently, we should take Berkeley to be explicating "being in the mind" in terms of "being perceived by the mind." As a quality is in the mind only by way of idea, that is, only as being perceived by that mind, there is no basis for predicating it of the mind as there would be were being perceived interpreted as inhering in. If this is a correct reading of Berkeley's initial response to the objection of Section 49, it thus far provides no evidence that he rejected the doctrine of substance.[17] He merely denies using it as his model for understanding perceiving.

The continuation of Section 49 seems to add a new element, an attack on the doctrine of predication that might be read as a general attack on the doctrine of substance:

> As to what philosophers say of subject and mode, that seems very groundless and unintelligible. For instance, in this proposition, a die is hard, extended and square, they will have it that the word die denotes a subject or substance, distinct from the hardness, extension and figure, which are predicated of it, and in which they exist. This I cannot comprehend: to me a die seems to be nothing distinct from those things which are termed its modes or accidents. And to say a die is hard, extended and square, is not to attribute those qualities to a subject distinct from and supporting them, but only an explication of the meaning of the word die.

This passage begins with the brief claim that what philosophers say of subjects and modes is groundless and unintelligible. Thereafter it contrasts the account routinely offered by philosophers of the logical structure of "A die is hard, extended, and square" and similar propositions, with the correct (Berkeleyan) account. On the basis of the expression, "As to what philosophers say of subject and mode; that seems very groundless and unintelligible," one might argue that Berkeley intends to provide a completely general argument regarding how one should analyze all singular propositions, an account that eliminates any logical subject corresponding to the grammatical subject. This supports the further claim that Berkeley implicitly eliminates the category of substance. If the grammatical subject is just a place marker for the several predicates used to explicate it, it does not denote a substance, spiritual or material, in addition to the qualities signified by the several adjectives predicated of the grammatical subject. From this line of thought one might be tempted to conclude that Berkeley implicitly reveals in Section 49 that spiritual substance is to be rejected along with material substance, because he explicitly replaces the substance analysis of predication with a bundle analysis.

This temptation should be resisted for two reasons, one having to do with abstraction, the other having to do with the import of Berkeley's handling of the example of the die. If one keeps in mind Berkeley's suspicion regarding very general terms that are not linked to determinate objects of experience, and his reluctance to assign univocal meaning to general terms that apply to both sensibles and their perceivers, it will not seem obvious that the comment about "subject and mode" is meant to reject the doctrine of substance. Neither will the comment about the proper analysis of "A die is hard, extended and square," once one realizes there are two reasonable alternatives to the position that it expresses a general rejection of the doctrine of substance. One is that they concern only singular propositions about sensible objects and are not meant to be taken as completely general comments about the logical structure or ontological implications of all singular propositions employing the "is" of predication. If this is so, nothing said about "A die is hard, extended and square," as representative of singular statements about sensible objects or bodies, applies to sentences like "I am sad" or "I am thinking."

The other alternative concedes that Berkeley's comments were intended to apply to all singular propositions that purport to employ an "is" of predication. On this interpretation, rather than signify a genuine distinction between subject and mode, such propositions in all cases in which they are employed appropriately and perspicuously merely use the predicate expression to explicate the subject term, which therefore does not signify a substance distinct from the qualities signified by the predicates that perform the explication. Even this general result is far more friendly to the category of substance than might be supposed. Assume that Berkeleyan minds are substances. They are, he claims, active beings, doers. They perceive, they think, they believe, they will. Hence, in rejecting the "is" of predication across the board, Berkeley may have meant that in the case of singular statements about minds, mental substances, the grammatical form that truly exhibits the ontological structure of facts about them is *subject – verb – object* rather than *subject – copula – adjective.* The perspicuous grammatical form for propositions about minds is illustrated by "I hear a sound" and "I love Jerry" rather than "I am sad" and "I am angry with my uncle." On this view, propositions of the form, *S* is *P*, subject – copula – predicate, never assign a quality to a distinct subject; they either explicate the subject term, reflecting a whole/part structure of sensible objects and their qualities, or, when applied to minds, have a misleading grammatical form and, thus, should be translated into the subject-verb-object form so as to perspicuously represent a state of affairs involving an active substance, its acts, and their objects. My conclusion is that Berkeley may well have envisioned a differential analysis of singular propositions, depending upon whether they concerned sensibles or perceivers, even if doing so would now universally be regarded as wrong-headed.

Because of Berkeley's comments about the relation of supporting, his comments about predication, and the links between supporting, instantiating, predication, and substance in its technical sense, one cannot take his rejection of material substance and endorsement of mental or perceiving substance at face value. There is abundant textual evidence that, at the very least, he tried to rethink the concept of substance in addition to assigning items to the category of substance nondualistically and, therefore, nontraditionally. On the other hand, it is far from obvious that his rethinking amounted to a repudiation or abandonment of the core notion of substance as the noncausal support for entities whose existence depends upon things other than themselves.

V. PROBLEMS RELATING TO AGENCY

There is nothing in Berkeley's few published comments on agency to suggest indecision, submerged doctrine, or inconsistency. He asserts that volitions – acts of will – produce ideas, and that minds perform volitions. Scholarly discussions of this position usually either speculate about how he might have filled in the gaps in this theoretical schema, or assess the plausibility of this position both in general and when combined with other Berkeleyan commitments. Most of the questions asked on the first approach and the problems raised on the second have in common Berkeley's silence about them in his published works.

Types of mental activity

An example of how unanswered questions are raised by Berkeley's published statements is Section 28 of the *Principles*. There, trying to establish that minds are qualified to be causes, he insists that,

> I find I can excite ideas in my mind at pleasure, and vary and shift the scene as oft as I think fit. It is no more than willing, and straightway this or that idea arises in my fancy: and by the same power it is obliterated, and makes way for another. This making and unmaking of ideas doth very properly denominate the mind active.[18]

Berkeley asserts awareness of his volitional control over some of his ideas of imagination and concludes his "making and unmaking of ideas" implies the mind is active. His argument portrays willing as an activity that causes ideas. It does not explicitly equate them, so the question arises, did Berkeley implicitly equate willing and acting (doing)? Notice, first, that nothing in the context of the argument adds anything concerning what it is for a mind to be active, and no other aspects or instances of mental activity are discussed or even mentioned. Nothing encourages a distinction between willing as causing (a robust kind of doing or acting) and other noncausal forms of mental activity. On the contrary, Berkeley's silence, while it logically permits such a distinction, suggests he has nothing more to say on the subject of agency, and so encourages the unwary reader to think that for Berkeley, to will is to be active, and to be active is to will.

In fact, it is highly misleading to equate Berkeleyan agency with volition or to discuss only causation under the heading of agency. Minds for him are active, but one should not assume, therefore, that their activity is exclusively volitional or exclusively causal. In the first place, one needs to consider the very difficult question of whether perceiving is for Berkeley a kind of doing. Mediate perceiving certainly seems to be so even though minds have little control and almost no conscious volitional control over what is mediately perceived. Even if I can train myself not to do so, it still seems that my attributing heat to what I see when I see a vivid red poker just removed from the fire, is an instance of mental activity. My attribution is, indeed, a result of experience, but still it is an anticipation of experience – tactile experience – and as such exhibits a mind that is more than passive. What about immediate perceiving? Because, as we just saw in the discussion of Section 49 of the *Principles*, Berkeley insisted that a mind's having an idea *just is* the mind's perceiving it, there is even some reason to think that it is also a kind of doing on the part of the mind. Other mental states raise further questions about the scope and varieties of mental activity. Berkeley says next to nothing about them as psychological states, so no firm conclusions are available, but it does not seem implausible to suggest that for him remembering and reasoning, for example, are also manifestations of mental activity even though they do not seem to be instances of causing. Provided one has not already equated willing with causing, and causing with acting, one can recognize these mental states as possible manifestations in Berkeley's philosophy of less robust but equally genuine kinds of mental activity.

Volition and nonblind agency

A different set of questions, undiscussed in Berkeley's published writings, concerns the nature of volitional causation. What is unique about a volition, and does a volitional cause have any special relationship to its effect in addition to the relation of causation? Many would answer, first, that what is unique about a volition or act of choosing is that it comprises a thought of something other than itself, and in addition, a resolution or effort to bring about the thing or state of affairs being thought about. The thought is of the intended result, the effort succeeds or fails to actualize it. In choosing to rub my hands I think about a state of affairs or process and set myself to realize it. Whether or not my volition succeeds, it has what might be called intentional representation. Intentional representation is noncausal because an object is conceived even in cases in which what is willed or chosen does not occur. This provides a key to answering the second question. A successful volition's intentional object begins to exist and stands to it as effect to cause, but besides the causal relationship there is the antecedent relationship of intentional representation of the object by the volition or some component of it. This relationship would have obtained even if the volition had failed as cause. In addition to the legitimate sense, then, recognized by Berkeley, in which an effect may be said to signify or represent its cause and a cause its effect, just in virtue of the causal relationship between them, there is – in the case of volition – a different relation of representation that is distinct from and antecedent to the relation of causation.

Berkeley denied all nonmental causation. He definitely acknowledged volitions as causes. There are no passages in which he affirmed nonvolitional mental causes. Despite this, the evidence that he denied all nonvolitional causes is not conclusive. Nonetheless, the most likely interpretation is that he identified mental causation with efficacious willing. This conclusion certainly comports with the assertion in his philosophical notebooks that there can be no blind agency.[19] Had some philosopher proposed to him nonintentional mental pulses as causes, it is highly likely that Berkeley would have rejected the hypothesis on the ground that such pulses are blind, whereas genuine causes are sighted, that is, intend their supposed effects.

In numerous entries to his philosophical notebooks, especially those usually considered late entries, Berkeley fretted about willing and the power to will. Many concern the relation of the will or acts of will to the self, will as substance or substance surrogate, or whether will and understanding are truly distinct. Berkeley also expressed questions about the relationship between acts of will and ideas, and proposed various answers.[20] Did he have reason to be concerned about this relationship, and if so why? To focus our attempt to answer these questions, let us consider what he might have regarded as a paradigm of human activity. Suppose, for example, that I choose to form an image of a canoe. No sooner do I make the effort than I succeed. The canoe's image is before my mind, as one says. What, if anything, is problematic about this situation from the perspective of Berkeley's account of volition? It will help to recall that he insisted minds are active, ideas passive, so that one cannot have an idea of a mind or any of its actions. From this it follows there can be no idea of an act of willing. The premise underlying this argument is that primary representation – being of something – is based on likeness.[21] So far so good.

Questions arise, however, when we turn to the requirement that volition, to avoid blind agency, must include a thought of its would-be effect. In our example, prior to my awareness of the image of a canoe there is an act of will. It selects a canoe image. Besides the mental effort to produce the image, a thought (of the canoe) is required to guide my image-making. However, on a likeness account of primary representation, the thought of the image must itself be an image. If the thought of something represents it by likeness, and the only thing like an idea is an idea, my thought of an idea of a canoe is itself an idea of a canoe. Berkeley's account of nonblind willing destroys the wall he has built between activities and ideas. If an act of volition includes an image, that is, an idea, it no longer seems to make sense to insist that acts of will are utterly different from ideas and so cannot be represented by them. Why can I not have an idea of an act of will if to have an act of will is, in part, to have an idea? One way of deflecting this question would be for Berkeley to hold that the will, properly speaking, is just the mental effort, not the image that accidentally accompanies it. Unfortunately, either this is utterly implausible – because the "accidental" image seems to have more to do with the effect, which always agrees with it, than what is alleged to be the willing, properly so-called – or it is to embrace blind agency, only recently banished. Of course, Berkeley could insist that the thought of a canoe intrinsic to my willing the idea does not represent it by likeness, so need not be an idea. Although this does avoid the problem, it seems decidedly ad hoc, because Berkeley routinely insists that sensible objects are represented by resemblance, and never states, by way of contrast, that ideas of imagination, images of sensible objects, represent or can be represented in some other way. When pressed to account for how the finite mind can conceive of other minds, Berkeley wrote that each mind is its own object of inner awareness and that, as such, each can be said to represent whatever resembles it. This certainly suggests unqualified acceptance of the principle that primary representation is by means of likeness. Given this, the element of the volition that intentionally represents the intended effect – the image of a canoe – seems to be of it because it is like it. Because the only thing like an idea is an idea, the resembling thought must be an idea. A volition, therefore, has an idea as a constituent, so once again Berkeley's radical contrast between volitions, as instances of activity, and ideas, as inherently passive, has been subverted.[22]

Ideas, volitions, and other minds

Several problems regarding Berkeley's proofs of other minds as causes of ideas of sense deserve our attention. The first concerns what must be supposed regarding the immediate objects of sense in order to sustain MQT, the Manifest Qualities Thesis, a principle without which Berkeley cannot deny activity to those objects. Even were one to grant that no immediate object of sense exhibits activity, one might insist that their activity is genuine, but unobserved. To block this Berkeley invokes MQT. Of the immediate objects of sense he writes, "For since they and every part of them exist only in the mind, it follows that there is nothing in them but what is perceived" (PHK 25). To say they and every part of them "exist only in the mind" must and need only mean they cannot exist unperceived. If that cannot validate MQT, nothing will. The problem is that if the immediate objects of sense cannot exist unperceived, then given Berkeley's principle that the only thing like an idea is an idea, no object of sense can exist unperceived. This seems to discredit Berkeley's proof of God's existence in the *Principles*, because given that result, it seems impossible to achieve the regularities among those sensible objects that are indispensable for an inference to a single cause of them all. Hume argued plausibly that we do not find the regularities supporting laws of nature in our actual sequences of immediate sensory experiences. Instead, we extrapolate them from partial broken sequences by positing unsensed instances to accompany sensed correlates for which we find no accompanying instance in immediate experience itself.[23]

What might be called the opposite problem arises because it is incumbent upon Berkeley in his causal proof of God to provide evidence that rules out the rival hypothesis that our ideas of sense are caused by two or more gods or two or more nondivine agents. Berkeley would have recognized this need because he was well aware of Bayle's arguments in the *Dictionnaire historique et critique* for the scandalous thesis that on rational grounds alone there is no basis for preferring orthodox theism to the Manichean hypothesis of two gods, one good, the other evil, neither all-powerful.[24] To block the multiple-agent hypothesis, it would seem, one must insist that the regularities of immediate sensory experience that support an inference to an unobserved mind are such that they can occur only with a single super-intelligent cause, or are best explained by supposing such a cause. If this is so, however, what can be our grounds for inferring other human agents? To be strong enough to succeed as a proof of a *single* God, the argument seemingly must prove too much as regards other human minds. Berkeley's account of our inferences to other human minds is so meager that it is not easy to tell how he would react to the above criticism, especially because his chief business is to establish that knowledge of God's existence is more certain than knowledge of our fellow humans. Indeed, his comments on how we arrive at belief in the existence of other humans are so few and underdeveloped that one cannot say precisely and confidently what his account is. One can speculate about it, but only while acknowledging that there is very little in the way of textual evidence to guide one's musings.

Before leaving these problems, and with them Berkeley's account of minds as substances and causes, I shall make two cautionary comments. The first is that for the very reason Berkeley wrote so little on these topics, we cannot without misplaced confidence conclude that he could not have answered the objections just rehearsed. The second is more general. In the wake of Hume's use of a regularity-based definition of "cause" to shatter the a priori contraints imposed on causation by his predecessors, so that thereafter only events within experience could be used to ground substantive causal judgments, it might seem appropriate to adopt toward Berkeley on causation an attitude similar to Hume's toward the occasionalists. With them, he wrote, "We are got into fairy land," where we have no reason to trust our common methods of argument.[25] From the historical perspective, at least, this would be a profound mistake.

Material causation was widely regarded as problematic. The followers of Descartes had difficulty reconciling genuine material causation with constant creation – his interpretation of God's sustaining the created world. Philosophers debated the nature of cohesion and how motion can be transmitted from one body to another. Locke had conceded, "Bodies, by our Senses, do not afford us so clear and distinct an *Idea* of *active Power*, as we have from reflection on the Operations of our Minds."[26] So strong was the bias in favor of the view that all genuine causation requires a mind, that even after Hume's revolution a philosopher as astute as Thomas Reid (the self-proclaimed defender of common sense), was unwilling to abandon it.[27] With the persistence of debates over free will and other minds, to mention just two, it is surely premature to declare Berkeley *passé* on the ground that philosophers today at last fully understand mind and its place in nature.

NOTES

1. Berkeley might not have regarded humans as animals, so he might not have framed the questions as I have.
2. Implicit, but equally important, was Berkeley's aim of presenting the argument for immaterialism without presupposing the way of ideas endorsed by virtually all the prominent new philosophers. Note the contrast between the early arguments of the first dialogue and those of the first seven sections of *PHK*.
3. See John Locke, *An Essay concerning Human Understanding*, ed. P. H. Nidditch (Oxford: Clarendon Press, 1975), II.vii.11, for an example of how a defender of ideas and material causes grounds causation in motion without distinguishing between sensed and material motion.
4. There is considerable discussion of causes, instruments, and occasions in the Second Dialogue, some of which could be thought to shed light on volitional causation. The latter, however, is not directly and explicitly analyzed.
5. See Locke, *Essay*, IV.ii.2–7 and IV. x, for Locke's notion of demonstration and his purported demonstration of God's existence. Berkeley may have used "demonstrate" in a less strict sense than Locke, and in that sense may have claimed to demonstrate the being of God.
6. Berkeley writes in the Third Dialogue (233), "It is granted we have neither an immediate evidence nor a demonstrative knowledge of the existence of other finite spirits; but it will not thence follow that such spirits are on a foot with material substances: if to suppose the one be inconsistent, and it be not inconsistent to suppose the other; if the one can be inferred by no argument, and there is a probability for the other; if

we see signs and effects indicating distinct finite agents like ourselves, and see no sign or symptom whatever that leads to a rational belief of matter."

7. Berkeley may be referring to Locke, who held the essence of mind is as unknown as the real essence of body, or to Nicholas Malebranche, who contrasted our knowledge of the real essence of body (extension) to our ignorance of the essence of mind. See Locke, *Essay* II.xxiii.32, and Malebranche, *Elucidations of the Search after Truth*, trans. Thomas M. Lennon, published with Malebranche, *The Search after Truth*, translated by Lennon and Paul J. Olscamp, Elucidation Eleven, "On the Seventh Chapter of the Second Part of the Third Book, Where I Prove that We have No Clear Idea Either of Our Soul's Nature or of its Modifications," (Columbus, OH: Ohio State University Press, 1980), 633–8.
8. In his unpublished philosophical notebooks, Berkeley did entertain the position that all significant words signify ideas and that all knowledge is of ideas, but there is powerful evidence that he abandoned it before the *Principles* appeared in print. See *Notebooks* 377–8 and David Berman, *George Berkeley: Idealism and the Man* (Oxford; Clarendon Press, 1994), chapter 1, especially 1–17.
9. In the first edition "or rather a notion" was absent.
10. In the second edition of the *Principles*, Berkeley made a significant addition to Section 142. It included these sentences: "I have some knowledge or notion of my mind, and its acts about ideas, inasmuch as I know or understand what is meant by those words. What I know, that I have some notion of."
11. Does the self, awareness of which permits us to think of other selves, include the passions and operations included among the objects of knowledge in Section 1? This question is not answered in Section 140 and is not explicitly considered elsewhere.
12. If I understand him correctly, this is the account given by at least one Berkeley scholar, Robert Muehlmann, in his *Berkeley's Ontology* (Indianapolis: Hackett, 1992). See especially chapter 6.
13. Here are some examples of Berkeley's doubts about substance:

    Qu: whether the substance of Body or any thing else, be more than the Collection of Ideas included in that thing. Thus the substance of any particular Body is extension solidity figure. of General Body no idea. (N 512)

    The very existence of Ideas constitutes the soul. (N 577)

    Mind is a congeries of Perceptions. Take away perceptions & you take away the Mind put the Perceptions & you put the mind. (N 580)

    Say you there must be a thinking substance. Somthing unknown wch perceives & supports & ties together the Ideas. Say I, make it appear there is

> any need of it & you shall have it for me. I care not to take away any thing I can see the least reason to think should exist. (N 637)
>
> The substance of Body we know, the substance of Spirit we do not know it not being knowable. it being purus actus. (N 701)

A brief but focused survey of the entries in the notebooks in which Berkeley struggles to find a coherent and defensible account of mind and mental substance is Charles J. McCracken's "Berkeley's Notion of Spirit," *History of European Ideas* 7 (1986): 597–602.

14. See PHK 8 on resemblance, PHK 25–26 on causation, the First Dialogue, 203–6, on immediately perceived ideas and mediately perceived bodies, and the Second Dialogue, 216–21, on material substance as cause, instrument, occasion, and substratum.
15. The final three sentences of section 17 do concern support or substance. They make the point that the unsensed material substratum is supposed to support figure, motion, and other sensible qualities, which are themselves supposed to exist unsensed. They cannot so exist, hence there are no qualities to be supported, and hence no need to examine further what is meant by "support" and "material substratum."
16. The paper that initiated discussion of the inherence interpretation is Edwin B. Allaire's "Berkeley's Idealism," *Theoria* 29 (1963): 229–44. The introduction to *Berkeley's Metaphysics: Structural, Interpretive, and Critical Essays*, ed. Robert G. Muehlmann (University Park: Pennsylvania State University Press, 1995), 1–4, provides a partial bibliography of the papers in which the inherence interpretation is developed or assessed.
17. It does, however, coincide with the interpretation of Sections 7 and 17, where "supporting" was explicated, for minds, as perceiving, so as to sustain existence.
18. In the next section Berkeley goes on to argue that one does not have the same volitional control over sensory perception that one has over imagination. This difference and the greater strength and liveliness of ideas of sense over ideas of imagination become the basis both of his causal argument for God's existence and his contention that the distinction between real and imaginary sensible objects can be drawn, despite *esse* is *percipi*, on the basis of the distinction between objects due to my own volitions and those over which I have no control. In *A Treatise of Human Nature* 1.4.2., "Of Scepticism with regard to the Senses," Hume asserted that neither strength and liveliness nor involuntariness can ground externality or reality. He wrote, "For 'tis evident our pains and pleasures, our passions and affections, which we never suppose to have any existence beyond our perception, operate with greater violence, and are equally involuntary, as the impressions of figure and extension,

colour and sound, which we suppose to be permanent beings" (1.4.2.16, in *A Treatise of Human Nature*, ed. David Fate Norton and Mary J. Norton [Oxford: Oxford University Press, 2000]). In his *Enquiry concerning Human Understanding*, Hume also questioned Berkeley's implicit claim that we have full volitional control of our imaginations (see 7.18 in *An Enquiry concerning Human Understanding*, ed. Tom L. Beauchamp [Oxford: Oxford University Press, 1999]).

19. The expression "blind agency" occurs in *Notebooks* 812. The passage reads "The propertys of all things are in God i.e. there is in the Deity Understanding as well as Will. He is no Blind agent & in truth a blind Agent is a Contradiction." Compare N 841 and 842 for a statement of the doctrine without the use of the term "blind agency." Although it occurs as part of an intricate discussion relating blind agency to issues concerning unperceived objects, Kenneth P. Winkler provides a useful guide both to Berkeley's comments on blind agency and to their immediate historical context. See his *Berkeley: An Interpretation* (Oxford: Clarendon Press), chapter 7, 204–37.
20. Especially in entries numbered above 600, as those numbers are usually assigned, Berkeley was preoccupied with substance, activity, and volition. He entertained on various occasions truly radical positions, most of them questioned or replaced by the final entry, number 888. This struggle to find acceptable positions relating to mind makes all the more poignant a statement of intention in entry 878 concerning "Book 2," presumably one of the envisioned, but never published, parts of the *Principles*.
21. Three types of representation are to be distinguished from one another: (a) When two types of thing are experienced in close succession or as cause and effect, one can be said to signify or represent the other. Effects are said to represent their causes and conversely. (b) In willing, we have claimed, a thought of the would-be effect occurs. This we have called intentional representation. (c) If one just considers how an ordinary thought is of its object, as when a cloud reminds me of my brother's profile, neither causation nor volition is invoked to account for how it is of him, though one may offer a causal explanation of why the cloud provoked my thought. An idea's being of its object is what is here being called primary representation. How is it achieved? This, perhaps, is the toughest question in philosophy. Berkeley's answer seems to be: by likeness or resemblance. In practice the distinctions just drawn between intentional representation, representation by causal connection, and primary representation frequently coincide. When an effect is said to represent its cause, one's experience of the effect may lead us to have a thought of its cause. The thought represents, Berkeley probably would

say, by likeness. We shall shortly see that problems arise concerning how primary representation is achieved in the intentional representation characteristic of willing.

22. At least one other option still might seem open to Berkeley. Why not say the thought of the image is linguistic, and thus unlike the idea even though of it? Perhaps we could, but could Berkeley?
23. In his account of belief in the external world in *Treatise* 1.4.2., Hume appealed to what he called "coherence." The belief in question is that some immediate object of sensory awareness exists unperceived and independently of oneself. See 1.4.2.20–22, especially 20.
24. See, especially, Remark D of Bayle's article on the Manicheans for arguments from experience (Pierre Bayle, *Historical and Critical Dictionary: Selections*, trans. Richard H. Popkin [Indianapolis: Hackett, 1991], 144–52). Compare PHK 151–4, especially the last.
25. See Hume, *Enquiry* 7.24.
26. Locke, *Essay* II.xxi.4. There were exceptions, of course. Hobbes, in particular, comes to mind.
27. Thomas Reid, *Essays on the Active Powers of Man*, Essay 1, "Of the Active Power in General," chapters 1–5, especially 5, in *The Works of Thomas Reid*, ed. Sir William Hamilton, 6th edition, two vols. (Edinburgh: McLachlan and Stewart, 1863).

LISA DOWNING

8 Berkeley's natural philosophy and philosophy of science

Although George Berkeley himself made no major scientific discoveries, nor formulated any novel theories, he was nonetheless actively concerned with the rapidly evolving science of the early eighteenth century. Berkeley's works display his keen interest in natural philosophy and mathematics from his earliest writings (*Arithmetica*, 1707) to his latest (*Siris*, 1744). Moreover, much of his philosophy is shaped fundamentally by his engagement with the science of his time. In Berkeley's best-known philosophical works, the *Principles of Human Knowledge* and *Three Dialogues between Hylas and Philonous*, he sets up his idealistic system in opposition to the materialist mechanism he finds in Descartes and Locke. In *De Motu*, Berkeley refines and extends his philosophy of science in the context of a critique of the dynamic accounts of motion offered by Newton and Leibniz. And in *Siris*, Berkeley's flirtation with neo-Platonism draws inspiration from the fire theory of Boerhaave, as well as Newton's aethereal speculations in the Queries of the *Opticks*. In examining Berkeley's critical engagement with the natural philosophy of his time, we thus will improve our understanding of not just his philosophy of science, but of his philosophical corpus as a whole.[1]

I. BERKELEY AND MECHANISM

ffall of Adam, rise of Idolatry, rise of Epicurism & Hobbism dispute about divisibility of matter &c expounded by material substances (N 17)[2]

Extension a sensation, therefore not without the mind. (N 18)

In y[e] immaterial hypothesis the wall is white, fire hot etc (N 19)

Primary ideas prov'd not to exist in matter, after the same manner y[t] secondary ones are prov[d] not to exist therein. (N 20)

Berkeley's immaterialist hypothesis was developed and formulated in opposition to materialist mechanism, as these early entries from his philosophical notebooks make clear. Berkeley aims his criticisms most frequently at Locke and Descartes, but the view he attacks was held, in one version or another, by most of the leaders of the new science of the seventeenth century, including Galileo, Hobbes, Gassendi, and Boyle. At the risk of obscuring important theoretical divisions among these natural philosophers, the core doctrines of materialist mechanism might be sketched as follows. In perception, human beings have ideas that are caused by material objects. The existence of these material objects is not dependent upon human beings or their acts of perception. Material objects are composed of submicroscopic particles possessing only a limited range of properties: size, shape, motion, and perhaps solidity. These properties are the primary qualities of bodies. Other properties (secondary qualities) that appear to belong to bodies, such as color, taste, sound, or smell, can be accounted for in terms of the effects of primary qualities upon our sensory systems. Nothing that *resembles* our ideas of color, taste, and so on, belongs to the bodies themselves.[3] As the secondary qualities of bodies are explained in terms of primary qualities, so all physical events ought to be explained in terms of the motions and collisions of these tiny particles or corpuscles.

An examination of Berkeley's arguments against materialism is beyond the scope of this chapter (they are examined by A. C. Grayling in Chapter 6), but we do need to consider here just what it is about materialist mechanism to which Berkeley is fundamentally opposed. Throughout the *Principles* and *Dialogues*, Berkeley attacks the mechanists' identification of physical bodies with mind-independent material objects. He rejects the claim that such objects (or their primary qualities) serve as causes of our ideas, or indeed, as any sort of causes (PHK 19, 25, 50, DHP 2 [216]). He aims also to subvert the ontologically loaded version of the primary/secondary quality distinction, according to which physical bodies are systematically and radically different from the way they appear to us (PHK 9–15, DHP 1 [187–9]). These are the doctrines that appear to Berkeley to lead inexorably to skepticism and atheism.

On the other hand, Berkeley does not specifically take issue with the core mechanist claim about explanation: that physical events should be explained in terms of the motions of corpuscles possessing primary qualities. Berkeley himself has no problem with the existence of a microworld; he clearly holds that it's often appropriate to explain macroscopic events in terms of microscopic mechanisms. This is evident from the seriousness with which he addresses a broadly mechanist objection to immaterialism in *Principles* 60:

It will be demanded to what purpose serves that curious organization of plants, and the admirable mechanism in the parts of animals; might not vegetables grow, and shoot forth leaves and blossoms, and animals perform all their motions, as well without as with all that variety of internal parts so elegantly contrived and put together, which being ideas have nothing powerful or operative in them, nor have any necessary connexion with the effects ascribed to them? If it be a spirit that immediately produces every effect by a *fiat*, or act of his will, we must think all that is fine and artificial in the works, whether of man or Nature, to be made in vain.... How comes it to pass, that whenever there is any fault in the going of a watch, there is some corresponding disorder to be found in the movements, which being mended by a skilful hand, all is right again? The like may be said of all the clockwork of Nature, great part whereof is so wonderfully fine and subtle, as scarce to be discerned by the best microscope. In short, it will be asked, how upon our principles any tolerable account can be given, or any final cause assigned of an innumerable multitude of bodies and machines framed with the most exquisite art, which in the common philosophy have very apposite uses assigned them, and serve to explain abundance of phenomena.

We might be tempted to sum up Berkeley's opposition to materialist mechanism by saying that what Berkeley rejects is the metaphysical side of such mechanism, rather than its scientific side. There is a danger of anachronism here, but we can avoid it by identifying the distinction that Berkeley himself seeks to impose between natural philosophy and metaphysics. We may begin by examining Berkeley's response to the mechanist challenge:

But to come nearer the difficulty, it must be observed, that though the fabrication of all those parts and organs be not absolutely necessary to the producing any effect, yet it is necessary to the producing of things in a constant, regular way, according to the Laws of Nature. There are certain general laws that run through the whole chain of natural effects: these are learned by the observation and study of Nature, and are by men applied as well to the framing artificial things for the use and ornament of life, as to the explaining the various phenomena: which explication consists only in shewing the conformity any particular phenomenon hath to the general Laws of Nature, or, which is the same thing, in discovering the *uniformity* there is in the production of natural effects; as well be evident to whoever shall attend to the several instances, wherein philosophers pretend to account for appearances. (PHK 62)

Though God could cause a watch to run with no internal mechanism, typically he will not do so, because he causes ideas according to set laws of nature, which he follows in order that nature should be intelligible to finite perceivers. Thus, a perceived disorder in the motions of a watch will be accompanied, given the appropriate circumstances, by a perceived disorder in the internal mechanism.

Here and elsewhere in the *Principles*, Berkeley gives us not just a response to an objection, but a developed account of the nature of scientific explanation and the status of laws of nature. Berkeley holds that laws of nature are regularities in the phenomena, regularities that "we learn by experience, which teaches us that such and such ideas are attended with such and such other ideas, in the ordinary course of things" (PHK 30). According to Berkeley's metaphysics, these are *mere* regularities, because physical phenomena are constituted by our perceptions and so caused directly by God. By observation we discover these regularities, which then permit us to explain phenomena. It seems, further, that any simple inductive generalization describes a law of nature for Berkeley, and that a phenomenon is explained when it is included in such a generalization:

So that any one of these or the like Phenomena, may not seem strange or surprising to a man who hath nicely observed and compared the effects of Nature. For that only is thought so which is uncommon, or a thing by it self, and out of the ordinary course of our observation. (PHK 104)

If therefore we consider the difference there is betwixt natural philosophers and other men, with regard to their knowledge of the phenomena, we shall find it consists, not in an exacter knowledge of the efficient cause that produces them, for that can be no other than the *will of a spirit*, but only in a greater largeness of comprehension, whereby analogies, harmonies, and agreements are discovered in the works of Nature, and the particular effects explained, that is, reduced to general rules.... (PHK 105)

Here we can see the distinction that Berkeley wants to draw between natural science and metaphysics. The role of the natural philosopher, for Berkeley, is to locate patterns in our ideas, not to examine the causes of those ideas, which are spiritual and properly treated by the metaphysician.[4] We can now return to the question raised earlier: Could Berkeley endorse mechanism as properly physical theory? Prima facie, it seems that the answer should be yes. If materialist mechanism can be stripped of its metaphysics (that is, its claims about the ontological status of physical bodies and their causal powers) and converted into an account of the succession of ideas, then Berkeley has no principled objection to it.[5] It seems that Berkeley has room for an idealistic corpuscularianism, as long as corpuscles are not held to be unperceivable in some very strong sense.[6] In fact, there's no reason Berkeley could not endorse an idealistic version of the primary/secondary quality distinction, according to which the secondary qualities of observable bodies can be correlated in a law-like way with the primary qualities of smaller particles.[7]

Does Berkeley *endorse* an idealistic corpuscularianism in the *Principles* or *Dialogues*, though? Pretty clearly the answer is no.[8] While it presumably could turn out that the most useful regularities for natural science involve correlations between primary qualities of tiny bodies and other qualities and events, Berkeley shows little enthusiasm for the full mechanist program in natural philosophy in these works:[9]

> Some have pretended to account for appearances by occult qualities, but of late they are mostly resolved into mechanical causes, to wit, the figure, motion, weight, and such like qualities of insensible particles; whereas in truth, there is no other agent or efficient cause than *spirit*, it being evident that motion, as well as all other *ideas*, is perfect inert. See *Sect*. 25. Hence, to endeavour to explain the production of colours or sounds, by figure, motion, magnitude and the like, must needs be labour in vain. And accordingly, we see the attempts of that kind are not at all satisfactory. Which may be said, in general, of those instances, wherein one idea or quality is assigned for the cause of another. I need not say, how many *hypotheses* and speculations are left out, and how much the study of Nature is abridged by this doctrine. (PHK 102)

While Berkeley's primary target here is again mechanist pretenses to *causal* explanation, his dismissive attitude toward "attempts of that kind" does not seem compatible with a personal commitment to an idealistic corpuscularianism. Moreover, despite Berkeley's reservations about Newtonianism, he clearly finds it much more promising, as a species of natural philosophy, than the corpuscularianism of Descartes or Boyle.[10]

II. BERKELEY AND DYNAMICS

Berkeley's Principles *and Newtonian dynamics*

Berkeley's philosophical engagement with Newton's *Principia Mathematica* began early in his career.[11] In the *Principia*, Newton had successfully reunited mechanics and astronomy by means of his laws of motion and theory of gravity. Berkeley's appreciation for Newton's achievement was profound. In the *Principles*, Berkeley cites Newton's mechanics as "the best key for... natural science" (PHK 110). His enthusiasm does not, however, prevent him from attempting to impose conceptual reforms upon the theory: He goes on to maintain that Newton's doctrine of absolute space and motion must be abandoned. Berkeley argues that conceiving of motion requires conceiving of two bodies; thus, absolute motion is inconceivable (PHK 112–14). Having declared absolute motion to be incomprehensible, there is no need to posit absolute space. Furthermore, pure space, independent of all body, is likewise inconceivable (PHK 116).[12]

Berkeley thus dismisses Newton's distinction between absolute and relative motion, suggesting that Newton has no real need for absolute motion, for relative motion will serve his purposes just as well.[13] Nevertheless, Berkeley wants to avoid concluding that whenever two bodies are in motion relative to one another, both bodies have an equal claim to be termed "moved." That is, he seeks to preserve the intuitive distinction between true and apparent motion (for example, when I look out the window of a speeding train and see trees rushing past, I want to say that their motion is merely apparent). It is in this context that one encounters the following striking passage:

> For to denominate a body *moved*, it is requisite, first, that it change its distance or situation with regard to some other body: and secondly, that the force or action occasioning that change be applied to it. If either of these

be wanting, I do not think that agreeably to the sense of mankind, or the propriety of language, a body can be said to be in motion. I grant indeed, that it is possible for us to think a body, which we see change its distance from some other, to be moved, though it have no force applied to it (in which sense there may be apparent motion), but then it is, because the force causing the change of distance, is imagined by us to be applied or impressed on that body thought to move. Which indeed shews we are capable of mistaking a thing to be in motion which is not, but does not prove that, in the common acceptation of *motion*, a body is moved meerly because it changes distance from another; since as soon as we are undeceiv'd, and find that the moving force was not communicated to it, we no longer hold it to be moved. So on the other hand, when one only body (the parts whereof preserve a given position between themselves) is imagin'd to exist; some there are who think that it can be moved all manner of ways, tho' without any change of distance or situation to any other bodies; which we shou'd not deny, if they meant only that it might have an impressed force, which, upon the bare creation of other bodies, wou'd produce a motion of some certain quantity and determination. But that an actual motion (distinct from the impressed force, or power productive of change of place in case there were bodies present whereby to define it) can exist in such a single body, I must confess I am not able to comprehend. (PHK 115, 1710 ed.)

This passage is surprising on two counts. First, Berkeley indicates that one body alone in the universe might have a force impressed upon it. Forces, then, must be distinct from all sensible effects, such as motions. Nor can a force be a mere disposition to motion if *it* would *produce* motion. Lacking the slightest caveat here, one must assume that Berkeley thought forces existed. Second, he defines impressed force as "*power productive* of change of place" (my emphasis). He thus appears to grant forces causal status.

This understanding of force conflicts, of course, with one of Berkeley's central metaphysical tenets, argued for in the *Principles* and elsewhere, that physical things (bodies) are inactive and only spirits have causal efficacy. It is reassuring to learn that Berkeley struck the second half of the section just quoted (from "but does not prove" forward) from the second edition of the *Principles* (published in 1734, 13 years after *De Motu*). Pretty clearly, it was sometime between 1710 and 1721 that Berkeley began to reflect on the problematic status of physical forces.[14] While the 1710 edition of the *Principles* includes, as we have seen, an uncritical reference to physical forces, the 1734 edition appears merely to rely on our everyday concept of force or action (rather than the dynamicists' unintelligible notion) to ground a merely pragmatic distinction between real and apparent motion.[15]

Berkeley's motivations for writing De Motu

We already have touched on some reasons why Berkeley, qua metaphysician, would have been pushed to consider the ontological status of physical forces. The existence of active corporeal forces contradicts Berkeley's doctrine that only spirits are causally active.[16] Moreover, Berkeley makes clear that his idealism directly implies that bodies, as bundles of ideas, are causally inactive:

> All our ideas, sensations, or the things which we perceive, by whatsoever names they may be distinguished, are visibly inactive, there is nothing of power or agency included in them. So that one idea or object of thought cannot produce, or make any alteration in another. To be satisfied of the truth of this, there is nothing else requisite but a bare observation of our ideas. For since they and every part of them exist only in the mind, it follows that there is nothing in them but what is perceived. But whoever shall attend to his ideas, whether of sense or reflection, will not perceive in them any power or activity; there is therefore no such thing contained in them. A little attention will discover to us that the very being of an idea implies passiveness and inertness in it, insomuch that it is impossible for an idea to do any thing, or, strictly speaking, to be the cause of any thing.... (PHK 25)

Interestingly, however, Berkeley makes no such arguments from metaphysics in *De Motu*. On the contrary, he seems to go out of his way to keep his immaterialism firmly under wraps. This is not so surprising given his intended audience. Berkeley wrote *De Motu* as a contribution to an ongoing debate among natural philosophers; he could not and did not expect a tract on the scientific consequences of immaterialism to be taken seriously by such an audience.[17] Moreover, Berkeley's first biographer tells us that *De Motu* was submitted to the Paris Academy of Sciences, which had inaugurated its illustrious series of essay competitions by offering a prize for the best essay on motion.[18] The judges, of course, would have been generally Cartesian in orientation, and Berkeley clearly crafts his work with this in mind.[19]

Despite the absence of idealism-based arguments against the existence of forces in *De Motu*, it is clear that Berkeley's attack on realism about dynamics is in part motivated by metaphysical concerns. Indeed, these concerns are made quite explicit in *Siris*:

> In strict truth, all agents are incorporeal, and as such are not properly of physical consideration. The astronomer, therefore, the mechanic, or the chemist, not as such, but by accident only, treat of real causes, agents, or efficients. Neither doth it seem, as is supposed by the greatest of mechanical philosophers, that the true way of proceeding in their science is, from known motions in nature to investigate the moving forces; forasmuch as force is neither corporeal nor belongs to any corporeal thing.... (S 247)

> Natural phenomena are only natural appearances. They are, therefore, such as we see and perceive them. Their real and objective natures are, therefore, the same–passive without anything active.... (S 292)

Berkeley found these doctrines threatened by the dynamic theories of motion put forward, most influentially, by Newton (in the *Principia Mathematica*) and Leibniz (in the *Specimen Dynamicum*, as well as other essays). In particular, Berkeley was concerned with a position that I will call dynamic realism: the view that forces are properly attributed to bodies, and that these forces are active, in other words that they are efficient causes of motion.[20] Leibniz certainly was the most forthright of dynamic realists, and so, unsurprisingly, he comes in for the lion's share of Berkeley's abuse in *De Motu*. Newton's attitude regarding dynamic realism is, of course, more problematic. Newton's *official* position in the *Principia* was to remain stubbornly neutral about what realities might underlie his mathematical laws, and indeed Berkeley himself frequently invokes Newton in support of his own position. Nevertheless, Berkeley was concerned that the success of Newtonian dynamics might be taken to support a dynamic conception of nature. His concern was not unwarranted, as is shown by the history of Newtonianism.[21]

Berkeley's case against dynamic realism

Berkeley pursues a two-pronged assault against the dynamic realist. In the first place, he invokes a number of loosely related philosophical views, each of which he takes to be widely held and to cast doubt on the plausibility of dynamic realism. Berkeley's strategy here is to point out some of the conceptual difficulties occasioned by attributing active (that is, efficient causal) qualities to corporeal bodies. The principles Berkeley invokes are chosen carefully so as both to cohere with Berkeley's metaphysical views and to secure the widest possible agreement. In the second place, Berkeley constructs a sustained argument that aims to show that dynamic realism is nonsensical. We will now look briefly at each aspect of Berkeley's campaign against realism about dynamics.

CHALLENGE FROM COMMON PHILOSOPHICAL PRINCIPLES

Antischolasticism. Perhaps the most widely held view that Berkeley appeals to in this context is antischolasticism. Berkeley accuses dynamicists of invoking occult qualities, using obscure terms, and in general falling back upon scholastic ways of thinking (DM 8, 19, 40). Berkeley specifically cites Leibniz in this context, and of course his accusations are well-grounded, as Leibniz himself forthrightly links his dynamics to the validity of certain scholastic notions.[22] However, as it stands these charges seem rather superficial; it is not clear exactly what features are shared (other than obscurity) by the theories Berkeley stigmatizes as neoscholastic, nor why they are objectionable. Fortunately, Berkeley's critique does not stop at this relatively superficial level.

Antivitalism and the heterogeneity thesis. If we examine some closely related passages, we begin to see more clearly what it is that Berkeley objects to in those dynamic theories he stigmatizes as neoscholastic:

> *Solicitation* and *effort* or *conation* [striving] belong properly to animate beings alone. When they are attributed to other things, they must be taken in a metaphorical sense; but a philosopher should abstain from metaphor. (DM 3)

> All those who, to explain the cause and origin of motion, make use of the hylarchic principle, or of a nature's want or appetite, or indeed of a natural instinct, are to be considered as having said something, rather than thought it. And from these they are not far removed who have supposed 'that the parts of the earth are self-moving, or even that spirits are implanted in them like a form' [Borelli] in order to assign the cause of the acceleration of heavy bodies falling. So too with him [Leibniz] who said 'that in the body besides solid extension, there must be something posited to serve as starting-point for the consideration of forces.' All these indeed either say nothing particular and determinate, or if there is anything in what they say, it will be as difficult to explain as that very thing it was brought forward to explain. (DM 20)

In effect, Berkeley accuses certain dynamic theorists of vitalism – in other words, of supposing that ordinary physical bodies are animate or ensouled. Berkeley maintains that vitalism is a thesis that withers under the light of philosophical scrutiny.

Berkeley's specific targets in *De Motu* 20 do appear to be open to charges of vitalism. In his first sentence, Berkeley seems to allude to the views of the Cambridge Platonists. Ralph Cudworth, for example, is willing to suppose that matter is moved by a "Subordinate Hylarchical Principle" or soul "vitally united" with bodies.[23] Giovanni Borelli, in his *De Vi Percussionis*, holds that the descent of heavy bodies is caused by an internal agent, and he supposes, as Berkeley reports, that particles of matter are self-moving or have self-moving spirits.[24] Leibniz sees his dynamics as tied to his metaphysical thesis that bodies are, in a sense, ensouled:

> ...I admit an active and, so to speak, vital principle superior to material notions everywhere in bodies....[25]
>
> Secondary matter is, indeed, a complete substance, but it is not merely passive; primary matter is merely passive, but it is not a complete substance. And so, we must add a soul or a form analogous to a soul....
>
> Something constitutive, substantial, enduring, what I usually call a *monad*, in which there is something like perception and appetite.[26]

Berkeley was not alone in finding Leibniz's position, for example, obviously absurd; in a paper published in the *Philosophical Transactions* of the Royal Society, Samuel Clarke mocks Leibniz for supposing "some *living Soul* essentially belonging to *every Particle of Matter*."[27]

But why exactly is it manifestly mistaken to suppose that bodies in general are ensouled or endowed with an active principle? Berkeley sheds some further light on this issue in a passage in which he uncharacteristically cites Descartes as an authority:

> A thinking, active thing is given which we experience as the principle of motion in ourselves. This we call *soul, mind*, and *spirit*. Also given is a thing extended, inert, impenetrable, moveable, totally different from the former and constituting a new genus. Anaxagoras, wisest of men, was the first to grasp the great difference between thinking things and extended things, and he asserted that the mind has nothing in common with bodies, as is established from the first book of Aristotle's *De Anima*. Of the moderns Descartes has put the same point most forcibly. What was left clear by him others have rendered involved and difficult by their obscure terms. (DM 30)

Berkeley here praises Cartesianism for its dualism, which makes body and mind heterogeneous. Berkeley clearly endorses the heterogeneity thesis, despite the fact that his underlying ontology differs greatly from Descartes'. The heterogeneity thesis explains the problem with vitalism – vitalism conflates two categories that ought to be kept distinct. Descartes, too, holds that certain sorts of dynamic realism violate the heterogeneity thesis; in the Sixth Set of Replies, Descartes cites the conflation of mind and body as the source of an illegitimate conception of gravity.[28]

Of course, for Descartes the heterogeneity thesis is grounded in a particular account of nature of body and mind, according to which all properties of body are modifications of extension, and all properties of mind are modifications of thought.[29] Thus, Descartes holds that bodies can possess only a very limited range of intrinsic qualities, and force, it would appear, cannot number among them. Louis de la Forge argues explicitly that because the concept of force does not include the concept of extension, force cannot belong to matter.[30]

Here, Berkeley is very much in accord with Descartes' conclusions, but for his own reasons. Berkeley, too, holds that bodies possess only a limited range of properties, although for him those properties include all the sensible qualities, not just the purely geometrical qualities of Cartesian mechanism. In DM 30, Berkeley focuses on Descartes' conclusions, and effectively underlines the fact that the conception of body put forward by his influential mechanical philosophy seems to leave no room for active force.

However, the fact that answering these further questions requires appeal to a more detailed metaphysical system limits the scope of Berkeley's objection. We might ask, for example, whether a Newtonian need be affected by Berkeley's appeal to the heterogeneity of mind and body. The Newtonian Samuel Clarke obviously rejects Leibniz's blatant attribution of a soul-like form to matter. Clarke certainly is disturbed by the prospect of conflating spirits with bodies. The question, however, is whether attributing forces to bodies *thereby* spiritualizes them. For the Cartesians and for Berkeley, this clearly is the case, because their ontologies dictate that only spirits are active. It is not clear, however, that this claim need secure general agreement.[31]

Inertia and the passivity principle. In addition, Berkeley provides us with one other way of spelling out what's wrong with animating bodies as some dynamicists do:

> But those who attribute a vital principle to bodies are imagining an obscure notion and one ill suited to the facts. For what is meant by being endowed with the vital principle, except to live? And to live, what is it but to move oneself, to stop, and to change one's state? (DM 33)

To suppose that bodies may contain a vital principle, Berkeley claims, is to suppose that they can move themselves, which violates the widely accepted principle that body is passive in the sense of being incapable of originating new motion. (This principle obviously is in harmony with Berkeley's metaphysical views, as it follows from the claim that bodies cannot be causes at all.)

I call this a widely accepted principle; it was not universally accepted: Gassendi, the influential seventeenth century atomist, for example, had rejected it.[32] I do want to claim, however, that in asserting that body cannot be self-moving, Berkeley was in accord with a spectrum of natural philosophers ranging well-beyond the Cartesian camp. Robert Boyle, for example, held that material bodies cannot be conceived of as self-moving or as the origins of motions; moreover, he associated the opposing view with vitalism.[33] In his study of materialism in eighteenth-century Britain, John Yolton cites a number of British natural philosophers in the early to mid-eighteenth century who maintained that bodies are passive in the sense of not intrinsically possessing any power to move themselves or to originate motion, including Samuel Colliber, Humphrey Ditton, Andrew Baxter, and William Porterfield.[34]

In assessing the scope of this challenge, however, it is crucial to notice that the sort of passivity that Berkeley appeals to here does not amount to *total* passivity, that is, complete causal inactivity. Those who maintained that bodies lacked active powers (to move themselves, to originate motion) often contrasted those powers with the passive powers that bodies evidently have (to move other bodies by means of impact, to transfer motion). Locke, for example, contrasts active with passive powers, and suggests that the power to transfer motion is not properly denominated an active power. Thus, the passivity principle does not by itself support the thesis that bodies have no causal powers, and so it does not ground a completely general worry about all attributions of force to body. (Positing impact forces, for example, does not conflict with this understanding of the passivity of body.)

Interestingly, Berkeley never charges Newton with the error of making bodies active in the sense of making them sources of new motion; rather, he cites Newton as an authority who implicitly acknowledges the passivity of body:

All heavy things by one and the same certain and constant law seek the centre of the earth, and we do not observe in them a principle or any faculty of halting that motion, of diminishing it or increasing it except in fixed proportion, or finally of altering it in any way. They behave quite passively. Again, in strict and accurate speech, the same must be said of percussive bodies. Those bodies as long as they are being moved, as also in the very moment of percussion, behave passively, exactly as when they are at rest. Inert body so acts as body moved acts, if the truth be told. Newton recognizes that fact when he says that the force of inertia is the same as impetus. But body, inert and at rest, does nothing; therefore body moved *does nothing*. (DM 26, my emphasis)

In this passage,[35] Berkeley alludes to Definition III of the *Principia*, where Newton defines the *vis insita* or inherent force of matter as "the power of resisting by which every body, so far as it is able, perseveres in its state either of resting or of moving uniformly straight forward."[36] From DM 26 it appears that Berkeley is appealing to Newton as support for his claim that bodies are passive in the sense of lacking all causal powers. Now, it is clear that in some sense Newton acknowledges the passivity of bodies in Definition III, for he attributes a force of inertia or inactivity to all bodies. However, it is equally clear that this force does not rule out causal interactions between bodies; rather, it appears to govern such causal interactions–as impulse, for example, it "endeavors to change the state" of other bodies. Newton provides a more explicit statement of his understanding of the passivity of body in a draft variant relating to Query 31 of the 1717–18 English edition of the *Opticks*:

For Bodies (alone considered as long, broad & thick . . .) are passive. By their vis inertiae they continue in their state of moving or resting & receive motion proportional to ye force impressing it & resist as much as they are resisted; but they cannot move themselves; & without some other principle than the vis inertiae there could be no motion in the world.[37]

Newton's understanding of the basic nature of body thus seems in accord with the passivity principle.[38] That view, however, does not rule out causal interactions between bodies at impact. In Newton's view the *vis inertiae*, although a *passive* principle in the sense that it does not permit bodies to originate motion, explains the causal interactions among bodies in accordance with his first three laws of motion.[39]

On the other hand, the considerations Berkeley raises here do pose a grave problem for a certain type of dynamic realism. It seems that Newton's own understanding of passivity rules out the view that *gravity*, *attraction*, or *repulsion* are intrinsic qualities of body.[40] Of course, this then raises a pressing problem about the status of such forces. Many early Newtonians were concerned to reconcile Newton's theory of gravity with their belief that body itself is not self-activating and cannot *originate* motion. Richard Bentley, for example, echoes Newton's view that "brute matter," as inanimate, can only transfer motion and cannot originate it.[41] Likewise, Benjamin Worster maintains that "the inertia of matter consists in its not being able to produce or destroy Motion in itself," and that "all Matter is sluggish and inactive, and unable to move itself."[42] One solution frequently proposed was to attribute such forces to God's activity – a move that Berkeley himself certainly would applaud as a step in the right direction. Samuel Clarke, for example, makes such a move,[43] as does Worster.[44]

Thus, while appealing to the principle that matter cannot move itself does not secure the conclusion that Berkeley ultimately wanted – that matter is passive in the sense of lacking any causal power – Berkeley's appeal does highlight a widespread worry about the status of attractive and repulsive forces that rendered outright realism about Newtonian dynamics unattractive.

God's relation to the physical world. This leads us to Berkeley's final line of attack, which is designed to undermine dynamic realism generally. In *De Motu* 34, Berkeley seems to imply that while the Newtonian conception of inertia *suggests* that bodies are causally inactive, a proper conception of God's relation to bodies leaves no doubt about their status:

> Modern thinkers consider motion and rest in bodies as two states of existence in either of which every body, without pressure from external force, would naturally remain passive; whence one might gather that the cause of the existence of bodies is also the cause of their motion and rest. *For no other cause of the successive existence of the body in different parts of space should be sought, it would seem, than that cause whence is derived the successive existence of the same body in different parts of time.* But to

treat of the good and great God, creator and preserver of all things ... is, however, rather the province of first philosophy or metaphysics and theology. (DM 34, my emphasis)

In this passage, Berkeley alludes to a well-known argument of Malebranche's designed to show that a proper conception of the dependence of the world on God entails that bodies are causally inactive. Malebranche's overall argument may be summarized as follows. Every body is perpetually causally dependent on God's conservation. (Thus, God is always a necessary cause of each body's existence.) But conservation is just continuous creation. (Thus, God is always a sufficient cause of each body's existence.) But, in causing a body's existence, necessarily God causes it to exist in a determinate state (in a particular place, for example). Therefore, God is the necessary and sufficient cause of all states of all bodies. In this picture, bodies are left with no causal role to play, except as the "occasional causes" of God's actions.[45]

This picture of the dependence of the physical world on God does, then, effectively motivate an occasionalist understanding of the passivity of body. It justifies Berkeley's assertion in *De Motu* 36 that God, qua conserving cause, is the true and efficient cause of all things. It thereby rules out attributing any (active) forces to body and so rules out the sort of dynamic realism Berkeley seeks to undermine in *De Motu*. The picture is a Cartesian one, traceable to Descartes' views on conservation and creation and found in the work of other prominent Cartesians, most notably Louis de la Forge.[46] It is also fully in harmony with Berkeley's metaphysics, because in Berkeley's view the ideas that make up physical bodies are caused by God. In causing their existence, he causes their properties and relations. There is thus no room left for bodies to cause motion among themselves.

In analyzing this aspect of *De Motu*, we have seen the remarkable extent to which Berkeley identifies some of the important philosophical tensions engendered by the emergence of force-based theories of motion in the seventeenth century. Most significantly, dynamic theories conflicted with a strict dualism according to which only minds or spirits could be characterized as active, with the widespread view that matter could not be self-moving or originate new motion, and with theological claims about the total dependence of the created world upon God. Furthermore, it was among the Cartesians that these doctrines were most strictly and firmly held. Thus, *De Motu* reveals an interesting affinity between Berkeley and the Cartesians at the intersection of physics and metaphysics, despite the deep ontological differences between them. In all these respects, Berkeley's *De Motu* is a crucial document for the history and philosophy of science.

THE ARGUMENT FROM UNIMAGINABILITY. In addition to the philosophical challenges detailed so far, Berkeley also puts forward a sustained argument designed to show that dynamical realism in untenable. The core of the argument is put forward in *De Motu* 22–4:[47]

> All that which we know to which we have given the name *body* contains nothing in itself which could be the principle of motion or its efficient cause; for impenetrability, extension, and figure neither include nor connote any power of producing motion; nay, on the contrary, if we review singly those qualities of body, and whatever other qualities there may be, we shall see that they are in fact passive and that there is nothing active in them which can be understood as the source and principle of motion....
>
> And so about body we can boldly state as established fact that it is not the principle of motion. But if anyone maintains that the term *body* covers in its meaning occult quality, virtue, form, and essence, besides solid extension and its modes, we must just leave him to his useless disputation with no ideas behind it, and to his abuse of names which express nothing distinctly. But the sounder philosophical method, it would seem, abstains as far as possible from abstract and general notions (if *notions* is the right term for things which cannot be understood).
>
> The contents of the idea of body we know; but what we know in body is agreed not to be the principle of motion. But those who as well maintain something unknown in body of which they have no idea and which they call the principle of motion, are in fact simply stating that the principle of motion is unknown, and one would be ashamed to linger long on subtleties of this sort.

Berkeley's argument here may be summarized as follows:

(1) Physical forces are supposed to be active qualities of body.
(2) But all the known qualities of body are passive.
Thus, (3) force is an unknown quality of bodies.
And therefore, (4) the term 'force' is empty: It does not refer.

The real grounds for Berkeley's argument are somewhat obscured by his presentation. It is crucial to notice that by 'known quality' here, Berkeley in effect means "sensed quality" (or better, "quality as sensed"); in recommending that we "review... those qualities of body," he is directing us to recollect our sensory experiences, not to attempt to consult intellectual or abstract concepts. Thus, (2) and (3) are relatively unproblematic; the major difficulty lies in justifying the leap to (4). Berkeley supplies the missing links elsewhere in *De Motu*, arguing in effect that (a) we cannot name what we cannot conceive, and (b) conceiving of something corporeal requires having a sense-based idea of it (either an idea of sense or an idea of imagination, which in turn must have its origin in sense).[48] Thus, Berkeley grounds this argument against dynamic realism in a restrictive empiricist epistemology and a claim about the conditions required for a term to refer. Because forces cannot be imagined (activity not being a sensible quality), they cannot be conceived. Dynamic terms therefore are not referential, and dynamic realism is untenable.

Berkeley's solution

Berkeley's conclusion, then, is that dynamic terms ("force," "gravity," "impetus," and so forth) do not refer to any active qualities of bodies, and thus we cannot suppose that dynamic theory provides us with a true description of the world. One response to this conclusion would be to suggest that because dynamics fails to describe the world, we ought to look for another theory of motion. This is not Berkeley's response, however. Berkeley clearly regards Newtonian dynamics, as presented in the *Principia Mathematica*, as an adequate and well-demonstrated mechanical theory; he goes so far as to cite Newton's laws and corollaries as paradigmatic of scientific principles (DM 69). It is clear, then, that Berkeley must have held some sort of antirealist understanding of Newton's dynamics. Indeed Berkeley's primary positive aim in *De Motu* is to advocate such an understanding of dynamics. We turn now to a closer examination of Berkeley's own view of the status of dynamics.

We should begin by examining some relevant passages:

> *Force, gravity, attraction,* and terms of this sort are useful for reasonings and computations about motion and bodies in motion, but not for understanding the simple nature of motion itself or for indicating so many distinct

qualities. As for attraction, it was certainly introduced by Newton, not as a true, physical quality, but only as a *mathematical hypothesis*. (DM 17, my emphasis)

A similar account must be given of the composition and resolution of any direct forces into any oblique ones by means of the diagonal and sides of the parallelogram. They serve the purpose of mechanical science and computation; but to be of service to computation and mathematical demonstrations is one thing, to set forth the nature of things is another. (DM 18)[49]

Action and reaction are said to be in bodies, and that way of speaking suits the purposes of mechanical demonstrations; but we must not on that account suppose that there is some real virtue in them which is the cause or principle of motion. For those terms are to be understood in the same way as the term *attraction*; and just as attraction is only a *mathematical hypothesis*, and not a physical quality, the same must be understood also about action and reaction, and for the same reason. For in mechanical philosophy the truth and use of theorems about the mutual attraction of bodies remain firm, as founded solely in the motion of bodies.... (DM 28, my emphasis)

The instrumentalist tone of these passages is unmistakable. Berkeley repeatedly emphasizes the utility of dynamics for calculations about the motions of bodies as contrasted with its unsuitability as a literal description of physical reality.

These passages raise two related questions, however, that are central to an adequate interpretation of Berkeley's position: How are the theorems of dynamics founded in the motion of bodies? What is a mathematical hypothesis? Berkeley provides the key to answers in Sections 38 and 39 of *De Motu*:

In mechanics also notions are premised, *i.e.* definitions and first and general statements about motion from which afterwards by mathematical method conclusions more remote and less general are deduced. And just as by the application of geometrical theorems, the sizes of particular bodies are measured, so also by the *application* of the universal theorems of mechanics, the movements of any parts of the mundane system, and the phenomena thereon depending, become known and are determined. And that is the sole mark at which the physicist must aim. (DM 38, my emphasis)

The mechanician makes use of certain abstract and general terms, supposing in bodies force, action, attraction, solicitation, etc. *which are of first utility for theories and formulations, as also for computations about motion*, even if in the truth of things, and in bodies actually existing, they would be looked for in vain, just like the geometers' *fictions* made by mathematical abstraction. (DM 39, my emphasis)

The theorems of mechanics are founded in the motions of bodies in that they are justified by their application to "the mundane system," by their ability to "determine" or predict the motions of bodies. From the universal "theorems" we can deduce concrete predictions. Mathematical hypotheses (force, attraction, and so on) are fictions.[50] The dynamic terms ("force," "attraction," and so on) function purely formally in the theory, like formal variables. The theory as a whole serves as an instrument or calculating device for making kinematic predictions. Berkeley's antirealism is thus full-fledged instrumentalism.[51]

Berkeley's recommended attitude toward dynamics is indeed modern-sounding, and it is not without provocation that some have characterized Berkeley as a proto-positivist. However, such descriptions run the risk of two sorts of problem. On the one hand, they tend to obscure the contextual motivation and significance of Berkeley's project as a contribution to an ongoing debate about the status of forces in mechanics and, more generally, about the activity/passivity of the natural world. And on the other, by encouraging a narrow focus on the modern-sounding aspects of Berkeley's philosophy of science, they obscure the connections between that philosophy of science and other aspects of his philosophy. In other words, they promote the neglect of both the historical and philosophical context of Berkeley's instrumentalism. As I have tried to show, both contexts are crucial to understanding Berkeley's case against dynamic realism and his intended alternative.[52]

Instrumentalism and the revised view of explanation

In Section I, we took note of Berkeley's account of laws of nature and explanation in the *Principles*; this account undergoes significant development in *De Motu*. The account in the *Principles* (according to which any simple inductive generalization counts as a law of nature, and phenomena are explained by inclusion in such generalizations) faces two major problems. The first is rather basic: Satisfactory scientific theorizing seldom stops with simple inductive generalizations. If, for example, I observe that the copper roof of a newly built building has begun to turn greenish, my generalization that this always seems to happen to copper that has been exposed to the elements clearly does not provide an adequate *scientific* explanation of my observation. The second difficulty is more specific: In the *Principles*,

Berkeley describes Newton's *Principia Mathematica* as "the best key" for natural science (PHK 110). However, Newton's laws of motion, the foundation of his mechanical system, are not the products of simple inductive generalization, and they do not each correspond to a simple regularity in the phenomena. Thus, in the *Principles*, it is unclear how Berkeley could regard Newton's laws as laws of nature that explain the motions of bodies.

In *De Motu*, Berkeley refines his account of natural laws and explanation in a way that alleviates these two problems and supports his dynamic instrumentalism. The key change in *De Motu* is Berkeley's new emphasis on the importance of the *generality* of scientific laws in properly scientific explanation:

> Similarly in mechanical philosophy those are to be called principles, in which the whole discipline is grounded and contained, those primary laws of motions which have been proved by experiments, elaborated by reason and rendered universal. These laws of motion are conveniently called principles, since from them are derived both general mechanical theorems and particular explanations of the phenomena.
>
> A thing can be said to be explained mechanically then indeed when it is reduced to those most simple and universal principles, and shown by accurate reasoning to be in agreement and connection with them. For once the laws of nature have been found out, then it is the philosopher's task to show that from the constant observance of these laws, that is from these principles, any phenomena necessarily follow. In that consist the explanation and solution of phenomena.... (DM 36–7)

Thus, in *De Motu*, Berkeley develops a specialized sense of "law of nature" according to which the laws of nature are the most general principles from which observed regularities in the phenomena can be deduced. A phenomenon is explained scientifically, then, when it is shown to follow from these most general principles.

In keeping with this revised conception of laws of nature, Berkeley no longer describes the scientist as merely inductively collecting laws from observation; rather the laws are "proved by experiments, elaborated by reason and rendered universal." Likewise, in *Siris* Berkeley states that "the natural or mechanic philosopher endeavours to discover those laws by experiment and reasoning" (S 234).

Because laws of nature may transcend simple inductive generalizations, Newton's laws become legitimate candidates for natural laws.

Berkeley's *De Motu* view of laws of nature and scientific explanation permits him to confer this status upon Newton's laws: We can deduce from them innumerable regularities in the motions of bodies, and observed motions can be explained by being shown to follow from Newton's laws (given initial conditions). Berkeley maintains that Newton's laws can play this role without having to be regarded as factual statements, because their importance lies in their applicability, not in descriptive content (which Berkeley ultimately thinks they lack). Thus Berkeley's *De Motu* view of laws of nature and scientific explanation legitimates his instrumentalist attitude toward Newtonian dynamics by dictating that Newton's laws, construed instrumentally, do count as laws of nature and do provide scientific explanations of kinematic phenomena. Moreover, the revised notions of laws of nature and scientific explanation that Berkeley puts forward in *De Motu* reflect more accurately the actual practice of science, which values generality in its theories, than his *Principles* view, which allowed that any inductive generalization explains its instances.

Although Berkeley's *De Motu* view of the aims of science clearly represents an improvement over his view in the *Principles*, it nevertheless provokes further questions. In particular, while Berkeley's *De Motu* view does capture the *fact* that science aims at general theories, one might well ask how Berkeley explains *why* science should seek generality – why more general laws provide more adequate scientific explanations. One response that might seem to be open to Berkeley is to assert that more general laws are more likely to accurately reflect God's volitions, because God's nature leads him to work in simple ways. This is not a response that Berkeley actually gives, however; in general, he seems reluctant to suppose that we can conclude much from our limited knowledge of God's nature.[53]

The response that seems most in accord with Berkeley's stated views is the following: General laws are preferable for pragmatic reasons; we can do more with them – make more predictions, correlate more data, and so forth. The nature of this response brings out the fact that Berkeley's notion of scientific explanation is a highly pragmatic one, so much so that one might wonder whether it really deserves to be called a notion of *explanation* at all. Certainly, Berkeley himself acknowledges a more full-bodied sort of explanation – causal explanation – which he holds to be the province of metaphysics or theology, rather than science:

Physically, therefore, a thing is explained *not by assigning its truly active and incorporeal cause*, but by showing its connection with mechanical principles.... (DM 69, my emphasis)

Only by meditation and reasoning can truly active causes be rescued from the surrounding darkness and be to some extent known. To deal with them is the business of first philosophy or metaphysics. And if each science were allotted its own province, its bounds assigned, the principles and objects belonging to it accurately distinguished, it would be possible to treat each with greater ease and clarity. (DM 72)[54]

Moreover, Berkeley holds that in order to truly and completely "account for the phenomena," we *must* treat their efficient cause:

We cannot make even one single step in accounting for the phenomena without admitting the immediate presence and immediate action of an incorporeal Agent, who connects, moves, and disposes all things according to such rules, and for such purposes, as seem good to Him. (S 237)

Although Berkeley describes himself as analyzing how science explains, it might be less misleading to describe him as putting forward a new view of the *aims* of science, rather than a new view of scientific explanation. Berkeley's position, under this description, is that science does not aim at *explanation* (which makes reference to causes) but rather at a certain sort of useful *understanding* of nature (which he is happy to call "explanation"), akin to the sort of understanding of a language that we gain from studying its grammar:

There is a certain analogy, constancy, and uniformity in the phenomena or appearances of nature, which are a foundation for general rules: and these are a grammar for the understanding of nature, or that series of effects in the visible world whereby we are enabled to foresee what will come to pass in the natural course of things. (S 252)

Newton's dynamics, construed instrumentally, provides precisely the sort of understanding that Berkeley takes to be the ultimate aim of science. Thus, Berkeley's considered view of the aims and workings of natural science complements and supports his instrumentalism about dynamics.

At this point, we are in a position to appreciate another problem with applying the proto-positivist tag to Berkeley, namely that it suggests a serious misreading of Berkeley's reformist project in *De Motu*. Berkeley's aim in *De Motu* is not, as the positivist label implies, to free physics from the tyranny of metaphysics. Indeed, Berkeley's aim is more nearly the reverse: Clearly Berkeley wishes to insulate metaphysics, and in particular, his idealist metaphysics, from the new science. Berkeley's prescription privileges metaphysics by placing causal explanation within its domain. Berkeley is quite blunt about this result in *Siris*:

Certainly, if the explaining a phenomenon be to assign its proper efficient and final cause, it should seem the mechanical philosophers never explained anything; their province being only to discover the laws of nature, that is, the general rules and methods of motions, and to account for particular phenomena by reducing them under, or shewing their conformity to, such general rules. (S 231)

Of course this should not be taken to suggest that Berkeley can be depicted as some sort of antiscience reactionary. On the contrary, he was a sincere and enthusiastic Newtonian precisely because his instrumentalist prescription for dynamics allowed him to be: If dynamics can be given an instrumentalist reading, then we have no a priori reason to prefer Newtonian physics to Cartesian physics – the theories must be judged by their results. It is clear what Berkeley thought the verdict should be:

Nature seems better known and explained by attractions and repulsions than by those other mechanical principles of size, figure, and the like; that is, by Sir Isaac Newton than Descartes. (S 243)

III. BERKELEY AND THE AETHER

This aether or pure invisible fire, the most subtle and elastic of all bodies, seems to pervade and expand itself throughout the whole universe. If air be the immediate agent or instrument in natural things, it is the pure invisible fire that is the first natural mover or spring from whence the air derives its power. This mighty agent is everywhere at hand, ready to break forth into action, if not restrained and governed with the greatest wisdom. Being always restless and in motion, it actuates and enlivens the whole visible mass, is equally fitted to produce and to destroy, distinguishes the various stages of nature, and keeps up the perpetual round of generations and corruptions, pregnant with forms which it constantly sends forth and resorbs. So quick in its motions, so subtle and penetrating in its nature, so extensive in its effects, it seemeth no other than the vegetative soul or vital spirit of the world. (S 152)

Siris, published in 1743, was Berkeley's last major work. It is undeniably an odd book, at least from the perspective of a student of Berkeley's early philosophical works; there are discontinuities of both style and substance between *Siris* and the *Principles*. The continuities, however, also are striking, and merit more scholarly attention than heretofore they have received.[55]

In particular, *Siris* exhibits very strongly Berkeley's lifelong interest in natural philosophy and, more specifically, his interest in Newton's works. Nevertheless, the result is a work of a very different character from *De Motu*. Whereas in *De Motu* Berkeley constructs a (narrowly) philosophical critique of the Newtonianism of the *Principia*, in *Siris* Berkeley produces a (broadly) philosophical meditation inspired by the Newtonianism of the Queries to the *Opticks*.

At the heart of *Siris* is the aether or invisible fire. Berkeley's enthusiasm for the aether clearly owes much to Newton, but his characterization of it is inspired more directly by the work of Hermann Boerhaave, the Dutch chemist, botanist, and physician whose teachings were highly influential in mid-eighteenth-century Britain.[56] Boerhaave, along with other Dutch natural philosophers cited by Berkeley, assigned a central role in accounting for physiochemical activity to fire – a subtle, insensible particulate substance sometimes identified with light.[57]

In order to understand why Berkeley accords this aether such a central role in *Siris*, we must take into consideration the aims of the book, which were three-fold: "to communicate to the public the salutary virtues of tar-water";[58] to provide scientific background supporting the efficacy of tar-water as a medicine; and to lead the mind of the reader, by gradual steps, toward contemplation of God.[59] The latter two aims shape Berkeley's extensive use of contemporary natural science in *Siris*: The "activity" of the aether, in his view, can both explain the miraculous virtues of a certain medicine, tar-water, and reveal God's divine order (S 237–9).

Limitations of space prevent us from following out the "chain of philosophical reflexions" that constitute *Siris*. We should touch briefly, though, on the relation of the philosophy of science in *Siris* to Berkeley's earlier views. In this area, the continuities with Berkeley's earlier work are very strong indeed.[60]

Berkeley makes heavy use of dynamic notions such as forces, attractions, and repulsions in *Siris*, most notably in his description of the aether, which is supposed to "operate" by means of forces (S 162). However, Berkeley also makes clear that the dynamic elements of his theorizing are to be understood instrumentally, not as literal attributions of real forces to particles; to say that certain particles attract or are attracted is just to say that their movements agree with certain laws (S 231). Indeed, some of Berkeley's most explicit declarations that physical bodies are not and cannot be invested with force are to be found in *Siris* (S 234).

Moreover, Berkeley makes clear that his tendency to dignify the aether with titles such as "mighty agent" should likewise not be taken at face value. The aether is, despite its subtlety, corporeal, and Berkeley remains firm in his conviction that no corporeal things can be true efficient causes:[61]

> We have no proof, either from experiment or reason, of any other agent or efficient cause than mind or spirit. When, therefore, we speak of corporeal agents or corporeal causes, this is to be understood in a different, subordinate, and improper sense. (S 154)

> Therefore, though we speak of this fiery substance as acting, yet it is to be understood only as a mean or instrument, which indeed is the case of all mechanical causes whatsoever. They are, nevertheless, sometimes termed agents and causes, although they are by no means active in a strict and proper signification.... In compliance with established language and the use of the world, we must employ the popular current phrase. But then in regard to truth we ought to distinguish its meaning. It may suffice to have made this declaration once for all, in order to avoid mistakes. (S 155)

What is more deeply puzzling about *Siris*, from this perspective, is Berkeley's apparent realism about the aether: He seems to treat the aether as something known to exist rather than as a "mathematical hypothesis" (S 281). This puzzle may be partially resolved by noting that Berkeley's reasons for treating forces as mere mathematical hypotheses center on their purported activity. Because the aether is not truly active, a realistic treatment of aether is not ruled out.[62] More specifically, accepting the existence of aether does not give rise to the sort of conceptual problems diagnosed by Berkeley in *De Motu*. Nor does it violate the epistemological and semantic doctrines appealed to in Berkeley's argument from unimaginability; the aether is corporeal and particulate – it possesses parts with size, shape, weight and so forth (S 162, 207). Because the aether possesses qualities of a sensible kind, it is imaginable and hence conceivable. Realism about aether is thus tenable in a way that realism about forces is not.

Thus, Berkeley's use of natural philosophy in *Siris* is not in obvious conflict with his philosophy of science laid out in *De Motu*. Moreover, aspects of that philosophy of science find their fullest and finest articulation only in *Siris*:[63]

> It passeth with many, I know not how, that mechanical principles give a clear solution of the phenomena. The Democritic hypothesis, saith Dr. Cudworth, doth much more handsomely and intelligibly solve the phenomena than that of Aristotle and Plato. But, things rightly considered, perhaps it will be found not to solve any phenomenon at all; for all phenomena are, to speak truly, appearances in the soul or mind; and it hath never been explained, nor can it be explained, how external bodies, figures, and motions, should produce an appearance in the mind. Those principles, therefore, do not solve, if by solving is meant assigning the real, either efficient or final, cause of appearances, but only reduce them to general rules. (S 251)

> The phenomena of nature, which strike on the senses and are understood by the mind, form not only a magnificent spectacle, but also a most coherent, entertaining, and instructive Discourse; and to effect this, they are conducted, adjusted, and ranged by the greatest wisdom. This Language or Discourse is studied with different attention, and interpreted with different degrees of skill. But so far as men have studied and remarked its rules, and can interpret right, so far they may be said to be knowing in nature. A beast is like a man who hears a strange tongue but understands nothing. (S 254)

NOTES

1. Of course one should also mention here Berkeley's works on vision, treated in Chapter 4 of this volume, which are certainly philosophical and are inspired in part by Berkeley's opposition to the geometrical theories of vision he found in Descartes and Malebranche.

2. Quotations from *De Motu* are from Luce's translation, which I have occasionally altered slightly for the sake of accuracy. I have also benefitted from Douglas Jesseph's translation in George Berkeley, *"De Motu" and "The Analyst": A Modern Edition with Introduction and Commentary*, ed. Douglas M. Jesseph (Dordrecht: Kluwer Academic Publishers, 1992).
3. Of course, this does not require the mechanist to deny that bodies are colored. Rather, as in Locke, color in bodies may be identified with powers (grounded in the body's primary qualities) to produce certain kinds of ideas.
4. See also DM 71, 72.
5. Here I agree with Daniel Garber, "Locke, Berkeley, and Corpuscular Scepticism," in *Berkeley: Critical and Interpretive Essays*, ed. Colin M. Turbayne (Minneapolis: University of Minnesota Press, 1982), 174–96; Kenneth P. Winkler, *Berkeley: An Interpretation* (Oxford: Clarendon Press, 1989), 238–75; and Margaret Atherton, "Corpuscles, Mechanism and Essentialism in Berkeley and Locke," *Journal of the History of Philosophy* 29 (1991): 47–67.
6. If corpuscles are unperceivable, then treating corpuscularianism as a description of regularities in our ideas becomes problematic; or, to put it another way, questions arise about the compatibility of the existence of corpuscles with Berkeley's *esse* is *percipi* principle. Here one must ask in what sense corpuscles are unperceivable. If, for example, they could be perceived with powerful microscopes (even if those microscopes are unlikely to be invented), then there doesn't seem to be much of a problem. For a more detailed discussion of this issue, see Margaret Wilson, "Berkeley and the Essences of the Corpuscularians," in *Essays on Berkeley: A Tercentennial Celebration*, ed. John Foster and Howard Robinson (Oxford: Clarendon Press, 1985), 131–48; Winkler, *Berkeley*, 263–75; and Lisa Downing, "*Siris* and the Scope of Berkeley's Instrumentalism," *British Journal for the History of Philosophy* 3 (1995): 279–300. Wilson also raises the interesting question of whether an acknowledgment of the scientific importance of the microworld is compatible with Berkeley's inclination to proclaim that according to his philosophy, we perfectly comprehend physical things (*Essays on Berkeley*, 146).
7. This comes in handy for interpreting *Siris* 266. See K. Winkler, *Berkeley*, 260–2.
8. Thus I agree with Wilson that Garber overreads *Principles* 60–6 somewhat. See *Essays on Berkeley*, 134–8 and Garber, "Corpuscular Scepticism," 182–7.
9. This of course does not prevent him from endorsing some obvious "mechanistic" claims about the behavior of plants and animals being correlated with an internal mechanical structure.

10. This is most explicit in *Siris* 243, but also seems evident in Berkeley's tendency, from the *Principles* onward, to reserve his praise in the area of natural philosophy for Newton.
11. Berkeley worries about the implications of Newton's doctrine of absolute motion as early as *Notebooks* 30.
12. Space does not permit a critical treatment of these claims. For further discussion see W. A. Suchting, "Berkeley's Criticism of Newton on Space and Time," *Isis* 58 (1967): 186–97; Gerd Buchdahl, *Metaphysics and the Philosophy of Science* (Cambridge, MA: MIT Press, 1969), 317–24; and Richard J. Brook, *Berkeley's Philosophy of Science* (The Hague: Martinus Nijhoff, 1973), 125–45.
13. It is presumably because Berkeley thinks that our clear conceptions of relative motion and space will stand in for Newton's unintelligible notions that he never raises the possibility of an instrumentalist treatment of absolute space, along the lines of his instrumentalist treatment of force. Berkeley argues that we implicitly rely on a relative conception of motion even when we suppose ourselves to be appealing to absolutes. See PHK 114, DM 64.
14. This position is, of course, necessarily somewhat speculative, but it is supported by the fact that Berkeley's pre-1721 writings include few remarks on physical force and show no signs of significant philosophical reflection on the status of dynamics. The only dynamic entry in his philosophical notebooks is 456, where Berkeley appeals to the notion of a *vis impressa* in what is apparently an attempt to defuse Newton's bucket argument as an argument for absolute space. (It may be that an allusion to a force-based response to the bucket experiment is preserved at the very end of *Principles* 114, in both the first and second editions. Berkeley is extremely cryptic here, however, so I do not take this as indicating a commitment to the existence of forces. See Suchting, "Berkeley's Criticism," 193. Neither the *New Theory of Vision* (1709) nor the *Three Dialogues* (1713) contain any significant use of dynamic concepts.

    More convincing (if still indirect) evidence that Berkeley, in this early stage of his career, had no well-thought-out philosophical attitude toward physical forces is provided by a look at the manuscript version of the *Principles* (George Berkeley, Add. MS. 39304 fol. 70r–78r, Department of Manuscripts, British Museum, London). The relevant portion of the manuscript is covered with deletions and insertions. Most tellingly, *Principles* 115 (including the problematic section) has no real ancestor in the manuscript version. It would seem, then, that *Principles* 115 represents a late decision by Berkeley to recapitulate his conclusions from *Principles* 113 and to elaborate upon the application of the notion of force to the problem at hand. Berkeley later came to regret the elaboration, and so dropped it from the second edition of the *Principles*. (I am indebted to Douglas Jesseph for suggesting to me the possible interest of this manuscript material.)

15. For different interpretations of this passage and the import of the changes in the second edition, see Kenneth P. Winkler, "Berkeley, Newton, and the Stars," *Studies in History and Philosophy of Science* 17 (1986): 23–42, and Warren O. Asher, "Berkeley on Absolute Motion," *History of Philosophy Quarterly* 4 (1987): 447–66.
16. At DHP 2 (217), for example, Philonous seeks to convince Hylas that "to suppose any efficient or active cause of our ideas, other than *spirit*, is highly absurd and unreasonable."
17. Thus I strongly disagree with Luce's assessment of *De Motu* as "the application of immaterialism to contemporary problems of motion" (Luce, Editor's Introduction to *De Motu*, *Works* 4: 3–4).
18. Joseph Stock, *An Account of the Life of George Berkeley*, in *George Berkeley: Eighteenth Century Responses*, ed. David Berman (New York: Garland, 1989), 1: 19. While no records of the submission remain (see Jesseph's editor's introduction to *"De Motu"* and *"The Analyst": A Modern Edition*, 3), certainly the timing of the essay and Berkeley's decision to write in Latin support this contention.
19. For example, in *De Motu* 25, Berkeley endorses a dualism of corporeal things and thinking things, not adding that in his own view corporeal things turn out to be bundles of ideas that are fundamentally ontologically dependent upon thinking things. Also in *De Motu* 53 Berkeley speaks somewhat uncharacteristically of a faculty of pure intellect (which, as it turns out, has spirit and the actions of spirits as its sole objects). Of course, here Berkeley is not saying anything that *contradicts* his own considered position, but he is certainly emphasizing his points of agreement with Cartesianism to the point that the reader might rashly assume more agreement than actually exists. The only passage in which it seems to me that Berkeley carries this strategy to the point of being disingenuous is *De Motu* 29, where he appears to suggest that the corpuscularian conception of body exhausts the real qualities of bodies. Of course, Berkeley himself holds that all the sensible qualities, including color, taste, sound, and so forth, are alike real qualities of bodies (a possibility that is left open by Berkeley's more cautious phrasing in *De Motu* 22).
20. Thus, while (as we will see) Berkeley attacks views that would invest bodies with spiritual powers or would merge body and spirit so as to activate the natural world, he does not address views that would attribute force only to spiritual substances entirely distinct from matter. Doubtless he assumes that the only sensible way of understanding the claim

that there are spiritual forces is as merely stating that minds cause the motions of bodies. He ultimately held, of course, that God's mind was the universal cause of such motions.

21. Indeed Cotes' preface to the second edition of the *Principia* (1713), wherein he speaks of gravity as a primary quality of matter, might well have fueled Berkeley's concern. Sir Isaac Newton, *The Principia: Mathematical Principles of Natural Philosophy*, ed. and trans. I. Bernard Cohen and Anne Whitman (Berkeley: University of California Press, 1999), 391–2. For relevant material on the history of Newtonianism see, among others, Robert E. Schofield, *Mechanism and Materialism: British Natural Philosophy in an Age of Reason* (Princeton: Princeton University Press, 1970), and P. M. Heimann and J. E. McGuire, "Newtonian Forces and Lockean Powers: Concepts of Matter in Eighteenth-Century Thought," *Historical Studies in the Physical Sciences* 3 (1971): 233–306.
22. See G. W. Leibniz, "A New System of Nature," in *Philosophical Essays*, trans. and ed. Roger Ariew and Daniel Garber (Indianapolis: Hackett Publishing Co., 1989), 139.
23. Ralph Cudworth, *Collected Works of Ralph Cudworth*, Volume 1, *The True Intellectual System of the Universe* (London: Richard Royston, 1678; reprinted Hildesheim: George Olms, 1977), 668–9. See also Jesseph's *"De Motu" and "The Analyst": A Modern Edition*, 81.
24. Giovanni Alfonso Borelli, *De vi percussionis liber* (Bononiae: Jacob Montij, 1667), 180–1. See R. S. Westfall's discussion in his *Force in Newton's Physics* (New York: American Elsevier Publishing Co., 1971), 228–9.
25. Leibniz, "A Specimen of Dynamics," *Philosophical Essays*, 125.
26. Leibniz, "On Nature Itself," *Philosophical Essays*, 162–3.
27. Samuel Clarke, "Letter Occasion'd by the present Controversy among Mathematicians, concerning the Proportion of Velocity and Force in Bodies in Motion," *Philosophical Transactions* 35 (1728): 381–8. Moreover, the second section (no. 2) of Clarke's appendix to the Leibniz-Clarke correspondence is clearly crafted to highlight what Clarke too sees as vitalism and neoscholasticism in the underpinnings of Leibniz's dynamics. Samuel Clarke and G. W. Leibniz, *The Leibniz-Clarke Correspondence*, ed. H. G. Alexander (Manchester: Manchester University Press, 1956) 127–31.
28. Rene Descartes, "Author's Replies to the Sixth Set of Objections," in *The Philosophical Writings of Descartes*, translated by John Cottingham, Robert Stoothoff, and Dugald Murdoch (Cambridge: Cambridge University Press, 1984), 2: 297–8. Murray Miles argues that Descartes' general opposition to positing underived forces in matter

stems from his conviction that to do so "involves an illicit conflation of the mental with the physical." See his "Descartes' Mechanism and the Medieval Doctrine of Causes, Qualities, and Forms," *The Modern Schoolman* 65 (1988): 101, 111.

29. Strictly speaking, this formulation must be qualified to take note of the fact that duration, existence, unity, and number are properties of both mind and body. Garber handles this by saying that all properties of body must be ways of being an extended substance. Daniel Garber, *Descartes' Metaphysical Physics* (Chicago: University of Chicago Press, 1992), 67–8.
30. Louis de la Forge, *Traité de l'esprit* (Amsterdam: Abraham Wolfgang, 1666; reprinted Hildesheim: Georg Olms, 1984), 251–2.
31. Of course, one might also simply reject the heterogeneity thesis altogether, as did Anne Conway in a treatise first published in Latin in 1690, eleven years after her death: *The Principles of the Most Ancient and Modern Philosophy*, ed. Allison P. Coudert and Taylor Corse (Cambridge: Cambridge University Press, 1996).
32. Even Gassendi, however, held that matter is not essentially self-moving, but that this attribute is bestowed on it by God at creation. Pierre Gassendi, *The Selected Works of Pierre Gassendi*, ed. and trans. Craig B. Brush (New York: Johnson Reprint Corporation, 1972), 399.
33. See Robert Boyle, *A Free Enquiry into the Vulgarly Received Notion of Nature*, ed. Edward P. Davis and Michael Hunter (Cambridge: Cambridge University Press, 1996), 25.
34. John Yolton, "Matter: Inert or Active," in *Thinking Matter: Materialism in Eighteenth-Century Britain* (Minneapolis: University of Minnesota Press, 1983), 90–106. Even Cudworth and More affirmed that matter is passive and unable to move itself. In their view spiritual principles must be introduced to explain activity. The result is the flagrant vitalism disparaged by Berkeley and Clarke.
35. See also *De Motu* 51.
36. Newton, *Principia*, 404.
37. Sir Isaac Newton, Add. 3970, fol. 620r, Cambridge University Library, quoted in J. E. McGuire, "Force, Active Principles, and Newton's Invisible Realm," *Ambix* 15 (1968): 170–1.
38. Here I am in agreement with Ernan McMullin, who argues that the core of Newton's conception of the passivity of matter is captured by the principle that matter cannot of itself be the source of new motion. Ernan McMullin, *Newton on Matter and Activity* (Notre Dame: University of Notre Dame Press, 1978), 35, 101–6.
39. See Alan Gabbey, "Force and Inertia in the Seventeenth Century: Descartes and Newton," in *Descartes: Philosophy, Mathematics, and*

Physics, ed. Stephen Gaukroger (Brighton: Harvester Press, 1980), 279 and 284.

40. Some of Newton's critics accused him of having such a view of gravity, although he vehemently rejected it in his now well-known letter to Bentley. Sir Isaac Newton, *Newton's Papers and Letters on Natural Philosophy*, ed. I. Bernard Cohen (Cambridge, MA: Harvard University Press, 1958), 302–3. To what extent this letter represented Newton's own view, as opposed to his desire to escape controversy, is, of course, a difficult question.
41. Richard Bentley, "Sermon VII," in *Eight Sermons* (Cambridge: Cornelius Crownfield, 1724) , 277–81.
42. *A Compendious and Methodical Account of the Principles of Natural Philosophy*, ed. Benjamin Worster, 2nd edition (London: Stephen Austen, 1730), xvi, 5.
43. Samuel Clarke, "A Discourse concerning the Unalterable Obligations of Natural Religion," in *The Works of Samuel Clarke* (London: J. and P. Knapton, 1738), 2: 601.
44. ". . . [It] is most evident and certain, that either these active Principles [attraction and repulsion] themselves, or at least that more general one from whence they result, is altogether immechanical and independent from Matter, and can only proceed from the first Cause and Author of all things. . . . " Worster, *Principles of Natural Philosophy*, 10.
45. Nicolas Malebranche, "Dialogue VII," in *Dialogues on Metaphysics*, trans. Willis Doney (New York: Arabis, 1980), 157.
46. Louis de la Forge, *Traité de l'Esprit de l'Homme*, in *Œuvres Philosophiques*, ed. Pierre Clair (Paris: Presses Universitaires de France, 1974), 242–3. It is, of course, a disputed question whether Descartes himself was committed to occasionalism. It suffices for my purposes that this be one obvious interpretation of certain of Descartes' tenets. Malebranche and de la Forge, among others, interpreted Descartes in this way. More recently Gary Hatfield has argued that Descartes does not, in the final analysis, attribute true forces to bodies, but rather holds that God is the source of the motions of bodies. Gary Hatfield, "Force (God) in Descartes' Physics," *Studies in the History and Philosophy of Science* 10 (1979): 113–40.
47. See also *De Motu* 29–31.
48. See *De Motu* 21 and 53, in addition to *De Motu* 22–24 and 29–31. For more detailed analysis of this argument, see Downing, "Berkeley's Case Against Realism About Dynamics," in *Berkeley's Metaphysics: Structural, Interpretive, and Critical Essays*, ed. Robert G. Muehlmann (University Park, PA: Pennsylvania State University Press, 1995), 197–214. Clearly (b) is the argument's weakest link.

49. Berkeley is referring to Newton's Corollaries I and II. See Newton, *Principia*, 417–18.
50. As passages quoted previously illustrate, in *De Motu* Berkeley most commonly uses "mathematical hypothesis" to mean something like "fictional entity admitted for the purposes of calculation." There are hints, however, of a broader usage according to which a mathematical hypothesis is a false supposition (or fiction) assumed for the purpose of calculation. Thus, the mathematical hypotheses involved in dynamics would not be forces and attractions, but rather that there are physical forces, that there are attractions, and so forth. This usage makes somewhat more perspicuous the parallels Berkeley sees between geometry and dynamics. Berkeley gives an example of a geometrical hypothesis in *De Motu* 61: "A curve can be considered as consisting of an infinite number of straight lines, though in fact it does not consist of them. That hypothesis is useful in geometry. . . . " The broader usage also appears in *Siris* 234: "But *what is said* of forces residing in bodies, whether attracting or repelling, is to be regarded only as a mathematical hypothesis, and not as anything really existing in nature" (my emphasis). For my purposes, however, nothing rides on this distinction between senses of 'mathematical hypothesis,' so I adhere to the narrower usage more prevalent in *De Motu*.
51. Many commentators have interpreted Berkeley as a reductionist (Hinrichs, Myhill, and Brook), rather than an instrumentalist, or as vacillating between the two (Buchdahl and Newton-Smith). On the reductionist interpretation, Berkeley would hold that dynamics is reducible to kinematics, that is, he would be committed to the possibility of translating any statement apparently invoking forces into a statement merely about the motions of bodies. Instrumentalism, on the other hand, avoids any claims about translatability by regarding the theory as a whole as a calculating device. In my view, several considerations militate against the reductionist interpretation, the most important being that Berkeley always *justifies* the use of mathematical hypotheses by the *utility* of dynamics, never by the *translatability* of dynamic terms into kinematic ones, nor does Berkeley offer anything like a manual for translation. Although certain passages of *De Motu* have a reductionist ring (DM 6, 7, 11, 22), one must keep in mind Berkeley's target. A realist Newtonian mechanist of the sort Berkeley is attacking holds that forces are distinct from all sensible effects. Berkeley supposes, however, that when such a person imagines having a nonvacuous concept of force, it must be an (illegitimate) thought of motion or the sensation of effort. Consequently, Berkeley repeatedly emphasizes that dynamical terms don't denote *anything other* than motion, felt impact, and so on; in this context,

to say that forces can't be separated from motions is just to say that *there aren't any distinct entities that are forces*. In *Siris*, it is clearer still that Berkeley is no reductionist; he straightforwardly declares that motion, but not force, belongs to bodies (S 234, S 250). For reductionist or quasireductionist interpretations of Berkeley see Gerard Hinrichs, "The Logical Positivism of Berkeley's *De Motu*," *Review of Metaphysics* 3 (1950): 492; John Myhill, "Berkeley's *De Motu*–An Anticipation of Mach," in *George Berkeley*, ed. S. C. Pepper, Karl Aschenbrenner, and Benson Mates, University of California Publications in Philosophy vol. 29 (Berkeley: University of California Press, 1957), 147; Brook, 117–18; Buchdahl, 287–8; W. H. Newton-Smith, "Berkeley's Philosophy of Science," in *Essays on Berkeley: A Tercentennial Celebration*, ed. John Foster and Howard Robinson (Oxford: Clarendon Press, 1985), 152.

52. I have room here only to gesture at one other important aspect of the philosophical context of Berkeley's instrumentalism. In the seventh dialogue of *Alciphron*, Berkeley develops a theory of significance according to which language can be significant, despite not suggesting ideas, by guiding or inspiring action. (This account is foreshadowed to some extent in the Draft Introduction to the *Principles*.) He specifically applies his account of action-guiding language to the case of dynamics, suggesting that dynamic terms acquire a sort of significance through their role in a system of action-guiding rules. Thus, Berkeley's views about language help to give further content to the instrumentalism he defends in *De Motu*.
53. Berkeley does, however, assume that we can know that God is benevolent and rational, and he maintains that this should give us confidence in our laws of nature.
54. See also *Siris* 231.
55. My own general interpretive attitude towards *Siris*, which I cannot defend at any length here, is that for the most part the book can be rendered consistent with the metaphysics of Berkeley's early works (as indeed Berkeley thought it could be), although the results are not always appealing. While Berkeley had not given up his idealism when he wrote *Siris*, he *had* abandoned some of his former motivations for it–strict empiricism and a desire to uphold common sense against skepticism, for example.
56. On Berkeley's debt to Boerhaave, see Jessop's introduction to *Siris*, *Works* 6: 11. Jessop also collects relevant passages from the *Elementa Chemiae* as Appendix II to *Siris*. See also I. C. Tipton, "The 'Philosopher by Fire' in Berkeley's *Alciphron*," in *Berkeley: Critical and Interpretive Essays*, ed. C. M. Turbayne (Minneapolis: University of Minnesota, 1982), 161. On Boerhaave's views and his influence in Britain, see

Schofield, 134–57. The *Elementa Chemiae* was published in 1732 and translated into English in 1735 and again in 1741. An unauthorized edition compiled from student lecture notes had been published in 1724 and translated into English in 1727.

57. Berkeley also mentions Nieuwentyt and Homberg, S 189–90.
58. *Siris*, Berkeley's introductory paragraph, *Works*, 5: 31.
59. On the last, see S 297, 303.
60. For a detailed treatment of aspects of Berkeley's natural philosophy in *Siris*, see Gabriel Moked, *Particles and Ideas: Bishop Berkeley's Corpuscularian Philosophy* (Oxford: Clarendon Press, 1988).
61. By "corporeal," Berkeley still ultimately means "ideal," as is made clear in *Siris* 251 and 292.
62. The question of the compatibility of the actual existence of the aether with Berkeley's *esse* is *percipi* principle is, however, a delicate one. See Wilson in *Essays on Berkeley*, 131–48; Winkler, *Berkeley*, 263–75; and Downing, "*Siris* and the Scope of Berkeley's Instrumentalism."
63. It has been some years since this chapter was composed, and it is difficult to reconstruct my numerous debts. My greatest debt is to the late Margaret Wilson, who helped shape early versions of this material, and always provided a model of the best scholarship. I am grateful for substantial help at some stage from Abraham Roth, Kenneth Winkler, Douglas Jesseph, and Ernan McMullin.

DOUGLAS M. JESSEPH

9 Berkeley's philosophy of mathematics

Berkeley was concerned with mathematics and its philosophical interpretation from the earliest stages of his intellectual life. As a student at Trinity College, Dublin, he became acquainted with the great mathematical advances of the seventeenth century (including analytic geometry and the calculus), and his interest in mathematics led him to devote his first publication to the subject. This book, *Arithmetica et Miscellanea Mathematica*, was part of Berkeley's campaign for a fellowship at Trinity, and although it is hardly a great mathematical contribution, it shows his familiarity with the arithmetical, algebraic, and geometric work of the early eighteenth century. Notwithstanding his proficiency in the mathematics of his day and his awareness of its philosophical background, Berkeley followed a decidedly independent and critical course in the philosophy of mathematics. There is, of course, nothing anomalous about this. Berkeley was always prepared to challenge the received views of his predecessors. Just as he approached the metaphysical, epistemological, or scientific doctrines of Descartes, Leibniz, or Newton with a critical (or even hostile) attitude, Berkeley was prepared to challenge their accounts of mathematics, even if this meant rejecting the most widely received principles and successful mathematical theories of his day.

His interest in mathematics remained with Berkeley throughout his career and eventually led him to publish a critique of the calculus in 1734 under the title of *The Analyst*. The publication of this treatise, which a noted historian of mathematics once called "the most spectacular event of the century in the history of British mathematics,"[1] led to a long and intense controversy over the foundations of the calculus. It is largely on the basis of *The Analyst* that Berkeley is known to historians of mathematics, and there is no question that this work is his most substantive and impressive mathematical publication. Nevertheless, it would be a mistake to see *The Analyst* as an isolated foray into mathematical terrain or as a work disconnected from other parts of Berkeley's philosophical enterprise. On the contrary, *The Analyst* is best seen as an application of Berkeley's philosophical principles to a particularly interesting case, namely the issue of how the techniques of the calculus can be reconciled with acknowledged criteria of mathematical rigor.

This chapter is divided into three parts. The first explores the background to Berkeley's philosophy of mathematics by sketching the main lines of the theory he opposed, as well as some of the contested philosophical questions raised by the mathematical developments of the seventeenth and eighteenth centuries. The second presents an overview of Berkeley's own conception of the object of mathematics and the principles appropriate to mathematical demonstration. The third contains a brief account of the infinitesimal calculus and Berkeley's objections to it, especially as they are formulated in *The Analyst*. The investigation leads into territory that is not generally covered in a study of Berkeley, but it will become clear that he did address issues central to the philosophy of mathematics, and that an adequate understanding of his philosophy necessitates an exploration of topics often ignored in the literature.[2]

I. SEVENTEENTH-CENTURY PHILOSOPHY AND MATHEMATICS

The seventeenth century was a period of intense and influential activity in philosophy and mathematics. In examining the philosophy and mathematics of this period, it is important to recognize that the two fields were associated much more closely than they are today, so that in that era a well-educated person could follow developments and do original work in both philosophy and mathematics. The contributions of Descartes and Leibniz are the most salient examples of this phenomenon, but these two were by no means the only thinkers to have turned their talents to the study of both mathematics and philosophy. In fact, such leading mathematicians as Isaac Barrow, John Wallis, and Isaac Newton devoted much of their published work to an examination and exposition of philosophical issues raised by mathematics. It is also remarkable that philosophers and philosophically minded mathematicians of the era shared a broadly defined philosophy of mathematics. This is not to say that there was unanimity of opinion on all issues – far from it, as I will argue later in this section. Nevertheless, there was widespread agreement on certain fundamental philosophical questions concerning mathematics. The "received view" in the philosophy of mathematics was, however, rejected by Berkeley, and it is important to devote some time to a study of it in order to clarify Berkeley's own views on the nature of mathematics.

The abstractionist philosophy of mathematics

The conventional wisdom in Berkeley's day held that mathematics was a science of abstractions. Although there were differences in points of detail, nearly every thinker who addressed the question held that the objects of mathematical investigation were, in some important sense, the products of human thought, and that they were produced by the abstraction or "stripping away" of irrelevant features. In contrast to a purely "Platonistic" doctrine according to which mathematical objects inhabit an extramundane domain of forms, or to a nominalistic theory that denies mathematical vocabulary any extralinguistic reference, abstractionism locates the objects of mathematics in a realm of pure concepts generated by the intellect.

The roots of the abstractionist philosophy of mathematics reach back to Aristotle, who adopted it as an alternative to the Platonic theory of forms.[3] In denying that mathematical objects reside in the realm of forms or serve as some kind of intermediary between the physical world and the formal domain, Aristotle was forced to give some account of the nature of mathematical objects without making them depend too closely upon specific features of the actual world. It is manifest that the truths of geometry should not depend upon the existence of material objects answering exactly to the definitions employed by geometers, and it seems equally obvious that there is no hope of developing a theory of arithmetic in which numbers are treated as actual physical objects. Aristotle's way around these difficulties was to declare that the objects of mathematical investigation begin with our perceptions of the physical world, but are generated by a process of abstraction. There are difficulties in accounting for exactly what is meant by the term "abstraction," but this much seems clear: Abstraction involves the mental removal of particular aspects of perceived objects. To abstract from the location of a tree, for example, is to think of it not as the tree in the park, but simply to conceive of it without reference to its location or any of its surroundings. More relevantly, at least for the mathematical case, the Euclidean definition of a line as "breadthless length" (*Elements* 1, Def. 2) can be taken as characterizing an abstraction in which the intellect separates the idea of length from breadth, thereby forming an object appropriate to the science of geometry. The result, according to Aristotle, is that

> ... The mathematician investigates abstractions (for in his investigation he eliminates all the sensible qualities, e.g. weight and lightness, hardness and its contrary, and also heat and cold and the other sensible contrarieties, and leaves only the quantitative and continuous, sometimes in one, sometimes in two, sometimes in three dimensions, and the attributes of things qua continuous, and does not consider them in any other respect, and examines the relative positions of some and the consequences of these, and the commensurability and incommensurability of others, and the ratios of others; but yet we say there is one and the same science of all these things – geometry).[4]

This approach to the philosophy of mathematics did not die with Aristotle. Many medieval thinkers (most notably Thomas Aquinas) found it quite congenial, for it has the virtue of linking mathematical knowledge to more ordinary kinds of knowledge without making mathematical truths depend upon contingent features of the actual world.[5] Furthermore, abstractionism gives important content to the claim that mathematical objects exist, without either tying their existence too closely to the physical world or removing the objects of mathematical investigation to a mysterious realm of pure forms.

The role of abstractionism in the scholastic philosophy of mathematics can perhaps best be seen in the work of Christopher Clavius (1537–1612), a Jesuit astronomer-mathematician who was a leading figure in development of sixteenth-century science and philosophy. The Jesuits followed a strongly Thomistic line in both metaphysics and epistemology, and Clavius was something of a champion of the mathematical sciences. One of his principal concerns was to find an appropriate place for mathematics in the Jesuit course of study at the *Collegio Romano*, a task made difficult by the fact that several influential Jesuits were openly hostile to mathematics, and regarded it as essentially inferior to such genuine sciences as physics. For instance, the Jesuit Benedict Pereira argued that mathematics fails to achieve the status of a genuine science because "mathematical things are abstracted from motion, therefore from all types of cause."[6] Because he regarded all scientific knowledge as grounded in the consideration of causes (a doctrine that has important Aristotelian roots), Pereira was prepared to conclude that mathematics could not properly be classed as a science. Clavius opposed this denigration of mathematics, and argued that the mathematical sciences occupy a kind of "middle ground" between physics and metaphysics, due to their peculiarly abstract character. As he explains:

> Because the mathematical sciences treat of things which are considered apart from all sensible matter, although they are themselves immersed in matter, this is the principal reason that they occupy a middle position between the metaphysical and natural sciences. If we consider [the sciences each according to its] subject,... the subject of metaphysics is indeed separated from all matter of any kind. But the subject of physics is always conjoined with some kind of matter. Whence, as the subject of the mathematical disciplines is considered apart from all matter, it is clear that it constitutes a mean between the other two.[7]

This theory also allows for a straightforward distinction between pure and applied mathematics in terms of the degree of abstraction found in each science. Because the objects of mathematics are abstracted from the contents of the physical world, pure mathematics deals with fully abstract objects, while applied mathematics treats partial abstractions that retain some of the sensible qualities of material objects. The application of mathematics to nature thus involves a reversal of the abstracting process that initially generated the objects of mathematics: We begin with a fully abstract result in pure mathematics but then regard the objects in nature as if they were the points, lines, or numbers of pure mathematics. This point is summed up nicely by Isaac Barrow, Cambridge's first Lucasian Professor of mathematics, when he remarks that "the parts of pure or abstract mathematics contemplate absolutely the general nature and proper affections of both number and magnitude, while the mixed or concrete parts consider the same as applied to certain bodies and special subjects, together with motive force and other physical accidents."[8]

The abstractionist philosophy of mathematics had become such a commonplace in Berkeley's day that Joseph Raphson's *Mathematical Dictionary* could define "Simple or Pure Mathematics" as "those parts of it which contemplate Quantity, simply as such, or abstracted from Matter, or any sensible Object."[9] Of course, Locke is notorious for his endorsement of the doctrine of abstract ideas, and there is nothing unusual or novel in his insistence that mathematical knowledge arises from the contemplation of abstract ideas of such mathematical objects as triangles or numbers.[10]

Berkeley's rejection of abstraction thus entails a repudiation of the dominant philosophy of mathematics in his day, and it is no exaggeration to say that his entire philosophy of mathematics is founded upon his critique of abstraction. In rejecting the abstractionist conception of mathematics, Berkeley set himself the task of developing an account of the metaphysics and epistemology of mathematics that does not rely upon the doctrine of abstract ideas. I will have more to say about these matters in Section II, but I must first outline some of the philosophical perplexities presented by seventeenth-century mathematics.

Disputed questions in seventeenth-century mathematics

Although the general framework of the abstractionist philosophy of mathematics was accepted almost universally in the seventeenth century, important issues still were contested by philosophers and mathematicians of the period. Two such questions are of interest for a study of Berkeley, for they bear crucially on his own program for the philosophy of mathematics. The first of these concerns the status of algebra and the related issue of whether arithmetic or geometry is the true foundation of all mathematics. The second concerns the rigor and reliability of infinitesimal methods. This subsection will address both questions briefly and indicate their connection to Berkeley's own philosophical project.

The development of algebra and its subsequent application to geometric problems (in the form of Descartes' "analytic geometry") is one of the most important advances in the history of mathematics. By the middle of the seventeenth century, mathematicians had available a powerful new tool that could readily solve problems previously deemed either extremely difficult or downright insoluble.[11] This great progress, though, was accompanied by unresolved difficulties that perhaps can best be expressed in terms of the problem of the classification of the sciences. According to traditional doctrine, the sciences are classified according to the objects with which they are concerned and the principles they employ. Traditionally, geometry and arithmetic were regarded as separate sciences, each with a distinct object: Geometry studies continuous magnitudes, while arithmetic is concerned with discrete magnitudes. Algebra does not fit particularly well into this scheme, because it does not appear to have a proper object. The general theory of equations applies to magnitudes of any kind, and yet the fundamental algebraic operations of addition, subtraction, multiplication, division, and the extraction of roots appear to be linked more closely to arithmetic. With the advent of analytic geometry and the resulting fusion of geometric and algebraic techniques, it became a matter of some importance to clarify the relationship between algebra, geometry, and arithmetic.

In his presentation of analytic geometry, Descartes held that the old opposition between geometry and arithmetic rested upon a failure to appreciate the power of the generalized conception of magnitude implicit in the use of algebra. The role of algebraic analysis in the new geometry is summed up on Descartes' remark in Book II of the *Geometry*:

> I could give here several other means to trace and conceive curved lines, which curves could become successively more complex without limit. But to take together all those which are in nature and to distinguish them by orders into certain types, I know of no better way than to say that all the points of those curves we can call "geometric", that is to say which admit of a precise and exact measure, necessarily have a definite relation to all the points of a right line, which relation can be expressed by a single equation.[12]

In emphasizing the role of algebraic equations in the classification and solution of geometric problems, the Cartesian program for geometry at once makes geometry amenable to algebraic investigation while challenging the traditional picture of the relationship between the different sciences. Another important difference between analytic and classical methods concerns the manner in which algebraic operations are interpreted in geometry. Classically, the geometric multiplication of two lines yields a rectangle, or the product of three lines a solid. But Descartes interprets multiplication as an operation that leaves the dimension of the product homogeneous with that of the multiplicands. Just as the product of two numbers is a number, Cartesian analytic geometry treats the product of two lines as a line. And in general, all operations in analytic geometry are operations on line segments that result in new line segments. This conception of geometry is underwritten by a strong thesis on the unity of arithmetical and geometric magnitudes. Descartes sees nothing peculiarly arithmetical about the operation of addition, or anything uniquely geometrical about the extraction of roots. The resulting application of algebra to geometry therefore treats algebra as a science of magnitude in general, and the specifically geometric content of a problem is removed when it is represented as a relation among various abstract magnitudes.

John Wallis took Descartes' results to show that arithmetic is ultimately the foundation of all mathematics, and he argued for the primacy of arithmetic over geometry in his 1657 *Mathesis Universalis*. This work marshals philosophical, historical, and philological arguments for the claim that arithmetic is the true foundation of all mathematics. Indeed, Wallis's point of view is evident in the full title of the *Mathesis Universalis*, which promises (among other things) "a complete Arithmetical work, presented both philologically and mathematically, encompassing both the numerical as well as the specious or symbolic arithmetic, or geometric calculus."[13] Part of his reasoning is the argument that universal algebra is fundamentally arithmetical and not geometrical. He insists that even the most basic geometric principles must ultimately be grounded in the universal truths of arithmetic. For instance, Wallis argues that the apparently geometrical fact that a line of two feet added to a line of three feet yields a line of five feet is really an arithmetical fact upon which a geometrical calculation is based.[14]

Barrow rejected this reasoning. In fact, he tried to turn the tables on Wallis by arguing that geometry is ultimately the foundation of all mathematics. In the third of his *Mathematical Lectures* Barrow considers Wallis's argument for the priority of arithmetic and issues the following rebuttal:[15]

> To this I respond by asking How does it happen that a line of two feet added to a line of two palms does not make a line of four feet, four palms, or four

of any denomination, if it is abstractly, *i.e.* universally and absolutely true that two plus two makes four? You will say, this is because the numbers are not applied to the same matter or measure. And I would say the same thing, from which I conclude that it is not from the abstract ratio of numbers that two and two make four, but from the condition of the matter to which they are applied. This is because any magnitude denominated by the name two added to a magnitude denominated two of the same kind will make a magnitude whose denomination will be four. Nor indeed can anything more absurd be imagined than to affirm that the proportions of magnitudes to one another depend upon the relations of the numbers by which they may be expressed.

Barrow's case for the primacy of geometry hinges on the claim that numbers, in and of themselves, are mere symbols whose content derives from their application to continuous geometric magnitude. To put it another way, there are no "numbers in the abstract" to serve as the object of arithmetic, except those that arise from the consideration of homogeneous magnitudes and their division.[16]

This difference of opinion is significant for understanding Berkeley's philosophy of mathematics. Berkeley can best be seen as trying to found geometry and arithmetic on separate kinds of principles and thereby avoid the kinds of difficulties and disputes in which Wallis and Barrow had become enmeshed. Furthermore, Barrow's conception of arithmetic and algebra as concerned solely with the manipulation of symbols reappears in Berkeley's own formalistic account of the nature and object of arithmetic, but he does not follow Barrow in taking this to indicate that arithmetic needs some further (that is, geometric) foundation.

The second major point of controversy in seventeenth-century mathematics concerned the admissibility of infinitesimal methods. We will investigate some of these issues more closely when we come to an account of Berkeley's critique of the calculus, but it is worthwhile at this stage to outline briefly the nature of the infinitesimal magnitudes and the conceptual difficulties they raise. The principles of classical geometry, particularly as formulated in the text of Euclid's *Elements*, confine the purview of geometry to the consideration of finite geometric magnitudes and finite differences between such magnitudes. Thus, to investigate a problem classically, there can be no recourse to treating geometric magnitudes as composed of an infinity of infinitely small parts. For example, the classical

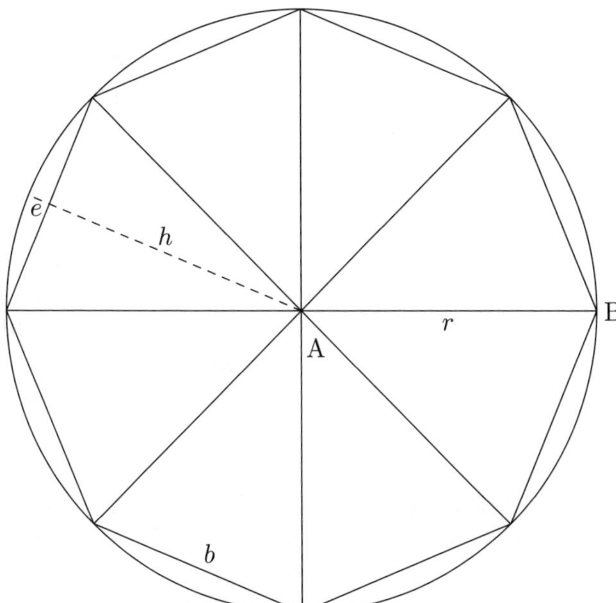

Fig. 1. Approximating the circle with isosceles triangles.

approach to the problem of determining the area of a figure (known as the problem of quadrature) can only consider finite lines, areas, or volumes that are produced by constructions from the standard axioms of Euclidean geometry.

This restriction to finitary methods makes the treatment of even very elementary results a matter of considerable complexity, and it renders a general approach to problems of quadrature all but impossible. In contrast, the use of infinitesimal methods can simplify matters quite considerably, and it is largely on account of their simplicity and relative generalizability that these methods were preferred by the "progressive" mathematicians of the seventeenth century. A simple example should illustrate the point. Let us consider the circle AB (as in Fig. 1) with center A, a radius of length r, and circumference c, and then use infinitesimal considerations to derive the formula πr^2 for its area. We first note that the area of the circle can be approximated by taking a collection of equal isosceles triangles inscribed within the circle, whose greater sides have length r. Moreover, if we consider ever-larger collections of such triangles, each with a progressively smaller base, we observe that they provide closer and closer approximations to the area. Letting b designate the length of the base of such a triangle and h designate the height, each triangle will have the area $\frac{1}{2}bh$. Then, taking e to represent the difference between h and r, we can express this area as $\frac{1}{2}b(r-e)$. If k represents the number of triangles used in the approximation, the value of c is approximated as kb and the area of the circle as $\frac{1}{2}kb(r-e)$.

It is tempting to think that, by taking an infinitely large collection of triangles with infinitesimally small sides, the above approximation will give way to an exact result. In the infinite case, our approximation to c (the circumference of the circle) becomes exact, so the term c can replace kb in our earlier area formula, while e (the difference between r and h) "vanishes." Replacing kb with c and $(r-e)$ with r, we get $\frac{1}{2}cr$ as the true area of the circle. However, because π is defined as the ratio between the circumference and diameter of the circle, and the diameter is equal to $2r$, we have $c = 2r$, and our formula for the area can be rewritten as $\frac{1}{2}rc = \frac{1}{2}r(2\pi r) = \pi r^2$.

Despite the fact that this argument is considerably shorter than a rigorous classical demonstration, and notwithstanding its fairly natural and intuitive appeal, the use of infinitesimals is not without its difficulties. The most pressing problem engendered by the use of infinitesimals is that of giving an account of what kind of thing infinitesimal magnitudes are. The infinitesimal appears to hover between something and nothing, because it is a magnitude less than any given (positive) quantity, and yet not equal to zero. Because the traditional conception of rigor requires that mathematics deal only with objects that are comprehended clearly, the use of the infinitesimal clearly requires some further justification if it is to be reconciled with the relevant canons of rigor and intelligibility. Those who introduced infinitesimal methods into seventeenth-century mathematics were well aware of these conceptual difficulties and sought (not with uniform success) to bring the infinitesimal within the purview of the classical standard of rigor, by arguing either that the infinitesimal could be made methodologically respectable, or that the results obtained by the use of infinitesimals could be obtained without them.[17] Berkeley was well aware of the conflicts surrounding the use of infinitesimals, and a major concern in his philosophy of mathematics is to show that the infinitesimal is both inadmissible and unnecessary in a properly developed mathematical theory.

II. BERKELEY'S PHILOSOPHY OF MATHEMATICS

The most general characterization of Berkeley's philosophy of mathematics identifies it as a denial of abstractionism. This level of description is too general to be very informative, however, because it says nothing about how Berkeley goes about the business of interpreting mathematics in nonabstract terms. The picture can be filled in more completely by observing that where the traditional account had declared abstractions to be the object of mathematical investigation, Berkeley treats mathematics as a science concerned with objects of sense. These sensible objects are of little interest in themselves, however, because the essential feature of mathematical knowledge is its generality. On Berkeley's view, the generality of mathematics arises from the capacity of perceived objects to function as signs. Linking mathematics to the theory of signs also permits Berkeley to accept the traditional division of mathematics into geometry and arithmetic, because he finds fundamentally different kinds of perceived objects to function as signs in the two principal mathematical sciences. Geometry takes (perceivable) extension as its object, while arithmetic will be interpreted nominalistically so that its immediate object will be symbols. This distinction of objects for the two sciences leads Berkeley to accept quite different accounts of geometrical and arithmetical truth. The theorems of geometry must answer to the facts of perception (because perceivable extension is its object), while arithmetical truths will have a conventional element (because they will be truths about the symbols themselves, and the choice of symbolic notation is largely arbitrary).

Berkeley's twofold approach to geometry and arithmetic also has the effect of sidestepping the traditional disputes over the relative priority of the two sciences. Where Wallis and Barrow had been concerned to show that either arithmetic or geometry occupied a privileged position as the foundation of mathematics, Berkeley is content to take them as independent, so that neither can claim priority over the other. It is also important to observe that in distinguishing sharply between arithmetic and geometry Berkeley does not mandate a strict theoretical segregation of the two domains: Because arithmetic (and its generalization in algebra) is a symbolic system applicable to anything, there is room for the use of algebraic techniques in geometry, although it is necessary that such an application proceed in accordance with principles consistent with the nature of geometric extension.

Not surprisingly, Berkeley's epistemological tenets also rule out the use of infinitesimal methods in mathematics. The objects of sense clearly are not infinite in nature, and Berkeley repeatedly insists that the capacity of the human mind does not extend to the comprehension of the infinite. Lacking an idea of the infinite, we thus are constrained to employ mathematical principles that are finitistic. Berkeley is certainly not alone in opposing infinitesimal mathematics, but his strict rejection of the infinite led him to deny even the infinite divisibility of geometric magnitudes, and in this respect his philosophy of mathematics was more radical than others of his day. The details of his philosophy can best be seen by first treating his account of geometry and contrasting it with his views on arithmetic.

Berkeley on geometry

A study of Berkeley's writings on geometry reveals that his thoughts on the subject underwent a significant change, particularly with respect to the question of how much of traditional geometry can be accommodated within his antiabstractionist epistemology. In his early notebooks, or *Philosophical Commentaries*, Berkeley outlined a radical program for geometry that would require the rejection of nearly all of classical geometry. In particular, during this period Berkeley opposed the doctrine of infinite divisibility and sought to found geometry on his doctrine of the minimum sensible – the smallest part of extension. By the time of the publication of the *Principles*, however, Berkeley had abandoned his plan for a new geometry of minima and had found the means to provide a nonabstract interpretation of classical geometry that left essentially all of the subject intact. This change in view can be understood best by contrasting the doctrine set forth in the notebooks with the pronouncements on geometry in the *Principles*.

When he wrote the notebooks, Berkeley was convinced that the doctrine of abstract ideas was a philosophical blunder that had led to a serious misunderstanding of the nature of geometry. "No Idea of Circle, etc. in abstract," he declares at N 238, and later elaborates: "Extension without breadth i.e. invisible, intangible length is not conceivable tis a mistake we are led into by the Doctrine of Abstraction" (N 365a). Here he is obviously challenging the claim that a Euclidean line can be conceived by abstracting breadth from length. As he expresses it, the doctrine of abstraction has led to the mistake of thinking that there could be such a thing as breadthless length, and the result of this mistake is a wholly misguided theory of the object of geometry. The entry also connects Berkeley's critique of abstract ideas to his *esse* is *percipi* thesis in an interesting way, because the "mistake" to which the doctrine of abstraction leads is that of supposing there could be an invisible and intangible (that is, unperceivable) length.

Berkeley's rejection of the standard account of geometry clearly develops out of his critique of abstraction, but it is not immediately clear what consequences this rejection has at the level of geometrical practice. As it turns out, Berkeley was led by his epistemology to deny the infinite divisibility of geometric magnitudes, and thence to propose a thoroughgoing revision of geometry designed to bring this science into line with his austere epistemological tenets. The connection between Berkeley's antiabstractionism and his rejection of infinite divisibility is readily explained. The abstractionist grants that perceived extension is not infinitely divisible, but the abstractionist theory of geometry makes room for the thesis of infinite divisibility by not requiring that geometry be restricted to the realm of the perceivable. There is surely a limit to the number of divisions we can make in any line actually drawn in the course of a geometric demonstration, but the thesis of infinite divisibility is unproblematic for abstractionism because it takes lines drawn in chalk or ink as mere physical representations of geometry's true objects, and these true geometric objects are abstractions from ordinary experience that do not suffer such physical limitations. Berkeley opposes such a move, and in the notebooks he insists that the truths of geometry be judged by appeal to the senses: "Sense rather than reason & demonstration ought to be employ'd about lines & figures, these being things sensible, for as for those you call insensible we have prov'd them to be nonsense, nothing" (N 466).

The thesis of infinite divisibility can be stated as the claim that every geometric magnitude, of whatever kind, is divisible into two magnitudes of the same kind. Thus, the infinite divisibility of the line is the thesis that every line can be divided into two lines, and a similar claim holds for other kinds of magnitude such as surfaces, angles, or solids. True to the principle that the object of geometry is perceived extension, Berkeley insists that there is a fundamental limit beyond which extension cannot be further divided. This limit, or minimum sensible, is therefore a kind of atom out of which Berkeley holds that geometric magnitudes can be constructed.

The significance of the thesis of infinite divisibility for traditional geometry can hardly be overstated. Versions of it are among the most elementary theorems proved in the first book of Euclid's *Elements*, and it was commonly held that such theorems suffice as incontestable proofs of the thesis of infinite divisibility itself.[18] Infinite divisibility is also implicated in the theory of incommensurable ("surd") magnitudes. A standard problem in classical geometry is to establish the proportion between two magnitudes, but such proportions cannot generally be expressed as ratios of integers. The most familiar example concerns the diagonal δ and side σ of a square; the proportion $\delta{:}\sigma :: \sqrt{2}{:}1$ is notoriously incapable of expression as a ratio of integers. If the thesis of infinite divisibility were false, though, then the side and the diagonal could be resolved into minimal parts, and the ratio between the two magnitudes could then be expressed as the ratio between the number of parts in the side and the diagonal, that is, as a ratio of integers.

In the notebooks, Berkeley proposed to take the minimum sensible as the foundation for geometry, and to let such minima play the role that the point plays in Euclidean geometry. Not surprisingly, his new geometry conflicts with the Euclidean system at every turn. The root of this conflict is the fact that Berkeley takes lines and figures to be composed of finite collections of minima, whereas Euclidean geometry requires that they contain an infinite number of points. Berkeley does not undertake a systematic exposition of his radical geometry of the minimum sensible, and there is no need for a detailed investigation of its claims.[19] The basic idea is that the features of any given geometric magnitude are determined exactly by the number of its minima (or "points" as Berkeley often calls them). The ordinarily difficult problem of comparing the lengths of a right line and a curve, for example, is easily solved: "If wth me you call those lines equal wch contain an equal number of points, then there will be no difficulty. that curve is equal to a right line wch contains as [many] points as the right one doth" (N 516). Similarly, Berkeley declares, "I can mean (for my part) nothing else by equal triangles than Triangles containing an equal number of points" (N 530). The scope of Berkeley's radical intentions for geometry in the notebooks can best be indicated by his remarks at N 469, where he announces that the doctrine of the minimum sensible will eliminate the doctrine of incommensurable magnitudes and make short work of any geometric problem. He writes:

> I say there are no incommensurables, no surds. I say the side of any square may be assign'd in numbers. Say you assign unto me the side of the square 10. I ask w^{t} 10, 10 feet, inches, etc. or 10 points. if the later; I deny there is any such square, tis impossible 10 points should compose a square. if the former, resolve y^{r} 10 square inches, feet, etc into points & the number of points must necessarily be a square number whose side is easily assignable. (N 469)

Naturally, such venerable results as the Pythagorean Theorem must also fall by the wayside in this new system of geometry: "One square cannot be double of another. Hence the Pythagoric Theorem is false" (N 500). And, of course, the theorem that any line can be bisected must be given up. A line consisting of an odd number of points, for example, cannot be divided into two equal lines (N 267, 276).

This program is unabashedly radical, but it is also hardly coherent. The idea that geometric magnitudes can be composed of finite collections of indivisible parts is not original with Berkeley,[20] but to take it seriously threatens to destroy anything worthy of the name of geometry. Beyond its manifest inconsistency with the accepted principles of classical geometry, Berkeley's geometry of minima faces serious objections even on its own terms. These need not be rehearsed in detail, but it suffices to indicate one such difficulty to show the kind of problem the doctrine encounters. Consider the problem of how to compose a line out of minima. The minima that compose the line must, it seems, be in immediate contact with one another, because otherwise an unbroken line must contain gaps. Then a single minimum in the interior of the line has at least two distinguishable parts: that part in contact with the adjacent minimum on either side. The indivisibility of minima, however, guarantees that they can have no parts. Hence, if the minima touch at all, they must coincide completely, and it is impossible that there can be a line consisting of more than one minimal part.

In light of such difficulties, Berkeley's proposal to overthrow classical geometry for the sake of a doctrine of minima seems entirely hopeless. Indeed, if the notebooks were Berkeley's only contribution to the philosophy of mathematics, his writings on the subject would be justly ignored. Fortunately, Berkeley abandoned this radical program and found the means to accommodate essentially all of classical geometry by exploiting his doctrine that universality consists not "in the absolute, positive nature or conception of anything, but in the relation it bears to the particulars signified or represented by it" (I 15). The Berkeleyan alternative to the theory of abstract ideas (which I call the theory of representative generalization) holds that the theoretical work previously assigned to abstract ideas can instead be taken over by particular ideas that stand as representatives of all other ideas of the same kind. The central tenet of the theory is summed up in Berkeley's declaration that "an idea, which is considered in itself is particular, becomes general by being made to represent or stand for all other particulars of the same sort" (I 12). In the geometric case, perceived lines or figures can be taken as representatives of all similar lines or figures, and the theorems proved of them can be applied generally to the class of things they represent, without supposing that the theorems deal either with abstract ideas or only the immediately perceived geometric objects.

If we take seriously the claim that one line can represent an entire class of line, then the number of minima in any particular line is largely irrelevant. It is the representative capacity of perceived lines that is of importance, and a particular line can represent not only all other actual lines, but presumably any line that might exist. This frees Berkeley from his earlier view that the truths of geometry must be restricted to what we immediately perceive, and his thesis that visual inspection of a particular suffices to establish a geometric result. The theory of representative generalization therefore introduces a significant change in Berkeley's conception of the object of geometry: Where earlier he had held that geometry could be concerned only with things immediately perceived, by taking diagrams as signs of other possible extended magnitudes, Berkeley allows any possibly perceived extension to count as an object of geometrical investigation. The clearest way to see the differences between the philosophy of geometry in the notebooks and that explored in the *Principles* is to start by observing that Berkeley uses the Euclidean theorem that every line can be bisected (*Elements* I 10) as a way of illustrating his theory of representative generalization:

> To make this plain by an example, suppose a geometrician is demonstrating the method, of cutting a line in two equal parts. He draws, for instance, a black line of an inch in length, this which in it self is a particular line is nevertheless with regard to its signification general, since as it is there used, it represents all particular lines whatsoever; for that what is demonstrated of it, is demonstrated of all lines or, in other words, of a line in general. (I 12)

This more liberal conception of geometry is also reflected in Berkeley's claim that the proposition "whatever has extension is divisible" should be understood to apply to extension in general, that is, to any particular extension (I 11).

These formulations seem to suggest that in the *Principles* Berkeley should accept the thesis of infinite divisibility because, as standardly formulated, infinite divisibility amounts to the claim that every geometric magnitude (or "extension") can be divided into two magnitudes of the same kind. However, Berkeley does not accept the infinite divisibility of extension in the *Principles* or later works. He insists that

> Every particular finite extension, which may possibly be the object of our thought, is an *idea* existing only in the mind, and consequently each part thereof must be perceived. If therefore I cannot perceive innumerable parts in any finite extension that I consider, it is certain they are not contained in it: but it is evident, that I cannot distinguish innumerable parts in any particular line, surface, or solid, which I either perceive by sense, or figure to my self in my mind: wherefore I conclude they are not contained in it. (PHK 124)

Berkeley is thus prepared to deny that every magnitude can be divided into two lesser magnitudes, but he does not see this as hindering the development of a more or less traditional geometric theory.

On Berkeley's account, the acceptance of infinite divisibility arises from a misunderstanding of the object of geometry and the nature of geometric proof, and more specifically from a failure to distinguish the line actually employed in a geometric demonstration from those lines it can be taken to represent. As he puts it:

> It hath been observed in another place, that the theorems and demonstrations in geometry are conversant about universal ideas [Section 15. Introduction]. Where it is explained in what sense this ought to be understood,

> to wit, that the particular lines and figures included in the diagram, are supposed to stand for innumerable others of different sizes: or in other words, the geometer considers them abstracting from their magnitude: which doth not imply that he forms an abstract idea, but only that he cares not what the particular magnitude is, whether great or small, but looks on that as a thing indifferent to the demonstration: hence it follows, that a line in the scheme, but an inch long, must be spoken of, as though it contained ten thousand parts, since it is regarded not in it self, but as it is universal; and it is universal only in its signification, whereby it represents innumerable lines greater than it self, in which there may be distinguished ten thousand parts or more, though there may not be above an inch in it. After this manner the properties of the lines signified are (by a very usual figure) transferred to the sign, and thence through mistake thought to appertain to it considered in its own nature. (PHK 126)

This doctrine thus allows nearly all of traditional geometry to be retained, although it requires that geometric theorems not be taken as true of the magnitudes employed in a demonstration, but only of those that can be represented by them. The required reinterpretation of Euclidean geometry thus contains an element of instrumentalism: It requires that "to the end any theorem may become universal in its use, it is necessary we speak of the lines described on paper, as though they contained parts which really they do not" (PHK 128).

This view of geometry as a "science of approximations" grounded in the representative generality of perceived lines and figures remained central to Berkeley's conception of geometry from the time of the publication of the *Principles*. The critique of the calculus in the *Analyst*, for example, takes place against the background of Berkeley's philosophy of geometry, because he regarded the calculus as a fundamentally geometric theory whose procedures must be judged in accordance with the criteria of rigor appropriate to geometry.

Berkeley on arithmetic and algebra

Berkeley's philosophy of arithmetic (which he extends without significant modification to include algebra) presents an important contrast to his views on geometry, although there are important elements in common to his treatment of both subjects. Antiabstractionism remains a key element in Berkeley's approach to arithmetic, but he adopts a nominalistic doctrine that led him to an account of arithmetical truth with a conventionalist element. Another point of contrast concerns the development of the two theories: Unlike the case of his philosophy of geometry, Berkeley's account of arithmetic did not undergo a significant revision, and the early views on arithmetic (as expressed in the notebooks, for instance) remain intact throughout his writings. The best way to investigate these issues is to begin with Berkeley's thesis that number is a creature of the mind, and then observe how this leads to a case for a thoroughgoing nominalism about arithmetic.

The Berkeleyan slogan "number is a creature of the mind" is intended to emphasize the fact that numbers are not the object of perception, but instead are imposed by the mind upon collections of ideas. Of course, every idea is a "creature of the mind" in the sense that only minds are active and capable of producing ideas, but Berkeley sees numbers as more radically mind-dependent than other objects of thought. His argument for the radical mind-dependence of number begins with the observation that the number properly attributed to an idea (or collection of ideas) depends upon the perceiving mind's choice of a unit. In the notebooks he announces that

> 2 Crowns are called ten shillings hence may appear the nature of Numbers. (N 759)
>
> Complex ideas are the Creatures of the Mind, hence may appear the nature of Numbers (N 760)

The idea here is that the same amount of money goes by two names, depending upon the choice of unit, and so there can be no number assigned to a collection unless some mind has antecedently chosen how it is to be counted.

These remarks foreshadow a more complete statement of the doctrine in the *Principles*:

> That number is entirely the creature of the mind, even though the other qualities be allowed to exist without, will be evident to whoever considers, that the same thing bears a different denomination of number, as the mind views it with different respects. Thus, the same extension is one or three or thirty six, according as the mind considers it with reference to a yard, a foot, or an inch. Number is so visibly relative, and dependent on men's understanding, that it is strange to think how any one should give it an absolute existence without the mind. We say one book, one page, one line;

all these are equally units though some contain several others. And in each instance it is plain, the unit relates to some particular combination of ideas arbitrarily put together by the mind. (PHK 12)

These sentiments echo Barrow's claim that nothing in nature determines what number applies to any given thing or collection, and it well may be that Berkeley's account of number derives in part from Barrow. Nevertheless, there is a crucial difference between Berkeley and Barrow on the status of arithmetic: Where Barrow concludes that the science of number must ultimately be founded on the principles of geometry, Berkeley is prepared to adopt an extremely nominalistic approach and to regard arithmetic as a purely formal science concerned with the manipulation of symbols.

The principal reason for Berkeley's arithmetical nominalism lies in the relative theoretical poverty of the assertion that numbers are "creatures of the mind." We clearly can reason about large numbers that correspond to no distinguishable collection of ideas, and Berkeley avoids the problem of large numbers by declaring that, in the first instance, it is the arithmetical notation itself that is the object of our thoughts. For example, there is presumably no distinct mental image of a collection of 23,177,414 things – or at least none that can be distinguished from that of a collection of 23,177,415; yet any reasonable theory of arithmetic will have to be able to distinguish these two numbers. Berkeley's solution to this difficulty is to allow that arithmetical signs can be employed without considering their referents. In a letter to Samuel Molyneux from December 8, 1709, Berkeley contends that

We may very well, and in my Opinion often do, reason without Ideas but only the Words us'd being us'd for the most part as Letters in Algebra, which tho they denote particular Quantities, Yet every step do not suggest them to our Thoughts, and for all that We may reason or perform operations intirly about them. Numbers we can frame no Notion of beyond a certain degree, and yet We can reason as well about a Thousand as about five, the truth on't is Numbers are nothing but Names. (*Works* 8: 25)

The declaration that numbers are "nothing but Names" figures in the notebooks as well. There, Berkeley observes that in making arithmetical calculations we attend only to the figures or symbols, rather than to collections of objects that are supposed to be designated by such signs. This leads him to the view that the ultimate foundation of arithmetic lies in the rules for the combination of arithmetical symbols, rather than in some abstract truths about a mysterious realm of numbers. He notes at one point

> I am better inform'd & shall know more by telling me there are 10000 men than by shewing me them all drawn up. I shall better be able to Judge of the Bargain you'd have me make when you tell me how much (i.e. the name of y^{e}) money lies on ye Table than by offering & shewing it without Naming. In short I regard not the Idea the looks but the Names. Hence may appear the Nature of Numbers. (N 761)

The investigation into the nature of numbers in the notebooks is not extensive, but the upshot is captured clearly in two entries: "Numbers are nothing but Names, meer Words" (N 763); and "Take away the signs from Arithmetic & Algebra, & pray wt remains?" (N 766). The mention of algebra at entry 766 shows that Berkeley conceives of algebra along the same lines as arithmetic. The only difference between them is that algebraic signs have an even higher level of generality than numerical signs, and can be taken to represent any quantity at all: "Algebraic Species or letters are denominations of Denominations, therefore arithmetic to be treated of before Algebra" (N 758).

The *Principles* gives a somewhat more extensive account of Berkeley's philosophy of arithmetic, including a more explicit link between his denial of abstraction and his conception of arithmetic as a science of signs. He asserts that by "taking a view of arithmetic in its infancy," we can see that it originated as a simple system of tally strokes, each of which was taken to designate a unit, where the unit is "some one thing of whatever kind [people] had occasion to reckon." In the course of time, more concise forms of notation were adopted, culminating in the Hindu-Arabic numerals, which Berkeley describes as a system "wherein by the repetition of a few characters or figures, and varying the signification of each figure according to the place it obtains, all numbers may be most aptly expressed" (PHK 121).

This system of notation was supplemented by a system of computational rules, which Berkeley characterizes as "methods of finding from the given figures or marks of the parts, what figures and how placed are proper to denote the whole or vice versa" (PHK 121). The symbols and rules for their manipulation are not, of course, of any great intrinsic interest, but are extremely useful because they allow us to accomplish by purely symbolic calculation many things that would be impossible if we were to try to work directly with the objects denoted by the symbols. As Berkeley puts it:

> For these signs being known, we can by the operations of arithmetic, know the signs or any part of the particular sums signified by them; and thus computing in signs (because of the connexion established betwixt them and the distinct multitudes of things, where of one is taken for an unit), we may be able rightly to sum up, divide, and proportion the things themselves that we intend to number. (PHK 121)

This account treats pure arithmetic as simply an exercise in the manipulation of symbols and gives pride of place to the application of arithmetic rather than to purely theoretical results. In applied arithmetic we begin with a collection of objects in the world and assign numbers to it in accordance with a specification of a unit. We then perform operations on the numerical signs, obtaining as a result a new sign that can be interpreted "back into the world" and used to guide our practice: "In arithmetic therefore we regard not the things but the signs, which nevertheless are not regarded for their own sake, but because they direct us how to act with relation to things and dispose rightly of them" (PHK 122).

The emphasis on the practical applications of arithmetic leads Berkeley to dismiss the study of pure arithmetic as a waste of time. Because the subject matter of arithmetic is the numerical symbols themselves (as opposed, say, to a mysterious abstract realm of numbers), Berkeley concludes that "to study them for their own sake would be just as wise, and to as good a purpose, as if a man, neglecting the true use or original intention and subserviency of language, should spend his time in impertinent criticisms upon worlds, or reasonings and controversies purely verbal" (PHK 122).

The Berkeleyan philosophy of arithmetic has clear points of similarity with the formalist conception of mathematics, which treats mathematical theories as "formal systems" of symbols and rules while denying that mathematical vocabulary has any reference to a realm of objects outside of the formal system.[21] One important aspect of formalism evident in Berkeley's account of arithmetic is the doctrine that the truth of an arithmetical statement consists in its derivability within the system of rules. Berkeley holds that the theorems of arithmetic are demonstrable precisely because the demonstrations concern only the manipulation of symbols in accordance with a specified set of rules. Thus, the truths of arithmetic concern only what combinations of symbols are constructible by using the rules, and are essentially true by definition.

This formalistic aspect of Berkeley's philosophy of arithmetic leads him to accept quite different accounts of arithmetical and geometric truth. As we have seen, Berkeley takes geometry to have a proper object (perceived extension), and although the figures that appear in geometric demonstrations are treated as signs, they are signs that must resemble the objects they represent. The difference here lies in what we might cautiously call the degree of abstraction involved in arithmetic as opposed to geometry. The theorems of arithmetic (although ultimately about the objects in the world) are immediately about what combinations of signs can be produced by following computational rules, and (unlike the geometric case) there is no presupposition that the arithmetical signs resemble the things they represent. This lack of resemblance between sign and thing signified injects an arbitrary or conventional element in the choice of arithmetical signs that is not matched by a similar arbitrariness or conventionality in geometry.

The difference is perhaps best brought out by considering that, on Berkeley's account, we can choose whatever signs we wish for numbers, while there is no similar freedom of choice in geometry. Berkeley was clearly aware of this difference between arithmetic and geometry in his system. He writes:

> Qu: whether Geometry may not be properly reckon'd among the Mixt Mathematics. Arithmetic and Algebra being the Only abstracted pure i.e. entirely Nominal. Geometry being an application of these to points. (N 770)

In another entry he connects the arbitrariness of our selection of signs to the nature of demonstration, arguing that it is by virtue of the fact that we create and choose such signs that we are able to demonstrate at all: "The reason why we can demonstrate So well about signs is that they are perfectly arbitrary & in our power, made at pleasure" (N 732).

Although there is a clear difference between Berkeley's treatments of arithmetic and geometry, the similarities are also significant. In each case Berkeley is concerned to develop an account of mathematics that does not rely upon the doctrine of abstract ideas, and in each case he avoids the use of abstractions by treating the objects of mathematics as signs. In his account of geometry he treats geometric figures as signs for classes of figures they resemble, and thus characterizes geometry as a science whose immediate objects are signs. Similarly, arithmetic is treated as a science whose immediate objects are signs, but in this case the signs are arbitrarily selected symbols that can stand for collections of objects. Although it is true that "all sciences, so far as they are universal and demonstrable by human reason, will be found conversant about signs as their immediate object" (*Alciphron* 7.13 [305]), this does not mean that arithmetic and geometry must be treated in exactly the same way. The signs used for geometry must themselves be geometric objects that represent other geometric objects, while the signs used in arithmetic and algebra are arbitrarily chosen symbols.

The significant differences between arithmetic and geometry do not, however, foreclose the possibility of analytic geometry. The application of algebraic methods to the solution of geometric problems is perfectly permissible, provided first that the application employ only assumptions that are consistent with the nature of the geometric magnitudes to which algebra is applied, and second that every algebraic operation used therein corresponds to a legitimate geometric construction. The calculus of Newton and Leibniz depends heavily upon the use of algebraic principles, and we now are in a position to appreciate Berkeley's criticism of their methods.

III. THE CRITIQUE OF THE CALCULUS

Berkeley's most famous contribution to the philosophy of mathematics is his attack on the foundations of the calculus in his 1734 treatise *The Analyst*. The principal object of his criticism is the Newtonian theory of fluxions, which evolved out of a "kinematic" treatment of geometric magnitudes and was developed into a powerful technique for investigating the properties of curves. A second target is Leibniz's differential calculus, which proceeds by considering "incomparably small" portions of curves. Although Berkeley is concerned more with the Newtonian presentation than with its Leibnizian counterpart, matters of exposition will be eased slightly if we start with an outline of the differential calculus and then compare it to the calculus of fluxions. As we will see, Berkeley's fundamental objections apply to both methods. Accordingly, this section is divided into three subsections: one concerned with the Leibnizian calculus; a second that presents the fundamentals of the Newtonian calculus; and a third that considers Berkeley's objections to both methods.

Leibniz and the differential calculus

As I mentioned in Section I, infinitesimal methods achieved a good deal of currency in seventeenth-century mathematics, largely because they enabled solutions to problems that had remained intractable when approached by the more austere methods of classical mathematics. Two kinds of problem are of particular significance: that of finding the area enclosed by a curve (known as the problem of quadrature in the parlance of the period); and that of finding the tangent to a curve at an arbitrary point (known as the problem of tangency). Leibniz introduced his differential calculus in a series of publications beginning in 1684, and he and his followers were spectacularly successful in employing it to extend the frontiers of mathematics. Leibniz himself did not publish a systematic treatise on the new method and he remained largely silent on foundational issues, which makes it somewhat problematic to discern his favored interpretation of the calculus.[22] On the other hand, the Marquis de L'Hôpital's 1696 treatise *Analyse des infiniment petits pour l'intelligence des lignes courbes* is a forthright and comprehensive statement of the method as understood by the "Continental" school of mathematicians working in the Leibnizian tradition.

L'Hôpital's account of the calculus is presented in a quasi-axiomatic form, and opens with definitions and postulates that are intended to set forth the foundations of the calculus. The definitions read:[23]

Definition I: *Variable* quantities are those which increase or diminish continually; and *constant* quantities are those which remain the same while others change. Thus in a parabola the ordinate and abscissa are variable quantities, while the parameter is a constant quantity.

Definition II: The infinitely small portion by which a variable quantity continually increases or diminishes is called its *difference*. Let there be, for

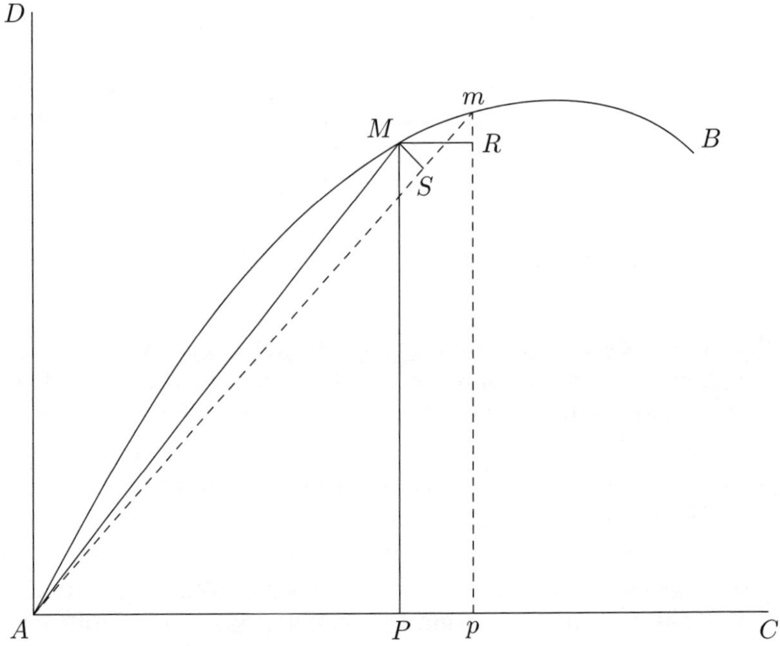

Fig. 2. L'Hôpital's doctrine of differences, adapted from *Analyse des infiniments petits*.

example, any curved line *AMB*, which has the line *AC* as its axis or diameter, and the right line *PM* as one of its ordinates, and let *pm* be another ordinate infinitely near to the former [Fig. 2]. This being granted, if *MR* is drawn parallel to *AC*, and the chords *AM*, *Am* are drawn; and about the center *A* with distance *AM* the small circular arc *MS* is described: then *Pp* will be the difference of *AP*, *Rm* that of *PM*, *Sm* that of *AM*, and *Mm* that of the arc *AM*. And similarly, the small triangle *MAm* which has as its base the arc *Mm* will be the difference of the segment *AM*; and the small space *MPpm* will be the difference of the space contained by the right lines *AP*, *PM*, and the arc *AM*.

The two postulates that follow declare how the key concept of a difference is to be employed:

Postulate or Supposition: It is postulated that one can take indifferently for one another two quantities which differ from one another by an infinitely small quantity: or (which is the same thing) that a quantity which is augmented or diminished by another quantity infinitely less than it can be considered as if it remained the same. It is postulated, for example, that one can take *Ap* for *AP*, *pm* for *PM*, the space *Apm* for the space *APM*, the small space *MPpm* for the rectangle *MPpR*, the small sector *AMm* for the small triangle *AMS*, the angle *pAm* for the angle *PAM*, etc.

Postulate or Supposition: It is postulated that a curved line can be considered as an infinite collection of right lines, each infinitely small: or (which is the same thing) as a polygon of an infinite number of sides, each infinitely small, which determine the curvature of the line by the angles they make with one another. It is postulated, for example, that the portion of the curve *Mm* and the arc of the circle *MS* can be considered as right lines because they are infinitely small, so that the small triangle *mSM* can be supposed to be rectilinear.

When combined with the techniques of analytic geometry, these basic concepts allow a wide variety of problems to be solved. Finding tangents to curves, for example, requires only that the curve be represented analytically by an equation and the differences between the variables x and y.

The great power of Leibniz's differential calculus is that it allows the problems of tangency and quadrature to be reduced to a relatively simple algorithmic procedure. Take as an example the curve with the analytic equation

$$y = \mathrm{a}x^3 + \mathrm{b}x^2 + \mathrm{c}x + \mathrm{d} \qquad [1]$$

with variables x, y and constants a, b, c, d. We then consider the "differential increment" of [1] obtained by replacing y and x with $y + dy$ and $x + dx$, respectively. The result is

$$(y + dy) = \mathrm{a}(x + dx)^3 + \mathrm{b}(x + dx)^2 + \mathrm{c}(x + dx) + \mathrm{d}. \qquad [2]$$

Expanding the right side of Equation [2] yields

$$y + dy = \mathrm{a}x^3 + 3\mathrm{a}x^2dx + 3\mathrm{a}xdx^2 + \mathrm{a}dx^3 + \mathrm{b}x^2 + 2\mathrm{b}xdx + \mathrm{b}dx^2 + \mathrm{c}x + \mathrm{c}dx + \mathrm{d}. \qquad [3]$$

Subtracting equation [1] from [2] gives the increment

$$dy = 3\mathrm{a}x^2dx + 3\mathrm{a}xdx^2 + \mathrm{a}dx^3 + 2\mathrm{b}xdx + \mathrm{b}dx^2 + \mathrm{c}dx. \qquad [4]$$

Dividing each side of [4] through by dx results in an equation expressing the ratio between dy and dx at any point on the curve, or:

$$\frac{dy}{dx} = 3\mathrm{a}x^2 + 3\mathrm{a}xdx + \mathrm{a}dx^2 + 2\mathrm{b}x + \mathrm{b}dx + \mathrm{c}. \qquad [5]$$

Because dx is infinitely small in comparison with x, the terms containing it can be disregarded in the right side of Equation [5], yielding

$$\frac{dy}{dx} = 3ax^2 + 2bx + c. \qquad [6]$$

The formula in [6] (known today as the "derivative" of [1]) gives the slope of the tangent at any point on the curve in Equation [1]. The algorithmic character of this procedure is especially important, because it makes the calculus applicable to a vast array of curves whose study had previously been undertaken in a piecemeal fashion, without an underlying unity of approach. In this example we have been concerned with a very simple third-degree equation, but the basic concepts can be extended to much more complex cases involving fractional or irrational powers and exponents, as well as more difficult "transcendental" functions. This is precisely the aspect of the calculus Leibniz trumpeted in his first publication on the subject, whose title promises a "New method for maxima and minima as well as tangents, which is not impeded by fractional or irrational quantities; and a remarkable type of calculus for them."

There is another important concept in the Leibnizian calculus that needs to be mentioned, namely that of higher-order differentials. In Leibniz's presentation, the differences dy and dx are themselves variable quantities, and they can be thought of as ranging over infinite sequences of values of x and y that are infinitely close to one another. Depending upon the nature of the curve, the infinitesimal quantities dy and dx can stand in any number of different relations, and because these quantities are themselves variable, it makes sense to inquire into the rates at which they vary. The second-order differences ddx and ddy can be introduced as infinitesimal differences between values of the variables dx and dy, and similar considerations would allow the construction of a sequence of differences of ever-higher orders. Higher-order differences are employed to consider the behavior of curves that themselves are derived from the taking of a first-order derivative, and this process can extend to a wide range of important cases. The means of introducing second-order differentials also can vary, depending on the style of presentation: Sometimes they are introduced as products of differences of the first order, or as magnitudes that stand in the same ratio to a first-order difference as the first-order difference stands to a finite quantity.

Newton and the calculus of fluxions

The Newtonian method of fluxions is founded on a set of basic concepts different from its Leibnizian counterpart, although it does deliver essentially the same results. Newton's presentation of the calculus takes geometric magnitudes to be produced by continuous motion, so that lines arise from the motion of points, surfaces from the motion of lines, and so forth. This contrasts with the Leibnizian theory in which such magnitudes are composed out of infinitesimal parts. In his treatise *On the Quadrature of Curves*, Newton is happy to draw attention to these apparent foundational differences:[24]

> I don't here consider Mathematical Quantities as composed of parts extreamly small, but as generated by a continual motion. Lines are described, and by describing are generated, not by any apposition of Parts, but by a continual motion of Points. Surfaces are generated by the motion of Lines, Solids by the motion of Surfaces, Angles by the Rotation of their Legs, Time by a continual flux, and so in the rest. These Geneses are founded upon Nature and are every Day seen in the motion of bodies.

An example can serve to clarify this doctrine. Take the curve $\alpha\beta$ as in Fig. 3, generated by the continuous motion of a point. As the point traces out the curve, its velocity can be resolved into two components $\dot{x}$ and $\dot{y}$, parallel to the axes OX and OY. Taken together, these components give the instantaneous velocity of the point at any stage in the generation of the curve, or (to use Newton's terminology)

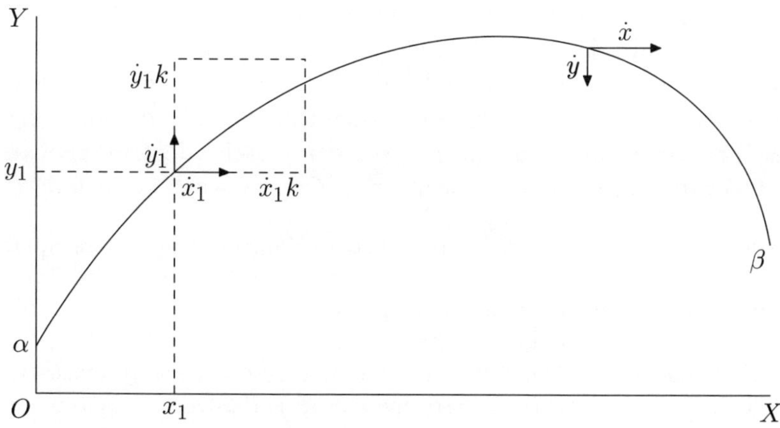

Fig. 3. Newton's doctrine of fluxions.

they determine the fluxion of the flowing quantity (or fluent) $\alpha\beta$. If we take a line of length κ, we can form the products $\dot{x}\kappa$ and $\dot{y}\kappa$ that stand in the same ratio as the fluxions; then the tangent to the curve at (x_1, y_1) can be determined by taking the diagonal of the parallelogram formed by the lines $\dot{x}_1\kappa$ and $\dot{y}_1\kappa$ and taking its diagonal. Just as the Leibnizian calculus employs higher-order differences, the fluxion itself can be treated as a fluent, and its rate of change can be calculated by finding its fluxion, that is to say a fluxion of a fluxion of a fluent quantity. Symbolically, the fluent x has a first fluxion $\dot{x}$, a second fluxion $\ddot{x}$, third fluxion $\dddot{x}$, and so forth. Given this conception of curves, the next step in the Newtonian development of the calculus is to devise a general method for finding tangents. Tangency problems thus become problems of finding the fluxions $\dot{x}$ and $\dot{y}$ when given an equation that describes the relationship between the fluents x and y. A quadrature is an inverse problem, namely that of determining the fluents when the fluxions are given.

Newton introduced two devices to help solve these problems: the doctrine of moments; and his theory of prime and ultimate ratios. He defines the moment of a fluent as its "momentaneous synchronal increment," or the amount by which it is increased in an "indefinitely small" time. These periods of time are represented by the symbol o and the moment of the fluent x is the product $o\dot{x}$. Thus, the increments of the fluents x and y become $x + o\dot{x}$ and $y + o\dot{y}$. The theory of prime and ultimate ratios is related closely to the kinematic conception of magnitudes, and involves the consideration of ratios between magnitudes as they are generated by motion. The prime ratio of two nascent magnitudes is that which holds just as the magnitudes are generated from nothing, while the ultimate ratio of evanescent magnitudes is that which obtains as the magnitudes vanish into nothingness. Newton's most straightforward account of this doctrine appears in the Introduction to the *Quadrature of Curves*, when he declares:[25]

Fluxions are very nearly as the augments of the Fluents, generated in equal, but infinitely small parts of Time; and to speak exactly, are in the *Prime Ratio* of the nascent Augments: but they may be expounded by any Lines that are proportional to 'em. As if the *Areas ABC, ABDG* [Fig. 4] be described by the Ordinates *BC, BD,* moving with an uniform motion along the base *AB,* the Fluxions of these Areas will be to one another as the describent Ordinates *BC* and *BD,* and may be expounded by these Ordinates; for those Ordinates

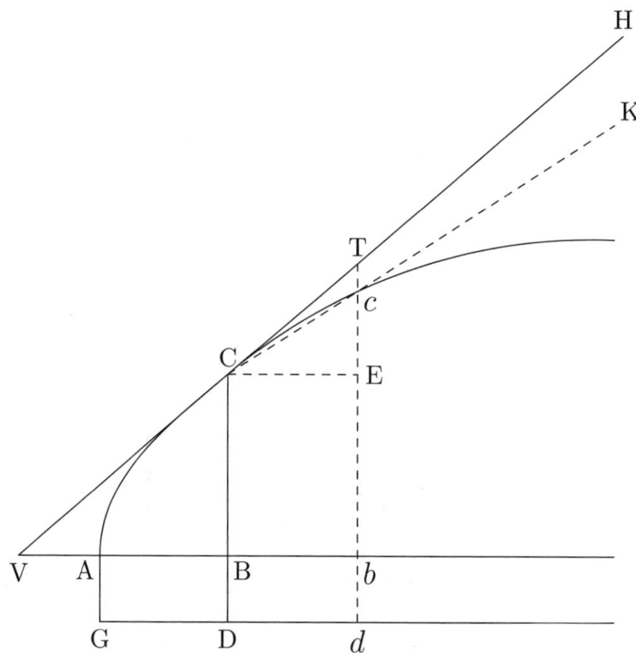

Fig. 4. Prime and ultimate ratios, adapted from Newton's *Quadrature of Curves.*

are in the same Proportion as the Nascent Augments of the Areas. Let the Ordinate *BC* move out of its Place *BC* into any new one *bc*: Compleat the Parallelogram *BCEb*, and the Right Line *VTH* be drawn which may touch the Curve [at] C and meet *bc* and *BA* produced in *T* and *V*; and then the just now generated Augments of the Abscissa *AB*, the Ordinate *BC*, and the Curve Line *ACc*, will be *Bb*, *Ec* and *Cc*; and the Sides of the Triangle *CET*, are in the *Prime Ratio* of these Nascent Augments, and therefore the Fluxions of *AB*, *BC* and *AC* are as the Sides *CE*, *ET* and *CT* of the Triangle *CET*, and may be expounded by those Sides, or which is much at one, by the Sides of the Triangle *VBC* similar to it.

As is evident from the contrast in the first sentence between the approximate truth of the doctrine of infinitesimals and the exact truth to be found by means of prime and ultimate ratios, Newton and his followers saw the method of prime and ultimate ratios as a more rigorous alternative to the Leibnizian calculus of infinitesimals. The Newtonian presentation of the calculus seems to avoid the use of infinitesimals altogether, as it apparently permits us to reason about fluxions by finite lines proportional to the fluxions and to do so without employing the extravagant apparatus of infinitesimal differences.

In actual practice, however, the fluxional calculus does not differ significantly from its Continental counterpart. This fact can be grasped most easily by considering the example Newton gives for the finding of a fluxion in the *Quadrature of Curves*. We begin with the equation

$$x^3 - xy^2 + a^2z - b^3 = 0, \tag{7}$$

with fluents x, y, z and constants a, b. We add the moments and $o\dot{x}$, $o\dot{y}$, and $o\dot{z}$ of the flowing quantities. This yields the augmented equation

$$(x + o\dot{x})^3 - (x + o\dot{x})(y + o\dot{y})^2 + a^2(z + o\dot{z}) - b^3 = 0. \tag{8}$$

Expanding equation [8] we have

$$\begin{aligned} &x^3 + 3x^2o\dot{x} + 3xo^2\dot{x}^2 + o^3\dot{x}^3 - xy^2 - o\dot{x}y^2 - 2xo\dot{y}y \\ &\quad - 2\dot{x}o^2\dot{y}y - xo^2\dot{y}^2 - \dot{x}o^3\dot{y}^2 + a^2z + a^2o\dot{z} - b^3 = 0. \end{aligned} \tag{9}$$

The difference between equations [9] and [7] will then give the increment of the original. Subtracting leaves

$$\begin{aligned} &3x^2o\dot{x} + 3xo^2\dot{x}^2 + o^3\dot{x}^3 - o\dot{x}y^2 - 2xo\dot{y}y - 2\dot{x}o^2\dot{y}y \\ &\quad - xo^2\dot{y}^2 - \dot{x}o^3\dot{y}^2 + a^2o\dot{z} = 0. \end{aligned} \tag{10}$$

Dividing by o, we obtain:

$$\begin{aligned} &3x^2\dot{x} + 3xo\dot{x}^2 + o^2\dot{x}^3 - \dot{x}y^2 - 2x\dot{y}y - 2\dot{x}o\dot{y}y \\ &\quad - xo\dot{y}^2 - \dot{x}o^2\dot{y}^2 + a^2\dot{z} = 0. \end{aligned} \tag{11}$$

Now we can "let the quantity o be lessened infinitely" and neglect the "evanescent terms" containing o as a factor, leaving the result

$$3x^2\dot{x} - \dot{x}y^2 - 2x\dot{y}y + a^2\dot{z} = 0. \tag{12}$$

Equation [12] thus determines the fluxion of equation [7] for any values of x, y, and z. This procedure can be extended to an algorithm in exact analogy with the procedure of differentiation in the Leibnizian calculus.

The case against the calculus

The definitive statement of Berkeley's objections to the calculus is his 1734 treatise *The Analyst*, but his reservations about the method were long-standing. The notebooks contain several entries critical of the new methods, while his 1709 essay "Of Infinites" (*Works* 4: 235–8) and the *Principles* contain more extensive attacks on the fundamental concepts of the calculus.[26] For my purposes, however, the argument of *The Analyst* is central, and I will concentrate exclusively upon it. Berkeley's basic complaint against the calculus is that its procedures offend against the most elementary standards of mathematical rigor, either by postulating a realm of incomprehensible objects or relying upon fallacious patterns of inference.

In charging that the calculus purports to study objects that are literally unintelligible, Berkeley makes use of a background criterion of rigor according to which the objects of mathematical investigation must be clearly conceived. There is certainly nothing idiosyncratic about this requirement. Part of the traditional conception of mathematics, and of the particularly exalted epistemological status attributed to it, is the claim that (unlike less certain areas of inquiry) mathematics is distinguished by the clarity of its concepts and the thoroughly intelligible nature of its objects. As Berkeley himself notes:

> It hath been an old remark that Geometry is an excellent Logic. And it must be owned, that when the Definitions are clear; when the Postulata cannot be refused, nor the Axioms denied; when from the distinct Contemplation and Comparison of Figures, their Properties are derived, by a perpetual well-connected chain of Consequence, the Objects being still kept in view, and the attention ever fixed upon them; there is acquired an habit of Reasoning, close and exact and methodical: which habit strengthens and sharpens the Mind, and being transferred to other Subjects, is of general use in the inquiry after Truth. (A 2)

The issue, then, is whether the objects of the calculus (in either its Leibnizian or Newtonian presentation) can be clearly conceived.

Berkeley is emphatic on this point: The objects postulated by the proponents of the calculus are entirely incomprehensible. Newton's moments, defined as "the nascent Principles of finite Quantities," are of no determinate magnitude, and yet the ratios between them are regarded as determinate quantities. Fluxions, defined as instantaneous velocities of fluents, "are said to be nearly as the Increments of the flowing quantities, generated in the least equal Particles of time; and to be accurately in the first Proportion of the nascent, or the last of the evanescent Increments" (A 3). Higher-order fluxions are yet more mysterious: They are the velocities with which fluxions of a lower order are produced, and therefore require the consideration of nascent increments of nascent increments. In Berkeley's estimation, our faculties are "very much strained and puzzled to frame clear Ideas of the least Particles of time, or the least increments generated therein: and much more so to comprehend the Moments, or those Increments of the flowing Quantities in statu nascenti, . . . before they become finite particles" (A 4). He concludes that "The further the Mind analyseth and pursueth these fugitive Ideas, the more it is lost and bewildered; the Objects, at first fleeting and minute, soon vanishing out of sight" (A 4).

The Leibnizian foundations for the calculus fare no better when judged against Berkeley's standard for clear conceivability. The very notion of an infinitesimal magnitude is famously difficult to comprehend, but the apparatus of higher-order infinitesimals, each infinitely less than its predecessor and yet still greater than nothing, is even more difficult to make sense of. Although there is no shortage of mathematicians who claim to comprehend the infinitely small, Berkeley suggests that comprehending this system of the infinitely small presents "an infinite Difficulty to any Man whatsoever; and will be allowed such by those who candidly say what they think; provided they really think and reflect, and do not take things upon trust" (A 5).

Although these complaints are essentially first-person reports of Berkeley's inability to frame the requisite ideas, they nevertheless have some force. The proponents of the calculus typically claimed that their methods were consonant with accepted criteria of rigor, and Berkeley's protests to the contrary cast such claims in doubt. The real strength of Berkeley's case against the calculus, though, lies in his charges of fallacious reasoning and logical error in the most elementary theorems of the calculus. These "logical" objections clearly supplement the earlier "metaphysical" critique of the calculus because they argue not simply for the unclarity or obscurity of the calculus but rather its logical inconsistency. As Berkeley puts it, such a further investigation will reveal "much Emptiness,

Darkness, and Confusion; nay, if I mistake not, direct Impossibilities and Contradictions" (A 8).

Berkeley focuses on two Newtonian proofs to make his logical case against the calculus. The first is an attempt to compute the fluxion of a product of two flowing quantities and is drawn from Book II of Newton's *Principia*; the second is a general rule for computing the fluxion of any power x^n of a flowing quantity x and is drawn from Newton's treatise *On the Quadrature of Curves*. Both can be set out quite succinctly. The *Principia* proof of the rule for determining the fluxion of a product is expressed in terms of the computation of the moment or "instantaneous difference" of a product. Newton assumes that there are two flowing quantities A and B, whose respective moments are a and b. To find the moment of the product AB, Newton begins by considering the two flowing quantities as lacking one-half of their moments, which yields the product

$$\left(A-\frac{1}{2}a\right)\times\left(B-\frac{1}{2}b\right). \qquad [13]$$

This expands to become

$$AB-\frac{1}{2}aB-\frac{1}{2}Ab+\frac{1}{4}ab. \qquad [14]$$

Newton then takes the quantities after they have gained one-half of their respective moments, which is to say the product

$$\left(A+\frac{1}{2}a\right)\times\left(B+\frac{1}{2}b\right). \qquad [15]$$

This becomes

$$AB+\frac{1}{2}aB+\frac{1}{2}Ab+\frac{1}{4}ab. \qquad [16]$$

The difference between equations [16] and [14] will be the moment or increment of the entire product AB, namely $aB+Ab$.

Berkeley's objection to this procedure is to point out that Newton does not compute the moment of the product AB, but rather the product $(A-\frac{1}{2}a)\times(B-\frac{1}{2}b)$. A moment is defined as the "momentaneous synchronal increment" of a flowing quantity, and Newton is evidently not concerned with the increment of the quantity AB. Had he been, he would have followed the "direct and true" method of comparing the product AB to the product $(A+a)\times(B+b)$. In this case, the augmented product expands to become $AB + aB + Ab + ab$, and the increment or moment of the original product becomes $aB + Ab + ab$. This result differs from Newton's by containing an additional term ab. Berkeley observes that the motivation for Newton's mysterious procedure is to avoid having to dismiss the term ab from the result (in the manner of the Continental analysts who routinely discard infinitesimal quantities); but this apparent rigor in the avoidance of infinitesimals is purchased at the cost of principles that seem quite inscrutable. In rendering his verdict on this part of Newton's calculus, Berkeley observes:

> And indeed, though much Artifice hath been employ'd to escape or avoid the admission of Quantities infinitely small, yet it seems ineffectual. For ought I see, you can admit no Quantity as a Medium between a finite Quantity and nothing, without admitting Infinitesimals. An increment generated in a finite Particle of Time, is it self a finite Particle; and cannot therefore be a Momentum. You must therfore take an Infinitesimal Part of Time wherein to generate your Momentum. It is said, the Magnitude of Moments is not considered: And yet these same Moments are supposed to be divided into Parts. This is not easy to conceive, no more than it is why we should take Quantities less than A and B in order to obtain the Increment of AB, of which proceeding it must be owned the final Cause or Motive is very obvious; but it is not so obvious or easy to explain a just and legitimate Reason for it, or shew it to be Geometrical. (A 11)

The sorry state of Newton's proof from the *Principia* is made manifest by Berkeley's criticisms, and the difficulty is made all the worse by the fact that this result is essential for the development of the calculus.

Having dealt with the *Principia* proof for the rule for finding the fluxion of a product, Berkeley goes on to consider Newton's rule for finding the fluxion of any power, as demonstrated in the Introduction to the *Quadrature of Curves*. His interest in this text is understandable: The *Quadrature of Curves* is a much more complete statement of the calculus than that contained in the *Principia*, and it uses a significantly different method of proof. Berkeley suggests that the flaws in the *Principia* proof led Newton to suffer "some inward Scruple or Consciousness of defect in the foregoing Demonstration," and in view of the fundamental importance of the result for the whole calculus, he resolved "to demonstrate the same in a manner independent of the foregoing Demonstration" (A 12).

Berkeley prefaces his objection to the second proof with a lemma he regards as "so plain as to need no Proof." It reads:

> If with a View to demonstrate an Proposition, a certain Point is supposed, by virtue of which certain other Points are attained; and such supposed Point be it self afterwards destroyed or rejected by a contrary Supposition; in that case, all the other Points, attained thereby and consequent thereupon, must also be destroyed and rejected, so as from thence forward to be no more supposed or applied in the Demonstration. (A 12)

This lemma is nothing more than the requirement that the premises of a demonstration be consistent, and as such it is an entirely unobjectionable logical requirement. The question of interest is whether Newton offends against it.

According to Berkeley, the proof in Newton's *Quadrature of Curves* violates the requirement by first introducing a positive increment (denominated "*o*") into a calculation and later dismissing the increment while retaining results that can be acquired only on the supposition that the increment is positive. Newton starts with a flowing quantity x and sets himself the task of finding the fluxion of the power x^n. Taking the positive increment o, Newton argues that as x becomes $(x + o)$ the quantity x^n becomes $(x + o)^n$. By binomial expansion, this latter quantity becomes

$$x^n + nox^{(n-1)} + \frac{(n^2 - n)}{2} o^2 x^{(n-2)} + \cdots. \qquad [17]$$

We now consider the increments of the quantities x and x^n and find that they are in the ratio

$$o : \left(nox^{(n-1)} + \frac{(n^2 - n)}{2} o^2 x^{(n-2)} + \cdots \right). \qquad [18]$$

Dividing each side of Equation [18] by the common term o yields the ratio

$$1 : \left(nx^{(n-1)} + \frac{(n^2 - n)}{2} ox^{(n-2)} + \cdots \right). \qquad [19]$$

Now we can let the augment o "vanish" and discard terms containing it, to get the ratio between the increments as o evanesces. This results in the ratio

$$1 : nx^{(n-1)}. \qquad [20]$$

From this we conclude that the fluxion of x is to the fluxion of xn as 1 to $nx^{(n-1)}$, or equivalently that the fluxion of the power x^n is $nx^{(n-1)}$.

Berkeley's objection to this way of proceeding is that Newton takes the quantity *o* first to be positive, and then zero, while nevertheless maintaining results that can be obtained only under the supposition that o is positive. In particular, the move from equation [18] to [19] is impossible without *o* being positive (because division by zero would otherwise result), but this is contradicted by the move from equation [19] to [20], which is permitted only if *o* is equal to zero. As Berkeley puts the matter:

> Hitherto I have supposed that x flows, that x hath a real Increment, that *o* is something. And I have proceeded all along on that Supposition, without which I should not have been able to have made so much as one single Step. From that Supposition it is, that I get at the Increment of x^n, that I am able to compare it with the Increment of x, and that I find the Proportion between the two Increments. I now beg leave to make a new Supposition contrary to the first, i.e. I will suppose that there is no Increment of x, or that *o* is nothing; which Supposition destroys my first, and is inconsistent with it, and therefore with every thing that supposeth it. I do nevertheless beg leave to retain nx^{n-1}, which is an Expression obtained in virtue of my first Supposition, which necessarily presupposeth such supposition, and which could not be obtained without it: All which seems a most inconsistent way of arguing, and such as would not be allowed of in Divinity. (A 14)

This passage raises issues that occupied the British mathematical community for much of the next twenty years, and although we cannot delve into them here, it suffices to note that Berkeley's objections are well-founded. The calculus as practiced by Newton and his followers certainly appears to violate Berkeley's lemma by treating the evanescent increment *o* as both positive and zero, according to convenience. It is this feature of evanescent magnitudes that led Berkeley to declare them "Ghosts of departed quantities" (A 35). Responses to Berkeley's critique generally tried to show that this appearance of inconsistency was illusory, and that when suitably interpreted, the calculus does not offend against accepted criteria of rigor.[27] These responses were so noticeably unsuccessful that the respondents themselves disagreed with each other and lent an air of considerable confusion to the already murky foundations of the calculus.

A few further points regarding Berkeley's critique of the calculus can be used to close this discussion. First, his attack does not depend upon peculiarities of Berkeley's epistemology or metaphysics: The standard of rigor he upholds was a commonplace among eighteenth-century mathematicians, and he does not object that fluxions or evanescent increments are impossible because they offend against the *esse* is *percipi* thesis or the denial of abstract ideas. The point is rather that the methods of the "modern analytics" are incomprehensible and logically incoherent, even taken on their defenders' own terms. Second, the Leibnizian calculus of infinitesimals faces a similar critique, because (as Berkeley himself notes) there is no formal difference between postulating an increment *o* that later vanishes, and assuming an infinitesimal quantity *dx* that can be introduced and discarded at will. This last point was of particular significance in the wake of the Newton-Leibniz dispute over the priority for the invention of the calculus. Defenders of Newton's priority claims charged Leibniz with both plagiarizing the calculus from Newton, and then making it unrigorous by founding it upon the extravagant hypothesis of infinitesimals.[28] Needless to say, Berkeley's suggestion that the two methods are equally unrigorous won him no admirers among the Newtonians.

Finally, Berkeley denies that the calculus can be rescued by opting either for instrumentalism (so as to accept it for its utility without regard to its coherence or truth) or for formalism (and thereby treat its objects as mere symbols). The rejection of an instrumentalistic interpretation is made clear when Berkeley replies to those who hope that because of its success in solving problems, "the Doctrine of Fluxions, as to the practical Part, stands clear of all such Difficulties" (A 32). He insists that "in such Case although you may pass for an Artist, a Computist, or Analyst, yet you may not be justly esteemed a man of Science and Demonstration" (A 33). Although Berkeley elsewhere endorses an instrumentalistic reading of physical sciences, his criteria for mathematical rigor make such an approach to the calculus impossible. Similarly, Berkeley denies the validity of a formalistic conception of the calculus. He frequently complains that the defenders of the calculus have devised a notation, but that the mere existence of a notation is insufficient to ground the procedures of the calculus. In other words, "Nothing is easier than to assign Names, Signs, or Expressions to these Fluxions, and it is not difficult to compute and operate by means of such signs," but because nothing can be found to correspond to the notation, the calculus lacks an adequate foundation (A 37). The grounds for this denial of formalism stem from the fact that Berkeley takes the calculus to be a fundamentally *geometric* method, so that (unlike arithmetic) it must have a proper object that is clearly conceived and must not be taken as a purely nominal science.

In the final analysis, Berkeley's engagement with the mathematics of his day led him to formulate a distinctive philosophy of mathematics that is in some ways strikingly modern. His application of this philosophy to the calculus and his resulting critique of the new methods set the agenda for a generation of British mathematicians. Although the resulting controversy is largely forgotten today, still it serves as a reminder of the impact Berkeley had on the intellectual world of the eighteenth century.

NOTES

1. Florian Cajori, *A History of the Conceptions of Limits and Fluxions From Berkeley to Woodhouse* (Chicago and London: Open Court, 1919), 230.
2. This is not to say that there has been no scholarly attention paid to these issues. My own book, Douglas M. Jesseph, *Berkeley's Philosophy of Mathematics* (Chicago: University of Chicago Press, 1993), deals with the subject in detail, as do Wolfgang Breidert, *George Berkeley, 1685–1753* (Basel: Birkhäuser, 1989), and Giulio Giorello, *Lo Spettro e il Libertino: Teologia, Matematica, Libero Pensiero* (Milan: Mondadori, 1985). An early work by G. A. Johnston, *The Development of Berkeley's Philosophy* (London: Macmillan, 1923) also contains an extended treatment of Berkeley's mathematical writings. See also Robert J. Baum, "The Instrumentalist and Formalist Elements in Berkeley's Philosophy of Mathematics," *Studies in History and Philosophy of Science* 3 (1972): 119–34; David Sherry, "The Wake of Berkeley's *Analyst*: Rigor Mathematicæ?" *Studies in History and Philosophy of Science* 18 (1987): 455–80; and Sherry, "Don't Take Me Half the Way: Berkeley on Mathematical Reasoning," *Studies in History and Philosophy of Science* 24 (1993): 207–22.
3. For more on Aristotle and the philosophy of mathematics see *Mathematics and Metaphysics in Aristotle*, ed. Andreas Graeser (Bern and Stuttgart: Paul Haupt, 1987); Edward Hussey, "Aristotle on Mathematical Objects," *Apeiron* 24 (1991): 105–33; J. F. Jones, III, "Intelligible Matter and Geometry in Aristotle," *Apeiron* 17 (1983): 94–102; Jonathan Lear, "Aristotle's Philosophy of Mathematics," *Philosophical Review* 91 (1982): 161–92; and Ian Mueller, "Aristotle on Geometrical Objects," *Archiv für Geschichte der Philosophie* 52 (1970): 156–71.

4. Aristotle, *Metaphysics* 11, 1061a29–1061b2, in *The Complete Works of Aristotle: The Revised Oxford Translation*, ed. Jonathan Barnes, 2 vols. (Princeton: Princeton University Press, 1984).
5. For Aquinas's treatment of mathematical abstraction, see Aquinas, *Thomas von Aquin in Librum Boethii de Trinitate Quæstiones Quinta et Sexta, Nach dem Autograph Cot. Vat. lat 9850*, ed. Paul Weyser (Fribourg: Société Philosophique; Louvain: Editions Nauvelaerts, 1948), 37–40. A useful study of Aquinas's views on geometry can be found in Vincent Edward Smith, *St. Thomas on the Object of Geometry* (Milwaukee: Marquette University Press, 1954), which can be supplemented by Joseph Owens, "Aristotle and Aquinas" (38–59), Norman Kretzmann, "Philosophy of Mind" (128–59), and Scott MacDonald, "Theory of Knowledge" (160–95), in *The Cambridge Companion to Aquinas*, ed. Norman Kretzmann and Eleonore Stump (Cambridge: Cambridge University Press, 1993). For the Jesuit background see Peter Dear, "Jesuit Mathematical Science and the Reconstitution of Experience in the Early Seventeenth Century," *Studies in History and Philosophy of Science* 18 (1987): 133–75.
6. Benedictus Pereira, *De communibus omnium rerum naturalium principiis et affectionibus libri quindecem* (Rome: 1576), 70.
7. Christopher Clavius, "Prolegomena to the Mathematical Disciplines," in *Christophori Clavii Bambergensis e Societate Iesu Operum Mathematicorum Tomus Primo-quintus* (Munich: A. Hierat, 1612), 1: 5.
8. Isaac Barrow, *The Mathematical Works of Isaac Barrow*, ed. W. Whewell, 2 vols. bound as one (Cambridge: Cambridge University Press, 1860; reprinted Hidesheim: Georg Olms Verlag, 1973), 31.
9. Joseph Raphson, *A Mathematical Dictionary; or, a Compendious Explication of all Mathematical Terms, Abridg'd from Monsieur Ozanam, and others* (London: Midwinter and Leigh, 1702), 2.
10. Locke is explicit in his acceptance of the common view at *Essay* IV.iv.6, where he declares, "I doubt not but it will be easily granted that the Knowledge we have of *Mathematical Truths*, is not only certain, but *real Knowledge*; and not the bare empty Vision of some vain insignificant *Chimeras* of the Brain: and yet, if we will consider, we shall find that it is only of our own *Ideas*. The Mathematician considers the Truth and Properties belonging to the Rectangle, or Circle, only as they are in *Idea* in his own Mind. for 'tis possible he never found either of them existing mathematically, i.e., precisely true, in his Life. But yet the knowledge he has of any Truths or Properties belonging to a Circle, or any other mathematical Figure, are nevertheless true and certain, even of real Things existing: because real Things are no farther concerned, nor intended to be meant by any such Propositions, than as Thing really agree to those *Archetypes* in his Mind." This passage

speaks only of "ideas" rather than "abstract ideas," but read in conjunction with his declaration that "General and certain Truths are founded in the Habitudes and Relations of abstract *Ideas*" (*Essay* IV.xii.7) and his accompanying praise of mathematical method, it is clear that he intends (IV.iv.6) to characterize mathematics as a science of abstract ideas. See John Locke, *An Essay concerning Human Understanding*, ed. P. H. Nidditch (Oxford: Clarendon Press, 1975).

11. See H. J. M. Bos, "The structure of Descartes' *Geométrie*," in *Descartes: Il metodo e I saggi*, ed. Giulia Belgioso (Rome: Instituta dell'Enciclopedia Italiana, 1990), 349–69; Paulo Mancosu, "Descartes' *Géométrie* and Revolutions in Mathematics," in *Revolutions in Mathematics*, ed. Donald Gillies (Oxford: Clarendon Press, 1992), 83–116; and A. G. Molland, "Shifting the Foundations: Descartes' Transformation of Ancient Geometry," *Historia Mathematica* 3 (1976): 21–49, for discussions of Descartes' program for geometry and its implications for seventeenth-century mathematics.
12. René Descartes, *Géométrie*, Book I; *Oeuvres de Descartes*, ed. Charles Adam and Paul Tannery, 12 vols., nouvelle presentation (Paris: Vrin, 1964–76), 6: 392.
13. Wallis, *Opera Mathematica*, 3 vols. (Oxford, 1693–99), 1: 5.
14. Thus he claims: "Indeed many geometric things can be discovered or elucidated by algebraic principles, and yet it does not follow that algebra is geometrical, or even that it is based on geometric principles (as some would seem to think). This close affinity of arithmetic and geometry comes about, rather, because geometry is as it were subordinate to arithmetic, and applies universal principles of arithmetic to its special objects. For, if someone asserts that a line of three feet added to a line of two feet makes a line five feet long, he asserts this because the numbers two and three added together make five; yet this calculation is not therefore geometrical, but clearly arithmetical, although it is used in geometric measurement. For the assertion of the equality of the number five with the numbers two and three taken together is a general assertion, applicable to other kinds of things whatever, no less than to geometrical objects. For also two angels and three angels make five angels. And the very same reasoning holds of all arithmetical and especially algebraic operations, which proceed from principles more general than those in geometry, which are restricted to measure" (*Opera Mathematica*, 1: 56).
15. Barrow, *Mathematical Works*, 1: 53.
16. "I say that mathematical number is not something having existence proper to itself, and really distinct from the magnitude it denominates, but is only a kind of note or sign of magnitude considered in a certain

manner; so far as the magnitude is considered as simply incomposite, or as composed out of certain homogenous equal parts, every one of which is taken simply and denominated a unit.... For in order to expound and declare our conception of a magnitude, we designate it by the name or character of a certain number, which consequently is nothing other than the note or symbol of such magnitude so taken. This is the general nature, meaning, and account of a mathematical number" (*Mathematical Works* 1: 56). See Michael S. Mahoney, "Barrow's Mathematics: Between Ancients and Moderns," in *Before Newton: The Life and Times of Isaac Barrow*, ed. Mordechai Feingold (Cambridge: Cambridge University Press, 1992), 83–116, and Helena Pycior, "Mathematics and Philosophy: Wallis, Hobbes, Barrow, and Berkeley," *Journal of the History of Ideas* 48 (1987): 265–86, for more on Barrow's account of number.

17. See Douglas M. Jesseph, "Philosophical Theory and Mathematical Practice in the Seventeenth Century," *Studies in History and Philosophy of Science* 20 (1989): 215–44, Antoni Malet, *From Indivisibles to Infinitesimals: Studies in Seventeenth-Century Mathematizations of Infinitely Small Quantities* (Barcelona: University of Barcelona Press, 1996), and Paolo Mancosu, *Philosophy of Mathematics and Mathematical Practice in the Seventeenth Century* (Oxford: Oxford University Press, 1996) for accounts of these problems.
18. The infinite divisibility of angles is proved in *Elements* I 9 as the theorem that every angle can be bisected; similarly, the infinite divisibility of lines follows from *Elements* I 10 as the theorem that every line can be bisected. See Euclid, *The Thirteen Books of Euclid's "Elements." Translated from the text of Heiberg*, ed. and trans. T. L. Heath, 3 vols. (Cambridge: Cambridge University Press, 1925; rep. New York: Dover, 1956), 1: 264–8. Both of these results follow from *Elements* I 1, which asserts that an equilateral triangle can be constructed upon any finite line segment. This most basic result actually depends upon a strong principle of continuity that is assumed only implicitly in Euclid's presentations. For more on this see Jesseph, *Berkeley's Philosophy of Mathematics*, 48–53.
19. See Jesseph, *Berkeley's Philosophy of Mathematics*, 57–67, for a more thorough analysis of the geometric doctrines of the notebooks.
20. A classical tradition of "geometrical atomism" with its roots in the Pre-Socratic atomists is reported in many ancient sources. For an overview of the atomistic background to the early modern period, see Kurd Lasswitz, *Geschichte der Atomistik von Mittelalter bis Newton*, 2 vols. (Hamburg: Leopold Voss, 1890; reprinted Hildesheim: Georg Olms, 1963).

21. The case for regarding Berkeley as a formalist, and indeed as the originator of the formalistic conception of mathematics, is made in Jesseph, *Berkeley's Philosophy of Mathematics*, chapter 3. See also Baum, "Instrumentalist and Formalist Elements in Berkeley's Philosophy of Mathematics," and Sherry, "Don't Take Me Half the Way: Berkeley on Mathematical Reasoning."
22. On Leibniz's account of the calculus, see Douglas M. Jesseph, "Leibniz on the Foundations of the Calculus: The Question of the Reality of Infinitesimal Magnitudes," *Perspectives on Science* 6 (1998): 6–40.
23. G. F. A. L'Hôpital, *Analyse des infiniment petits pour l'intelligence de lignes courbes* (Paris, 1696), 1–2. The following quotation appears on 3–4.
24. Isaac Newton, *The Mathematical Works of Isaac Newton*, ed. Derek T. Whiteside, 2 vols. (New York and London: Johnson Reprint, 1964–67), 1: 141.
25. Newton, *Mathematical Works* 1: 141.
26. See Jesseph, *Berkeley's Philosophy of Mathematics*, chapter 5, for a study of these pre-1734 writings and their relationship to the argument of *The Analyst*.
27. See Jesseph, *Berkeley's Philosophy of Mathematics*, chapter 7, for a fuller account of the aftermath of Berkeley's *Analyst*.
28. See A. R. Hall, *Philosophers at War: The Quarrel Between Newton and Leibniz* (Cambridge: Cambridge University Press, 1980), for an account of this dispute and its many charges.

STEPHEN DARWALL

10 Berkeley's moral and political philosophy

Relatively little of Berkeley's published work is devoted explicitly to the philosophy of ethics and politics. Berkeley did project a Part II of his *Principles* that would have included ethics, but he lost the manuscript while traveling in Italy in 1715, and Part II never appeared. This leaves *Passive Obedience* (a brief treatment of the duty to obey the sovereign), Dialogues 2 and 3 of *Alciphron*, which deal with the ethics of Mandeville and Shaftesbury, respectively, and various passages scattered throughout his other works.

At the same time, however, a profoundly ethical interest infuses virtually the whole of Berkeley's corpus. For example, Berkeley begins the Preface to the *Dialogues* by insisting, against "men of leisure" who are "addicted to speculative studies," that it should be a commonplace that "the end of speculation [is] practice, or the improvement of our lives and actions." If his readers can be convinced by his arguments in the *Dialogues*, he adds, they will be shown how speculation can be "referred to practice" (DHP 1 [168]). The point is not that the *Dialogues* explicitly discuss practical matters; to the contrary, they are taken up almost entirely with issues of epistemology and metaphysics. Rather, Berkeley believes that only by refuting the doctrine of material substance can he establish securely the existence of a benevolent, "all-seeing God" and the immortality of the soul, both of which he thinks necessary to ground morality and secure it from the attacks and distracting counsels of atheistic, freethinking libertines (DHP 1[167–8]).

That is why, having made arguments to the same metaphysical and epistemological conclusions in the *Principles*, Berkeley ends that work by saying that "the main drift and design of [his] labours" had been to encourage the "consideration of *God,* and our *duty.*" Unless his readers have been "inspire[d]... with a pious sense of the presence of God... [to] dispose them to reverence and embrace the salutary truths of the Gospel, which to know and to practise is the highest perfection of human nature," the speculative arguments of the *Principles* will have been "altogether useless and ineffectual" (PHK 156).

All this would be thoroughly unexceptional if Berkeley's motive were simply a bishop's desire to foster piety in his flock. What makes his project profoundly more interesting is what lies behind it – an analysis of the sources of, and interrelations between, all the following: materialism; religious unbelief; class affectation; disdain for morality; and the causes of widespread human suffering. Implicit throughout Berkeley's works is what might be called, if anachronistically, an anti-Nietzschean account of materialism, unbelief, and moral critique. Men of fashion and fellow-traveling intellectuals affect, Berkeley believes, a libertine style of life, along with an indulgence in purely theoretical speculation, because they wish to distinguish themselves from vulgar folk (DHP 1 [167–8,171–2]). This affectation leads to studied skepticism, atheistic materialism, and contempt for common morality.[1] Atheism both distinguishes "men of parts" from the "common herd" and rationalizes their libertine ways: Without a watchful God, what would otherwise be sinful can go unpunished.[2] Believing in material substance and denying an immaterial, incorruptible soul does similar service. "How great a friend material substance has been to *atheists* in all ages, were needless to relate," Berkeley declares (PHK 92). It is "very natural" that "impious and profane persons should readily fall in with those systems which favour their inclinations, by... supposing the soul to be divisible and subject to corruption as the body," and by denying the "inspection of a superior mind over the affairs of the world" (PHK 93). Thus, while Berkeley insists that the great mass of common people have nothing to fear from denying the doctrine of material substance, he allows that "[t]he atheist indeed will want the colour of an empty name to support his impiety" (PHK 35).

Actually, Berkeley's point is not just that the metaphysical doctrines he aims to establish in the *Principles* and the *Dialogues* will be harmless to the vulgar. On the contrary, he believes their widespread acceptance to be utterly crucial to relieving the human suffering he sees all around him – especially in Ireland, where a wealthy class spends its money aping English and foreign fashion, wasting money that could have been used to discharge their duty of alms to the poor or invested in the home economy. It would be one thing if the consequences of materialism and atheism were restricted to the professors of these doctrines. It is quite another when they "draw after them ... consequences of general disadvantage to mankind" (DHP 1 [171]).[3]

Berkeley thought that fashionable affectations caused poverty and suffering in various different ways. In addition to neglect and disinvestment, he believed that disdain for common values of industry and practicality encouraged speculative fever in early eighteenth-century Britain of the sort that caused the South Sea Bubble and its disastrous burst in 1720.[4] Further, he saw the syndrome as causing declining attachment to morality and religious belief among the elite, and regarded widespread suffering as the inevitable consequence of this.

Berkeley worried also about the effects of studied skepticism on the common folk themselves.

> [W]hen men of less leisure see them who are supposed to have spent their whole time in the pursuits of knowledge, professing an entire ignorance of all things, or advancing such notions as are repugnant to plain and commonly received principles, they will be tempted to entertain suspicions concerning the most important truths, which they had hitherto held sacred and unquestionable. (DHP 1 [172])

The vulgar can no more afford decline in morality among themselves than they can afford it among "men of parts." Only by cleaving to values of industry and sobriety (in, of course, employment that calls for these virtues), Berkeley believed, could common people hope to escape the poverty that was rife in early eighteenth-century Ireland and elsewhere.[5]

The most urgent step to advancing the general prosperity, therefore, was to secure respect for morality; as Berkeley saw it, this required securing beliefs in a benevolent, "all-seeing" God and in the immortality of the soul. This sets the agenda for the *Principles* and the *Dialogues*. The refutation of material substance provides the readiest route to both demonstrating these morality-supporting beliefs, and removing the atheist's most cherished cloak to immorality.

I. BERKELEY ON THE THREATS TO MORALITY

Thus although Berkeley's philosophical reputation is due almost wholly to his metaphysical and epistemological writings, much of his motivation in these works was to remove obstacles to widespread respect for *morality*. But what, exactly, was Berkeley's own moral philosophy? How did it fit within the metaphysical idealism for which he is so much better known? The remarkable thing is that despite the relatively little explicit treatment he gave to these questions, Berkeley actually had coherent, reasonably comprehensive, and extraordinarily interesting answers to them. On the side of normative theory (concerning what is good and right, respectively), Berkeley defended a sophisticated version of hedonism, together with what may be claimed to be the first formulation of rule-utilitarianism (as it is called in contemporary philosophy). On the metaethical side (concerning the metaphysical questions of what goodness and rightness themselves, respectively, *are*), Berkeley put forward a reductionist account of the former together with a theological voluntarist theory of the latter, but one advanced within an ingenious version of the kind of *internalist* account of oughtness or normativity characteristic of empirical naturalist moral philosophy in Britain in the modern period, and which has deeply influenced English-speaking ethics ever since.[6]

We shall consider these different aspects of Berkeley's ethics, treating his metaethical views first in Section II, and then, in the context of his argument in *Passive Obedience*, in Section III. Section IV shall be devoted to Berkeley's normative theory as advanced in *Passive Obedience*. Finally, in Section V, we shall consider briefly the specific moral and political doctrines Berkeley was concerned to defend within this framework. To prepare the way for considering Berkeley's own views, however, we shall begin here with his critique of the ideas he thought most threatening to the conception of morality he wished to defend – the ethics of Mandeville and Shaftesbury. Although they are quite different, Berkeley saw both as expressing a disdain for morality as a divinely sanctioned law, one that characterized "men of parts" more generally. He undertook to lampoon their theories in Dialogues 2 and 3 of *Alciphron*, respectively.

Bernard Mandeville was the author of the *Fables of the Bees*, a work that shocked but also profoundly influenced early eighteenth-century Britain.[7] First published as a poem in 1706 and later supplemented with philosophical commentary, this work was famous for two theses. The first is a version of what would become the important economic idea that the consequences of a set of individual actions, taken in the aggregate, are frequently very different from those intended by any individual. Mandeville's thesis was that the unintended, combined effect of widespread individual vice is net public gain; and correlatively, that widespread virtue, in the aggregate, is publicly harmful. By virtue, Mandeville meant the attempt to surmount natural selfish impulses to benefit others; by vice, he meant the gratifying of such impulses when doing so is (in the individual case) socially disadvantageous (*Fable*, 34). The actual, if unintended, effects of everyone's trying to help others at his own cost, Mandeville argued, is significant public harm. Prosperity is likelier if people are self-serving and "endeavou[r] to supply each other's lust and vanity." This creates wealth, the fruits of which all can enjoy. With no desire for luxuries, avarice, or vanity, the engine of productive activity is stilled, and all are left in poverty.

The second thesis was that whichever traits people count as virtues depends on the vagaries of fashion – on what people (especially those with the power to shape moral opinion) actually praise others for. "Moral virtues," he famously proclaimed, are "the political offspring which flattery begot upon pride" (*Fable*, 37).

Lysicles is the character who makes Mandeville's argument in Dialogue 2 of *Alciphron*, with Euphranor and Crito responding on Berkeley's behalf. Lysicles argues, for instance, that drunkenness is reckoned a vice by "sober moralists," but that the trade in beer, wine, and spirits greatly benefits the public (ALC 2.2 [66–7]). Noting that Lysicles is asserting only that vice is useful because of the productive activity it causes, Euphranor asks "whether money spent innocently doth not circulate as well as that spent upon vice?" (ALC 2.5 [72]). By considering only the actual economic benefits of alcoholic excess, Euphranor complains, Lysicles ignores economic benefits that would have arisen from other uses of the resources expended. He ignores what economists call "opportunity costs." Euphranor challenges Lysicles: "[U]pon the whole then, compute and say, which is most likely to promote the industry of his countrymen, a virtuous married man with a healthy numerous offspring, and who feeds and clothes the orphans in his neighbourhood, or a fashionable rake about town?" (A 2.5 [72]).

Euphranor and Crito argue that Lysicles also underestimates the costs of vice. Vice only seems to benefit those who practice it so long as a crude hedonism is assumed that overestimates the relative value of sensual pleasures to "rational pleasures" that call upon distinctively human aspects of personality. "Notional pleasures" are better, both extrinsically and intrinsically, for human beings. They "neither hurt the health, nor waste the fortune, nor gall the conscience. By them the mind is long entertained without loathing or satiety" (ALC 2.16 [89]). Because they are better suited to our nature, then, we enjoy them more (ALC 2.14 [86]).

Most worrisome, though, are the costs the vicious – worse, the freethinking advocates for vice – impose on others. "If a man spoils my corn, or hurts my cattle," Crito remarks, "I have a remedy against him; but if he spoils my children I have none" (A2.20 [98]). Mandevillian disdain for morality advertises a seductive rationalization for more proximate and vivid sensory pleasures. This spoils rather than cultivates, by confirming habits that make genuniely better lives difficult if not impossible for us to achieve, both collectively and individually.

Berkeley's other main target in *Alciphron* was Anthony Ashley Cooper, the Third Earl of Shaftesbury, whose *Characteristics* (1714) advanced an ethics of virtue based on a theory of moral sense.[8] The threat Berkeley regarded Shaftesbury as posing to morality was quite different, but also far subtler and more pernicious than that posed by Mandeville. Unlike Mandeville, Shaftesbury voiced no disdain for morality per se. On the contrary, Shaftesbury regarded himself as defending morality, including against the attacks of Mandeville.[9] Shaftesbury *was* sharply critical, though, of any attempt to model morality on law, whether Hobbist or theological voluntarist. He had special scorn as well for the idea that the distinctive motive to morality is fear of sanctions, whether these be imposed civilly or by God.[10] In opposition, Shaftesbury carried forward the Cambridge Platonist idea that morality fundamentally concerns character rather than acts forbidden or required by a moral law. The morality of conduct, he believed, derives entirely from the vice or virtue of the motives and affections from which it arises. Vice and virtue, he held, are a kind of deformity or beauty that we perceive with what he called a "moral sense." The distinctively moral motive thus is not any fear of sanction; it is something beautiful of which moral sense approves, together with the motivating appreciation of its beauty that moral sense itself provides.

Berkeley believed that such a view trivializes morality by recommending it "on the same foot with manners" (ALC 3.13 [133]). If the immoralist can be convicted of no more than bad taste, then morality can hardly protect the vulnerable, the innocent, and the poor from those who prey upon them or who damage them less wittingly. With friends like Shaftesbury, Berkeley must have thought, morality may not need enemies.

Berkeley's general line of objection to Shaftesbury includes several strands that are worth distinguishing. First, he thought that the reflective responses that Shaftesbury attributed to a "natural moral sense" could be explained better on other grounds. To the suggestion that we detest villainy spontaneously when we contemplate it, Euphranor replies: "[M]ay not this be sufficiently accounted for by conscience, affection, passion, education, reason, custom, religion; which principles and habits, for aught I know, may be what you metaphorically call a moral sense?" (ALC 3.6 [121]). By "conscience" Berkeley means an awareness that the act is contrary to God's will, together with a knowledge of the sanctions God will apply. What worries Berkeley most is that "moral sense" may be simply a cover for fashion: an arbitrary distinction of manners employed by "people of fashion" or "ingenious men" who wish to separate themselves from "the middle sort" and the poor (ALC 2.3, 3.2 [69, 115]). Not only would this make morality depend on an arbitrary basis; worse, it would rest it on something that had been used to take advantage of the innocent, the vulnerable, and the poor.

Second, even if moral sense faithfully tracks morality as Berkeley reckons it (by divine command), without sanctions there can be no generally adequate motive to be moral. Shaftesbury's proposal, he writes,

> ...seems just as wise as if a monarch should give out that there was neither jail nor executioner in his kingdom to enforce the laws, but that it would be beautiful to observe them, and that in so doing men would taste the pure delight which results from order and decorum. (ALC 3.13 [133])

By pretending to make men "heroically virtuous," Shaftesbury has "destroy[ed] the means of making them reasonably and humanly so" (ALC 3.13 [132]). Shaftesbury does not see this, Berkeley suggests, because of his own distance from ordinary folk. He is from "a rank above most men's ambitions," and has "a conceited mind, which will ever be its own object, and contemplate mankind in its own mirror!" (ALC 3.13 [132]).[11]

If Shaftesbury's views gain wide acceptance, then, the consequences for common people will be disastrous. Actually, this creates an internal problem for Shaftesbury, because he accepts some form of the doctrine of divine providence. Indeed, an important theme of his *Inquiry* is that anyone lacking a belief in the well-governedness of the universe also lacks the capacity for the "noble enthusiasm" of moral sense.[12] The prospect of a God who does not reward virtue and punish vice can hardly be pleasing and beautiful, Berkeley urges. A system "wherein men thrive by wickedness and suffer by virtue,... which neither protects the innocent, punishes the wicked, nor rewards the virtuous," is an "ugly system" (ALC 3.11 [129–30]). So, third, if ethics depends in any way on the assumption of the well-governedness of things, as Shaftesbury accepts, then this will entail a conception of morality as involving divine sanctions.

To sum up, then, Berkeley maintains that Shaftesbury's ethical philosophy already has had pernicious effects, and were it more widely accepted the results could be catastrophic, especially for the innocent and the vulnerable. These are precisely the people that morality's function is to protect, though, and it can do so only if morality is understood to consist in the will and sanctions of a benevolent, "all seeing" God.

II. BERKELEY'S METAETHICS

At this point we can turn to trying to comprehend Berkeley's own philosophy of morals, and to seeing how it fits within his philosophy more generally. Ultimately, we shall want to understand Berkeley's normative and metaethical theories of morality and his account of the moral and the rational 'ought.' First, however, we should begin with his theory of nonmoral good.

For Berkeley, what there is is exhausted by minds and their ideas (PHK 89). It follows, therefore, that ethical properties and facts, if there be any, must somehow be constructed out of these. Nonmoral good presents the easiest case, because Berkeley thinks it is identical with pleasure. "Good" is an example of a term that people are apt to think stands for some general notion or abstract idea, but, like all such terms, its function is to refer variably to any of some set of particulars – in this case, to any "particular pleasure" (PHK 100).[13] That an experience is a pleasure and that it is good are not, therefore, two different properties of it. Being good and being pleasurable are the very same (sensible) quality.

This position gives Berkeley both a metaethical and a normative hedonism of nonmoral good. As G. E. Moore would have been quick to point out, however, such a metaethical view cannot account for what contemporary philosophers call *normativity*; it cannot explain why something good *ought* to be sought, or even desired. We should set aside this issue for the moment, however. We will return to it when we consider Berkeley's account of the rational and the moral *ought*.

Berkeley makes two different distinctions within nonmoral goods that are important to his own ethics as well as to his criticisms of the views of freethinking libertines. One distinction is between "natural" and "fantastical pleasures."[14] The former, natural pleasures, are independent of the "fashion and caprice of any particular age or nation" and are "suited to human nature in general"; the latter please owing to "some particular whim or taste accidentally prevailing in a sett of people."[15] The relevance of this distinction to Berkeley's critique of "affected" fashionable ethics is obvious enough. The goods they praise are arbitrary: Were the fashion not to exist, neither would the good, and correlatively for fantastical pains and evils. When it comes to natural pleasures and pains, however, these are stable aspects of the human condition and independent of any arbitrary feature. Were Berkeley right about the relation of Shaftesburyan moral sense to fashion, a virtuous woman's contemplation of her own beautiful character would be no less "fantastical" than the pleasure a dandy takes in his fashionable dress.

The other distinction is one we have already met in passing, namely the distinction between pleasures of sense and "rational" or "notional" pleasures that Euphranor urges against Lysicles (Mandeville). It is clear that Berkeley thinks the latter are "more agreeable to human-kind" than the former because they call on distinctively human faculties. It is not clear, however, whether he thinks this entails a qualitative dimension of the value of pleasure that might compete with a quantitative dimension. All we know is that Berkeley thinks that notional pleasures are, other things being equal, better for a person, both extrinsically and intrinsically – not that they would be better even if less pleasurable.

We should return now to the issue we set aside, namely, why the good, on Berkeley's account, is something anyone should care about – from what does its normative claim on us derive? This raises a more general question: What, for Berkeley, can *any* "ought" derive from or consist in? If the quality of nonmoral goodness is identical with pleasure, then it is a sensible quality or idea. In what, though, can the normativity of this idea consist? If all there are are minds and ideas, what is oughtness?

We can approach this question by considering a number of passages in which Berkeley discusses the function of "laws of nature" and the "language of nature" in *regulating* human action.

> [T]he proper objects of vision constitute an universal language of the Author of nature, whereby we are instructed how to regulate our actions in order to attain those things that are necessary to the preservation and well-being of our bodies....[16]

> Now the set rules or established methods, wherein the mind we depend on excites in us the ideas of sense, are called the *Laws of nature*: and these we learn by experience, which teaches us that such and such ideas are attended with such and such other ideas, in the ordinary course of things. (PHK 30)

> This gives us a sort of foresight, which enables us to regulate our actions for the benefit of life. (PHK 30–1; see also PHK 44, 62, 65, 146.)

> It is clear from what we have elsewhere observed, that the operating according to general and stated laws, is so necessary for our guidance in the affairs of life, and letting us into the secret of Nature. (PHK 151)

In these and other passages, Berkeley develops the idea that God causes ideas in us by *general rules* we learn by experience. These ideas amount to a *language*, because what we call "cause" and "effect" are really related as sign to thing signified. I come to learn, for example, that the ideas that together make up a falling rock headed for my toe are usually followed, "in the ordinary course," by a painful idea in my toe. I take the former as a sign of the latter, or rather, as a sign that the latter will occur unless I do something to alter the normal course of events. This enables me to take evasive action. Wanting to avoid a pain in my toe, I know to move it to evade the falling rock.

If, however, God did not cause ideas in me by general rules, my future ideas would be entirely unpredictable. In such a situation my wanting to avoid painful ideas could give me no deliberative basis for action, because I would not be able to predict what I might do to avoid having them. "[A] grown man [would] no more know how to manage himself in the affairs of life, than an infant just born" (PHK 31). It is, Berkeley thinks, some of the most impressive evidence we have of God's wisdom and benevolence that he causes our ideas by "the never enough admired laws of pain and pleasure" (PHK 146).

The laws of nature, then, are the general rules according to which ideas are caused in us by God. In learning these we learn which ideas signify which others; the laws are "stated," Berkeley says, in "the language of the Author of nature." Natural laws in this sense, however, are not directly prescriptive or normative (for us, anyway). They do not tell us what to do or what we should do. They only say what will happen in the normal course. However, although they don't *directly regulate* conduct, Berkeley believes they are necessary to enable *us* to regulate our conduct.

But how? If we can answer that, we can see how Berkeley is thinking about normativity or oughtness. We should note, first, that Berkeley thinks that no agents are indifferent to (their own) pain or pleasure, and therefore to (their own) good or evil.[17] Indeed, in the sermon "On Immortality," Berkeley briefly develops an account of "rational desire" as proportional to expected net pleasure (goodness).[18] Ideas of good and evil thus have an inherent practical relevance; they provide a motivational framework for deliberation about what to do, casting favorable light on alternatives related to them in relevant ways. Because I want to avoid pain, the knowledge that falling rocks headed for toes give rise, in the normal course, to pain puts evasive action in a favorable light in my deliberations about what to do. I can then *act* for that reason.

This suggests that Berkeley understands *regulation* in terms of means/end rationality, together with the idea that the agent's own good is an inescapable end, or that one desires one's own greatest good when one deliberates rationally. If so, Berkeley holds a version of the same empirical naturalist, internalist theory of normativity found in Hobbes, Cumberland, and sometimes Locke, and (later) in John Clarke, Hutcheson, and John Gay, among others.[19] For these writers, what it is for it to be the case that someone *ought* to do something – say, an action necessary to one's (nonmoral) good – is that this is what a person would be dominantly *moved* to do if he or she deliberated rationally, where the deliberation is understood to involve means/end rationality and, perhaps, the calm use of theoretical reason. The normativity of nonmoral good then would consist in a fact about its role in motivating minds, at least when they are thinking in a certain way.

A problem with such empirical naturalist internalisms is that in reducing claims about what a person *ought* to desire or do to facts about what they *would* desire or do under conditions specifiable in a nonnormative vocabulary, these internalisms can seem to change the subject. For any such desire or action, it seems we can always think: Yes, that is what a person would do, but is it what one *should* do? In the twentieth century, this line of thought was an important source of support for noncognitivism, the view that the function of normative language is to express some affective or conative state of mind, or to insinuate or make some demand on others, rather than to assert anything that might be true or false.[20]

Now, while it certainly goes beyond what is warranted to say that Berkeley was himself a noncognitivist, or even that he had any well-worked-out view on these matters – or indeed that he (or anyone else in the eighteenth century) saw the alternatives clearly – there are places where Berkeley does indeed suggest such a picture. In the Introduction to the *Principles*, Berkeley remarks that "the communicating ideas marked by words is not the chief and only end of language" (I 20).[21] Language use can have other functions, among which he lists "the raising of some passion, the exciting to, or deterring from an action" (I 20). He gives the following example: "May we not... be affected with the promise of a *good thing*, though we have not an idea of what it is?"

Recall, at this point, the concern that identifying nonmoral goodness with pleasure does not yet explain why someone ought to pursue it: It does not yet account for goodness's normativity, that what is good ought to be desired or pursued. On the present suggestion, the reason the additional (normative) claim is not included in any proposition or fact about pleasure is that the additional claim is noncognitive. Its function is not to communicate any idea, even the idea of pleasure, but rather to express some affective or motivating state or, perhaps, to elicit it in others. As intriguing as this suggestion is, Berkeley does not follow it up. In the end, the most we can say is that he appears to think either that the normativity of good is to be explained *internally* in terms of the motives of a deliberating agent, or that there is nothing in which oughtness or normativity consists, "ought" claims being expressive, rather, of noncognitive states of mind.

III. PRUDENTIAL REASONS

This line of thought finally puts us onto the terrain of Berkeley's most important ethical and political work, *Passive Obedience*, and enables us to engage its main line of argument. Berkeley's aim in *Passive Obedience* is to defend a position somewhere between the Whig doctrine that subjects have no more than a conditional duty to obey their sovereign, and the view that subjects must do whatever the sovereign commands, even if doing so violates other moral duties. The key to Berkeley's position is a distinction he makes between positive and negative duties. The former enjoin "positive actions," the latter, that a person forbear from certain specified positive actions. The duty of obedience, he argues, is both negative and unconditional. It enjoins, not any particular positive action, but forbearance from all *resistance* to the sovereign. Specifically, it requires one not to "mak[e] use of force and open violence, either to withstand the execution of the laws, or ward off the penalties appointed by the supreme power" (PO 3). From this, however, it does not follow that subjects should always act as the sovereign commands. There may be things the sovereign may command a subject that would be wrong for a person to do. The (absolute) duty of obedience is a duty of non*resistance*; it is a duty of *passive* obedience.

Berkeley can claim Biblical authority for his position in St. Paul's dictum that "whosoever resisteth the power, resisteth the ordinance of God."[22] But, although he will argue from divine command, Berkeley wishes "to build ... altogether on the principles of reason common to all mankind" (PO 2). Nor is he prepared to rest with the consensus of "all wise men" that "there are certain moral rules or laws of nature, which carry with them an eternal and indispensable obligation" (PO 4).[23] Even if there is agreement about this, there is disagreement about how we know these, or about what exactly they include. Any argument from this basis for an absolute duty of passive obedience will therefore be unsatisfying. Consequently,

> in order to lay the foundation of that duty the deeper, we [must] make some inquiry into the origin, nature, and obligation of moral duties in general, and the criteria whereby they are to be known. (PO 4)

This is where we came in. Berkeley begins with the premise that self-love (that "principle of all others the most universal, and the most deeply engraven in our hearts") leads us to "regard things as they are fitted to augment or impair our own happiness; and accordingly [to] denominate them *good* or *evil*" (PO 5).[24] It is, he says, "the whole business of our lives to endeavour, by a proper application of our faculties, to procure the one and avoid the other" (PO 5).[25] As will become clear, by "whole business" Berkeley does not mean a vocation that we are charged with by God and consequently have a duty to pursue. On the contrary, he will explain the obliging force of God's commands by appeal to the agent's "whole business" of procuring his happiness or nonmoral good. Berkeley's thought seems to be that this is the end that agents do in fact pursue, either necessarily or contingently, at least when we are thinking clearly and deliberating rationally.

As we learn from experience about the nature of things (through God's "language"), we come to see that immediate goods can be followed by greater evils and vice versa. We also learn that rational pleasures give us greater satisfactions than those of sense. Having our greatest good as end, therefore, and seeing that distant, more lasting goods are necessary to achieving this, we are "*oblige[d]* . . . frequently to overlook present momentary enjoyments" (PO 5, emphasis added). For Berkeley, this is where oughtness or normativity first gets a hold. The "obligation of moral duties in general" will be derived from this.

Berkeley helps himself at this point to various propositions concerning the existence of an omniscient, omnipotent, and omnibenevolent God and the immortality of the soul that his later metaphysical works aim either to prove or to remove obstacles from accepting. Having established that proximity in time is no ground for preferring a present good or for dispreferring a present evil, he argues that this principle extends to our eternal interests as well. Just as we are obliged to forego present goods when doing so is necessary to our greatest earthly good, so likewise are we obligated when deferred gratification is necessary to our greatest good on the whole, counting both earthly and eternal interests. Our earthly interests, though, are "altogether inconsiderable" in relation to our eternal interests. Because it is evident "by the light of nature" that a God exists,

> ...who alone can make us for ever happy, or for ever miserable; it plainly follows that a conformity to His will, and not any prospect of temporal advantage, is the sole rule whereby every man who acts up to the principles of reason must govern and square his actions. (PO 6)

God wills the relations between ideas in "the ordinary course of things" – the "laws of nature," as this phrase is used in Berkeley's nonethical works. Plainly it cannot be *this* will of God to which Berkeley says our eternal interest obliges us to conform. Ideas cannot fail to conform to the laws of God's natural language. As Berkeley is evidently thinking of it, God also wills that *we act* in certain ways. This is a will that he can only have for *agents*, for active minds.

The picture that emerges is that while we are obliged to take account of laws of nature in regulating ourselves by our own greatest good, we do not regulate ourselves by these laws directly. Rather it is our end of our own greatest good, together with what the laws show to be the necessary means to it, that obligate us. God also wills that we *act* in certain ways, and because he makes our eternal interest conditional on conformance, we are also obliged by our interest to regulate ourselves by his will.

The question then becomes what God's will is for us. There can be no doubt, Berkeley thinks, that God wills the greatest happiness of his creatures overall. This leaves two possibilities: Either God wills that we do what (we ourselves think) will promote the greatest overall happiness; or God wills that we follow "some determinate, established laws, which, if universally practised," will best promote the happiness of all (PO 8). For reasons we will explore in the next section, Berkeley embraces the latter alternative. God wills that we follow "certain universal rules of morality" rather than that we try, each of us individually, to promote the greatest good overall. These "certain universal rules" are the "laws of nature" to which Berkeley refers at *Passive Obedience* 4 as objects of general consensus.[26]

Moral duties and the moral 'ought' are determined in the first instance, then, by the rules by which God wills all human agents be governed. Ultimately, however, the normativity of the moral 'ought' – its power to obligate – derives from the very same source as that of prudential obligation. It is because we inescapably seek our own greatest good (and because conforming to God's rules is necessary to realize that), that morality obligates. This is the "deeper" foundation of the "obligation of moral duties," as we are obliged to prefer any greater distant good to a lesser nearer one.

IV. A THEOLOGICAL VOLUNTARIST RULE-UTILITARIANISM

In order for morality to obligate, therefore, there must be inescapably conclusive reasons of (eternal) self-interest for doing what it demands. Berkeley does believe that moral rules promote the public good, but he says clearly that a rule has normative force – "is a law" – not on this ground, but only "because it is decreed by the will of God, which alone can give the sanction of a law of nature to any precept" (PO 31). It is only because moral duties are backed by God's eternal sanctions that they obligate. This explains why Euphranor comments in *Alciphron* that "when the fear of God is quite extinguished the mind must be very easy with respect to other duties," and that "conscience always supposeth the being of a God" (ALC 1.12 [52]). As well, it is why Berkeley says in his notebooks (also known as *Philosophical Commentaries*), in a remark that looks forward to the contemplated Part II of the *Principles*: "The 2 great Principles of Morality. the Being of a God & the Freedom of Man: these to be handled in the beginning of the Second Book" (N 508). The will of God, which establishes the moral law, is directed to *agents*. It is only because we can freely follow or flout his will that our eternal interest is staked on conformance; again, it is only because our eternal interests *are* at stake that it obligates.[27]

In this section we turn to what Berkeley thinks God's will, hence morality, commands. Ultimately, Berkeley's aim is to show that God's will commands unconditional passive obedience to the supreme civil governing power. To establish that claim, however, Berkeley first sets out an overall normative theory, based on what God commands in general. Its premise is that as God is a being of infinite goodness, his end is the good of all his creatures. The question then becomes, if God's end is the greatest good of all (henceforth: the good), what does he prescribe that we do?

Berkeley thinks there are only two possibilities:

W1 God wills that each person aim to do all *he or she* can, in each instance, to promote the good *directly*. Each is obliged "upon each particular occasion to consult the public good, and always ... do that which to him shall seem, in the present time and circumstances, most to conduce to it." (PO 8)

W2 God wills that each observe "some determinate, established laws, which, if universally practised, have from the nature of things, an essential fitness to procure the well-being of mankind." (PO 8)

Corresponding to these two propositions about God's will are the following claims about right and wrong.

R1 On each occasion, what it is right for a person to do is what that person believes (or, perhaps, would believe on available evidence) would best promote the good.

R2 On each occasion, what it is right for a person to do is what would be required by those rules which, if universally accepted and followed, would best promote the good.

It is a mark of Berkeley's philosophical subtlety that he is able to see the difference between these alternatives. So far as I know, he is the first philosopher to do so and, consequently, the first to distinguish, much less defend, a rule-utilitarian theory of right (henceforth: RU). From a contemporary vantage point, however, it may seem that these two are not the only possiblities. As an alternative to *W1*, there seems to be:

W1′ God wills that each person, on each occasion, do whichever available act would actually promote the good.

A corresponding *R1′* would be a familiar form of act-utilitarianism (henceforth: AU). *R1* and *R1′* are *subjective* and *objective* forms of AU, respectively.

In addition, recent writers also distinguish between *direct* and *indirect* forms of utilitarianism. Direct utilitarianism judges the rightness of an agent's act by its direct contribution, assessed relative to other available alternatives either subjectively or objectively, to promoting the good. Indirect forms, of which RU is one example, judge an act right only if something else to which it is related maximizes the good: a motive producing it, a trait it expresses, a deliberative procedure calling for it, or a rule that requires it. Moreover, there can be different forms depending on whether what is required are acts relevantly related to motives, traits, rules, and so forth, that it would maximize the good for the *individual* in question to have, taking other people's actual motives, traits, rules, and the others, as fixed; or acts relevantly related to motives, traits, rules, and the rest, that it would maximize the good for *everyone* to have. *R2*, corresponding to *W2*, is one form of indirect utilitarianism, but might not God's will correspond to some other form? Here are only two of many possibilities:

W2′ God wills that each person have *traits* it would maximize the good for her to have and that each person do, on each occasion, what would express these traits.

W2″ God wills that each person accept those rules it would maximize the good for *her* to accept and that each person do, on each occasion, what such rules would require.

Finally, the form of RU that Berkeley defends is a particular form of ideal rule-utilitarianism. It differs, however, from a currently popular form of ideal rule-utilitarianism that takes account of the costs and benefits not only of a rule's being accepted and followed (acceptance-utility and conformance-utility),[28] but also of its being taught.[29]

W2a God wills that each person do, on each occasion, what would be required by rules, the universal teaching of which would maximize the good.

I have set out these distinctions partly to provide some insight into the structure of Berkeley's own proposals, but also because it is worth considering whether Berkeley could have had good reasons to prefer alternatives *W1* and *W2* to the others I have mentioned, as well as good reasons for selecting *W2* over *W1*, and hence, *R2* over *R1*. I believe that, whether or not he saw the other alternatives clearly, he had principled reasons for excluding them.

The key to seeing what Berkeley was about is to appreciate that in order for his whole system to work, human agents have to be able to give sense to the idea that God holds them *accountable* for acting in certain ways. Berkeley thinks we can believe our eternal interests to be staked on our conformance to God's will only if we can regard God as reasonably holding us responsible for conformance. Or, to put the point another way, whatever it is that God wills us to do, such that whether we do it or not affects our eternal interests, must be something we can regard him as reasonably holding us responsible for doing. This rules out *W1′* and *R1′*. We cannot reasonably be held responsible for consequences of our actions we could not have known about, so God cannot make our eternal benefit depend upon whether our actions *actually* promote the good. Berkeley writes in his notebooks, "[A]ctions leading to heaven are in my power if I will them, therefore I will them," and further, "Men impute their actions to themselves because they will'd them & that not out of ignorance but whereas they knew the consequences, of them whether good or bad."[30]

This is an important point for understanding Berkeley's ethics. Morality consists of demands God makes of us, laying up eternal bliss and torment, respectively, for conformance and violation. Thus, while the greatest good of all is God's end in making these demands, it can be an end *morality gives to us* only if it is possible for God to hold us accountable for promoting it directly, and if it would maximize the good for us to try to do so. Plainly Berkeley thinks it would be inconsistent with God's goodness and mercy for him to hold us accountable for success at promoting the good when how successful we are is not in our own hands. It accords with God's nature to stake our eternal interest on what we have only to will to do. Various principles under the heading of the rule of law fall out of this idea, for example that God's law must be promulgated, must be possible to obey by a sufficient effort of will, and so on.

This is why Berkeley fixes on *W1* rather than *W1′*. In effect, *W1* is a *rule* that agents can conform to *if they will*, whereas *W1′* is not. It also explains why the form of indirect utilitarianism Berkeley considers as an alternative to direct utilitarianism is RU (*R2*), rather than some form of motive or trait utilitarianism. God cannot reasonably hold us responsible for having particular motives or traits (*W2′*), because we cannot acquire these at will. He might hold us responsible for doing what we would do if we had such traits, but that would be the same thing as holding us responsible for following a rule that dictates such acts. Given God's desire that the good of all be realized, he would prescribe *that* rule only if our accepting and following it would best promote the good. That seems, however, to be no different from *W2*, and hence, from RU (*R2*).

Well, perhaps not. Perhaps God's will is that each individual follow whatever rule it would best promote the good for *that person* to accept and follow. That is, perhaps God's will is that expressed in *W2″*. As we shall see, Berkeley thinks that together we can discover what rules are such that it would maximize the good for us *all* to follow. But if *W2″* were true, we could follow God's will only if each person knew what rules it would be best for *that individual* to follow, taking as given the actual actions and rule-conformance of others. Even were it possible to know this, the need for coordination will exert a strong push in the direction of common rules. We will want, as well, common rules to provide a common standard for earthy praise and blame, even if only to confirm beneficial, coordinating public practices. Considerations of this sort tell in favor of *W2* rather than *W2″*.

But why *W2* rather than *W2a*? Why should we not be held, and hold each other, not to rules it would be best for all to accept and follow – as though creating and recreating their acceptance were cost-free – but to rules it would be best to *teach*, taking account of the costs of teaching as well as the benefits and costs of accepting and following them? Here we might distinguish the costs of socially identifying the rules from the costs involved in inducing people actually to follow them. Berkeley presumably means to include the former costs: He takes seriously the objection that trying to follow his form of RU leaves individuals "to their own private judgments as much as ever" (PO 29). His response is that "candid rational inquirers after truth" will come fairly easily to agreement in identifying the most beneficial rules. So we might think of their calculations as factoring in the costs of their own investigation. Once these have been accounted for, though, Berkeley must believe that the remaining costs are those any flourishing society will be committed to paying anyway to bring everyone to a vivid "pious Sense of the Presence of God" (PHK 156), together with educating them in the relation of God's will – and hence their eternal interests – to these rules. There is no reason, then, to consider *W2a* rather than *W2*.

This leaves the field to *W1* and *W2*. Actually, if the foregoing reflections have been correct, there's a sense in which the field is left to (the most general form of) *W2* alone. If God can reasonably hold us only to prescriptions that are rules already in effect, then *W1* would express his will only if it would best promote the good for every individual to accept and follow the rule of doing what that person believes (or would reasonably believe) would best promote the good, on each occasion. If that were true, there would be no difference between *W1* and a generalized form of *W2* – in other words, that God wills that everyone accept and follow rules, the acceptance and following of which would best promote the good.

Of course, Berkeley has a more specific alternative in mind in *W2*, namely that God wills that everyone follow certain "determinate, established laws," among which would be an absolute prohibition on resistance and, consequently, a duty of passive obedience. That, then, becomes the issue on which Berkeley concentrates. Does God will that everyone attempt to promote the good on a case-by-case basis, or does he will that everyone follow certain "determinate, established laws," the universal following of which (each believes) will best promote the good? Berkeley's answer, now famous, is that God must will the latter; because He wills the latter, these determinate laws determine what we morally must do.

Berkeley gives various arguments. The first one, that we rarely know all the "hidden circumstances and consequences of an action," may seem directed at an objective rather than a subjective reading of *W1* (*W1′* rather than *W1*) (PO 9). However, because we rarely even have *beliefs* about which of our actions will have the best consequences, from here to eternity, this phrase can find a target in *W1* as well. I've already briefly mentioned Berkeley's second argument, namely that *W1* gives us no "sure standard" for assessing the conduct of others. To evaluate their conduct, we would need to know others' "private disinterested opinion of what makes most for the public good at that juncture," and we rarely do know this (PO 9).

The consideration that weighs most heavily with Berkeley, however, is the same that lies behind his account of why God fashions laws of nature and speaks to us in the language of nature – *predictability*. God operates by general rules in each case for very similar reasons. We could not act in our own interest at all unless God caused ideas in us in some regular, predictable way. Similarly, different individuals cannot promote the good together unless their actions – specifically, the "actions of good men" – are mutually predictable. Productive social activity must be coordinated, but if every person were to try to promote the good as each saw it, there could "be no harmony or agreement between the actions of good men" (PO 10). God's will for human action, then, must be that they follow certain common, general rules as well.

It can be objected to an ideal rule-utilitarianism such as Berkeley's that it is actually unable to provide an adequate basis for coordination. If every person follows rules each believes it would maximally promote the good for all to accept, what reason is there to think that everyone will fix on the same rules?[31] As I already mentioned in passing, Berkeley considers this objection, that "men will be left to their own private judgments as much as ever" (PO 29). His answer is that although there is great uncertainty regarding the relation of particular acts to the greatest good, "candid rational inquirers after truth" will not find significant disagreement in their beliefs about what general rules would be best for all to accept (PO 29).

Even aside from whether Berkeley is correct about this, how does he think such agreement would arise? Here *Passive Obedience* and remarks in other writings give somewhat mixed signals. Berkeley says in *Passive Obedience* that the moral "'laws of nature'... are said to be 'stamped on the mind,' to be 'engraven on the tables of the heart,'" but that is "because they are well known to mankind" (PO 12). Although he adds that the moral laws are "suggested and inculcated by conscience," Berkeley does not suggest there that conscience is an additional source of moral knowledge (PO 11). Thus, when he goes on to argue that there are duties of truth-telling, justice, and chastity, Berkeley does not appeal to his readers' consciences but asserts:

> Let any one who hath the use of reason take but an impartial survey of the general frame and circumstances of human nature, and it will appear plainly to him that the constant observation of truth, for instance, of justice, and chastity, hath a necessary connexion with their [humans'] universal well-being. (PO 15)

In his sermon "On the Will of God," however, Berkeley says reason is not the only "natural means to discovering the will of God."[32] We also have "a natural conscience" that "previous to all deductions of reason" gives us a spontaneous "distaste" in contemplating certain evil actions.

However we know which rules God wills us to follow, Berkeley is clear that they have the property of being rules it would maximize the good for all to accept and follow, *and* that they must be followed even in situations where doing so will occasion "great sufferings and misfortunates... to very many good men" (PO 8). This raises a question familiar from recent discussions of RU. If what justifies establishing general rules is simply the instrumental benefits of doing so, then how can actually obeying the rules be justified when doing so would be detrimental? When the question facing an agent is what *to do*, the objection goes, the relevant question concerns the instrumental benefits and costs of *the action*, including, of course, those mediated by instrumentally beneficial, rule-structured practices the actions may affect.

Whether contemporary forms of RU can deal adequately with this objection or not, Berkelely's metaethic gives him a way of avoiding it. For Berkelely, no rule has normative force "merely because it conduceth to the public good, but because it is decreed by the will of God" (PO 31). The public good is God's end in decreeing the moral law, but that doesn't make the public good normative *for us*. It would be only if God willed that we make it our end, and conditioned our eternal interest on our doing so. God would do that only if it would be best for us all to aim directly at this end; because it would not be, he does not will it. He wills that we accept and follow generally useful rules even on those occasions when the consequences of following them would be worse. Precisely because that is what God wills, and conditions our eternal interest on conformance, we must conform.

V. BERKELEY'S NORMATIVE VIEWS

We can now, in closing, briefly consider the moral and political doctrines Berkelely wished to set in the framework we have been investigating in the last two sections. Central to his defense of passive obedience is his distinction between *positive* and *negative* moral precepts. What this amounts to is a distinction between duties (positive) that "allow room for human prudence and discretion in the execution of them," and those (negative) that "must by everyone, in all times and places, be all actually observed" (PO 26). As Berkeley conceives it, if there are any duties of beneficence at all, there will be positive duties, because any duty that requires us to do good will effectively require us to use our discretion in determining what would actually be beneficial. Once the contrast is put this way, the contrast between positive and negative duties becomes akin to the contrast between *W1* and *W2*, and Berkeley's argument that not all duties can be positive works similarly. He has already shown, he argues, that the "great end of morality" is not furthered by "leaving each particular person to promote the public in such a manner as he shall think most convenient" (PO 27). Rather, to coordinate socially beneficial activity there must be specific rules enjoining certain specific acts, regardless of whether individuals think they could more beneficially act otherwise. Therefore there must be rules that everyone is to observe "in all times and places." Because "it is not possible for one man to perform several" conflicting actions at the same time, such rules must be ones someone can obey by doing nothing: by abstaining, for example, from lying, stealing, or harming another, or – in the instance in which Berkeley is primarily interested in *Passive Obedience* – from resisting the sovereign's authority.

Because individuals are so inept at "avert[ing] the evils, or procur[ing] the blessings of life" by themselves, and because they are so apt to disagree about the best ways of doing so collectively, the public good requires that they be "combined together, under the direction... of one and the same will" (PO 16), wherever "this supreme power of making [and enforcing] laws" may happen to be located in a "civil community" (PO 3). Leaving it to individual discretion whether to rebel against the Supreme Power inevitably leads to violent clashes (PO 20). The general case for specific negative duties applies with special force here. Any rule that makes political obedience conditional on the sovereign power's meeting some standard cannot establish "any determinate, agreed, common measure of loyalty," because it "leave[s] every subject to the guidance of his own particular mutable fancy" (PO 20).

Thus Berkeley regarded the argument for an absolute duty of loyalty or nonresistance as a special instance of the general case for "determinate, established laws, which, if universally practised" will "procure the well-being of mankind" (PO 8). This argument supports only a negative duty of nonresistance, however, not any positive duty. The only duty of obedience that is unconditional on individual discretion is the duty *not to rebel*. Subjects remain obligated by the rest of morality; no earthly sovereign, only God, can suspend *that*. If a temporal sovereign commands something that violates one of God's "determinate, established laws," there is no obligation to obey.

Ultimately, Berkeley's argument for an absolute duty of passive obedience derives from the same premises (the existence of a benevolent, "all seeing" God and the immortality of the soul) that he takes to undergird all of morality. Because these are required to support the legitimacy of the state as well as the whole moral system, Berkeley declares that the state cannot tolerate the dissemination of contrary doctrines. Although "common sense, as well as Christian charity" may recommend toleration on "some points of religion, yet the public safety requireth that the avowed contemners of all religion should be severely chastised."[33] Perhaps, he remarks ominously, blasphemy should be punished "with the same rigour as treason against the king."[34]

Berkeley's political doctrines no doubt will strike most contemporary readers as wrongheaded and dangerous. In judging him on that basis, however, we should bear in mind that Berkeley thought nothing less was necessary to protect morality itself and, therefore, the interests of the innocent and the vulnerable.

NOTES

1. The charge that unorthodox or opposing views result from affectation is a recurrent polemical device in early eighteenth-century philosophical controversy, one well worth further study.
2. See ALC 1.15 (59). See also ALC 1.2 (35) and DHP 1 (167).
3. The continuation of the passage makes it clear that Berkeley is also worried about the spreading of skepticism and unbelief to common folk themselves.
4. As Jessop says in his introduction to Berkeley's *An Essay towards Preventing the Ruin of Great Britain*, first published in London in 1721, the bursting of the Bubble "haunts almost every line of the essay" (*Works* 6: 63). For more on the bursting of the Bubble and its consequences, see Chapter 11, Patrick Kelly's contribution to this volume.
5. On Berkeley's formulation of this point in the context of his critique of Mandeville, see Section I. For his economic diagnosis of the causes of poverty and his proposals for combatting it, see *The Querist* and *A Word to the Wise*, both in *Works* 6. For the context and argument of *The Querist*, see Chapter 11 of this *Companion*.
6. I discuss Berkeley's internalism in Section II. In the present context, internalism is the view that what it is for someone to be under an

obligation (or for it to be the case that a person ought to do something) must somehow be understood in relation to that person's motives (actual or hypothetical). I describe the development of internalism within two different traditions in early modern Britain – one, empirical naturalist, the other, tying obligation to autonomy or self-regulation – in Stephen Darwall, *The British Moralists and the Internal 'Ought' 1640–1740* (Cambridge: Cambridge University Press, 1995). I do not there discuss Berkeley. The present essay may be viewed as placing Berkeley in relation to the framework of that book.

7. Bernard Mandeville, *The Fable of the Bees: of Private Vices, Publick Benefits*, ed. F. B. Kaye (Indianapolis: Liberty Classics, 1988), based on the 6th edition, published in London in 1729.
8. *Characteristics of Men, Manners, Opinons, and Times*, ed. Lawrence E. Klein (Cambridge: Cambridge University Press, 1999). This text is based on the 2nd edition (London, 1714); the 1st edition was published in 1711.
9. Francis Hutcheson subtitled the first edition of *An Inquiry into the Original of our Ideas of Beauty and Virtue* (London, 1725) thus: "In which the Principles of the late Earl of Shaftesbury are Explain'd and Defended, against the Author of the *Fable of the Bees*."
10. I discuss Shaftesbury's views in chapter 7 of *The British Moralists and the Internal 'Ought.'*
11. It seems likely that what moved Berkeley to such an ungenerous interpretation of Shaftesbury's thought was the latter's ridicule for much of instituted religion. As Jessop put it, although Berkeley "did not mind religion's being seriously argued against . . . he would not have it laughed at" (*Works* 6: 11).
12. *An Inquiry Concerning Virtue or Merit*, Book I, in *Characteristics*, ed. L. Klein, 163–93.
13. See also *Passive Obedience* 5.
14. See, for example, "Pleasures," an essay Berkeley published in the *Guardian*, May 7, 1713, in *Works* 7: 193–7.
15. *Works* 7: 193.
16. NTV 147.
17. N 143; see also N 166.
18. In *Works* 7:11. Bishop Richard Cumberland worked out similar ideas in his *A Treatise of the Law of Nature*, originally published as *De Legibus Naturæ Disquisitio Philosophica* in 1672, trans. John Maxwell (London, 1727; reprinted New York: Garland Publishing, 1978). See also Francis Hutcheson's "natural laws of calm desire" in *An Essay on the Nature and Conduct of the Passions and Affections* (London: 1728; rep. Gainesville, FL: Scholars' Facsimiles & Reprints, 1969).

19. I discuss the development of this idea in Hobbes, Cumberland, Locke, and Hutcheson in *The British Moralists and the Internal 'Ought.'*
20. Noncognitivism has been advanced in a variety of forms: (a) *emotivism*: A. J. Ayer, *Language, Truth and Logic* (New York: Dover Publications, Inc., 1952); and C. L. Stevenson, "The Emotive Meaning of Ethical Terms," *Mind* 46 (1937): 14–31, and *Ethics and Language* (New Haven: Yale University Press, 1944); (b) *prescriptivism*: R. M. Hare, *The Language of Morals* (Oxford: Clarendon Press, 1952), and *Freedom and Reason* (Oxford: Clarendon Press, 1963); and *norm-expressivism*: Allan Gibbard, *Wise Choices, Apt Feelings* (Cambridge: Harvard University Press, 1990); and Simon Blackburn, *Ruling Passions: A Theory of Practical Reasoning* (Oxford: Clarendon Press, 1998).
21. See also Berkeley's "Draft Introduction to the Principles of Human Knowledge," MS #3, the "Chapman" MS, Trinity College Library, Dublin, 145–7. Paul J. Olscamp discusses these passages in the context of the general question of whether Berkeley was an emotivist in *The Moral Philosophy of George Berkeley* (The Hague: Martinus Nijhoff, 1970), 130–53. See also I. A. Richards and C. K. Ogden, *The Meaning of Meaning* (New York: Harcourt, Brace, and World Co., 1923), 42; and A. P. Stroll, *The Emotive Theory of Ethics* (Berkeley and Los Angeles: University of California Press, 1954), 24–5.
22. *Romans* 13: 2.
23. "Law of nature" here means a directly prescriptive norm rather than the descriptive or predictive laws of nature, stated in the language of nature. This distinction will be discussed further.
24. Here is a parallel passage from Berkeley's notebooks: "I'd never blame a Man for acting upon Interest. he's a fool that acts on any other Principle. the not understanding these things has been of ill consequence in Morality" (N 542).
25. Compare this with Euphranor's statement to Alciphron in the first dialogue of *Alciphron* that "the general happiness of mankind [is] a greater good than the private happiness of one man," and thus "the most excellent end" (ALC 1.16 [61]). This echoes a line of thought in Cumberland's *Treatise of the Law of Nature* that I discuss in Chapter 4 of *The British Moralists and the Internal 'Ought.'*
26. See PO 14–15 for the distinction between these two kinds of law of nature.
27. See ALC 7.16–20 (309–18) for some discussion of free will.
28. On these notions, see David Lyons, *Forms and Limits of Utilitarianism* (Oxford: Clarendon Press, 1970), 139–40.
29. See, for example, Richard B. Brandt, *A Theory of the Good and the Right* (Oxford: Clarendon Press, 1979), 286–305.

30. N 160, 157. Consider also: "Sin or moral turpitude doth not consist in the outward physical action or motion, but in the internal deviation of the will from the laws of reason and religion" (DHP 3 [236–7]).
31. For this objection, see, for instance, Conrad D. Johnson, *Moral Legislation* (Cambridge: Cambridge Univerity Press, 1991), 36–7.
32. *Works* 7: 130. Here Berkeley also discusses revelation as a source of knowledge about God's will.
33. *The Ruin of Great Britain*, in *Works* 6: 70–1.
34. *Works* 6: 70–1.

PATRICK KELLY

11 Berkeley's economic writings

I. INTRODUCTION

To feed the hungry and clothe the naked, by promoting an honest industry, will, perhaps, be deemed no improper employment for a clergyman who still thinks himself a member of the commonwealth.[1]

This note prefacing the second edition of *The Querist* suggests that when Berkeley came to set his name to the tract he had first published anonymously some fifteen years earlier, he felt that discussion of economic problems might not seem appropriate for a bishop. In considering such matters, though, Berkeley was far from unique amongst the clergy of the Church of Ireland in the eighteenth century. The papers of Archbishop King reveal him as one of the most percipient analysts of Ireland's economic and social problems from the 1690s to the 1720s.[2] Berkeley's friend, the Reverend Samuel Madden, was active in the encouragement of agriculture and industry, as well as being the author of an important economic tract, *Reflections and Resolutions Proper for the Gentlemen of Ireland* (1738).[3] The most famous writer on Irish economic and social problems of this period in the eyes of posterity was Jonathan Swift, Dean of St Patrick's.[4] The only one of this galaxy of Irish clerical economists to figure in textbooks on the history of economics is, however, Berkeley, who has long earned a place for his innovative conception of the "true idea of money, as . . . a ticket or counter" (Q 23), though today he equally commands attention as a pioneer of development economics.

Before discussing Berkeley's economic ideas, it may not be amiss to recall that in the early eighteenth century economics had not yet emerged as a separate, defined field of inquiry. Questions of foreign trade, currency management, employment and banking, and so forth, were regarded as sub-fields of politics, whose interrelations were still not altogether clearly delineated.[5] In asking "Whether there can be a greater mistake in politics than to measure the wealth of the nation by its gold and silver?" *The Querist* (562) showed that Berkeley, too, regarded economic matters as falling within the domain of politics. However, despite the ambiguous status of "economics," by the early eighteenth century there was already an established body of literature dealing with commercial and monetary questions stretching back to the work of Malynes, Misselden, and Mun in the 1620s. This represented not so much a coherent theory as a common stock of ideas and definitions on which writers on questions involving trade and money were accustomed to draw. Though as yet lacking a specific name (and differing in important ways from the later science of political economy), this discourse about money and trade was ready to hand for those who wished to discuss the economic problems that beset their society. As *The Querist* and his other economic writings make clear, it was a discourse with which Berkeley was undoubtedly familiar, despite the paucity of his references to specific works.[6]

The ambiguous status of "economics" in the early eighteenth century helps explain why economic issues were often somewhat puzzlingly combined in Berkeley's writings with discussions of education, political arrangements, ethics, and morality.[7] Despite its unusual format of a series of apparently randomly linked questions, Berkeley's *Querist* belonged to a particular genre of later seventeenth- and early eighteenth-century economic literature, namely the "improvement" tract.[8] Such works devoted themselves to the "improvement" of the country's welfare in a variety of fields – economic, educational, moral, and political, as well as agricultural and horticultural. What imparts particular interest to Berkeley's work is his concern not only with the range of subjects normally covered by improvement tracts, but the way such matters relate to his general ideas on how society should be organised, and the questions he raised as to the true purpose of economic activity and its limits – questions that reflect the basically Aristotelian perspective from which he considered economic matters.[9]

II. *THE QUERIST* AND BERKELEY'S OTHER ECONOMIC WRITINGS

Though Berkeley's reputation as an economic thinker rests mainly on *The Querist*, he was also the author of a number of other economic works. Most important were *An Essay towards Preventing the Ruine of Great Britain* (1721), the second dialogue of *Alciphron* (1732); and *A Word to the Wise* (1749); minor pieces included the separate publication of many of the queries relating to banking under the title, *A Plan, or Sketch of a National Bank* (1738), *The Irish Patriot, or Queries upon Queries* (1739), and *Maxims concerning Patriotism* (1750).[10] *The Querist* was published anonymously in Dublin in three separate parts in 1735, 1736, and 1737.[11] However, the text on which assessments of Berkeley's economic ideas have generally been based is the revised and consolidated edition of 1750. This omitted 345 of the original queries (mostly dealing with the proposed national bank), together with the cross-referencing between queries, and added 45 entirely new queries.[12] The sometimes randomly connected questions of *The Querist* shift backwards and forwards over a number of broad themes such as the employment of the poor, the role of the Irish landed gentry, the position of the Roman Catholics, regulation of the coinage, and the function of a national bank, punctuated by occasional gnomic references to the need to think seriously about Ireland's position.[13] While demonstrating Berkeley's considerable literary skills,[14] the format is undeniably repetitive; indeed, Query 41, "Whether a single hint be sufficient to overcome a prejudice? And whether even obvious truths will not sometimes bear repeating?" suggests the repetition was deliberate.[15] Furthermore, Query 315 of the first edition – "Whether one, whose end is to make his countrymen think, may not gain his end, even though they should not think as he doth?" – suggests Berkeley was originally more interested in stimulating public debate than in advocating his own detailed policies. More importantly, the query format makes it difficult to establish Berkeley's precise views on certain complex issues, notably the role of land-backing for the paper money to be issued by the National Bank. In other cases, such as whether Ireland would benefit from engaging in foreign trade, we are confronted by unreconciled assertions for and against the matters raised.[16] Various candidates have been put forward as the model for the format of *The Querist*. Berkeley's twentieth-century editor, T. E. Jessop, favored the queries at the end of Newton's *Optics*, while T. W. Hutchison has urged the case for William Petty's *Quantulumque concerning Money* (1695); a more recent Irish model may have been Swift's *Queries Relating to the Sacramental Test* (1732).[17]

An Essay towards Preventing the Ruine of Great Britain was written in the aftermath of the South Sea Bubble of 1720, probably during the inquiries conducted by the British Parliament early in 1721.[18] The Bubble was the English manifestation of Europe's first stock market crisis (also embracing Law's Mississippi disaster in France and a similar collapse in Amsterdam), and resulted in the ruin of many would-be speculators as well as a credit crisis that severely affected the prosperity of Britain and Ireland for a prolonged period. This disastrous episode provoked widespread reappraisal of financial and commercial developments in England since the late seventeenth century, such as the growth of banking and fractionary credit, the emergence of a stock market and the relations between the new financial class of "monied men" and the mass of ordinary property owners who had suffered in the Bubble. Setting its face against many of these recent developments, Berkeley's *Essay* sought to demonstrate that a nation could only be weakened by a financial system that divorced wealth and prosperity from trade, industry, and labor. It condemned the South Sea directors as deliberate architects of their country's ruin, and argued that only by returning to religion, frugality, industry, and public spirit could the nation hope to avoid disaster. In parallel with this moral and political analysis, Berkeley also displayed a competent (though as yet in no way remarkable) understanding of the operations of the economy. He emphasized the role of human industry in the creation of wealth and the significance of the demand-inducing function of the circulation of money. He also proffered a number of specific recommendations such as the promotion of new manufactures and the reorganization of poor relief, all conceived in terms of state intervention through the machinery of the legislature. Berkeley's main message was that a well-ordered society depended on provision for moderate wants through individual industry and frugality, and that to encourage things to function otherwise (particularly in breaking the link between prosperity and industry) was to court ruin both moral and political.[19]

A major interest of the 1721 *Essay* is the quantum leap in economic understanding it showed Berkeley to have achieved by the time he came to write *The Querist* fourteen years later. The fundamental preoccupations with labour and industry, the unique demand-creating function of monetary circulation, the moral and economic dangers of luxury and idleness, and the crucial role of the state in directing the economy were all to be clearly distinguished in the later work.[20] What was new was a far sharper awareness of the realities of the economic process: The unique field of comparison afforded by what he had learned of economic and social conditions in his two-year sojourn in New England in 1729–31 provided the insights in Berkeley's consideration of the malfunctioning of the poorer economy of Ireland.[21] A further fruit of Berkeley's American visit had been the writing of *Alciphron, or the Minute Philosopher*, published in 1732 after his return to London. The second of its seven dialogues was directed at refuting the thesis that economic prosperity was the result of extravagance and debauchery rather than industry and frugality, as argued by Mandeville in *The Fable of the Bees* (1724) on the principle of what Lysicles (the minute philosopher of the dialogues) termed "the beautiful and never-enough-admired connexion of the vices."[22] In contrast, Berkeley sought to demonstrate that luxury and extravagance brought only a temporary benefit to the economy, whereas the temperate and prudent citizen, in establishing a household and family, created a longer-enduring and thus greater demand (as well as a socially more beneficial one). Berkeley's final important economic pamphlet, *A Word to the Wise* of 1749, was a reiteration of the call in *The Querist* to set the Irish poor to work for the benefit of their country, recast in the novel form of an appeal addressed to the Irish Catholic clergy as fellow citizens and Christians by a bishop of the established church. Though the harsh tones of protestant ascendancy occasionally broke through the diction of enlightened benevolence, *A Word to the Wise* urged the Catholic clergy to use their undoubted influence to promote the material as well as the spiritual welfare of their flocks, citing the example of the promotion of industry and agriculture the youthful Berkeley had witnessed three decades earlier on his travels in the Papal States.[23]

III. CONDITIONS IN MID-EIGHTEENTH-CENTURY IRELAND

Given that the main concern of *The Querist* was the solution of Ireland's economic difficulties, it seems appropriate to preface discussion of Berkeley's ideas by considering conditions in Ireland at the time. The underlying trend of the Irish economy in first half of the eighteenth century, particularly the 1720s and 1730s, was largely unfavorable.[24] Lack of demand for Irish products both in Britain and on the continent, together with a growing population, resulted in a fall in per capita income from the beginning of the eighteenth century to the 1750s, despite the stagnation in population growth after 1739. While there were occasional spurts of prosperity in the second decade of the century, the twenty-five years following the South Sea Bubble in 1720 were particularly depressed. The successive harvest failures of the late 1720s resulted in widespread famine. The proportion of good harvests in the 1730s was sufficient to avert the famine's renewal, but the early 1740s saw its recurrence on a devastating scale. The main difficulty of the early and mid-1730s was that the abundant harvests which kept famine at arm's length made for low agricultural prices which prolonged stagnation in the economy. By the mid-1740s, however, things began to improve, in that for the first time the possibility of food imports staved off the prospect of starvation. From then on, revival of foreign trade (despite a succession of wet seasons in the 1750s) began to stimulate the general recovery that led to a modest prosperity in the later part of the century. The stagnation of foreign trade in the form of inadequate demand for Irish products is considered by Louis Cullen, the foremost economic historian of Ireland's eighteenth century, to have been the main factor underlying the pessimism of the economic writings of the 1720s and 1730s.[25] It was this that led to the hopes expressed by Berkeley and others for expansion in the linen industry, the sole sector of Irish manufactures that seemed to promise a growth in exports as well as prospects for the expansion of employment (Q 74, 164, 492, 516–23). Periodic harvest failure, so critical for the early eighteenth-century economy in terms of subsistence crises, was also crucial in terms of credit crises, particularly those of the late 1720s, whose consequences continued to be felt in the form of depressed circulation and bank failure as late as 1735, and probably helped provide the stimulus for writing *The Querist*.[26]

Also crucial to Ireland's difficulties from the South Sea Bubble to the later 1730s was the country's extraordinarily unsatisfactory currency provision. As in the American colonies, Britain refused to permit setting up a local mint for gold and silver – despite a succession of Irish demands from the Restoration onwards.[27] The Irish economy was thus dependent for its circulating medium on what English gold and silver coins could be attracted through trade, supplemented by a wide variety of European moneys current at values established by the Irish administration at British direction. From the beginning of the eighteenth century, a combination of the adverse foreign trade pattern and the burden of remittances to absentees in England resulted in periodic severe shortages of specie, aggravated by the lack of small change and the overvaluing (in pro rata specie terms) of certain foreign gold coins, especially high denomination Portuguese pieces.[28] Among the solutions proposed were the issue of various copper coinages and the creation of a national bank, together with the devaluation of specific foreign gold moneys, and the revaluation (that is, enhancement) of silver coins.[29] Such proposals, however, proved explosive in political terms. The first half of the 1720s saw violent controversy over a project for a national bank in 1720–1, followed by the even more contentious issue of a copper currency under a patent granted to William Wood in 1722. Alarm amongst a section of the Anglo-Irish nobility and gentry led by Archbishop King and Jonathan Swift eventually forced withdrawal of both proposals, not because their opponents saw no need for remedial action but because of a deep-seated distrust of the motives behind any form of British intervention. This view stemmed from a conviction, going back to the 1699 English act prohibiting the export of woollen cloth, that English ministers could in no way be trusted to advance Ireland's welfare.[30] Further proposals for an issue of copper currency in 1729, together with a call for devaluation of foreign gold moneys, sparked off a fresh wave of pamphleteering, which included some very restricted proposals for the issue of paper money.[31] The latter evoked widespread hostility on the part of leading Irish writers on monetary questions, such as Swift, Thomas Prior, and Sir John Browne. Apart from the idea of a national bank canvassed by the anonymous *Proposal for the Relief of Ireland* (Dublin, 1734) cited by Berkeley, only the obscure Daniel Webb favoured an issue of small interest-bearing bills to the value of £30,000 to assist artisans and tradesmen.[32] This general fear of paper supplements in Ireland was in notable contrast to the inventiveness displayed by various American colonies – though by no means had all the American experiments been successful. Among the most effective paper money issues, however, was that in the Rhode Island, of which Berkeley had acquired first-hand knowledge in 1729–31.[33]

In the early 1730s Ireland experienced its first significant failures by private bankers, and these seriously affected liquidity as well as confidence in the economy.[34] The problem of such failures greatly exercised Berkeley in the original edition of *The Querist*, particularly in Part II; as II 9 (Q 275) asked, "Whether the wealth and prosperity of our country do not hang by a hair, the probity of one banker, the caution of another and the lives of all?" Also crucial was the problem caused by lack of appropriate small denomination pieces to service local markets and pay laborers and artisans, in particular for the needs of the linen industry in the North (the sole flourishing Irish export product in these years).[35] This led once more to calls to devalue foreign gold moneys with the intention of discouraging the import of moiodores and other high-value gold pieces with low rates of circulation, and replacing them with lower-value gold moneys more adapted to the needs of the Irish economy. In 1736 even the Irish Privy Council urged the London government to authorize the devaluation, leading to a further wave of pamphleteering which provided the immediate context of the second and third parts of *The Querist*. Despite the opposition of Swift amongst others, the London government finally agreed to the devaluation of gold in August 1737.[36] In consequence, though silver remained in short supply (as was also the case in England for much of the eighteenth century), the shortage of appropriate coin to service transactions eventually eased.

IV. THE TRUE NATURE OF WEALTH AND OF MONEY

Berkeley's approach in *The Querist* highlights the salient features of this depressed economy, emphasizing the need for providing for basic subsistence, stimulating the industry of the population, and creating an adequate circulating medium. His solution reflected prevailing mercantilist views in accepting that the most effective means of stimulating economic activity depended on increasing the circulation of money, but in two very important ways Berkeley departed from accepted wisdom. Not only did he reject the notion that gold and silver alone could serve as the effective form of money (though he was by no means a pioneer in this respect), but he claimed that under certain circumstances foreign trade might actually impoverish rather than enrich a nation, an assertion which struck at the central postulate of more than a century of mercantilist argument.

Berkeley's theoretical principles were sketched out in the opening forty queries of the book.[37] They set forth: the nature of wealth; its origin in human industry; the objective of full employment for the population; the function of money (independent of its substance); the primacy of will or opinion in getting men to labor; and the resulting need to motivate this will through arousing the appetite to consume. Given the absence of any conception of the achievement of equilibrium through hidden harmony or the design of nature, a pivotal responsibility was accorded to the state in bringing about the necessary conditions to promote what Berkeley asserted to be the public objective of full employment.[38] Central to the state's function was the provision of an adequate circulating medium without which industry and natural resources could not be set in motion. Such a means of facilitating commerce need not depend on Ireland's inelastic supply of gold and silver, because through translating wants into effective demand by means of paper money the state could promote real wealth without any resort to foreign trade.

In another sense, however, Berkeley's real starting point was the mind. At numerous places in *The Querist* he reiterated the need for a new way of thinking about Ireland's economic problems, involving a clear identification of the problems to be solved, and a well-defined goal to be achieved (Q 495, 568). "Whether," as Query 48 put it "reflection in the better sort might not soon remedy our evils? And whether our real defect be not a wrong way of thinking?" It is tempting to speculate that Berkeley may have found the inspiration for his novel approach in one of the best-known recent pamphlets on Ireland's economic problems, namely Swift's *A Short View of the State of Ireland* (1727–8). This examined fourteen factors (comprising both natural advantages and government policies) that had been effective in promoting national prosperity in other countries. In Ireland all fourteen either had failed to bring about the expected result, or had been frustrated by English malevolence or by the ignorance and folly of the Irish themselves. While offering a similar diagnosis of Irish conditions, Berkeley, however, drew very different conclusions. In place of Swift's despair, he was able to perceive that the reason very different consequences had ensued in Ireland was due to its underdeveloped condition, and that the basic mercantilist assumption that foreign trade was the sole key to wealth did not and could not hold good in Ireland's case. As Query 108 asked, "Whether there is not a great difference between Holland and Ireland? And whether foreign commerce, without which the one could not subsist, be so necessary for the other?" For a poor agricultural nation such as Ireland to export the resources so desperately needed to sustain and employ its own starving masses, in order to gratify the luxurious appetites of an ignorant and unheeding gentry, was the path not to wealth but to destruction (Q 145, 146, 173, 175). What was necessary was to provide a solution to Ireland's problems appropriate to Ireland's circumstances, above all meeting the needs of the mass of her people by providing the basic requirements of subsistence and employment. To make effective policy prescriptions, though, it was necessary to understand the basis from which one must start by determining the true nature of wealth and the true nature of money.

In considering the true nature of wealth, Berkeley rejected the current identification of wealth with gold and silver in favour of what satisfied real human needs, namely "plenty of all the necessaries and comforts of life" (Q 542). As Query 562 asked, "Whether there can be a greater mistake in politics than to measure the wealth of a nation by its gold and silver?" This conclusion, brought home to Berkeley by his experience in Ireland and America (Query 251), also accorded with his philosophical position on the nonexistence of abstract general ideas. The "universal" wealth, represented for earlier economists such as Petty by gold and silver, yielded place to what they had characterised as "domestic" or "local" wealth in the form of food, clothing, houses, lands, tools, capital goods, and the rest.[39] Because, unlike gold and silver, this "real wealth" was the immediate creation of human industry, it could be provided from the nation's internal resources without any recourse to foreign trade: "Might we not put a hand to the plough, or the spade, although we had no foreign commerce?" (Q 109).

The question in creating the wealth necessary to sustain the population became therefore how to promote the industry of all the inhabitants of the state so as to advance the common welfare (Q 329, 352). In terms of individual motivation, industry could be "stirred" only by awakening the will to labor, which in turn depended on creating an appetite for the product of labour, that is, stimulating the desire to consume. Thus the creation of economic prosperity turned out to be fundamentally a psychological matter, "the immediate mover," as Query 590 expressed it, "[is] the blood and the spirits... not money [whether] paper or metal." It therefore became the business of the state to direct people's appetites by controlling fashion, which was far too important a matter to be left "to the management of women and fops, tailors and vintners" (Q 13). However, though wealth was derived from human industry (without which even land remained without value), unless the product of industry could be exchanged it remained incapable of giving rise to further activity in the economy. What was needed was a means of transferring and exchanging the power over the industry of others represented by the product; that is, its value must become capable of being circulated in the market through being symbolically represented by money. As Query 31 asked, "Whether it be not the opinion or will of the people, exciting them to industry, that truly enricheth a nation? And whether this doth not principally depend on the means for counting, transferring, and preserving this power...?"

Berkeley thus clearly perceived how money enabled the wants and desires of people to be transformed into effective demand by creating entitlements to goods and services in direct proportion to the value of their labor product. This insight was prefigured in the strictly functional definition of the utility of money in Query 5, "Whether money be not only so far useful, as it stirreth up industry, enabling men mutually to participate in the fruits of each other's labour?" From the assertion that those who could command all that money would enable them to obtain would not need gold and silver, Berkeley was able to show that the substance of the circulating medium was largely immaterial (Q 6, 7, 34).[40] In practical respects paper money had many advantages over the precious metals, while the prevention of forgery through careful control of printing and signatures would ensure its acceptability within the country (Q 440, 445). What was crucial in stimulating industry, however, was the role of monetary circulation rather than simply money as such (Q 424). The money set in motion must remain in circulation and not be allowed to slip into hoard or to stagnate (Q 242, 472); there was also a danger of sterile (meaning nonproductive) circulation in the form of stock-jobbing or gambling (Q 239, 305, 424). Equally damaging would be an excess of money circulating in proportion to industry (Q 310, 313; Om. Q. I. 215), though a deficiency in the volume of the circulating medium might to an extent be made up by an increase in the velocity of circulation (Q 22, 478–80).

By analyzing the function of money in facilitating the circulation of goods and services, Berkeley was thus able to show that the contemporary obsession with gold and silver was nothing but "prejudices" (Q 439). For him, money primarily represented power over the labor product of others through its capacity to function as "a ticket or counter."[41] The concept of the ticket or counter was contrasted in Query 23 with the views of other writers that money "ha[d] an intrinsic value, or [was] a commodity, a standard, a measure, or a pledge,"[42] a criticism presumably directed at Locke.[43] Berkeley's conception of money as a ticket is not, as some have suggested, to be understood as equivalent to the neutral, inert function of money in exchange favored by classical economists, but rather represents the mercantilist conception of money as an active, independent variable in the economic process. The distinction is clear from Query 441, where Berkeley spoke of the "true and just idea" of money being "a ticket entitling to power," in addition to serving merely "to record and transfer such power."[44] In order to satisfy people's urge to consume, the government should ensure that the members of society received this power in correct proportion to the value of their labor product (Q 8). This could most readily be achieved by the issue of paper money, which would facilitate the translation of natural wants into effective demand in economic terms.

Berkeley was by no means the first writer to propose the adoption of a paper currency as a means of overcoming the shortage of specie in a given country. Notable proposals along these lines had been made for England as early as the Cromwellian period by William Potter and Thomas Violet, while at the beginning of the eighteenth century the later originator of the Mississippi scheme, John Law, had proposed a paper currency based on land values as the solution to the problems of the violently impoverished economy of Scotland following the collapse of the Darien scheme in the 1690s.[45] What was novel about the proposals in *The Querist* was the linking of the paper money solution to the problem of economic growth with the creation in Ireland of what was virtually a closed economy (Q 127, 129). Such a proposal was dependent on the perception that Ireland's export of raw agricultural produce in return for luxury imports deprived the bulk of the population of basic foodstuffs and prevented them from ever becoming productive members of society: Query 173 asks, "Whether the quantities of beef, butter, wool, and leather, exported from this island, can be reckoned the superfluities of a country, where there are so many natives naked and famished?" Retaining these commodities at home would enable the unemployed masses to combine their labour with Ireland's natural resources so as to satisfy their needs (Q 119), which would be transformed into effective demand through the adoption of paper money. This would in turn bring them into the market economy, where their wants would provide the stimulus to set an expanding cycle of production and consumption on its way (Q 107).

V. INDUSTRY, CONSUMPTION, AND CLASS DIFFERENTIALS

In the Ireland of Berkeley's day the implementation of this elegant theoretical solution faced considerable practical difficulties. There seemed to be an institutional constraint in that the bulk of the population apparently preferred idleness, however wretched, to honest toil. Though Berkeley's description of the Irish as "the most indolent and supine people in Christendom" might seem a mere echo of more than a century's colonialist strictures on Irish sloth (Q 19, 357), what was offered in Query 61 ("Whether nastiness and beggary do not... extinguish all such ambition [of aspiring to wealth], making men listless, hopeless, and slothful?") was a more serious analysis of the way misery and despair inhibited efforts to better their condition. Given reasonable opportunity to enjoy the fruit of their labor, however, even the Irish poor might be stimulated to industry and self-respect, through awakening an appetite for wearing shoes and eating beef (Q 19–20, 132, 353, 355, 378). Such a process called for enlightened self-interest on the part of the upper classes and a realization that the required solution was as much political as economic in accepting that they themselves could never be prosperous as long as the bulk of the population lived in misery (Q 167, 255). Although some commentators have argued that this emphasis on creating an appetite amongst the poor for eating beef and wearing shoes made Berkeley an advocate of luxury as the key to consumption, such an interpretation is in practical terms hard to sustain. Not only did he generally condemn luxury, but the modest "comfortable living" which he envisaged the Irish poor as aspiring to enjoy was clearly to remain at that level (Q 18, 107). Berkeley had no desire to abolish the distinction between the gentry and the people at large; indeed in Query 119 he spoke in almost medieval tones of domestic manufacture being able to produce high quality goods sufficient to sustain the necessary differences of status in society.[46]

The reference to the need for an enlightened ruling class to provide the necessary direction and example in economic activity (Q 201), particularly through its activities in the legislature, is an important reminder that for all his advanced ideas on money, Berkeley's thought remained firmly within the traditional mercantilist framework, which envisaged the state taking the lead in directing economic activity.[47] This accorded with the achievement of the happiness (that is, the well-being) of the mass of the inhabitants of the country, which he identified as the proper goal of state activity (Q 345). Berkeley saw the matter in terms of the legislature having certain mechanisms at its disposal to direct the members of society towards the goal of the provision of employment for all – mechanisms which essentially depended on human nature and needs.[48] By means of inducements in terms of modest prosperity backed, where such inducements failed to activate individuals, by the power of state coercion, the legislature could stimulate the industry of the population. Berkeley was quite uncompromising in his acceptance of the fact that where emulation failed to promote the necessary industry amongst the poor, harsher measures on the part of the state were undoubtedly justified, indeed going so far as to advocate a period of temporary slavery (Q 383–6). The state had not only the right to appropriate the labor of the lower orders in order to advance the well-being of the public, but indeed the duty to do so, because the well-being of the state and the prosperity of the upper classes depended on the surplus labor of the poor over and above what was required to maintain their modest "comfortable living" (Q 59, 331, 383, 487).

Industry was a frequently recurring term in *The Querist* and Berkeley's other economic writings and represented both an economic resource and a moral good. In the 1721 *Essay* and the second dialogue of *Alciphron*, industry was frequently coupled or equated with virtue, as luxury was with vice.[49] All possible means were to be harnessed towards promoting industry, even morally questionable ones such as the disposition to follow fashion (Q 99, 361). In place of imported luxuries, the gentry (as the consumption class) were to be encouraged to display their wealth by consuming native products, in building fine houses and laying out gardens, orchards, and agricultural improvements which would both employ native labor and add to the nation's capital stock.[50] Arts and crafts using native raw materials were particularly to be fostered through the direction of fashion and, where necessary, direct state subvention (Q 115–21, 397–414). The habit of industry moreover was something that needed to be encouraged for its own sake and, like all good habits, was best inculcated in childhood (Q 371, 378). As well as being of economic benefit to its individual practitioners and to the nation as a whole, the habit of industry further developed a sense of self-respect that was essential if individuals were to escape from the debilitating cycle of deprivation and misery (Q 58–61).[51] We fail to understand Berkeley's position, however, if we assume that for him industry was merely a virtue for the poor. On the contrary, he believed that society had no room for drones or nonproductive consumers at any social level: "[W]hether those who employ neither head nor hands for the common benefit deserve not to be expelled like drones out of a well-governed State?" (Q 3; see also 360). Indeed his strongest strictures were reserved for gentry extravagance, asking whether "a woman of fashion [is not] a public enemy" and a "fine gentleman . . . a public nuisance" (Q 141, Om. Q. I. 62; see also Q 149). He also attempted to use shame as a means of directing people to their true economic interest, and even on occasion exploited religious prejudice in pointing out that by importing Flemish lace, Irish protestant ladies provided a livelihood for Catholic nuns (Q 453). The cure for gentry extravagance and idleness was seen to lie in education, particularly of elder sons who would become the future legislators of their country (Q 15, 330, 346). The enlightened legislation which was the key to national prosperity depended on a properly educated gentry capable of understanding complicated economic and fiscal problems (Q 183). Effective policy moreover required proper understanding of conditions at home and abroad, and that the resources of political arithmetic should be brought to bear on decisions relating to trade (Q 346, 530, Om. Q. II. 199).

VI. A NATIONAL BANK, FORMS OF MONEY, AND THE ISOLATED ECONOMY

One of the most important functions Berkeley envisaged for the legislature was the establishment and regulation of the national bank, which would be required to manage the paper money.[52] Although it is often asserted that Berkeley's chief debt in this regard was to John Law's *Money and Trade Considered* (1705), there were crucial differences between their proposals. Indeed some of Berkeley's criticisms of what he saw as the shortcomings of Law's proposals for Scotland suggest a certain lack of familiarity with the detail of Law's book.[53] A further important distinction arose in relation to the constitution and status of the bank. Where Law envisaged a private bank serving the needs of the Scottish economy, Berkeley was insistent that what Ireland needed was a truly national bank, that is, one fully owned by the public and answering to the legislature (Om. Q. I. 222).[54] Because the public would be the sole shareholder and owner, the possibility of bank collapse (a fear that reflected Berkeley's concern over the crises in the private banking sector in Ireland in the early 1730s) should be virtually impossible Q 223, 245). Though responsibility for setting up the bank and laying down the principles on which it operated would rest with parliament, day-to-day management would be carried out by experienced persons appointed by the legislature and subject to their constant inspection (Om. Q. III. 120–6). Detailed information was provided as to what had gone wrong with Law's *Banque Royale* in France, as well as in various American paper money schemes, but Berkeley was confident that with "a little sense and honesty," a bank issuing paper money would indeed prove Ireland's "philosopher's stone" (Q 247, 459).[55]

The chief practical problem would be to maintain a constant value for the bank's notes through keeping a proper balance between the quantity of notes and the volume of trade. Drawing on Locke's quantity theorem, Berkeley held that the value of the notes would be proportional to the total volume of goods traded in the economy (Q 465). However, backing for the bank's notes was also to be provided by mortgaging land in exchange for notes issued. Care would have to be taken that excessive amounts of land were not pledged (as Berkeley claimed had happened in Scotland), through ensuring that mortgaged lands were sold regularly to maintain liquidity. As land values could be expected to rise both because of the additional value this new mortgageability conferred on land and also because of the general increase in economic activity (Om. Q. I. 237–46), this would particularly exercise the skill of the managers. Given Berkeley's concept of the truly national bank owned by the public and answerable to the legislature (which would thus have the whole stock of the nation behind it), it is not altogether clear why he still clung to the need to back the bank's notes with land. It is impossible to disentangle from the inherent ambiguity of the *Querist* format whether Berkeley's concern was merely the need to maintain public confidence through concrete backing of the bank's notes with a tangible intrinsic value, or whether he himself did not accept the apparent logic of his own arguments, which pointed to a truly cartalist form of money. That he advocated an intrinsic backing for the bank's notes, however, cannot be denied, and this ultimately established Berkeley as a covert metallist, as Joseph Schumpeter pointed out.[56]

Besides his proposal for the creation of a national bank to issue paper money, Berkeley was also concerned about ensuring an adequate supply of small change for everyday transactions, asking in Query 231 "Whether plenty of cash be not absolutely necessary for keeping up a circulation among the people; that is, whether copper be not more necessary than gold?" (Cf. Q 468, 571). Further awareness of the need for different forms of money to service different forms and levels of transaction (and the institutional implications this had for the performance of local markets and the employment of artisans and others) was revealed in Berkeley's comments on the differing rates of circulation of large-denomination gold pieces (often foreign) and smaller silver coins (Q 469–70, 473, 482–3).[57] Small retail transactions in local markets required an abundance of small units of denomination, and it was particularly important for the value of the coins or notes to be in due proportion to the units of the money of account, so as to avoid unwieldy fractions (Q 461).[58] Thus the state should ensure a sufficiency of the appropriate medium to sustain the various branches of trade (Q 572). This concern with the appropriateness of monetary forms to service different levels of transactions makes clear that Berkeley did not simply equate money with credit, as has sometimes been asserted.[59]

A further problem in relation to the proposals for the adoption of paper money is whether its "local value" (Q 440), in Ireland at least, in some way depends on the maintenance of an isolated economy. Certainly the arguments in support of the isolated economy seemingly represented a departure from the policies advocated in the 1721 *Essay*, where Berkeley's specifically economic proposals emphasized the need for promoting manufactures for export. Because attention was first drawn to Berkeley's concept of the closed economy by Joseph Johnston in the 1930s, when ideas of autarchy were the prevailing wisdom, some writers have been unhappy with the notion of reading such a meaning into Berkeley's text.[60] However, the frequency of Berkeley's claims that it was possible for a country to enjoy a reasonable standard of living without any foreign trade whatsoever suggests that he was indeed serious in making such a proposal (Q 107, 12). Moreover, as we have seen, in Ireland's case Berkeley particularly equated foreign trade with the selfish desire of the gentry to import expensive foreign luxuries at the expense of the most basic well-being of their poorer fellow citizens (Q 57–8, 102, 145, 149). Yet against this should be set the numerous proposals in *The Querist* for promoting manufactures for export, especially the emphasis on the production of items such as carpet and tapestry, with low raw material needs and high-value labor inputs (Q 64–9). Comparing the two positions, we are probably justified in concluding that Berkeley's image of an Ireland prospering behind "a wall of brass a thousand cubits high" (Q 134) was offered in the spirit of Locke's discussion of what would happen on an island cut off from all commerce with mankind, which "serve[s] rather to give us some light into the nature of Money, than to teach here a new Measure of Traffick."[61] The export of agricultural produce and raw materials from a country with a mass of unemployed and starving paupers had resulted in the Irish becoming the "people who so contrive as to be impoverished by their [foreign] trade" of Query 325. While it might not be possible to eliminate all foreign trade, Berkeley insisted that it should consist largely of imports which served as raw materials for domestic production rather than corrupting luxuries (Q 170–6, 554).

The discussion of Berkeley's apparently contradictory statements on foreign trade seems an appropriate place to refer to his view of Ireland's commercial relations with Great Britain. His attitude, in striking contrast to that of the previous generation of patriots such as Swift and Archbishop King, was one of urging cooperation wherever possible, and particularly avoiding competition with England's traditional monopoly of the woollen industry (Q 73, 81, 89–90, 323). Although the nineteenth-century patriot John Mitchel accused Berkeley of a slave mentality in adopting this approach,[62] such was also the view of his friends Thomas Prior and Samuel Madden, and was strongly advocated by their associate, Arthur Dobbs, who even supported political union.[63] In what seems very probably an implicit criticism of Swift, Query 317 asked "Whether it be not delightful to complain? And whether there be not many who had rather utter their complaints than redress their evils?" Berkeley also saw Ireland's dependent status as conferring economic advantages, such as not having to provide for its own defence (Q 322). Like the writers mentioned, Berkeley further believed in an imperial system of which Great Britain was the hub, but which served to promote the welfare of the colonies as long as this did not come in direct competition with its own (Q 434, 578). Ireland's vast labor force could produce hemp and flax for the British navy with benefit to the imperial balance of payments, while London already constituted the centre of Ireland's monetary circulation (Q 75–7, 433).

VII. SOURCES AND INFLUENCES

Berkeley stands out even amongst early writers on economics in the paucity of specific references in his writings – nor, as in some other cases, can this deficiency be made good from library catalogues. Despite this, the question of sources is of importance in light of the aspiration voiced in the Advertisement to the Reader in the second edition of *The Querist*, that Berkeley's studies would help promote "the sum of human happiness . . . in the goods of mind, body, and fortune," while comparison with experience in other countries (presumably acquired from books) was an important part of his method (Q 346, 495, 499, 530, Om. Q. I. 223). Interestingly, however, as suggested in Section VI, Berkeley did not seem to have made a very careful study of the most significant work alluded to in *The Querist* – John Law's *Money and Trade Considered* (1705). Other figures who can be reasonably certainly identified as of importance to Berkeley included John Locke, William Petty, and Charles Davenant. The last is particularly interesting in that not only did "Davenant on Trade 1698" figure in the sale catalogue of the Berkeley family's library in 1796, but Davenant was also a writer much cited by Berkeley's Irish contemporaries.[64] His perhaps most significant debt would seem to have been to Locke's *Some Considerations concerning the Lowering of Interest, and Raising the Value of Money* (1692), both as a source of specific concepts and as something to react against (see Section IV).[65] Not only did Berkeley rely on Locke's version of the quantity theorem and the significance of the velocity of circulation (compare to Q 465), but Locke may also be plausibly considered as the inspiration for the concept of the isolated island economy.[66] One aspect of Locke's thought not reflected in Berkeley, however, was Locke's implacable hostility to altering the value of the currency. In several places *The Querist* argued for periodic revaluation of metallic coin (Q 462–4, Om. Q. II. 143; III. 163–9),[67] though interestingly Query 28 and omitted Query III. 143 conceded the Lockian claim that invasion of contract might well be a valid objection to reducing the precious metal content of coin. Petty, too, would seem to have been an important source, with his distinction between "local" and "universal" wealth and his implicit acceptance that the Irish economy posed significantly different problems to those of Britain and Holland.[68] From Davenant Berkeley derived his emphasis on the importance of the circulation of money, together with the analogy between this and the circulation of the blood in the body (Q 484, 579–80).[69] Further indirect light on Berkeley's sources is provided by a pamphlet written by the go-between for the publication of *The Querist*, Berkeley's college contemporary Samuel Madden. The latter's *Reflections and Resolutions Proper for the Gentlemen of Ireland* (1738) covered many of the issues raised in *The Querist*, and was unusually frank in identifying its sources. Among the authors Madden cited most frequently, other than Locke, Petty, and Davenant, were Thomas Prior's *List of Absentees* (1729), Arthur Dobbs's *Essay on the Trade of Ireland* (two parts, 1729–31), Samuel Hartlib's

Legacie of Husbandrie (1651), and "Captain" [Andrew] Yarrington's *The Improvement of England* (1679). Other writers referred to included Samuel Fortrey, Josiah Child, Sir William Temple, Lewes Roberts, William Potter, Dr Chamberlain, and Jonathan Swift. It is hard to believe that anyone concerned with Ireland's economic problems in the 1720s and 1730s could have failed to be aware of the latter's writings. However, though Swift's *Short View of Ireland* may have had a crucial role in enabling Berkeley to perceive the fallacy in Ireland's case of the mercantilist doctrine that foreign trade was the sole path to national riches, Swift and Berkeley's attitudes to Ireland's economic dependence on Great Britain differed strongly.[70]

Mention of Swift brings up the question of the influence of other friends and associates on Berkeley's economic writings. As well as Madden, Thomas Prior (who acted as Berkeley's agent in Ireland from 1724 to 1733) assisted in bringing out *The Querist*.[71] Prior was the author not only of the widely-read *List of Absentees*, but also of the important *Observations on the Coin in General* (both 1729). George Caffentzis has interestingly suggested that *The Querist* was published as part of a campaign to influence government policy in Ireland in promoting tillage, employment, and manufactures – the goals of the Dublin Society founded in 1731.[72] The opponents of this policy were the graziers and sheep-raisers, who stood to benefit from the export of cattle and wool, together with landlords who saw large-scale ranching as more beneficial than a multitude of small, impoverished tenants. The conflict extended to the controversy over agistment tithes[73] in the Irish parliament, where the landlords sought to defend their interests against the clergy by a Commons' Resolution of March 1736, stating that such tithes were a novel and illegal demand.[74] Swift, too, became involved in the agistment tithe controversy, which confirmed his long-standing grievance against the Irish gentry for failing to support the Church of Ireland.[75] Though tithes did not form as substantial a part of Berkeley's personal income as Bishop of Cloyne as they did for the majority of the Irish clergy (and had done for Berkeley when Dean of Derry), one may be fairly sure that he would have rallied to the cause against the graziers.[76] There are several hostile references in *The Querist* to grazing both as an economically undesirable practice inherited by the native Irish from their Tartar ancestors and as a manifestation of the selfish interests of a section of the gentry (Q 85, 87, 489, 513).

There are as well vaguer references to unnamed opponents in the guise of those who seek "to puzzle plain causes" and gentlemen who would oppose any proposal they could not turn into a job (Om. Q III. 62, 47).

VIII. PURPOSE AND LIMITATIONS OF ECONOMIC ACTIVITY

The outcome of the policies proposed in *The Querist* would be to increase population, diversify forms of economic activity, and generally promote prosperity through the achievement of full employment for the population at large (Q 62, 128, 352, 403). Ultimately the poor nation would, through these means, achieve parity with its prosperous neighbors and be able to stand on its own feet, engaging on equal terms in trade with the rest of the world (Q 172). Despite his understanding of the development from poor to wealthy nation, Berkeley retained his distaste for foreign trade, asserting that even after the achievement of parity with developed nations, external trade should still be carefully monitored and regulated (Q 128, 170, 554). This latent hostility to all forms of foreign trade derived from Berkeley's equating it with the import of luxury products, which he considered undesirable for the nation at large and damaging to the interests of their particular consumers, namely the gentry.[77] However, the expansion of the industrious population through economic growth was something which Berkeley viewed without Malthusian misgivings (Q 62, 352). For him, as for the preindustrial world generally, prosperity did not imply any radical change in the social structure. While the mass of the population would be rendered happy through full employment and modest prosperity, there is no question of their aspiring to the lifestyle enjoyed by the gentry. It is taken as axiomatic that only a small portion of the population can be supported at a higher level: "What," Query 286 asked, could be worse than "a nation of gentlemen?" This brings us to the fact that for Berkeley, economic activity was clearly limited in its objectives. Because the human capacity to consume was finite, there could be no point in pursuing limitless accumulation. Berkeley saw a stark contradiction between the seemingly infinite appetite for money, and the purpose money was intended to serve in society, as well as the individual's capacity to consume (Q 304, 306). Those who became obsessed by "this capricious tyrant, which usurps the place of reason," such as "usurers, stockjobbers and [financial] projectors," were condemned to "gathering counters... multiplying figures [and] enlarging denominations, without knowing what they would be at, and without having a proper regard to the use, or end or nature of things." For individuals this could only be the path to madness in "endless pursuits and wild labyrinths" (Q 308–9). For whole societies, the domination of such values (as during the South Sea Bubble) undermined political stability through promoting luxury and corruption, and would ultimately result in absolute government and the loss of liberty.[78] Moreover, unlike many mid-eighteenth-century writers obsessed by favorable trade balances computed in terms of labor values, Berkeley was convinced that the happiness (that is, the well-being) of society could not be considered in the abstract apart from the happiness of the individuals who make it up (Q 345).[79]

Such an approach to economics reflected Berkeley's overall priorities and the rather limited role he accorded to economics in his general scheme of things. Unlike the majority of eighteenth-century thinkers, Berkeley did not subscribe to the view that we never act more beneficially towards our fellows than in the pursuit of profit.[80] For Berkeley, economics remained subordinate to politics and social organization, and for this reason businessmen and traders were ill-fitted to serve as statesmen or direct the destinies of a nation.[81] In the overall design of God for man, which it was seemingly Berkeley's goal to illuminate for his contemporaries, while economic activities provided the material basis for society, the competing interests of individuals required careful reconciling by the legislator if society were to provide for all its members in the fashion God intended.[82] By the mid-eighteenth century, such a view seemed little different from the generally superseded Aristotelian model of national economics as household management writ large. Moreover, it revealed Berkeley as fundamentally out of sympathy with the growth of commercial society, and perhaps accounts for the relatively slight impact his views had on his contemporaries and immediate successors, bar a few marginal figures such as Robert Wallace.[83] Even in Ireland, the impact of *The Querist* in Berkeley's lifetime was distinctly marginal, despite the enthusiasm of the pioneer Catholic pamphleteer Arthur O'Connor of Belnagare.[84] With the prospect of seemingly open-ended development afforded by the beginnings of industrialization, economists put aside concerns about the purpose of economic activity in favor of the promotion of untrammelled growth, unaware that the issues they were ignoring would return to the forefront of attention as the consequences of unrestricted industrial expansion came to threaten humankind's very existence in the later twentieth century.

NOTES

1. Advertisement by the Author, *The Querist*, 2nd edition (Dublin, 1750). Citations are from the text of the 1750 edition, as printed in *Bishop Berkeley's* Querist *in Historical Perspective*, ed. Joseph Johnston (Dundalk: Dundalgan Press, 1970), followed by the omitted queries from the 1st edition. To reduce footnotes, references to *The Querist* are henceforth given in text in the form "(Q 000)" and "(Om[itted]. Q. I. 000)," with the Roman numeral indicating Part I, II, or III of the original edition as appropriate.
2. See Patrick Kelly, "A Pamphlet attributed to John Toland and an Unpublished Reply by Archbishop William King," *Topoi* 4 (1985): 81–90, and "Some Observations on the Taxes Pay'd by Ireland to support the Government," Trinity College, Dublin, MS 1488 (extract in Jonathan Swift and Thomas Sheridan, *The Intelligencer*, ed. James Woolley [Oxford: Clarendon Press, 1992], Appendix A).
3. *Dictionary of National Biography*, sv Madden, and further Toby Barnard, "Improving Clergymen," in *As By Law Established: The Church of Ireland since the Reformation*, ed. Alan Ford, James McGuire, and Kenneth Milne (Dublin: Lilliput Press, 1995), 136–51.
4. Though economists have tended to dismiss the significance of Swift's work, see James Kelly, "Jonathan Swift and the Irish economy in the 1720s," *Eighteenth-Century Ireland* 6 (1991): 7–36.
5. See Lars Magnusson, *Mercantilism: the Shaping of an Economic Language* (London: Routledge, 1994), 9–11; *Locke on Money*, ed. P. H. Kelly, two volumes, (Oxford: Clarendon Press, 1991), Introduction, 1: 67–70; and literature cited therein.
6. For a discussion of Berkeley's sources, see Section VII.
7. It would be misleading to regard Berkeley's discussion of noneconomic factors as on a par with their role in current development theory, where there is a coherent theoretical perception of their significance for economic development as such.
8. Notable examples include Carew Reynell, *The True English Interest* (London, 1674); Andrew Yarranton, *England's Improvement by Sea and Land* (London, 1677); Richard Lawrence, *Interest of Ireland* (Dublin, 1682), and the manuscript Jacobite tract *The Improvement of Ireland* (1698), printed in *Analecta Hibernica* 35 (1992): 45–84. This last item

has striking affinities with *The Querist*, especially in relation to the economic role of the gentry in the countryside.

9. See Section VIII.
10. For bibliographical details, see Geoffrey Keynes, *A Bibliography of George Berkeley, Bishop of Cloyne* (Oxford: Clarendon Press, 1976).
11. Each part was subsequently issued in London the year following its Dublin publication. The London issue of Part I contained an interesting "Preface to the Reader," probably by Berkeley's friend, John Percival, first Earl of Egmont.
12. Part I contained 317 queries; Part II, 254, and Part III, 324; the 1750 edition had 595 queries. The most striking new element in 1750 was a section on eugenics (Q 206–16).
13. For examples of gnomic queries, see queries 41, 48, 51,317, 568, 595, and Om. Q. I. 52, 55, 312, 315–17; II. 11; III. 62; III. 80, 88.
14. Cf. A. J. Balfour, introduction to *The Works of George Berkeley, D. D., Bishop of Cloyne*, ed. George Sampson, 3 vols. (London and New York, 1898), 1: xlix–l.
15. Cf. Om. Q. III. 88.
16. See Section VI below.
17. Cf. *Works*, 6: 90, where Jessop drew attention to the 67 queries which conclude *The Analyst* (1734); T. W. Hutchison, "Berkeley's *Querist* and its Place in the Economic Thought of the Eighteenth Century," *British Journal of the Philosophy of Science*: 4 (1953–4): 52–77, 54. For an interesting discussion of what Berkeley may have intended in adopting such a format, see C. George Caffentzis, "Querying the Querist," *Maine Scholar* 3 (1990): 287–307.
18. For the background to the *Essay* and the circumstances of its production, see Patrick Kelly, "'Industry and Virtue versus Luxury and Corruption': Berkeley, Walpole, and the South Sea Bubble Crisis," *Eighteenth-Century Ireland* 7 (1992): 57–74, esp. 70.
19. *Works* 6: 69, 77, 82.
20. Noticeably absent from *The Querist* was the *Essay's* concern with religion as a key factor for the proper functioning of society; cf. *Works* 6: 69–70.
21. Query 449 suggests that it was specifically as a result of his American experience that Berkeley came to favor the use of paper money as a means of stimulating the inadequate circulation of poorer economies.
22. *Works* 3: 68.
23. *Works* 6, esp. 233–9, 245, 247.
24. For a description of the early eighteenth-century Irish economy, see the various writings of L. M. Cullen, especially *An Economic History of Ireland*, 2nd edition (London: B. T. Batsford, 1987), 39–49; "Landlords,

Bankers, and Merchants: The Early Irish Banking World" in *Economists and Irish Economy*, ed. A. E. Murphy (Dublin: Irish Academic Press, 1984): and *A New History of Ireland* (Oxford: Clarendon Press, 1991–), Volume 4, *Eighteenth-Century Ireland, 1691–1800*, chapter 6, "Economic Development, 1691–1750"; as well as S. J. Connolly, *Religion, Law and Power: the Making of Protestant Ireland, 1660–1760* (Oxford: Clarendon Press, 1992), 41–59.

25. Cullen, *Economic History*, 47.
26. Cullen, "Landlords, Bankers, and Merchants," 28–9. Little can be discovered about the precise circumstances that led Berkeley to publish. For what it is worth, an advertisement in the *Dublin Newsletter*, March 8–12, 1735, suggests that Berkeley may have arranged for the appearance of Part I to coincide with his fiftieth birthday on March 12, 1735.
27. Joseph Johnston, "The Irish currency in the Eighteenth Century," reprinted as *Berkeley's* Querist *in Historical Perspective*, chapter 6. Cf. Queries 94, 485, 573.
28. Cullen, *Economic History*, 42–3.
29. The range of proposals was discussed in Sir John Browne, *A Short Review of the Several Pamphlets...on the Subject of Coin* (Dublin, 1730).
30. Irvin Ehrenpreis, *Swift: the Man, his Works, and the Age*, Volume 3 (Cambridge, MA: Harvard University Press, 1983), 152–313 throughout, and Isolde Victory, "The Development of Colonial Nationalism, 1692–1725," doctoral thesis, Trinity College, Dublin, 1985, chapters 5–6.
31. For titles, see *Irish Economics: 1700–1783*, ed. H. R. Wagner (London: J. Davy, 1907), 33–42 throughout. For an appreciative assessment of this literature, see Salim Rashid, "The Irish School of Economic Development: 1720–1750," *Manchester School of Economic and Social Studies* 56 (1988): 345–69.
32. Om. Q. I. 226. Wagner's suggestion that Berkeley was the author is contradicted by the *Proposal's* call for a bank with private subscribers on the model of the Bank of England (see Section VI). Daniel Webb, *An Enquiry into the Reasons of the Decay of Credit, Trade and Manufactures in Ireland* (Dublin, 1735).
33. For details, see Richard A.Lester, *Monetary Experiments: Early American and Recent Scandinavian* (Princeton: Princeton University Press, 1939), chapters 3–4. Cf. Berkeley's comments in queries 240, 247, 251–2, 449, and Om. Q. I. 212.
34. Cullen, "Landlords, Bankers, and Merchants," 28–9. In the late 1720s, informed contemporaries put the volume of private bankers' notes at roughly equal to the total specie circulation. Cf. Query 33.

35. Thomas Prior, *Observations on the Coin in General* (Dublin, 1729), 45; [Jonathan Swift], *A Letter from a Gentleman in the North of Ireland... In Relation to the Regulation of the Coin* (Dublin, 1736) (reprinted from *The Intelligencer* 19 [1728]).
36. Archbishop Boulter to Sir R.Walpole, May 25, 1736, *Letters Written by his Excellency, Hugh Boulter, D.D.*, 2 vols. (Dublin, 1770), 2: 121–2.
37. See Patrick Kelly, "Ireland and the critique of Mercantilism in Berkeley's *Querist*," *George Berkeley: Essays and Replies*, ed. D. Berman (Dublin: Irish Academic Press, 1986), 109–12.
38. On the need for intervention to secure effective cooperation between the various interests in the economy, see Queries 346, 587.
39. Petty, *The Political Anatomy of Ireland*, in *The Economic Writings of Sir William Petty*, ed. C. H. Hull, 2 vols. (Cambridge: Cambridge University Press, 1899; reprinted New York: A. M. Kelley, 1963–4), 1: 147.
40. Different forms of transaction, however, may require different forms of medium of exchange to service them (see Section VI).
41. For an illuminating discussion of the concept of money as a "ticket or counter" in relation to Berkeley's theory of signs, see David Berman, *George Berkeley: Idealism and the Man* (Oxford: Clarendon Press, 1994), 168–9.
42. A ticket differs from a pledge in that the latter must possess a value independent of the goods the money represents. Query 24 went on to establish Berkeley's theory of price as "a compounded proportion, directly as the demand, and reciprocally as the plenty," though little further reference was made to this, other than indirectly in relation to the quantity theorem in Query 465.
43. See *Some Considerations concerning the Lowering of Interest, and Raising the Value of Money* (London, 1692), 32 (*Locke on Money*, 1: 234); and *Further Considerations concerning Raising the Value of Money* (London, 1695), 1–4 (*Locke on Money*, 2: 402–4).
44. See Hutchison, "Berkeley's *Querist*," 68–9; Douglas Vickers, *Studies in the Theory of Money* (London: Peter Owen, 1960), 142–3.
45. Potter was among the authors referred to by Berkeley's friend Samuel Madden in *Reflections and Resolutions Proper for the Gentlemen of Ireland* (Dublin, 1738) (see Section VII).
46. Cf. Barry Gordon, *Economic Analysis before Adam Smith* (London: Macmillan, 1975), 228.
47. Sir James Steuart would later argue that implementing the goal of full employment involved state direction and control of all aspects of

society: *An Inquiry into the Principles of Political Oeconomy*, two volumes (London, 1767), 1: 15.

48. Query 590 described the legislature in traditional Aristotelian terminology as "the soul and will of the community."
49. *Works* 6: 70–1, 75–6; 3: 104.
50. Hutchison sees Berkeley as unsuccessfully grasping here at a distinction between beneficial and harmful luxury, "Berkeley's *Querist*," 69–72.
51. *A Word to the Wise* urged that even where there was no immediate prospect of employment, the habit of cleanliness should be fostered to raise the poor out of despair and misery: *Works* 6: 242–3.
52. The bank proposal figured more prominently in the first edition of *The Querist*. Much of the detail relating to foreign banks such as those of Amsterdam, Venice, and Genoa was omitted in 1750, as well as was the extensive commentary on the failure of Law's *Banque Royale* in France in 1720. The only indication given as to sources for this information on banks was to [John Broughton's] *Vindication and Advancement of a National Constitution and Credit* (London, 1710) (Om. Q. I. 214), on the Bank of Genoa.
53. John Law, *Money and Trade Considered* (Edinburgh, 1705), 73–5, explicitly addressed the main points which Om. Q. I. 215 accused Law of having ignored, namely the proportion between the volume of notes and the quantity of trade, and the rise that might be expected in land values. I discuss these further on.
54. Cf. Om. Q. I. 216.
55. Cf. Om. Q. I. 223.
56. Berkeley was a metallist in believing that in order to represent value money must consist of, or at least be backed by, something that was in itself valuable. Cf. Joseph Schumpeter, *A History of Economic Analysis* (New York: Oxford University Press, 1954), 288–9.
57. Query 445 further listed the stages through which the process of exchange had evolved, starting from simple barter, to the use of a common medium of exchange, to coin, and finally "the use of paper, with proper marks and signatures . . . the last . . . [and] greatest improvement." Query 486 raises the problem of increased wear on small coin.
58. The discrepancy between the (foreign) monies in circulation and the units in which prices were expressed had been identified by David Bindon, *An Essay on the Gold and Silver Coin Currant in Ireland* (Dublin, 1729), 12–15, as the major disadvantage arising from Ireland's not being permitted to coin its own money.
59. Queries 231, 571. Cf. Hutchison, "Berkeley's *Querist*," 64; Vickers, *Studies*, 152.

60. Johnston, "Locke, Berkeley and Hume as Monetary Theorists," 68–9, reprinted in *Bishop Berkeley's* Querist *in Historical Perspective*, 86; Vickers, *Studies*, 146, 162–4.
61. *Locke on Money*, 1: 264. Cf. the assertion in Query 269 as to the Utopian character of some of Berkeley's proposals.
62. Jonathan Swift and George Berkeley, *Irish Political Economy*, ed. John Mitchel (Dublin, 1847), 27–28 nn.
63. Prior, *A List of the Absentees of Ireland* (Dublin, 1729), 63–72; Madden, *Reflections and Resolutions Proper for the Gentlemen of Ireland* (Dublin, 1738), 24–31; Dobbs, *Essay on Trade and Improvement of Ireland*, two volumes (Dublin, 1729–32), 1: 52, 56–72 throughout. Dobbs, *Essay on Trade and Improvement*, 1: 69–70, probably was the source of the idea of London as the center of Ireland's monetary circulation in Query 433.
64. "*Catalogue of the Valuable Library of the Late . . . Dr Berkeley Lord Bishop of Cloyne*, Leigh and Sotheby, June 6, 1796; the three other economic titles listed are "Graunt on the Bills of Mortality 1665," "Child on Trade 1693," and "Decker on Foreign Trade 1749." Cf. Prior, *List of Absentees*, 62–3; Dobbs, *Essay on Trade*, 2: 14.
65. Locke was enormously influential generally amongst early eighteenth-century Irish writers on money; see Patrick Kelly "Perceptions of Locke in Eighteenth-Century Ireland," *Proceedings of the Royal Irish Academy* 89 C (1989), no. 2, 21.
66. *Locke on Money*, 1: 235, 264. Berkeley's frequently reiterated fear of money lying dead or failing to circulate is also probably derived from Locke.
67. Om. Q. I. 29–30 favoured introducing the English monetary standard in Ireland (the English, and later British, shilling coin being rated at 13 pence Irish between 1701 and 1826).
68. Petty, *Political Anatomy of Ireland* (1691), in *Economic Writings*, 1: 147, 183–201, 295.
69. Cf. Davenant, *An Essay upon . . . the Balance of Trade* (1699), in *The Political and Commercial Works of that Celebrated Writer*, ed. C. Whitworth, 5 vols. (London, 1771), 2: 169–70, 273–5.
70. See Section VI.
71. Berkeley to Prior, March 5, 1736/7 (*Works* 8: 244).
72. This context is explored in Constantine George Caffentzis, *Exciting the Industry of Mankind: George Berkeley's Philosophy of Money* (Dordrecht: Kluwer Academic Press, 2000), 111–19. I am indebted to Professor Caffentzis for alerting me to this, as well as for stimulating discussions of other aspects of Berkeley's economics. Cf. Dobbs, *Essay on Trade*, 1: 25–7, on the advantages of tillage.

73. These were tithes payable on grazing for dry cattle – a growing form of agricultural exploitation in the 1720s and 1730s.
74. Louis A. Landa, *Swift and the Church of Ireland* (Oxford: Clarendon Press 1964), 135–42; Giles Jacob, *A New Law Dictionary* (London, 1739), under agistment; *Journals of the House of Commons* [Ireland], 6: 184, 219.
75. Notably in publishing the poem, *The Legion Club* (1736); see Ehrenpreis, *Swift*, 3: 171–4, 827–9: Landa, *Swift and the Church*, 100–69 throughout.
76. Cf. James Maziere Brady, *Clerical and Parochial Records of Cork, Cloyne and Ross*, three volumes (Dublin, 1863), 28–9; Berkeley to Prior, January 26, 1733/4: "The bulk of the Deanery [of Derry] is in tithes, and a very inconsiderable part in land" (*Works* 8: 26).
77. See Section V.
78. *Essay* (1721), in *Works* 6, esp. 77–85.
79. See Patrick Kelly, "Between Politics and Economics; Concepts of Wealth in English Mercantilism in the Seventeenth and Eighteenth Centuries," *Studi Settecenteschi* 5 (1984): 20–6.
80. Cf. A. O. Hirschman, *The Passions and the Interests* (Princeton: Princeton University Press, 1977), 58–63.
81. *Alciphron*, *Works* 3: 80, 96; *Siris* 350; *Querist* 183.
82. *Money, Obedience, and Affection: Essays on Berkeley's Moral and Political Thought*, ed. Stephen R. L. Clark (New York: Garland, 1989), xix–xxi, xxviii–xxx in the introduction, and papers by David E. Leary and Frank Petrella.
83. Robert Wallace, *Characteristics of the Present State of Great Britain* (London, 1758), throughout. On the subsequent influence of Berkeley's economics, see Salim Rashid, "Berkeley's *Querist* and its Influence," *Journal of the History of Economic Thought* 12 (1990): 38–60.
84. See Patrick Kelly, "Berkeley and Ireland," *Études Irlandaises* 11 (1986): 22–3.

STEPHEN R. L. CLARK

12 Berkeley on religion

I. INTRODUCTION

Berkeley was a religious philosopher throughout his working life, and much of his philosophical work has interesting implications for the proper understanding of that "watchful, active, intelligent, free Spirit, with whom we have to do, and in whom we live, and move and have our being" (TVV 2).[1] There may still be critics who imagine that God only entered his philosophy to fill the gaps between one finite observer's perceptions and the next, or to save his episcopal reputation. The truth is that the works for which he is still chiefly known were written when he was a struggling research fellow at Trinity College, Dublin, but already deeply religious. "Strange impotence of man. Man without God. Wretcheder than a stone or tree, he having only the power to be miserable by his unperformed wills, these having no power at all" (N 107). He later rejected the aphorism, presumably because it might easily have given the wrong impression. He also rejected the wording of the commitment he made in his notebooks (or *Philosophical Commentaries*): "Actions leading to heaven are in my power if I will them, therefore I will will them" (N 160). Both remarks remained close to his conviction. "The man can see neither deep nor far who is not sensible of his own misery, sinfulness, and dependence... and who would not be glad of getting into a better state; and who would not be overjoyed to find that the road leading thither was the love of God and man" (ALC 5.5 [178]). Like Socrates, he therefore devoted himself to "the turning men aside from vice, impertinence, and trifling speculations to the study of solid wisdom, temperance, justice and piety, which is the true business of the philosopher."[2] None of his writings can be understood without bearing that in mind.

There are, nonetheless, particular texts relevant to his philosophical understanding of religion – its content, grounds and social importance. These are *Passive Obedience* (1713), *Alciphron* (1732), *Discourse to Magistrates* (1738),[3] a letter to Sir John James (1741),[4] Siris (1744), and a sermon on the Will of God (1751).[5] There are also particular topics which deserve examination. The second part of *A Treatise concerning the Principles of Human Knowledge* would have dealt, amongst other things, with "the 2 great Principles of Morality: the Being of a God & the Freedom of Man" (N 508).[6] We can reasonably suspect that they also would have dealt with other issues that concerned him: the proper role of prejudice; faith (not as "an indolent perception, but [as] an operative persuasion of mind which ever worketh some suitable action, disposition, or emotion in those who have it" [ALC 7.10 (301)]); religion as the chief bond of society; the way God must be supposed to speak to us through nature; and eternal happiness. Here I shall discuss Berkeley's conception of religion – its foundation, meaning, content, object, and importance. No doubt his conception varied over time. It does not follow that we can now identify the precise progress of his mind, as though he always said "exactly what he thought (and nothing that he did not absolutely think)."[7] Like other philosophers he tried out ideas; like other polemicists, he often argued from principles he did not himself endorse in order to comply with "established language and the use of the world" (S 155). Thus, although I shall often give the publication date of the arguments and aphorisms I cite, I make no claim to know exactly when Berkeley formulated them, nor whether he would *always* at that time have said the same.

II. THE VEILS OF PREJUDICE[8]

Berkeley was a philosopher at the beginning of the Cartesian Era (so to call it), that period when philosophers were expected to divest themselves of prejudice, even if only to place their commonsense beliefs on a more secure foundation. "Our affections should grow from inquiry and deliberation else there is danger of our being superstitious or Enthusiasts.... It is our duty to strive to divest our selves of all byas whatsoever."[9]

In our nonage while our minds are empty and unoccupied many notions easily find admittance, and as they grow with us and become familiar to our understandings we continue a fondness for them.... But we would do well to consider that other men have imbibed early notions, that they as well as we have a country, friends, and persons whom they esteem. These are pleas which may be made for any opinion, and are consequently good pleas for none.[10]

To strip the soul of prejudice is an ancient nostrum. Witness Edward Herbert, British rationalist: "Those who would enter the shrine of truth must leave their trinkets, in other words their opinions, at the entrance, or as one might say in the cloakroom. They will find that everything is open or revealed to perception as long as they do not approach it with prejudice."[11] This is a commonplace (also to be found in John Colet and in Luther),[12] derived from Philo of Alexandria's allegory whereby the High Priest must strip off the soul's tunic of opinion and imagery to enter the Holy of Holies,[13] and from Plato's story of Glaucus.[14] It is very difficult to strip, "since the veils of prejudice and error are slowly and singly taken off one by one" (S 296).

It is, on the other hand, very easy to *think* that one has done it, and that our own, conscientiously "modern" opinions are so obviously founded on right reason that we do not need to argue for them. "Freethinkers" despise people who do not dare (or care) to question what they have been taught – but are themselves as fond of the fashionable opinions by which they define their own identity. "Nor, if we consider the proclivity of mankind to realize their notions, will it seem strange that mechanic philosophers and geometricians should, like other men, be misled by prejudice, and take mathematical hypotheses for real beings existing in their own right" (S 250).[15] Ulysses Cosmopolita, investigating the mind of a fashionable freethinker with the aid of "Philosophical Snuff," "discovered Prejudice in the figure of a woman standing in a corner, with her eyes close shut, and her fore-fingers stuck in her ears; many words in a confused order, but spoken with great emphasis, issued from her mouth."[16] In another of his *Guardian* essays Berkeley refers to gentlemen (likewise "freethinkers") who "did not think themselves obliged to prove all they said, or else proved their assertions, by saying or swearing they were all fools that believed the contrary."[17] Euphranor justly rebukes Alciphron for his credulity in believing "most incredible things on most slender authority" (ALC 6.21 [261]), so long as they are inconsistent with the Hebrew scriptures. It is a fault quite commonly encountered even now. It is one thing to recognize that we may have imbibed errors, quite another to discover some rule by which we may identify them.

That rule clearly cannot simply be to "weed out of [our] minds and extirpate all such notions or prejudices as were planted in them before they arrived at the free and entire use of reason."[18] There may be many things we cannot ourselves prove which are still true, and which we have good reason to accept as true. "The not distinguishing between prejudices and errors is a prevailing oversight among our modern free-thinkers."[19] If we really attempted to put aside all "prejudice", all opinions taken upon trust, we should find ourselves entirely destitute. "If we were left, every one to his own experience, [we] could know little either of the earth it self or of those things the Almighty has placed thereon: so swift is our progress from the womb to the grave."[20] Even if a few brilliant intelligences could cope with believing all and only what they themselves have "proved," that cannot be the normal condition of humanity.

It follows that those of us who do attempt to follow Philo's rule must still accept some propositions without proof, and those (the majority) who do not had better hope that they have all been well enough brought up.

> There must ... of necessity, in every State, be a certain system of salutary notions, a prevailing set of opinions, acquired either by private reason and reflection or taught and instilled by the general reason of the public, that is, by the law of the land.... Nor will it be any objection to say that these are prejudices; inasmuch as they are therefore neither less useful nor less true, athough their proofs may not be understood by all men.... The mind of a young creature cannot remain empty; if you do not put into it that which is good, it will be sure to receive that which is bad. Do what you can, there will still be a bias from education; and if so, is it not better this bias should lie towards things laudable and useful to society? ... If you strip men of these their notions, or, if you will, prejudices, with regard to modesty, decency, justice, charity, and the like, you will soon find them so many monsters, utterly unfit for human society.[21]

We cannot simply abandon all traditional beliefs. Nor can we rely only on a version of the Cartesian rule: to believe only those propositions which it is impossible ("logically impossible") to deny. It is true, no doubt, that I cannot coherently deny that I exist, nor that there is a truth which transcends my thought of it.[22] It may even be true, as Berkeley also believed, that this Truth must be God – the infinite free Spirit. But "nothing could be more vain and imaginary than to suppose ... that the whole world ... might be produced by a necessary consequence of the laws of motion" (or the original structure of the world; S 232f.). We may wish to insist that the Truth does, after all, contain all truths, and that God, in knowing them, makes them definite, but they remain, for us, beyond all argument. It does not follow that we cannot, with patience, "know" them, but not with "scientific or demonstrative knowledge". Maybe even God cannot know them save by observation – though not of a sensory kind (as "there is no sense nor sensory in God" [S 289, *contra* Newton]) – and enactment.

> Without all doubt this world could arise from nothing but the perfectly free will of God.... From this fountain ... [what] we call the laws of nature have flowed, in which there appear many traces indeed of wise contrivance, but not the least shadow of necessity. These therefore we must not seek from uncertain conjectures, but learn them from observations and experiments. He who is presumptuous enough to think that he can find the true principles of physics and the laws of natural things by the force alone of his own mind, and the internal light of reason, must either suppose that the world exists by necessity, and by the same necessity follows the laws proposed; or if the order of Nature was established by the will of God, that himself, a miserable reptile, can tell what was fittest to be done.[23]

We cannot expect to demonstrate the truth of everything worth believing. We cannot even suppose that we should only believe what has always been believed by everyone: "Diversity of opinions about a thing doth not hinder but that thing may be, and one of the opinions concerning it may be true" (ALC 1.15 [59], Euphranor speaking).[24] Nor can we evade our own responsibility for what we choose to accept as true. As Berkeley wrote to his friend John James, on the occasion of James's conversion to the Church of Rome: Even if it were true that there is an objectively infallible guide, we could not locate such a guide without a prior trust in our own capacity to do so. "Of what use is an infallible guide without an infallible sign to know him by?"[25] "We see . . . with our own eyes, by a common light but each with his own private eyes. And so must you or you will not see at all. And not seeing at all how can you chuse a Church? Why prefer that of Rome to that of England? Thus far, and in this sense every man's judgment is private as well as ours."[26]

On the one hand, it must be I who judge what to believe; on the other hand, this "I" and the principles on which it acts are as debatable as any. "We would do well to consider that other men have imbibed early notions, that they as well as we have a country, friends, and persons whom they esteem . . ." – and an identity. So must I conclude that my conclusions are not to be relied upon? They may not be, but I can no more conclude to this, in practice, than to a denial that I exist or think. I must suppose that there is that in me which can be trusted, and must also reject all theories which deny that fundamental faith. "True it is that prejudices early imbibed and sunk deep in the mind are not immediately got ridd of; but it is as true that in every Humane Creature there is a ray of common sense, an original light of reason and nature which the worst and most bigoted education, although it may impair, can never quite extinguish."[27] "There is an indwelling of Christ and the Holy Spirit, there is an inward light. If there be an *ignis fatuus* that misleads wild and conceited men, no man can thence infer there is no light of the sun."[28] "Intellect and reason are alone the sure guides to truth" (S 264) – which is, emphatically, not to say that secular reason is.

"I, among a number of persons who have debauched their natural taste, see things in a peculiar light, which I have arrived at, not by any uncommon force of genius or acquired knowledge, but only by unlearning the false notions instilled by custom and education."[29] This youthful boast relies upon the notion of "natural taste," true light – a reliance Berkeley did not surrender. In trusting that original light, though, we must, as he made clear, accept that it is not just our own. "Our present impending danger is from the setting up of private judgement, or an inward light, *in opposition to human and divine laws.*"[30] Those who "flatter themselves that they alone are the elect and predestinate of God, though in their lives and actions they show a very small degree either of piety toward God or charity toward man" are not good models.[31] If there is a light in me, it must also be in others, and in the original judgment of humanity, however far defiled or damaged. There are false and dangerous opinions loose in the world, and many failures of intelligence, but if we are not to despair entirely of ever speaking truth, we must believe that there is a truth within tradition, and that, by faithful obedience to the light, we can uncover more. Unlearning *everything* on the plea that it might be false is both impossible and self-defeating. As Herbert said: "Reason is the process of applying common notions as far as it can, and has nothing beyond them to which it can appeal. Common Notions, therefore, are principles which it is not legitimate to dispute." "Anyone who prefers persistently and stubbornly to reject these principles might as well stop his ears, shut his eyes amd strip himself of all humanity."[32] "We who believe a God are entrenched within tradition, custom, authority and law": Why abandon that advantage at the will of a freethinker? (ALC 4.3 [143], Euphranor speaking).

> The more we think, the more difficult shall we find it to conceive how mere man, grown up in the vulgar habits of life, and weighed down by sensuality, should ever be able to arrive at science without some tradition or teaching, which might either sow the seeds of knowledge, or call forth and excite those latent seeds that were originally sown in the soul. (S 339)

In sum: Self-styled freethinkers who spoke out against "religious prejudice" necessarily relied on prejudice themselves, while simultaneously denying themselves the right to do so (ALC 6.19 [255], Euphranor speaking). Those who say there is no inner light at all cannot coherently trust their own judgment; those who say that testimony and inherited opinion must all be abandoned condemn themselves to an incorrigible ignorance. Those who claim the inner light entirely for themselves (as though the Truth should enlighten them and no one else) are the first victims of "an inward conceited principle... sufficient to dissolve any human fabric of polity or civil government."[33] If we should believe what cannot (coherently) be denied, we should believe in the possibility of finding truth "by consulting [our] own minds, and looking into [our] own thoughts"[34] – always recalling that those thoughts were conveyed to us by others.

III. EMOTION AND RELIGIOUS KNOWLEDGE

What I have said so far is true of every sort of human knowledge. Its relevance to religion is twofold. First, it is absurd to mock the religious for their reliance on testimony and reliable judgment, when all of us are bound to do as much. "This is a plea which may be made against any opinion, and is consequently a good plea against none."[35] Second, it is absurd to adopt as one's own a doctrine which denies the possibility, or high probability, of ever achieving truth. If there is no infinite free spirit with whom we have to do, we can neither conceive what Truth might be, nor give ourselves any good reason to believe that we could reach it. To that second point I shall return.

But what sort of truths, if any, do religious utterances convey? We cannot dismiss them, as freethinkers do, merely because we cannot "prove" them (cannot show that they follow, by freethinkers' rules, from axioms accepted by freethinkers).[36] The rules and axioms of freethinkers are also taken upon trust, and are less acceptable than religious rules and axioms just because they claim that nothing should be taken upon trust. But perhaps religious utterances (or those of some traditions) are so obscure, or so absurd, that we should, after all, abandon them. We may sensibly believe what cannot be proved; can we sensibly believe what cannot be understood? It must seem clear that we cannot.

Berkeley's response, as so often, is *ad hominem*: "That philosopher is not free from bias and prejudice who shall maintain the doctrine of force and reject that of grace, who shall admit the abstract idea of a triangle, and at the same time ridicule the Holy Trinity" (ALC 7.8 [296], Euphranor speaking). And again: "With what appearance of reason shall any man presume to say that mysteries may not be objects of faith, at the same time that he himself admits such obscure mysteries to be the objects of science?" (A 7).

> To me it seems evident that if none but those who had nicely examined, and could themselves explain, the principle of individuation in man, or untie the knots and answer the objections which may be raised even about human personal identity, would require of us to explain the divine mysteries, we should not often be called upon for a clear and distinct idea of a person in relation to the Trinity, nor would the difficulties on that head be often objected to our faith. (ALC 7.8 [298], Euphranor speaking)

At least two answers are possible. First, we might agree that there is much that we do not understand, in science and common sense, and yet deny that we should therefore pretend to accept yet more uncomprehended dicta. Second, we might insist that the oddities of current physical theory, the contradictions of mathematical practice, or the difficulty of giving an acceptable analysis of current common sense, are all temporary failings. We cannot imagine eleven-dimensional space-time; we may not (yet) be able to do without such contradictions as Berkeley identified in Newton's calculus; we may not have a good account of personal identity for the same reason that we have no good account of bogeys. Some day (perhaps) we shall discover "God's true language" or "the Mind of God." The fact that our present language has its flaws is no good reason to retreat to a still earlier, worse one. "Science" (as a general title) is progressive; "religion" is conservative. Failings in science will be corrected; those of religion are inescapable.

To the first reply, Berkeley might respond in turn that the issue is not about what we should *add* to our belief-system, but about what we have reason to reject. The argument is not that because physicists believe in wave-particle duality they might equally believe that borogoves are mimsy. Berkeley is himself responding to an attack: If it is difficult to analyze the doctrine of the Trinity, or be sure exactly what its implications are, this is itself no reason to reject the doctrine. If it were, we should have exactly the same reason to reject much physical and mathematical theory, as well as common sense. "I do not therefore conclude a thing to be absolutely invisible, because it is so to me . . . [and] dare not pronounce a thing to be nonsense because I do not understand it" (ALC 6.7 [229], Euphranor speaking). Berkeley's prejudice is to keep as close to common sense[37] as possible, even if that sense should also be purged of outright error and infidelity. We are entitled (as above) to go on believing things we cannot prove, and ones whose implications we do not altogether understand. We are entitled to prove sophisms false by doing the things that sophists say we cannot.[38] Belief, of course, is not displayed in verbal repetition, and certainly not the repetition of abstract formulae.

> There is . . . a practical faith, or assent, which sheweth itself in the will and actions of a man, although his understanding may not be furnished with those abstract, precise, distinct ideas, which, whatever a philosopher may pretend, are acknowledged to be above the talents of common men. (ALC 7.9 [299], Euphranor speaking)

What we do not "understand" we may still believe, and act on.

It is this latter claim which forms the basis of Berkeley's chief contribution to the study of "religious meaning" – a contribution that sometimes is misunderstood. Berkeley, it is suggested, thought that "moral and religious utterances" had an *emotive*, even if not an assertoric meaning. "Truth. 3 sorts thereof Natural, Mathematical & Moral" (N 676). Of those three sorts, only the "natural" involves any accurate reproduction of a fact distinct from any utterance of ours (as it might be, "there are children playing in the street outside"). Mathematical truths are functions only of the words we use. "Moral truths", so called, are measured by "the general good of mankind", and "believed" simply in being acted on. On this account, Berkeley came close to saying that moral and religious utterances were just devices for awakening appropriate emotions – as it might be, "love, hope, gratitude, and obedience . . . agreeably to that notion of saving faith which is required in a Christian" (ALC 7.8 [197], Euphranor speaking). Accordingly, *to believe* the doctrine is only to act accordingly, and not to make an assertoric claim about the world or any being in or out of it.

> May not Christians . . . be allowed to believe the divinity of our Saviour, or that in Him God and man make one Person, and be verily persuaded thereof, so far as for such faith or belief to become a real principle of life and conduct? inasmuch as, by virtue of such persuasion, they submit to His government, believe His doctrine, and practise His precepts, although they form no abstract idea of the union between the divine and human nature; nor may be able to clear up the notion of *person* to the contentment of a minute philosopher. (ALC 7.8 [198], Euphranor speaking)

On this account, perhaps, to say that Christ is King is only to commit ourselves to living in love and charity with our neighbor, while encouraging ourselves in this by fantasy and verbal music. We can certainly agree that "the faith of a true Christian must be a lively faith that sanctifies the heart and shews it self in the fruits of the Spirit."[39] "Religion is no such speculative knowledge which rests merely in the understanding. She makes her residence in the heart, warms the affections and engages the will."[40] "A Man may frame the most accurate Notions, and in one Sense attain the exactest Knowledge of God and Christ that human Faculties can reach, and yet, notwithstanding all this, be far from knowing them in that saving Sense. . . . To know God as we ought, we must love him; and love him so as withal to love our Brethren, his Creatures and his Children."[41] We can also agree that much religious utterance is difficult or impossible to translate into less "musical" form. "The Apostle himself, who was caught up into the 3rd heaven, could give us no other than this empty tho emphatical description of it. 'tis wt eye hath not seen nor ear heard neither hath it enter'd into the heart of man to conceive."[42] We can even agree that most attempts at theological analysis will be futile or divisive:

The Christian religion was calculated for the Bulk of Mankind, and therefore cannot reasonably be supposed to consist in subtle and nice notions.... The making of Religion a notional Thing, hath been of infinite Disservice. And whereas its holy Mysteries are rather to be received with Humility of Faith, than defined and measured by the Accuracy of human Reason; all Attempts of this Kind, however well intended, have visibly failed in the Event; and instead of reconciling Infidels, have by creating Disputes and Heats among the Professors of Christianity, given no small Advantage to its Enemies.[43]

Berkeley does not therefore contend that such doctrines have no "assertoric" significance. On the contrary. Although he emphasizes the importance of "worship in spirit & in truth... not lip worship, not will-worship, but inward and Evangelical",[44] his point is rather that we should be moved by what we also understand.

How can we recite that noble Hymn We praise thee O God, we acknowledge thee to be the Lord, without some elevation and transport of Soul?... Shall we condemn the lip-worship of a poor ignorant papist who is not affected *with what he does not understand,* and at the same time our selves run over the most apt and significant form of words *which we perfectly understand* without suitable impulses of devotion.[45]

His argument, rather, is that we have reason, in the emotions they excite, to think that words convey a meaning not to be equated with any present *ideas* we may or may not have. Words do not "mean" by standing for or exciting clear and distinct ideas. Sometimes they are no more than place-holders, or expressions of a lively hope for something more. We cannot exclude such utterances without paradox:

Let us suppose a person blind and deaf from his birth, who being grown to man's estate, is... deprived of his feeling, tasting and smelling, and at the same time has the impediment of his hearing removed, and the film taken from his eyes.... It would be just as reasonable in him to conclude that the loss of those three senses could not possibly be succeeded by any new inlets of perception, as in a modern Free-thinker to imagine there can be no state of life and perception without the senses he enjoys at present.[46]

There are truths (who can deny it?) that we do not know and cannot even delineate. "Methinks it may consist with all due deference to the greatest of human understandings, to suppose them ignorant of many things, which are not suited to their faculties, or lie out of their reach" (ALC 2.5 [72], Euphranor speaking). We can properly believe what we do not understand, because it would be insane to think that what *we* cannot understand cannot express a truth.[47] So might "borogoves are mimsy"? No one worth believing has told us this is true, nor does it play a part in moral and religious life, such that to reject or to abandon it would lessen our chances of holding to that "saving faith which is required in a Christian." A religion wholly "reasonable" in containing nothing that we could not "understand" (could not form representative ideas of) would have less force. "It may be owned that the Gentiles might by a due use of their reason, by thought and study, observing the beauty and order of the world, and the excellency and profitableness of vertue, have obtained some sense of a Providence and of Religion.... But how few were they who made this use of their reason, or lived according to it!"[48] It would have less force; it would also be far less likely to be true. We must believe that there is that in us which can attain to truth. It does not follow that we must believe that only what is now attainable is true.

Nor does Berkeley accept a merely negative theology, for which the terms applied to God must always have another, unknown sense than any term applied to creatures. His reply (mediated through Crito) to the puzzle about the attributes of God, is that terms such as "wise" are applied to God "proportionably, that is, preserving a proportion to the infinite nature of God," who is "wise and good in the true and formal acceptation of the words" (ALC 4.21 [170]). It is God who is really wise; finite beings are wise only in their degree, by courtesy.

In sum: Religious knowledge requires a movement of the heart, and must transcend what can be clearly understood. We have no idea of heaven, beyond those images that best, for us, excite delight. Eternal happiness will be

...a happyness large as our desires, & those desires not stinted to ye few objects we at present receive from some dull inlets of perception, but

> proportionate to wt our faculties shall be wn God has given the finishing stroke to our nature & made us fit inhabitants for heaven, a happiness which we narrow-sighted mortals wretchedly point out to our selves by green meadows, fragrant groves, refreshing shades, crystal streams & wt other pleasant ideas our fancys can glean up in this Vale of misery.[49]

We have no idea of God himself, any more than of our selves. What we say of heaven, of God, and of ourselves is meaningful because it has a use in holding us to the straight way. How those doctrines will eventually be "cashed" can be as obscure to us here and now as any algebraic calculation: Untill that day their meaning, for us, is protreptic.[50] We need no "clear and distinct idea marked by the word *grace*" to be able to speak intelligibly and helpfully of God's grace. The Athanasian Creed requires us not to think of God as Three Gods nor as One God with three names. The fact that we cannot (now or ever) analyze the riddle does not mean that we may safely abandon the recipe. "The main end was not . . . to convey positive ideas to the minds of men . . . but rather a negative sense, tending to exclude Polytheism on the one hand, and Sabellianism [the heretical doctrine that the different persons of the Trinity are merely some amongst many different appearances or modes of the one god] on the other" (ALC 7.9 [300–1], Crito speaking). The wrongness of those excluded doctrines is revealed in the moral confusions of their advocates (in the theory that there are many incommensurable values, on the one hand, or that the best life is unique and solitary on the other). What we do not yet fully understand, in science as well as in religion, may still be believed.

IV. NATURE AS GOD'S SPEECH

It is reasonable to believe what we cannot "prove"; it is even reasonable to believe, and feel, what we can't understand. Both theses depend upon a further "religious" axiom, that the Origin is to be trusted. If we could not sensibly believe the testimony of ages, nor trust our common sense or "natural taste," we should have no escape from chaos. To that extent, we *must* live on faith. If we could not sensibly believe that what is now obscure may still have a solution, and may guide our hearts, we must remain "*minute* philosophers."[51] "This being the case, how can it be questioned what course a wise man should take? Whether the principles of Christians or infidels are truest may be made a question; but which are safest can be none."[52] Those who are moved neither by the past nor by the hope of a future they do not yet understand have nothing to sustain or occupy them but their present pains or pleasures. We had better at least pretend that testimony can be relied on, that our thoughts are not limited to what we now perceive, and that we can properly predict our futures on the basis of our remembered past. Maybe a "freethinker" can concede so much, yet still contend there is no Providence, nor any natural norm. Stephen Jay Gould, for example, is ready to welcome the corollary, that "we are an improbable and fragile entity . . . not the predictable result of a global tendency."[53] Not only we as individuals, but we as a species and as a natural kind (the kind of Rational Being) may perish utterly, and "who would tell the difference? . . . . Some find the prospect depressing. I [he says] have always regarded it as exhilarating, and a source of both freedom and consequent moral responsibility."[54] Gould's reasoning is perhaps as follows. If we were the product of a plan, if anyone or anything had intended us to be, then on the one hand our designer was both cruel and astoundingly circuitous; on the other, there would be a way of being which was ineluctably intended for us. We would be someone else's plan, and compelled to think our planner was monstrous.

As to the latter conclusion, Berkeley's mockery is perhaps the only answer: "He who undertakes to measure without knowing either [the measure or the thing to be measured] can be no more exact than he is modest, . . . who having neither an abstract idea of moral fitness nor an adequate idea of the divine economy shall yet pretend to measure the one by the other" (ALC 6.17 [251–2], Crito speaking).

But suppose that it is true (or that we come to believe it true) that there is no admirable plan. "What beauty can be found in a moral system, formed, and governed by chance, fate or any other blind, unthinking principle?" (ALC 3.10 [128], Euphranor speaking). Why should we suppose that the impulses accidentally bred into us form any sort of coherent, admirable, or long-lasting whole? If what "we" are (whoever we may be) is so accidental, we have, Berkeley suspects, no reason to believe that we could find out truths (not even the truth that we are accidental), nor that we could ever live peaceably together. All rules of common decency, all rules of reason, would be founded in unreason. What possible reason have we to believe that a society of people who believed what Gould believes could even comprehend his reasons for believing it? It is not as easy as some modern thinkers suppose to do without a trust in Providence. To that extent Berkeley was justified.

According to Berkeley "it is not possible for free intellectual agents to propose a nobler pattern for their imitation than nature, which is nothing else but a series of free actions produced by the best and wisest Agent."[55] Natural phenomena are caused directly by that best and wisest agent, so as to convey information to his creatures. Berkeley's objection to Alciphron's ecstatic apostrophes to "nature"[56] is not that "nature" should not be admired at all, but that Alciphron has no reason to admire it. Phenomena are a form of speech, in that the connection between (say) visible phenomena and the tactile phenomena they intimate to us is something that we can only learn from experience. There is, according to Berkeley, no "common sense" (in Aristotle's sense), that can discern *the same* shape in a visible square and a felt one. Someone born blind and then given sight would have to learn the connection, like anyone confronted by an unknown language. This is not, moreover, the only way in which phenomena must be interpreted as speech (specifically, as God's speech).[57] The point is not only that we learn from experience how God will complete his sentences (a "grammar for the understanding of nature"),[58] but that we learn what he intended to convey. "The phenomena of nature... form not only a magnificent spectacle, but also a most coherent, entertaining and instructive Discourse" (S 254). We learn, for example, that he wishes us to act on general rules. We learn that phenomena are symbolical of moral law. Examining gravitational attraction, "if we carry our thoughts from the corporeal to the moral world, we may observe in the Spirits or Minds of men a like principle of attraction, whereby they are drawn together in communities, clubs, families, friendships, and all the various species of society."[59] We learn that he intends us to be active, rather than supine. "All nature will furnish you with arguments and examples against sloth."[60]

Berkeley's arguments are twofold. On the one hand, the order and reliability of "natural phenomena" give us reason to believe that there is some single cause of all that happens – a cause that must be "an active, free Spirit" (as "we have no proof, either from experience or reason, of any other agent or efficient cause than mind or spirit" [S 154]). "We cannot make even one single step in accounting for the phenomena without admitting the immediate presence and immediate action of an incorporeal Agent, who connects, moves, and disposes all things according to such rules, and for such purposes, as seem good to Him" (S 237). We have as good reason to believe in some one, infinite agent as the author of all phenomena as we do to believe in any finite agent as the author of particular phenomena. "Neither is the soul of man any more than the Spirit of Christ visible to the eyes of flesh and blood, they are nevertheless both of them plainly to be seen in their effects."[61] On the other hand, if there were no such providential cause, no "meaning" in phenomena, we could not sensibly take our moral cue from them – and if not from them, from where?

His conviction that God intends us to learn moral messages from what he makes appear to us even allows him to learn from things that we do not strictly *see*.

> Astronomy is peculiarly adapted to remedy a little and narrow spirit.... There is something in the immensity [of astronomical distances] that shocks and overwhelms the imagination; it is too big for the grasp of a human intellect: estates, provinces and kingdoms vanish in its presence.[62]

Simple critics could reply that it is only physicists who tell us that there are such distances, such unseen globes. If it is absurd to claim that "the Wall is not white, Fire is not hot & c,"[63] why is not absurd to say that the stars of the night sky are really vaster than the Earth itself? (ALC 4.10 [154]). Why isn't astronomy just a record of mammalian sense data (as Frank Ramsey said)?[64] Herbert's mystical rationalism concluded that our souls could reach out to the stars, and far beyond:

> When you have left the womb of the lower world, will you not attain to what you formerly conceived as ideal? On this journey you will first encounter the blue which is commonly supposed to be the ceiling of heaven; but this is ignorance. For in reality it consists of the most refined region of the air which appears to be this colour owing to its distance, as experts in optics tell us. When you have passed through this tract you will discover the stars to have been created not merely to sparkle but to be new worlds. And at last, to prolong the account no further, the infinite itself will unfold.[65]

Malebranche, on the other hand, uses as an argument against the imputation of secondary qualities to the things themselves that if they were in the objects, our souls would reach out to the heavens: "It seems to me beyond question that our souls do not occupy a space so vast as that between us and the fixed stars ... thus, it is unreasonable to think that our souls are in the heavens when they see stars there."[66] It would seem that Berkeley should think, with Herbert, that our souls reach to the heavens, for the very reason that Malebranche sought to refute. That, after all, is why he can say that "he is the true possessor of a thing who enjoys it, and not he that owns it without the enjoyment of it":[67] We *own* the sights we see, the scents we savor – because there is nothing else to own than those ideas, and no stars beside the ones that shine for us.

It may be, of course, that Berkeley's remarks about astronomy were youthful indiscretions (though he had already formulated his philosophy at that time), or else that he was being disingenuous: Knowing that other people thought the stars were far away he used their error to suggest a moral point. But it seems more likely that he felt the same humility before the "distant" stars as they. Why not? The infinite free Spirit chose to tell a story – of "astronomical distances" – and he did so to provide us with a symbol of Infinity, of something we can know but not embrace. Geological eons, in the imagination of geologists, might have a similar function – though Berkeley actually dismissed the evidence for those eons for quite unmetaphysical reasons (ALC 6.221 [298 ff.]). Both are symbols, and echoes, of an older discovery:

> Astronomy opens the mind, and alters our judgement, but Christianity produceth an universal greatness of soul.... How mean must the most exalted potentate upon earth appear to that eye which takes in innumerable orders of blessed spirits, differing in glory and perfection. How little must the amusements of sense, and the ordinary occupations of mortal men, seem to one who is engaged in so noble a pursuit as the assimilation of himself to the Deity, which is the proper employment of every Christian![68]

Nature is an array of useful symbols. "Resurrection, I say, how strange soever at first sight will be found natural, that is conformable to the course of nature in her ordinary productions, which nature is the work of God."[69] It is also a complex of divine suggestions. We are urged to act on general principles, but also to feel particular, self-sacrificial attachments: "That prevalent love in parents towards their children, which is neither founded on the merit of the object, nor yet on self-interest" is at once a symbol and a duty.[70] What we are generally required to feel we can be sure is what we ought to feel. *"Providence hath with a bountiful hand prepared variety of pleasures for the various stages of life,"*[71] but not everything we call "a pleasure" is naturally, or really, pleasant.

> *Natural pleasures* I call those, which, not depending on the fashion or caprice of any particular age or nation, are suited to human nature in general, and were intended by Providence as rewards for using our faculties agreeably to the ends for which they were given us. *Fantastical pleasures* are those which, having no natural fitness to delight our minds, presuppose some particular whim or taste accidentally prevailing in a sett of people, to which it is owing that they please.[72]

From all of which it follows that we can learn moral lessons from "nature", and that those lessons are to take account of "natural impulses" of loyalty and affection, "native inbred notions" (S 309, in defense of Plato's "innate ideas"), and to be led by general laws, those laws that we can conceive to be incumbent on all rational creatures – laws that "a reasonable agent would choose to obey if he were perfectly fair and not biased."[73]

> As God is the common father of us all, it follows that it cannot be his intention, that we should each of us promote his own private interest, to the wrong and damage of his neighbour, but that such conduct or behaviour as tends to procure the general well-being of mankind, is most acceptable to him. From whence it follows, that all the particular laws of nature or morality are to be looked upon, as so many decrees of the divine will, inasmuch as they are evidently calculated to promote the common good of all men.... *All these natural tendencies and impressions on the conscience, are so many marks to direct and inform the mind, of the will of the author of nature.*[74]

If all this were not so, we would have no "reason" to rely upon any "natural" impulses to be ones that any "reasonable" agent would require, nor any grasp of what such agents would or should desire. "If God is not in Nature, He is not in you," as Plotinus pointed out to the Gnostics.[75] If what is "natural" is not rationally required, what is?

V. HONOR AMONG INFIDELS?

Monotheism, in its cosmological aspect, is the thesis that "all things are made for the supreme good" and correctly understood only when we see how all is for the best (S 260). In its moral or political aspect, it is the thesis that there is, despite appearances, a single and discoverable synthesis of interests. If there is no universal Providence, we have no reason to believe that there is any such confluence of interests, nor any "duty" to assent to, or reject, any impulse that we chance to feel. What else could any of us expect to pursue than "profit and pleasure, [which] are the ends that a reasonable creature would propose to obtain by study, or indeed by any other undertaking"?[76] This would not, in a thoroughly atheistical universe, be our *duty*, but it would be what we did.

The issue is twofold. First, what would we do, under this or that hypothesis? Second, what makes this or that our *duty*? According to Berkeley, something is our *duty* if and only if it is required by God. "Nothing is a law merely because it conduceth to the public good, but because it is decreed by the will of God, which alone can give the sanction of law to any precept" (PO 31). What God requires must be the good of all his creatures: What reason could such an infinite Spirit have to discriminate? The rules we should live by must therefore be ones obedience to which would serve the interest of all those whom we can affect (a class that Berkeley, unwisely, equates with human beings). "It is not therefore the private good of this or that man, nation, or age, but the general well-being of all men, of all nations, of all ages of the world, which God designs should be procured by the concurring actions of each individual" (PO 7). It is in the real interest of each of us to be guided by that common good, which includes our own: It is our duty because it is God's will.

> It is the duty and interest of each individual to cherish and improve [the social inclinations] to the benefit of mankind; the duty, because it is agreeable to the intention of the Author of our being, who aims at the common good of his creatures, and as an indication of his will, hath implanted the seeds of mutual benevolence in our souls; the interest, because the good of the whole is inseparable from that of the parts; in promoting therefore the common good, every one doth at the same time promote his own private interest.[77]

"Everyone knows the prevailing principle in human nature is self-love. This under the direction of well-informed reason should lead us into the true methods of obtaining happiness; but it is a blind principle that takes part with our passions and flatters us in the enjoyment of ease and pleasure."[78] Each of us would prosper – at least with reference to "natural pleasures" – in a world obedient to such laws. Unfortunately, we are also susceptible to the lure of the fantastical, and strongly inclined to misjudge or be too little moved by our own temporal interest. "The depraved condition of humane nature was no secret to the wise among the heathen, it being evident by the light of reason in all times and places, that the understanding of man was obscure, his will perverse, and his passions irregular."[79] Berkeley concludes that we must be disciplined into obedience, and encouraged by the thought of a more than temporal reward, even to do what "reasonable people" would, in the abstract, agree was in our interest. "It will be very evident that we are too imperfect creatures to be governed by our own wills. For where each particular person is governed by his own will, intent on his own interest, and often mistaking that, such conduct can produce nothing but public confusion and private misery."[80] The importance of an obedient spirit I shall discuss below.

"Interest and duty go together so we cannot practise the one without promoting the other."[81] "Mankind are, by all the ties of duty, no less than of interest, bound to obey [God's] laws" (PO 6). "Interest", or "self-interest", is an ambiguous term, though. "I'd never blame a Man for acting upon Interest. He's a fool that acts on any other principle" (N 542). However, "in valuing Good we reckon too much the present and our own" (N 851). "We must learn to wean ourselves from self-interest, or rather learn wherein our true interest consists.... A man who considers things with any fairness or impartiality will be easily convinced that his chief interest consists in obeying Almighty God."[82]

Berkeley sometimes suggests that reasonable beings would expect "wrong-doing" (commonly so-called) to be against their interests, but may easily be misled by a corruption of the will and judgment. "There is hardly a spirit upon earth so mean and contracted as to center all regards on its own interest, exclusive of the rest of mankind."[83] "A wise and good Man wuld therefore be frugal in the Management of his Charity; that is, contrive it so as that it might extend to the greatest Wants of the greatest Number of his Fellow-creatures."[84] Elsewhere Berkeley wonders whether "wrong-doing" might not actually be in our interests, were it not that God forbids it (and will punish us). "It should even seem that a man who believes no future state, would act a foolish part in being thoroughly honest. For what reason is there why such a one should postpone his own private interest or pleasure to the doing his duty?"[85] In the first place, no atheist can reasonably think that anything is a duty; in the second, an individual's own particular interest may, after all, be served by doing what that same person would seek to prevent in others. "Common mutual faith is the great support of society; and an oath, as it is the highest obligation to keep our faith inviolate, becomes the great instrument of justice and intercourse between men."[86] Why *should* atheists acknowledge the force of oaths? Occasionally, Berkeley acknowledges that some atheists may be so well-conditioned as to act generously or heroically, but adds that "they act foolishly who pretend to advance the interest of [virtue] by destroying or weakening the strongest motives to it, which are accommodated to all capacities, and fitted to work on all dispositions, and enforcing those alone which can affect only a generous and exalted mind."[87] It may take a while for the full effects of radical scepticism to be observed, but they can be imagined.

> The morals of a people are in this like their fortunes; when they feel a national shock, the worst doth not shew itself immediately. Things make a shift for a time on the credit of old notions and dying opinions. But the youth born and brought up in wicked times, without any bias to good from early principle or instilled opinion, when they grow ripe must be monsters indeed. And it is to be feared, that age of monsters is not far off.[88]

Honest, well-meaning atheists are usually scornful of such prophecies. They find it easy to believe that people (their kind of people) have moderate passions, and that scientific theorizing is a matter of simple, dispassionate observation, unhampered by priestcraft, superstition, or personal desire. They believe, in effect, that "natural humanity" needs no religion. But those very notions of a "natural humanity," "reason," and "intelligible natures" are what is under threat. If there is no Providence, no correspondence between any "natural impulse" of humanity (ethical or epistemic) and the way the Great World works, their own notions of humanity and nature are as accidental, and as temporary, as the rest. What is "natural" (if this is to be a normative idea) need not (and cannot) be "original, universal and invariable" (ALC 1.14 [57], Euphranor speaking) – but such naturalness requires that there be transcendent norms and final causes. How is it possible to believe both that "scientific fact" is value-free, and that "being scientific" is a sufficient condition for being honest, honorable, and at ease? It is customary for liberals to mock the efforts of Roman moral theologians to defend, on presently fashionable principles, moral judgments first made on other grounds. Why not just admit that those judgments were mistaken? Atheistical liberals are in the same position: The morals and epistemology we have inherited distinguish what is "natural" from what is not, rational religion from chance superstition, waking life from dream; they embody a conviction that there is a real identity of interest amongst all human beings, and some nonviolent way of resolving personal and tribal conflicts. If there is no Providence, Berkeley believes, then all this is false, or might as well be.

Berkeley insists that "religion" is a vitally important element of civil peace. "Obedience to all civil power is rooted in the religious fear of God: it is propagated, preserved, and nourished by religion."[89]

> Religion hath in former days been cherished and reverenced by wise patriots and lawgivers, as knowing it to be impossible that a nation should thrive and flourish without virtue, or that virtue should subsist without conscience, or conscience without religion; inasmuch that an atheist or infidel was looked on with abhorrence, and treated as an enemy to his country.[90]

Atheism, as Berkeley interprets it, at once diminishes our reason to believe that we *should* obey, and our motive for doing so. "The same atheistical, narrow spirit, centering all our cares upon private interest, and contracting all our hopes within the enjoyment of this present life, equally produceth a neglect of what we owe to God and our country."[91] "The modern schemes of our free-thinkers, who pretend to separate morality from religion, how rational soever they seem to their admirers, are in truth and effect, most irrational and pernicious to civil society."[92]

"Is it not visible that we are less knowing, less virtuous, less reasonable, in Proportion as we are less religious?"[93] The claim may not be entirely convincing, and Berkeley also acknowledges (as above) that people may be put off wrong-doing, and even encouraged to right-doing, by the residual effect of past beliefs. "The frequent denouncing of God's judgements against sinners hath some effect on our consciences; and even the reprobate who hath extinguished in himself all notion of religion is oft restrained by a sense of decency & shame from those actions that are held in abhorrence by all good

Christians."[94] Berkeley was also conscious of the ills of misplaced enthusiasm: "We do not contend for superstitious follies, or for the rage of bigots" (ALC 5.6 [179], Crito speaking). It is not surprising that "there should be half-believers, mistaken bigots, holy frauds, ambitious, interested, disputing, conceited, schismatical, heretical, absurd men among the professors of such revealed religion" (ALC 6.28 [274], Crito speaking). For that very reason we should hold fast to the revelation. "For Heaven's sake if we have any religion at all let not us who are commanded to love our enemies hate one another."[95] "As difference of opinion can never justify an uncharitable conduct towards those who differ from us, so neither can difference of interests."[96] "Our zeal must not be directed against persons but things."[97] Enmity can be founded upon religious difference, and upon corrupt interpretation of the scriptures: "Our first Planters imagined they had a right to treat Indians on the foot of Canaanites or Amalekites."[98] There are those who identify themselves, and their interests, solely with a particular nation, which they then idolatrously worship. It is humankind as a whole that God would have us consider, though, reckoning national differences as valuable only in providing a necessary variety and mutual support. "As different countries are by <their re>spective products fitted to sup<ply each> other's wants: so the all-wise <provi>dence of God hath ordered <that> different men are endowed w<ith> various talents whereby they are mutually enabled to assist and promote the happiness of one another."[99] Thinking that God is like ourselves, that he has the same narrow (individualist or nationalist) views as ourselves, we misidentify what He requires of us. "What is the sum and substance, scope and end of Christ's religion, but the love of God and man?" (ALC 5.15 [189], Crito speaking).

> He doth not require from us costly sacrifices, magnificent temples or tedious pilgrimages, but only that we shou'd love one another.... There must be an inward, sincere disinterested affection that takes root in the heart and shews itself in acts of kindness and benevolence.[100]

"I will even own", says Crito, "that the Gospel and the Christian religion have often been the pretexts for [feuds, factions, massacres, and wars]; but it will not thence follow they were the cause. On the contrary, it is plain they could not be the real proper cause of these evils; because a rebellious, proud, revengeful, quarrelsome spirit is directly opposite to the whole tenor and most express precepts of Christianity.... And secondly, because all those evils... were as frequent, nay, much more frequent, before the Christian religion was known in the world" (ALC 5.16 [190]).

Disinterested affection may be present "naturally" in some, without the support of religious instruction and practice, but without religion it cannot be a "duty," nor anything but one of the impulses bred in us.

> That men have certain instinctive sensations or passions from nature, which make them amiable and useful to each other, I am clearly convinced. Such are a fellow-feeling with the distressed, a tenderness for our offspring, an affection towards our friends, our neighbours and our country, an indignation against things base, cruel, or unjust. These passions are implanted in the human soul, with several other fears and appetites, aversions, and desires, some of which are strongest and uppermost in one mind, others in another. Should it not therefore seem a very uncertain guide in morals, for a man to follow his passion or inward feeling? And would this rule not infallibly lead different men in different ways, according to the prevalency of this or that appetite or passion? (ALC 3.5 [120])

If we were all kind, no doubt, we would all prosper, or prosper as well as any mortals could. Our kindness is limited, alas, and insecure: If others are not kind, why would we be; if we stand to gain here and now by not being quite so kind, why not? "What but this hope [of everlasting life] could inspire men with courage to undergo the most cruel torments, and lay down their lives, rather than transgress the laws of God?"[101]

In sum: It is our duty and our interest to do what the infinite free Spirit, our maker and sustainer, asks of us. If there were in fact no such Spirit, we should have less reason to do what such a Spirit *would* require of us, and less reason to believe that there was any such coherent set of demands. Why believe that there is anything at all that all rational or reasonable beings would or could agree to do or refrain from doing? Why be concerned about what, if anything, such unimaginable abstractions do? Even if we agree that, in the end, our own civil society would be more prosperous if everyone, or nearly everyone, were well-behaved, so what? What reason does that give me to behave well even to fellow-members of my civil society, let alone to fellow-members of that "great City, whose author and founder is God, in which the civil laws are no other than the rules of virtue and the duties of religion, and where every one's true interest is combined with his duty"? (ALC 3.10 [129]; see also S 279). According to Lysicles, "benevolence to mankind is perhaps pretended, but benevolence to himself is practised, by the wise" (ALC 3.12 [131]). Is he, on atheistical assumptions, wrong? Alciphron thinks "honour" will be enough to secure a form of good behavior – but such "honour among infidels is like honesty among pirates; something confined to themselves, and which the fraternity may find their account in, but every one else should be on his guard against" (ALC 3.2 [115]).

VI. OBEDIENCE AND ETERNAL LIFE

Charity is our duty and our interest: our duty because it is required of us by an impartial law-giver; our interest because we probably will prosper in this life if enough of us are charitable, and certainly will prosper in the future life. "A Benefaction of this Kind seems to enlarge the very Being of a Man, extending it to distant Places and to future Times; inasmuch as unseen Countries and after Ages, may feel the Effects of his Bounty, while he himself reaps the Reward in the blessed Society of all those who, *having turned many to Righteousness, shine as the Stars for ever and ever.*"[102] Even the heathen will be better off if they do good: "A Good life as it includes piety towards God, temperance towards ourselves and justice towards our neighbour is most indispensibly necessary to intitle a man to the Favor of him who is holy in all his ways.... Tho [good works] may not purchase to a Heathen that everlasting inheritance which is the sure expectation of every good Christian, yet it cannot be denied that they will at least mitigate the wrath of God, and make his state easier and better than it would otherwise have been."[103] Modern moralists, even if they seek to found such duties of benevolence elsewhere, are likely to praise charity. They are less likely to think well of Berkeley's passionate defence of obedience, his conviction that "a peaceful submission and compliance in things lawful is the indispensable duty of every Christian."[104] He would not have been surprised: If once we forget to fear God, why should we honour the king? "'Fear God' and 'Honour the King,'" said Lysicles, "are a pair of slavish maxims" (ALC 1.12 [52]). The maxims of "free thought" require us to preserve our own good judgment – as Berkeley himself insisted in his letter to John James. "We see . . . with our own eyes, by a common light but each with his own private eyes. And so must you or you will not see at all."[105] No one (we now insist) can excuse evil-doing by appealing to superior command.

That argument, of course, appeals only to those who think there really is such a thing as evil-doing, that we actually have a *duty* (amongst other things) to govern our lives in accordance with such rules as are conducive to the general good. Even those without such moral qualms may object to the notion of "a Mind, which knows all things, and beholds human actions, like some judge or magistrate, with infinite observation and intelligence. The belief of a God in this sense fills a man's mind with scruples, lays him under constraints, and embitters his very being" (ALC 4.16 [163], Lysicles speaking). And that would never do. Lysicles, for that reason, professes that he would not trouble to disprove the existence of a God whose attributes (though verbally identical with those we might discern in finite beings) were intended in some different sense. Belief in a God who would not really trouble itself about us and our doings, and which is "an unknown subject of attributes absolutely unknown is a very innocent doctrine" (ALC 4.17 [164]; see also 7.26 [324], against Spinoza, where Crito is speaking). The God of some modern theologians is as harmless, because it is now reckoned to be a vulgar error that God acts, judges, or decrees.

The God whom we might find it easier to accept – but need not really obey – is a merely ideal and inactive one – the impartial judge by whose ideal judgments all rational beings everywhere would abide. "Religion is nothing else but the conforming our faith and practice to the will of god, . . . which is the freedom and perfection of a rational creature."[106] In doing what an ideal god wills, we do only and entirely what "reason" requires for the common good, what we would ourselves judge best if we were genuinely impartial, as well as well-informed. What is lacking in later rationalist moralising is any hint as to why, being decidedly ill-informed and partial creatures, we should feel any impulse to act as if we were not. How could we tell what an ideal god would wish? What sanction could there be against disobedience, and (if there could be none) what reason is there to obey?

Instead of an ideal, or allegorical, or unknown god, Berkeley affirms the real, effective existence of an infinite free spirit who makes his wishes known to us, through nature, conscience, and revelation. "It is certain that <the prac>tice of any vice or the co<mmision> of any crime is att<ended> with an immediate punish<ment> in this life. The infinitely <wise> providence of God hath joyned moral and <natural> evil together"[107] – but the practice of vice is wrong because God forbids it, and not because it leads to disaster. On the contrary, it leads to disaster because God has forbidden it, and chooses that way to make his displeasure clear. On this account, we cannot argue that if there be some occasion when the vicious act does not lead to disaster it is not "really" wrong on that occasion: It remains wrong even if God delays or ameliorates the punishment.

We should therefore obey those laws which, by reason and experience, we can see are generally required for the common good, even if some particular disobedience does not always (to our weak judgment) seem to be so bad.

> Men, having strong passions and weak judgements, are for the most part blind to their own interests.... From all which, we may certainly conclude, it is not our true interest to be governed by our own carnal and irregular wills, but rather to square and suit our actions, to the supreme will of him, whose understanding is infinite, comprehending in one clear view the remotest events and consequences of things.[108]

We should therefore, Berkeley contends, obey the actual rulers (monarchical or republican) whom God has allowed to power – or rather we should not seek their overthrow. "The ills of rebellion are certain, but the event doubtful"[109] – which is not merely an argument from prudence, but further evidence that God does not desire us to rebel. Such obedience need not always be active: If the sovereign commands us to blaspheme, or murder, or commit some other offense to divine law, we must not do it, but endure what punishment the sovereign imposes, passively. More modern moralists may think themselves more "moral" in advocating active disobedience, but Berkeley thought he knew better what the ills of rebellion were, and that those same modern moralists would be outraged if anyone rebelled against their favored rulers.

Obedience to God and the king (which is to say, any ruler in actual control of the land) is no great hardship, just because it is evident, in Berkeley's view, that indiscipline is bound to be an evil. For the same reason, Berkeley, to a later age, seems strangely indifferent to the evil of slavery, contenting himself with urging planters to allow their slaves to be baptized, and arguing against "an erroneous notion, that the being baptized is inconsistent with a State of Slavery."[110] His college in Bermuda, for the education of colonists and Indians alike, was to depend on forcible abduction: "Young *Americans*, educated in an Island at some Distance from their own Country, will more easily be kept under Discipline till they have attained a compleat Education, than on the Continent; where they might find Opportunities of running away to their Countrymen, and returning to their brutal Customs, before they were thoroughly imbued with good Principles and Habits."[111] Purported savages are not alone in being less free because they are less disciplined. "That gloomy empire of the spleen, which tyrannizeth over the better sort (as they are called) of the free nations" makes them "more wretched slaves than even the subjects of absolute power" (S 106). Outward slavery is of little importance compared with that inward misery, which should be cured by wholesome discipline (and, of course, whatever corporeal aids, like tar-water, can be found).

Obedience to God is to be manifested in two ways. In the first place, "we ought not . . . to repine at the dispensations of providence, or charge god foolishly. I say it becomes us with thankfulness to use the good things we receive from the hand of God, and patiently to abide the evil, which when thoroughly considered and understood may perhaps appear to be good, it being no sure sign that a thing is good, because we desire, or evil, because we are displeased with it."[112] "Excesses, defects, and contrary qualities conspire to the beauty and harmony of the world" (S 262) – however ill-disposed we are to remember it. To believe in God is, in part, to live thankfully, and not demand more of what we wish than we are given, or expressly permitted to pursue. In the second place, and as a corollary, we should not object to living "under discipline", even if we have good reason to believe that those who exercise the discipline (slave-owners, rulers, rectors) are themselves wrong-doers. Disobedience, as a general practice, would bring about such ills as even we could recognize. "What is it that renders this world habitable, but the prevailing notions of order, virtue, duty, and Providence?"[113] "As for unbounded liberty, I leave it to savages, among whom alone I believe it is to be found" (ALC 5.35 [215], Crito speaking). But we are unlikely to be much moved by this, even if we acknowledge it, unless we recall that there is a world to come.

> We should not therefore repine at the divine laws, or show a frowardness or impatience of those transient sufferings they accidentally expose us to, which, however grating to flesh and blood, will yet seem of small moment, if we compare the littleness and fleetingness of this present world with the glory and eternity of the next. (PO 42)

It is that literal belief which sets the seal on Berkeley's account of religion: "I can easily overlook any present momentary sorrow, when I reflect that it is in my power to be happy a thousand years hence. If it were not for this thought, I had rather be an oyster than a man, the most stupid and senseless of animals than a reasonable mind tortured with an extreme innate desire of that perfection which it despairs to obtain."[114] Our duty of obedience prepares us for that life. What happens here is at once much more and much less important than we think: much more, because our immortal life rests on it; much less, because "if we knew what it was to be an angel for one hour, we should return to this world, though it were to sit on the brightest throne in it, with vastly more loathing and reluctance than we would now descend into a loathsome dungeon or sepulchre" (ALC 4.23 [172], Euphranor speaking). As Socrates suggested, we are in jail, and it is wise to accept that discipline, and enjoy its occasional blessings. "The worst prison is the body of an indolent epicure" (S 104) – or that of any who have debauched their natural tastes.

"That impious and profane men should expect divine punishment doth not seem so absurd to conceive" (ALC 6.13 [243–4], Crito speaking), but Berkeley's more usual emphasis is not on Hell, but Heaven. "He that acts not in order to the obtaining of eternal Happyness must be an infidel at least he is not certain of a future Judgment" (N 776). "Eternal life is the ultimate end of all our views: It is for this, we deny our appetites, subdue our passions and forgo the interests of this present world. Nor is this at all inconsistent with the glory of God being the last end of our actions, forasmuch as this very glory constitutes our heaven or felicity in the other world."[115]

Berkeley does not trouble to argue directly for the truth of this expectation, content to take it on trust. After all, "the hazard tho never so small & uncertain, of a good so ineffably so inconceivably great, ought to be more valu'd and sought after than the greatest assurance we can have of any sublunary good."[116] "Whether the principles of Christians or infidels are truest may be made a question; but which are safest can be none. Certainly if you doubt all opinions you must doubt of your own; and then, for aught you know, the Christian may be true. The more doubt the more room there is for faith, a sceptic of all men having the least right to demand evidence" (ALC 7.24 [322]). In accepting what is now known as Pascal's Wager, Berkeley reverted to his oldest trick, accepting his opponent's premisses to establish a conclusion opposite to theirs. From scepticism he established faith, while also subverting in great detail all the customary arguments against such faith. "Either there is or is not a God: there is or is not a revelation: man either is or is not an agent: the soul is or is not immortal. If the negatives are not sure, the affirmatives are possible. If the negatives are improbable, the affirmatives are probable" (ALC 7.24 [322], Crito speaking). Philosophy, so Socrates declared, is the practice of death; religion, Berkeley might have answered, is the practice of immortality.

On the one hand, that hoped-for happiness produces pleasures even in this life: "The pleasure which naturally affects a human mind with the most lively and transporting touches, I take to be the sense that we act in the eye of infinite wisdom, power and goodness, that will crown our virtuous endeavours here with a happiness hereafter, large as our desires, and lasting as our immortal souls."[117] On the other hand, such a hope helps preserve the civil peace, in which alone we have any reasonable hope of any of our goals. "Is it of any use to the publick that good men should lose the comfortable prospect of a reward to their virtue, or the wicked be encouraged to persist in their impiety, from an assurance that they shall not be punished for it hereafter?"[118]

The one positive argument for the truth of this useful doctrine he suggests is that the frustration of a natural desire would be absurd: "Shall that appetite of immortality, natural to all mankind, be alone misplaced, or designed to be frustrated?"[119] "Man alone of all animals hath understanding to know his God. What availeth this knowledge unless it be to enoble man, and raise him to an imitation and participation of the Divinity?" (ALC 5.28 [207], Crito speaking). His complaint against Celsus is that he supposed that brutes "have a nearer commerce and union with the Divinity; that they know more than men; and that elephants, in particular, are of all others most religious animals and strict observers of an oath" (ALC 6.25 [267], Euphranor speaking).[120] Better, Berkeley thinks, to think that we are unlike beasts – if only because those who disagree end by treating themselves and others as badly as they treat beasts. Our goal lies in eternity, not in the pleasures for which beasts are well adapted. "The zeal which is animated with the hopes and fears of eternity must never terminate in worldly ends."[121]

That there actually is in the Mind of Man a strong Instinct and Desire, an Appetite and Tendency towards another and a better State, incomparably superior to the present, both in point of Happiness and Duration, is no more than every one's Experience and inward Feeling may inform him. The Satiety and Disrelish attending sensual Enjoyments, the Relish for Things of a more pure and spiritual Kind, the restless Motion of the Mind from one terrene Object or Pursuit to another, and often a Flight or Endeavour above them all towards something unknown, and perfective of its Nature, are so many Signs or Tokens of this better State, which in the stile of the Gospel is termed Life Eternal.... Every Man, who knows and acts up to his true Interest, must make it his principal Care and Study to obtain it.[122]

In sum: Berkeley's God is an individual but infinite free Spirit who really requires of us an obedience to discipline, while simultaneously blessing us with manifold pleasures of sense, and promising far larger pleasure in eternity to those who endure to the end. God is more than an ideal vision of what (we think) might be. We may think to evade his judgment, but "whatever Men may think, the Arm of the Lord is not shortened."[123] Berkeley's belief is sustained by metaphysical argument, by a careful trust in testimony, and through the conviction that so strong a desire – for immortal being – could not be so absurdly doomed to absolute frustration.

NOTES

1. See also his *Guardian* essay on "The Christian Idea of God," *Works* 7: 219, and *Alciphron* 4.14 (159), Euphranor speaking.
2. Letter to Percival, December 27, 1709, *Works* 8: 28; also in Benjamin Rand, *Berkeley and Percival* (Cambridge: Cambridge University Press, 1914), 68.
3. *Works* 6: 201–22.
4. *Works* 7: 143–55.

5. *Works* 7: 129–38.
6. The freedom of man is discussed in *Alciphron* 7.16–20 (309–18).
7. *Pace*, amongst others, John Wild, *George Berkeley: A Study of His Life and Philosophy* (Cambridge, MA: Harvard University Press, 1936), 155f., who proposes that "the Berkeley of the *Principles* and the early sermons is a typical mouthpiece of the Enlightenment," who later became enamored of more mystical and emotional doctrines. Berkeley's actual writings are more complex than Wild imagined.
8. Much of this and the following section were delivered as the Aquinas Lecture for 1994 at Blackfriars, Oxford. I am grateful for comments by Brian Davies and others.
9. Letter to Sir John James (1741), *Works* 7: 147.
10. Sermon on Religious Zeal (1709–12), *Works* 7: 20.
11. Edward Herbert, *De Veritate*, trans. M. H. Carré (Bristol: Arrowsmith, 1937), 72.
12. Leland Miles, *John Colet and the Platonic Tradition* (London: Allen and Unwin, 1961), 128, 141.
13. Philo, *Legum Allegoriae* 2.56 (*Collected Works*, trans. F. H. Colson, G. H. Whitaker et al. (Heinemann: London, 1929–62), 2: 259). See also Plotinus, *Enneads* 1.6.7, 5–7, and J. M. Rist, *Plotinus: The Road to Reality* (Cambridge: Cambridge University Press, 1967), 188–98.
14. *Siris* 313f., citing Proclus's *Commentary* on *Alcibiades* I, after Plato's *Republic* 10.611c ff.; see also Plotinus, *Enneads* 1.1.12.
15. See *Siris* 193 on phantoms such as "corporeal forces, absolute motions, and real spaces."
16. *Guardian* essay "On the Pineal Gland," *Works* 7: 188; see *Alciphron* 3.13 (158), Crito speaking.
17. "The Pineal Gland (continued)," *Works* 7: 191.
18. *Alciphron* 1.5 (39); see also 1.2 (34f.).
19. *Discourse to Magistrates, Works* 6: 205.
20. Sermon on Immortality, *Works* 7: 14.
21. *Discourse to Magistrates, Works* 6: 203f.
22. See Stephen R. L. Clark, "Descartes' Debt to Augustine," in *Philosophy, Religion and the Spiritual Life*, ed. M. McGhee (Cambridge: Cambridge University Press, 1992), 73–88.
23. Isaac Newton, represented by Hooykaas, after Cotes's preface to 2nd edition of *Principia*: R. Hooykaas, *Religion and the Rise of Modern Science* (Edinburgh: Scottish Academic Press, 1972), 49. On this point Berkeley sided with Newton against Descartes.
24. Cf. *Alciphron* 4.2 (221), Alciphron speaking.
25. Letter to Sir John James, *Works* 7: 148.

26. Letter to Sir John James, *Works* 7: 146. Further pejorative remarks on popery occur in *Alciphron* (2.9 [78f.], 2.26 [109], 5.20 [195], 5.29–30 [209]), and in his letters to the Roman clergy of Ireland (*Works* 6: 229–49).
27. *Primary Visitation Charge* (1734–7), *Works* 7: 163.
28. Letter to Sir John James, *Works* 7: 145; see also *Alciphron* 6.5 (226), Euphranor speaking.
29. *Guardian* essay on "Pleasures," *Works* 7: 194.
30. *Discourse to Magistrates*, *Works* 6: 217 (my emphasis).
31. Sermon on the Mystery of Godliness (1731), *Works* 7: 91.
32. Herbert, *De Veritate*, 120, 131.
33. *Discourse to Magistrates*, *Works* 6: 217.
34. Letter to Samuel Johnson, *Works* 2: 282.
35. Sermon on Religious Zeal (1709–12), *Works* 7: 20.
36. Especially if no freethinker will accept an axiom from which God's existence follows.
37. "By common sense . . . should be meant, either the general sense of mankind, or the improved reason of thinking men" (ALC 6.12 [241], Crito speaking).
38. *Alciphron*, Euphranor speaking (7.18 [314]): "Walking before them was thought the proper way to confute those ingenious men [who undertook to prove that motion was impossible]."
39. Sermon on the Mission of Christ, *Works* 7: 48.
40. Sermon on Religious Zeal, *Works* 7: 16.
41. Anniversary S. P. G. Sermon, *Works* 7: 116.
42. Sermon on Immortality, *Works* 7: 12.
43. Anniversary S. P. G. Sermon, *Works* 7: 127f.
44. Sermon at Newport (1730), *Works* 7: 71.
45. Sermon on Religious Zeal, *Works* 7: 25 (my emphasis).
46. *Guardian* essay on "The Future State," *Works* 7: 183f.
47. See *Alciphron* 6.20 (257–8), Euphranor speaking.
48. Sermon on the Mission of Christ (1714), *Works* 7: 41.
49. Sermon on Immortality, *Works* 7: 12.
50. See *Alciphron* 7.3 (288ff.); Berkeley's "doctrine of signs" has influenced many later philosophers unconvinced by his theology.
51. *Alciphron* 1.10 (46), after Cicero, *De Senectute* 86.
52. *Alciphron* 7.24 (322), Crito speaking. Crito's argument is to a slightly different point, which I shall soon address.
53. Stephen Jay Gould, *Wonderful Life: The Burgess Shale and the Nature of History* (Penguin: Harmondsworth, 1991), 319.
54. Gould, *Wonderful Life*, 291.
55. *Passive Obedience*, *Works* 6: 24; see also 32.

56. "Oh nature! The genuine beauty of pure nature!": *Alciphron* 1.13 (55); and see *Alciphron* 3.6 (120–1).
57. *Alciphron* 4.7 (149ff.), an issue discussed elsewhere in this volume, Chapters 4 and 5.
58. *Siris* 252; after Plotinus, *Enneads* 3.3.6.
59. *Guardian* essay on "The Bond of Society," *Works* 7: 226; see also *Siris* 242f.
60. *Discourse to Magistrates, Works* 6: 237; see also *The Querist* (discussed in Chapter 11 of this volume), and the Sermon on the Mystery of Godliness, *Works* 7: 91.
61. Sermon on the Mystery of Godliness, *Works* 7: 90; see also *Alciphron* 4.4 (145ff.).
62. *Guardian* essay on "Minute Philosophers," *Works* 7: 207f.
63. *Notebooks* 392. Berkeley adds: "We Irish Men cannot attain to these truths."
64. F. P. Ramsey, *Foundations of Mathematics* (London: Routledge & Kegan Paul, 1931), 35f.
65. Herbert, *De Veritate*, 329.
66. Nicolas Malebranche, *The Search after Truth*, trans. T. M. Lennon and Paul J. Olscamp (Columbus: Ohio State University Press, 1980), I. xiv. 1 (67); see also IIIb. i. 1 (217).
67. *Guardian* essay on "Pleasures," *Works* 7: 195.
68. *Guardian* essay on "Minute Philosophers," *Works* 7: 207f.; see *Alciphron* 4.23 (172) on the "innumerable orders of intelligent beings more happy and perfect than man" (Euphranor speaking).
69. Sermon on Eternal Life, *Works* 7: 107; see also *Alciphron* 6.11 (241), Euphranor speaking.
70. *Guardian* essay on "The Bond of Society," *Works* 7: 227.
71. *Guardian* essay on "Public Schools and Universities," *Works* 7: 203.
72. *Guardian* essay on "Pleasures," *Works* 7: 193; see also *Alciphron* 7.31 (329), Crito speaking.
73. See Joseph Kupfer, "Universalization in Berkeley's Rule-Utilitarianism," *Revue Internationale de Philosophie* 28 (1974): 511–21, reprinted in *Berkeley: Money, Obedience and Affection*, ed. Stephen R. L. Clark (New York: Garland, 1989), 93–114, after *Alciphron* 3.10 (129).
74. Sermon on the Will of God (1751), *Works* 7: 129f., my emphasis.
75. Plotinus, *Enneads* 2.9.16; see Stephen R. L. Clark, *God's World and the Great Awakening* (Oxford: Clarendon Press, 1991), 36.
76. *Guardian* essay on "Short-sightedness," *Works* 7: 211.
77. *Guardian* essay on "The Bond of Society," *Works* 7: 227.
78. Sermon on the Mystery of Godliness, *Works* 7: 90.
79. Sermon on the Mystery of Godliness, *Works* 7: 86.

80. Sermon on the Will of God (1751), *Works* 7: 131.
81. Sermon on Charity (1714), *Works* 7: 30.
82. Sermon on Charity, *Works* 7: 33.
83. *Guardian* essay on "Happiness," *Works* 7: 214.
84. *Proposal for the Better Supplying of Churches in Our Foreign Plantations* (1725), *Works* 7: 358.
85. *Guardian* essay on "The Sanctions of Religion," *Works* 7: 200; see also *Alciphron* 7.10 (303), Crito speaking.
86. *Advice to the Tories* (1715), *Works* 6: 54.
87. *Guardian* essay on "The Sanctions of Religion," *Works* 7: 199.
88. *Discourse to Magistrates, Works* 6: 221; see also *Alciphron* 3.12 (130f.), Crito speaking.
89. *Discourse to Magistrates, Works* 6: 208.
90. *Essay towards Preventing the Ruin of Great Britain, Works* 6: 89.
91. *Essay towards Preventing the Ruin of Great Britain, Works* 6: 79.
92. *Discourse to Magistrates, Works* 6: 206.
93. Anniversary S. P. G. Sermon, *Works* 7: 126.
94. Sermon on the Mission of Christ, *Works* 7: 42.
95. Sermon on Religious Zeal, *Works* 7: 23.
96. Sermon on Charity, *Works* 7: 33.
97. Sermon on Religious Zeal, *Works* 7: 17.
98. Anniversary S. P. G. Sermon, *Works* 7: 122.
99. Sermon on Charity (1714), *Works* 7: 35; the manuscript is in parts illegible.
100. Sermon on Charity, *Works* 7: 28.
101. Sermon on Eternal Life, *Works* 7: 112.
102. *Proposal, Works* 7: 359f.
103. Sermon on Religious Zeal, *Works* 7: 22.
104. Sermon on Religious Zeal, *Works* 7: 26.
105. Letter to Sir John James, *Works* 7: 146.
106. Sermon on the Will of God, *Works* 7: 136, 134.
107. Sermon on Charity, *Works* 7: 36.
108. Sermon on the Will of God, *Works* 7: 134f.
109. *Advice to the Tories, Works* 6: 55.
110. Anniversary S. P. G. Sermon, *Works* 7: 122; see also his *Proposal, Works* 7: 346 ("Gospel Liberty consists with temporal servitude").
111. *Proposal, Works* 7: 357.
112. Sermon on the Will of God, *Works* 7: 134.
113. *Discourse to Magistrates, Works* 6: 202.
114. *Guardian* essay on "Immortality," *Works* 7: 222.
115. Sermon on Eternal Life, *Works* 7: 105–6.
116. Sermon on Immortality, *Works* 7: 12.

117. *Guardian* essay on "Pleasures," *Works* 7: 196.
118. *Guardian* essay on "Happiness," *Works* 7: 216.
119. *Guardian* essay on "The Future State," *Works* 7: 182; see also *Alciphron* 6.11 (241), Euphranor speaking.
120. It is an unfortunate effect of Stoic influence on Christian thought that the pious have found it necessary to distance themselves from God's other, nonhuman creatures.
121. Sermon on Religious Zeal, *Works* 7: 19.
122. Anniversary S. P. G. Sermon, *Works* 7: 114–15.
123. Anniversary S. P. G. Sermon, *Works* 7: 124.

APPENDIX: BERKELEY'S VERSES ON AMERICA[1]

VERSES BY THE AUTHOR, ON THE PROSPECT OF PLANTING ARTS AND LEARNING IN *AMERICA*.

The Muse, disgusted at an Age and Clime,
  Barren of every glorious Theme,
In distant Lands now waits a better Time,
  Producing Subjects worthy Fame:

In happy Climes, where from the genial Sun
  And virgin Earth such Scenes ensue,
The Force of Art by Nature seems outdone,
  And fancied Beauties by the true:

In happy Climes the Seat of Innocence,
  Where Nature guides and Virtue rules,
Where Men shall not impose for Truth and Sense,
  The Pedantry of Courts and Schools:

There shall be sung another golden Age,
  The rise of Empire and of Arts,
The Good and Great inspiring epic Rage,
  The wisest Heads and noblest Hearts.

Not such as *Europe* breeds in her decay;
  Such as she bred when fresh and young,
When heav'nly Flame did animate her Clay,
  By future Poets shall be sung.

Westward the Course of Empire takes its Way;
  The four first Acts already past,
A fifth shall close the Drama with the Day;
  Time's noblest Offspring is the last.

NOTE

1. From *A Miscellany, containing Several Tracts on Various Subjects. By the Bishop of Cloyne* (London: J. and R. Tonson and S. Draper, 1752), 186–7.

BIBLIOGRAPHY

I. BERKELEY'S WRITINGS

A. Early editions of Berkeley's principal works, in order of first publication; with selected modern editions

The modern editions listed contain useful introductory or supplementary material.

An essay towards a new theory of vision. Dublin: J. Pepyat, 1709. A revised version was published with *Alciphron* (1732). Modern editions: in *Works on Vision*, ed. Colin M. Turbayne, Indianapolis: Bobbs-Merrill, 1963 (reprinted Westport, CT: Greenwood Press, 1981); in *Works*, ed. A. A. Luce and T. E. Jessop, volume 1.

A treatise concerning the principles of human knowledge, part I, wherein the chief causes of error and difficulty in the sciences, with the grounds of skepticism, atheism, and irreligion, are inquir'd into. Dublin: J. Pepyat, 1710. 2nd edition (bound with the 3rd edition of the *Three Dialogues*), London: J. Tonson, 1734. Modern editions: with *Dialogues*, ed. Colin M. Turbayne, Indianapolis: Bobbs-Merrill, 1965; ed. Kenneth P. Winkler, Indianapolis: Hackett Publishing Company, 1982; with *Dialogues*, ed. Roger Woolhouse, London: Penguin: 1988; ed. Jonathan Dancy, Oxford: Oxford University Press, 1998; in *Works*, ed. A. A. Luce and T. E. Jessop, volume 2.

Passive obedience. Dublin: J. Pepyat, 1712. In *Works*, ed. A. A. Luce and T. E. Jessop, volume 6.

Three dialogues between Hylas and Philonous. The design of which is plainly to demonstrate the reality and perfection of humane knowledge, the incorporeal nature of the soul, and the immediate providence of a deity: in opposition to sceptics and atheists. Also, to open a method for rendering the sciences more easy, useful, and compendious. London: H. Clements, 1713. 2nd edition, London: W. and J. Innys, 1725. 3rd edition (bound with the 2nd edition of the *Principles*), London: J. Tonson, 1734. Modern editions: with *Principles*, ed. Colin M. Turbayne, Indianapolis: Bobbs-Merrill, 1965; ed. Robert Merrihew Adams, Indianapolis: Hackett Publishing Company, 1979; with *Principles*, ed. Roger Woolhouse, London: Penguin, 1988; ed. David Hilbert and John Perry, Claremont, CA: Arete Press, 1994; ed. Jonathan Dancy, Oxford: Oxford University Press, 1998; in *Works*, ed. A. A. Luce and T. E. Jessop, volume 2.

De motu sive de motus principio & natura, et de causa communicationis motuum [Of motion, or the principle and nature of motion, and the cause of the communication of motions]. London: J. Tonson, 1721. Republished in Berkeley's *Miscellany* (1752). Modern editions: George Berkeley, De Motu *and* The Analyst: *A Modern Edition, with Introductions and Commentary*, ed. Douglas M. Jesseph, Dordrecht: Kluwer, 1992; in *Works*, ed. A. A. Luce and T. E. Jessop, volume 4, with translation by A. A. Luce.

A proposal for the better supplying of churches in our foreign plantations, and for converting the savage Americans to Christianity. London: H. Woodfall, 1724. In the 2nd edition (London: H. Woodfall, 1725), the title continues with the words, "*by a college to be erected in the Summer Islands, otherwise called the Isles of Bermuda.*" Republished with revisions in Berkeley's *Miscellany* (1752). In *Works*, ed. A. A. Luce and T. E. Jessop. volume 7.

Alciphron, or the Minute Philosopher, 2 vols. (London: J. Tonson, 1732). Modern edition of the first, third, fourth, and seventh dialogues: *George Berkeley: Alciphron, or The Minute Philosopher, in Focus*, ed. David Berman, London: Routledge, 1993. In *Works*, ed. A. A. Luce and T. E. Jessop, volume 3.

The theory of vision, or visual language, shewing the immediate presence and providence of a Deity, vindicated and explained. London: J. Tonson, 1733. Modern editions: in *Works on Vision*, ed. Colin M. Turbayne, Indianapolis: Bobbs-Merrill, 1963; reprinted Westport, CT: Greenwood Press, 1981; in *Works*, ed. A. A. Luce and T. E. Jessop, volume 1.

The analyst; or, a discourse addressed to an infidel mathematician. Wherein it is examined whether the object, principles, and inferences of the modern analysis are more distinctly conceived, or more evidently deduced, than religious mysteries and points of faith. London: J. Tonson, 1734. Modern editions: George Berkeley, De Motu *and* The Analyst: *A Modern Edition, with Introductions and Commentary*, ed. by Douglas M. Jesseph, Dordrecht: Kluwer, 1992; in *Works*, ed. A. A. Luce and T. E. Jessop, volume 4.

A defence of free-thinking in mathematics. London: J. Tonson, 1735. In *Works*, ed. A. A. Luce and T. E. Jessop, volume 4.

The querist; containing several queries, proposed to the consideration of the public. Part I, Dublin: G. Risk, G. Ewing, and W. Smith, 1735. Part II,

Dublin: G. Risk, G. Ewing, and W. Smith, 1736. Part III, Dublin; J. Leathley, 1737. Republished in Berkeley's *Miscellany* (1752). Modern editions: *Bishop Berkeley's* Querist *in Historical Perspective*, ed. Joseph Johnston, Dundalk: Dundalgan Press, 1970; in *Works*, ed. A. A. Luce and T. E. Jessop, volume 6.

Siris: a chain of philosophical reflexions and inquiries concerning the virtues of tar-water, and divers other subjects connected together and arising one from another. Dublin: R. Gunn, 1744, and London: C. Hitch and C. Davis, 1744. In *Works*, ed. A. A. Luce and T. E. Jessop, volume 5.

A miscellany, containing several tracts on various subjects. By the Bishop of Cloyne. London: J. and R. Tonson, 1752.

B. Writings published after Berkeley's death

Three posthumously published pieces have been especially important in recent discussions of Berkeley's views: the notebooks he kept in 1706–8; his draft introduction to the *Principles of Human Knowledge*; and an exchange of four letters with his American follower Samuel Johnson, author of *Elementa Philosophica* (see II.C., *Eighteenth-century responses to immaterialism*).

1. Editions of the notebooks, in order of publication

"Commonplace Book of Occasional Metaphysical Thoughts." In *Works*, ed. A. C. Fraser (1871), volume 4, and in *Life and Letters* (see II.A., *Biographies and source materials*). The first publication of the notebooks.

Berkeley's Commonplace Book. Ed. G. A. Johnston. London: Faber and Faber, 1930.

Philosophical Commentaries, Generally Called the Commonplace Book[,] *George Berkeley, Bishop of Cloyne*. Ed. A. A. Luce. London: Thomas Nelson, 1944. The basis for the text appearing in *Works*, ed. A. A. Luce and T. E. Jessop, volume 1.

Philosophical Commentaries. Ed. George H. Thomas, with explanatory notes by A. A. Luce. Alliance, OH: Mount Union College, 1976; reprinted New York: Garland, 1989.

The Notebooks of George Berkeley, Bishop of Cloyne. Facsimile of Add. MS 39305 in the British Museum, with a postscript by Désirée Park. Oxford: Alden Press, 1984.

2. Editions of the Draft Introduction to the *Principles*

"First Draft of the Introduction to the Principles." In *Works*, ed. A. A. Luce and T. E. Jessop, volume 2.

George Berkeley's Manuscript Introduction. Ed. Bertil Belfrage. Oxford: Doxa, 1987.

3. Berkeley's correspondence with Samuel Johnson

Johnson, Samuel. *Samuel Johnson, President of King's College: His Career and Writings*. Ed. H. W. Schneider. 4 vols. New York: Columbia University Press, 1929. In volume 2.

"Philosophical Correspondence between Berkeley and Samuel Johnson 1729–30." In *Works*, ed. A. A. Luce and T. E. Jessop, volume 2.

C. Editions of Berkeley's collected works, in order of publication

The Works of George Berkeley, late Bishop of Cloyne in Ireland. 2 vols. London: L. Exshaw, 1784.

The Works of George Berkeley. Ed. G. N. Wright. 2 vols. London: T. Tegg, 1843.

The Works of George Berkeley, D.D. Ed. A. C. Fraser. 4 vols. Oxford: Clarendon Press, 1871. Revised edition, Oxford: Clarendon Press, 1901.

The Works of George Berkeley, Bishop of Cloyne. Ed. A. A. Luce and T. E. Jessop, 9 vols. London: Thomas Nelson: 1948–57. A critical edition and the standard source for scholars; used for the most part throughout this *Companion*.

D. Anthologies of Berkeley's writings

Essay, Principles, Dialogues, with Selections from other Writings. Ed. Mary Whiton Calkins. New York: Scribner's, 1929. (Includes the *New Theory of Vision*, the *Principles*, the *Dialogues*, *Passive Obedience*, and selections from *Alciphron*, *The Querist*, and *Siris*.)

Berkeley's Philosophical Writings. Ed. David M. Armstrong. London: Macmillan, 1965. Includes the notebooks, the *New Theory of Vision*, the *Principles*, the *Dialogues*, *De Motu*, and the correspondence with Johnson.

Philosophical Works, including the Works on Vision. Ed. Michael R. Ayers. London: J. M. Dent, 1993. Includes the notebooks, the *New Theory of Vision*, the *Principles*, the *Dialogues*, *De Motu*, *The Theory of Vision Vindicated and Explained*, and the correspondence with Johnson.

E. Electronic texts

A database containing every text represented in *Works*, ed. A. A. Luce and T. E. Jessop, is published by the InteLex Corporation of Charlottesville, VA (www.nlx.com) in its "Past Masters" series. The *New Theory of Vision*, the *Principles*, the *Dialogues*, and *Alciphron* are also available as part of its "Locke-Berkeley-Hume" and "British Philosophy: 1600–1900" databases.

II. WRITINGS ABOUT BERKELEY

A. Biographies and source materials

Aaron, Richard I. "A Catalogue of Berkeley's Library." *Mind* 41 (1932): 465–75.

Berman, David. *George Berkeley: Idealism and the Man*. Oxford: Clarendon Press, 1994.

———. "George Berkeley: Pictures by Goldsmith, Yeats, and Luce." In Berman, ed. (see II.G., *Collections of essays*).

A catalogue of the valuable library of the late Right Reverend Dr Berkeley, Lord Bishop of Cloyne, together with the libraries of his son and grandson. London: Leigh and Sotheby, 1796.

Fraser, Alexander Campbell, ed. *Life and Letters of George Berkeley*. Oxford: Clarendon Press, 1871. Reprinted, New York: Garland, 1988.

Gaustad, Edwin S. *George Berkeley in America*. New Haven: Yale University Press, 1979.

Hone, J. M. and M. M. Rossi. *Bishop Berkeley: His Life, Writings, and Philosophy*. London: Faber and Faber, 1931.

Houghton, Raymond W., David Berman, and Maureen T. Lapan, eds. *Images of Berkeley*. Dublin: National Gallery of Ireland, 1986.

Jessop, T. E. *George Berkeley*. London: British Council and Longmans, Green, 1959.

Luce, A. A. *The Life of George Berkeley. Bishop of Cloyne*. London: Thomas Nelson, 1949.

McCracken. C. J. and I. C. Tipton, eds. *Berkeley's* Principles *and* Dialogues: *Background Source Materials*. Cambridge: Cambridge University Press, 2000.

Rand, Benjamin. *Berkeley and Percival*. Cambridge: Cambridge University Press 1914.

———. *Berkeley's American Sojourn*. Cambridge, MA: Harvard University Press, 1932.

Stock, Joseph. *An Account of the Life of George Berkeley*. London: J. Murray, 1776.

Wild, John. *George Berkeley: A Study of His Life and Philosophy*. Cambridge, MA: Harvard University Press, 1936.

Winkler, Kenneth P. "Empiricism and Multiculturalism," *Philosophic Exchange* 34 (2003–4): 55–84.

———. "George Berkeley (1685–1753)." In *British Prose Writers, 1660–1800, First Series*, ed. Donald T. Seibert. Dictionary of Literary Biography, volume 101. Detroit: Gale Research, 1991.

B. Bibliographies, in order of period covered

Keynes, Geoffrey. *A Bibliography of George Berkeley, Bishop of Cloyne: His Works and His Critics in the Eighteenth Century.* Oxford: Clarendon Press, 1976.

Jessop, T. E. *A Bibliography of George Berkeley*. London: Oxford University Press, 1934. Revised edition, The Hague: Martinus Nijhoff, 1973. Covers both Berkeley's writings and writings about Berkeley. Supplemented by the sources listed below.

Turbayne, Colin M. and Robert Ware. "A Bibliography of George Berkeley, 1933–62." *Journal of Philosophy* 60 (1963): 93–112.

Turbayne, Colin M. and R. Appelbaum. "A Bibliography of George Berkeley, 1963–1974." *Journal of the History of Philosophy* 15 (1977): 83–95.

Turbayne, Colin M. "A Bibliography of George Berkeley 1963–1979." In C. M. Turbayne, ed. (see II.G., *Collections of essays*).

Kapstein, Matthew. "A Bibliography of George Berkeley 1980–1985." In E. Sosa, ed. (see II.G., *Collections of essays*).

Items published since 1985 are listed in the *Berkeley Newsletter* (published from 1977–78 through 1997–98) and indexed in *The Philosopher's Index.* As of July, 2005, the Berkeley Newsletter has been revived as an on-line journal (http://people.hsc.edu/berkeleynews/index.php). The site includes electronic files of past issues.

C. Eighteenth-Century responses to immaterialism

Ancillon, Louis Frédéric. "Dialogue between Berkeley and Hume." Translated by Charlotte Stanley. *Hume Studies* 27 (2001): 99–127.

Baxter, Andrew. *An Enquiry into the Nature of the Human Soul.* London: A. Baxter and J. Bettenham, 1733. 2nd edition. 2 vols. London: A. Baxter and A. Millar, 1737; reprinted Bristol: Thoemmes, 1990.

Berman, David, ed. *George Berkeley: Eighteenth-Century Responses.* 2 vols. New York: Garland, 1989.

Eschenbach, Johann Christian. *Samlung der vornehmsten Schriftsteller die die Würklichkeit ihres Eignenkörpers und der ganzen Körperwelt Läugnen.* Rostock: A. F. Rose, 1756. A German translation of the *Dialogues*, with extensive commentary.

[Garve, Christian, and Johann Georg Heinrich Feder.] "The Göttingen Review." In *Kant's Early Critics: The Empiricist Critique of Transcendental Philosophy*, ed. Brigitte Sassen. Cambridge: Cambridge University Press,

2000. A review of Kant's *Critique of Pure Reason*, claiming that the principal foundation of Berkeley's idealism is also "one basic pillar" of Kant's (53–4). Kant responds in the *Prolegomena*.

Hume, David. *An Enquiry concerning Human Understanding*. Ed. Tom L. Beauchamp. Oxford: Oxford University Press, 1999. See Section 12.

———. *A Treatise of Human Nature*. Ed. David Fate Norton and Mary J. Norton. Oxford: Oxford University Press, 2000. See especially 1.1.7, 1.4.2., and 1.4.4.

Hutcheson, Francis. Letter to William Mace. *The European Magazine and London Review* 14 (1788): 158–60.

Johnson, Samuel. *Elementa Philosophica*. Philadelphia: B. Franklin and D. Hall, 1752. Reprinted, New York: Kraus, 1969.

Kant, Immanuel. *Critique of Pure Reason*. Translated by Paul Guyer and Allen W. Wood. Cambridge: Cambridge University Press, 1998. See in particular "Refutation of Idealism" (B 274–9) and "The Transcendental Aesthetic," B 69–71.

———. *Prolegomena to Any Future Metaphysics*. Translated by Gary Hatfield. Revised edition. Cambridge: Cambridge University Press, 2004. See in particular "Note III" (41–5) and, in the Appendix, "Specimen of a judgment about the *Critique* which precedes the investigation," 125–7.

Reid, Thomas. *Essays on the Intellectual Powers of Man, A Critical Edition*. Ed. Derek R. Brookes and Knud Haakonssen. University Park, PA: Pennsylvania State University Press, 2000. See Essay 2, chapters 10 and 11.

———. *An Inquiry into the Human Mind*. Ed. Derek R. Brookes. University Park, PA: Pennsylvania State University Press, 1997.

D. General studies of Berkeley

Ardley, Gavin W. R. *Berkeley's Renovation of Philosophy*. The Hague: Martinus Nijhoff, 1968.

Bender, F. *George Berkeley's Philosophy Re-examined*. Amsterdam: Uitgeverij H. J. Paris, 1944.

Berman, David. *George Berkeley: Idealism and the Man*. Oxford: Clarendon Press, 1994.

———. *Berkeley: Experimental Philosophy*. London: Phoenix, 1997.

Bracken, H. M. *Berkeley*.London: Macmillan, 1974.

Dancy, Jonathan. *Berkeley: An Introduction*. Oxford: Blackwell, 1987.

Fogelin, Robert J. *Berkeley and the* Principles of Human Knowledge. London: Routledge, 2001.

Grayling, A. C. *Berkeley: The Central Arguments*. London: Duckworth, 1986.

Hedenius, Ingemar. *Sensationalism and Theology in Berkeley's Philosophy*. Uppsala: Almqvist and Wiksells, 1936.

Hicks, G. Dawes. *Berkeley.* London: Ernest Benn, 1932. Reprinted, New York: Garland, 1988.

Johnston, G. A. *The Development of Berkeley's Philosophy*. London: Macmillan, 1923. Reprinted, New York: Garland, 1988.

Kingston, F. T. *The Metaphysics of George Berkeley, 1685–1753: Irish Philosopher*. Lewiston, NY: Edwin Mellen Press, 1992.

Luce, A. A. *Berkeley and Malebranche: A Study in the Origins of Berkeley's Thought.* London: Oxford University Press, 1934. Reprinted, New York: Garland, 1988.

———. *Berkeley's Immaterialism: A Commentary on His "A Treatise concerning the Principles of Human Knowledge."* London: Thomas Nelson, 1945.

———. *The Dialectic of Immaterialism*. London: Hodder and Stoughton, 1963.

Muehlmann, Robert G. *Berkeley's Ontology*. Indianapolis: Hackett, 1992.

Pappas, George S. *Berkeley's Thought*. Ithaca: Cornell University Press, 2000.

Park, Désirée. *Complementary Notions: A Critical Study of Berkeley's Theory of Concepts*. The Hague: Martinus Nijhoff, 1972.

Pitcher, George. *Berkeley*. London: Routledge and Kegan Paul, 1977.

Porter, Noah. *The Two-Hundredth Birthday of Bishop George Berkeley: A Discourse Given at Yale College*. New York: Scribner's, 1885.

Ritchie, A. D. *George Berkeley: A Reappraisal*. Manchester: Manchester University Press, 1967.

Stack, George J. *Berkeley's Analysis of Perception*. The Hague: Martinus Nijhoff, 1970.

Stoneham, Tom. *Berkeley's World: An Examination of the* Three Dialogues. Oxford: Oxford University Press, 2003.

Tipton, I. C. *Berkeley: The Philosophy of Immaterialism*. London: Methuen, 1974. Reprinted, New York: Garland, 1988.

Umbaugh, Bruce. *On Berkeley*. Belmont, CA: Wadsworth/Thomson, 2000.

Urmson, J. O. *Berkeley*. Oxford: Oxford University Press, 1982.

Vesey, Godfrey. *Berkeley: Reason and Experience*. Milton Keynes: Open University Press, 1982.

Walmsley, Peter. *The Rhetoric of Berkeley's Philosophy.* Cambridge: Cambridge University Press, 1990.

Warnock. G. J. *Berkeley*. 3rd edition. Oxford: Blackwell, 1982.

Wild, John. *George Berkeley: A Study of His Life and Philosophy*. Cambridge, MA: Harvard University Press, 1936.

Winkler, Kenneth P. *Berkeley: An Interpretation*. Oxford: Clarendon Press, 1989.

Wisdom, J. O. *The Unconscious Origin of Berkeley's Philosophy.* London: Hogarth, 1953.

Young, Theodore A. *Completing Berkeley's Project: Classical vs. Modern Philosophy*. Lanham, MD: University Press of America, 1985.

E. Other books relating to immaterialism

Bennett, Jonathan. *Learning from Six Philosophers*. volume 2, *Locke, Berkeley, Hume*. Oxford: Clarendon Press, 2001.

———. *Locke, Berkeley, Hume: Central Themes.* Oxford: Clarendon Press, 1971.

Foster, John. *The Case for Idealism*. London: Routledge, 1982.

Hausman, David G., and Alan Hausman. *Descartes's Legacy: Minds and Meaning in Early Modern Philosophy*. Toronto: University of Toronto Press, 1997.

Huxley, Thomas H. *Hume: With Helps to the Study of Berkeley*. London: Macmillan, 1894.

Loeb, Louis. *From Descartes to Hume: Continental Metaphysics and the Development of Modern Philosophy*. Ithaca: Cornell University Press, 1981.

McCosh, James. *Locke's Theory of Knowledge with a Notice of Berkeley.* New York: Scribner's, 1884.

McCracken, Charles J. *Malebranche and British Philosophy.* Oxford: Clarendon Press, 1983.

Morris, C. R. *Locke, Berkeley, Hume*. London: Oxford University Press, 1931. Reprinted, Westport, CT: Greenwood, 1980.

Priest, Stephen. *The British Empiricists: Hobbes to Ayer*. London: Penguin, 1970.

Richetti, John. *Philosophical Writing: Locke, Berkeley, Hume*. Cambridge, MA: Harvard University Press, 1983.

Shepherd, Lady Mary. *Essays on the Perception of an External Universe.* London: J. Hatchard, 1827. Excerpted in *Women Philosophers of the Early Modern Period*. Ed. Margaret Atherton. Indianapolis: Hackett, 1994.

Turbayne, Colin M. *The Myth of Metaphor.* New Haven: Yale University Press, 1962. Revised edition. Columbia: University of South Carolina Press, 1970.

Waxman, Wayne. *Kant and the Empiricists: Understanding Understanding.* Oxford: Clarendon Press, 2005.

Wilson, Margaret Dauler. *Ideas and Mechanism: Essays in Modern Philosophy*. Princeton: Princeton University Press, 1999.

Woolhouse, Roger. *The Empiricists*. A History of Western Philosophy, volume 5. New York: Oxford University Press, 1988.

Yolton, John W. *Perceptual Acquaintance from Descartes to Reid.* Minneapolis: University of Minnesota Press, 1984.

———. *Realism and Appearances: An Essay in Ontology.* Cambridge: Cambridge University Press, 2000.

F. Selected works in languages other than english

Berlioz, Dominique. *Berkeley: un nominalisme réaliste.* Paris: Vrin, 2000.

———, ed. *Berkeley: langage de la perception et art de voir.* Paris: Presses universitaires de France, 2003.

Bouveresse-Quillot, Renée, ed. *Berkeley.* Dijon: Centre Gaston Bachelard, 2000.

Breidert, Wolfgang. *George Berkeley, 1685–1753.* Vita Mathematica, no. 4. Basel: Birkäuser, 1989.

Brykman, Geneviève. *Berkeley: philosophie et apologétique.* 2 vols. Paris: Vrin, 1984.

———. *Berkeley et le voile de mots.* Paris: J. Vrin, 1993.

Charles, Sébastien, ed. *Épistémologie et science selon Berkeley.* Québec: Presses de l'Université Laval, 2004.

Glauser, Richard. *Berkeley et les philosophes du XVIIe siècle: perception et scepticisme.* Sprimont, Belgium: Mardaga, 1999.

Gueroult, Martial. *Berkeley: Quatre études sur la perception et sur Dieu.* Aubier: Éditions Montaigne, 1956.

Leroy, André-Louis. *George Berkeley.* Paris: Presses universitaires de France, 1959.

Metz, Rudolf. *George Berkeley, Leben and Lehre.* Stuttgart: Fr. Frommanns (H. Kurtz), 1925.

Parigi, Silvia. *Il mondo visibile: George Berkeley e la 'perspectiva.'* Firenze: L. S. Olschki, 1995.

Robles, José Antonio. *Estudios Berkeleyanos.* Mexico City: Universidad Nacional Autónoma de México, 1990.

Rossi, Mario M. *Introduzione a Berkeley.* Bari: Laterza, 1970. 2nd edition. Bari: Laterza, 1986.

———. *Saggio su Berkeley.* Bari: Laterza, 1955.

G. Collections of essays on Berkeley

Berman, David, ed. *George Berkeley: Essays and Replies.* Dublin: Irish Academic Press, 1985. A reprint of *Hermathena* 139 (1985): 1–171.

British Journal for the Philosophy of Science 4, no. 13 (1953). Reprinted as *George Berkeley Bicententary.* Ed. A. C. Crombie. New York: Garland, 1988.

Creery, Walter E., ed. *George Berkeley: Critical Assessments*. 3 vols. London: Routledge, 1991.

Engle, Gale W., and Gabriele Taylor, eds. *Berkeley's* Principles of Human Knowledge: *Critical Studies*. Belmont, CA: Wadsworth, 1968.

Foster, John, and Howard Robinson, eds. *Essays on Berkeley: A Tercentennial Celebration*. Oxford: Clarendon Press, 1985.

Hermathena, no. 82 (1953). *Homage to George Berkeley (1685–1753).*

Hermathena, no. 139 (1985). *George Berkeley: Essays and Replies*. Reprinted as *George Berkeley: Essays and Replies*. Ed. David Berman. Dublin: Irish Academic Press, 1986.

History of European Ideas 7, no. 6 (1986). *George Berkeley 1685: 1985*. Ed. Geneviève Brykman.

Martin, C. B., and David Armstrong, eds. *Locke and Berkeley: A Collection of Critical Essays*. Garden City, NY: Doubleday, 1968. Contents on Berkeley rep. as *Berkeley: A Collection of Critical Essays*. Ed. C. B. Martin and David Armstrong. New York: Garland, 1988.

Muehlmann, Robert G., ed. *Berkeley's Metaphysics: Structural, Interpretive, and Critical Essays*. University Park, PA: Pennsylvania State University Press, 1995.

Pepper, S. C., Karl Aschenbrenner, and Benson Mates, eds. *George Berkeley; Lectures Delivered before the Philosophical Union of the University of California in Honor of the Two Hundredth Anniversary of the Death of George Berkeley, Bishop of Cloyne (1685–1753).* Berkeley: University of California Press, 1957.

Revue internationale de philosophie 7, no. 23–4 (1953).

Revue internationale de philosophie, no. 154 (1985). *Berkeley 1685–1985.*

Sosa, Ernest, ed. *Essays on the Philosophy of George Berkeley*. Dordrecht: Reidel, 1987.

Steinkraus, Warren, ed. *New Studies in Berkeley's Philosophy*. New York: Holt, Rinehart and Winston, 1966. Reprinted, with updated bibliography, Washington, DC: University Press of America, 1981.

Turbayne, Colin M., ed. *Berkeley: Critical and Interpretive Essays*. Minneapolis: University of Minnesota Press, 1982.

———. *A Treatise Concerning the Principles of Human Knowledge/George Berkeley, with Critical Essays*. Indianapolis: Bobbs-Merrill, 1970.

H. Essays relating to immaterialism

Adams, Robert M. "Berkeley and Epistemology." In E. Sosa, ed. (see II.G., *Collections of essays*).

Airaksinen, Timo. "Berkeley and the Justification of Beliefs." *Philosophy and Phenomenological Research* 48 (1987): 235–56.

Allaire, Edwin B. "Berkeley's Idealism." *Theoria* 29 (1963): 229–44.

———. "Berkeley's Idealism Revisited." In C. M. Turbayne, ed. 1982 (see II.G., *Collections of essays*).

———. "Berkeley's Idealism: Yet Another Visit." In R. G. Muehlmann, ed. (see II.G., *Collections of essays*).

Anscombe, G. E. M. "The Intentionality of Sensation." In G. E. M. Anscombe, *Metaphysics and the Philosophy of Mind*. Minneapolis: University of Minnesota Press, 1981.

Armstrong, David M. "The Heart of Berkeley's Metaphysics? A Reply to Ernest Sosa." *Hermathena* 139 (1985): 162–4.

Atherton, Margaret. "How Berkeley Can Maintain that Snow Is White." *Philosophy and Phenomenological Research* 67 (2003): 101–13.

———. "Lady Mary Shepherd's Case against George Berkeley." *British Journal for the History of Philosophy* 4 (1996): 347–66.

Ayer, A. J. "Berkeleianism and Physicalism as Constructively Critical." In *The Nature of Philosophical Inquiry*, ed. Joseph Bobik. Notre Dame: University of Notre Dame Press, 1970.

Ayers, M. R. "Berkeley on the Meaning of Existence." *History of European Ideas* 7 (1986): 567–73.

———. "Divine Ideas and Berkeley's Proof of God's Existence." In E. Sosa, ed. (see II.G., *Collections of essays*).

———. "Substance, Reality, and the Great, Dead Philosophers." *American Philosophical Quarterly* 7 (1970): 38–49.

Barnes, Winston H. F. "Did Berkeley Misunderstand Locke?" *Mind* 49 (1940): 52–7.

Baxter, Donald L. M. "Berkeley, Perception, and Identity." *Philosophy and Phenomenological Research* 51 (1991): 85–98.

Bennett, Jonathan. "Substance, Reality and Primary Qualities." *American Philosophical Quarterly* 2 (1965): 1–17.

Bouwsma, O. K. "Notes on Berkeley's Idealism." In his *Toward a New Sensibility*, ed. J. L. Craft and Ronald E. Hustwit. Lincoln: University of Nebraska Press, 1982.

Bracken, Harry M. "Berkeley and Malebranche on Ideas." *Modern Schoolman* 41 (1963): 1–15.

———. "Berkeley's Realisms." *Philosophical Quarterly* 8 (1958): 41–57.

Broad, C. D. "Berkeley's Denial of Material Substance." *Philosophical Review* 63 (1954): 155–81.

Brykman, Geneviève. "Berkeley on 'Archetype.'" In E. Sosa, ed. (see II.G., *Collections of essays*).

Burnyeat, Myles. "Idealism and Greek Philosophy: What Descartes Saw and Berkeley Missed." *Philosophical Review* 91 (1982): 3–40.

Carriero, John. "Berkeley, Resemblance, and Sensible Things." *Philosophical Topics* 31 (2003): 21–46.

Cummins, Phillip. "Berkeley's Ideas of Sense." *Nous* 9 (1975): 55–72.

———. "Berkeley's Likeness Principle." *Journal of the History of Philosophy* 4 (1966): 63–9.

———. "Berkeley's Manifest Qualities Thesis." *Journal of the History of Philosophy* 28 (1990): 385–401.

———. "Perceptual Relativity and Ideas in the Mind." *Philosophy and Phenomenological Research* 24 (1963–4): 202–14.

———. "Berkeley's Unstable Ontology." *Modern Schoolman* 67 (1989): 15–32.

Daniel, Stephen H. "Berkeley, Suarez, and the *Esse-Existere* Distinction." *American Catholic Philosophical Quarterly* 74 (2000): 621–36.

———. "Berkeley's Christian Neoplatonism, Archetypes and Divine Ideas." *Journal of the History of Philosophy* 39 (2001): 239–56.

———. "The Ramist Context of Berkeley's Philosophy." *British Journal for the History of Philosophy* 9 (2001): 487–505.

Davis, John W. "Berkeley and Phenomenalism." *Dialogue* 1 (1962): 67–80.

Dicker, Georges. "Berkeley on the Immediate Perception of Objects." In *Minds, Ideas, and Objects: Essays on the Theory of Representation in Modern Philosophy*, ed. Phillip D. Cummins and Guenter Zoeller. Atascadero, CA: Ridgeview, 1992.

———. "The Concept of Immediate Perception in Berkeley's Immaterialism." In C. M. Turbayne, ed. 1982 (see II.G., *Collections of essays*).

Doney, Willis. "Two Questions about Berkeley." *Philosophical Review* 61 (1952): 382–91.

Elugardo, Reinaldo. "An Alleged Incoherence in Berkeley's Philosophy." In *New Essays on Rationalism and Empiricism*, ed. Charles E. Jarrett, John King-Farlow, and F. J. Pelletier. *Canadian Journal of Philosophy*, Supplementary Volume 4 (1978): 177–89.

Faaborg, Robert. "Berkeley and the Argument from Microscopes." *Pacific Philosophical Quarterly* 80 (1991): 301–23.

Fleming, Noel. "Berkeley and Idealism." *Philosophy* 60 (1985): 309–25.

———. "The Tree in the Quad." *American Philosophical Quarterly* 22 (1985): 25–36.

Flage, Daniel E. "Berkeley's Epistemic Ontology: The *Principles*." *Canadian Journal of Philosophy* 34 (2004): 25–60.

———. "Berkeley, Individuation, and Physical Objects." *Individuation and Identity in Early Modern Philosophy: Descartes to Kant*, ed. Kenneth R. Barber and J. M. Gracia. Albany: State University of New York Press, 1994.

———. "Berkeley's *Principles*, Section 10." *Journal of the History of Philosophy* 41 (2003): 543–51.

Fogelin, Robert. "Hume and Berkeley on the Proofs of Infinite Divisibility." *Philosophical Review* 97 (1988): 47–69.

Furlong, E. J. "An Ambiguity in Berkeley's *Principles.*" *Philosophical Quarterly* 14 (1964): 334–44.

———. "On Being 'Embrangled' in Time." In C. M. Turbayne, ed. 1982 (see II.G., *Collections of essays*).

Gallois, André. "Berkeley's Master Argument." *Philosophical Review* 83 (1974): 55–69.

Garber, Daniel. "Something-I-Know-Not-What: Berkeley on Locke on Substance." In E. Sosa, ed. (see II.G., *Collections of essays*).

Graham, Jody. "Common Sense and Berkeley's Perception by Suggestion." *International Journal of Philosophical Studies* 5 (1997): 397–423.

Grave, S. A. "The Mind and Its Ideas: Some Problems in the Interpretation of Berkeley." *Australasian Journal of Philosophy* 42 (1964): 199–210.

Grey, Denis. "The Solipsism of Bishop Berkeley." *Philosophical Quarterly* 2 (1952): 338–49.

Greco, John. "Reid's Critique of Berkeley and Hume: What's the Big Idea?" *Philosophy and Phenomenological Research* 55 (1995): 279–96.

Harris, Stephen. "Berkeley's Argument from Perceptual Relativity." *History of Philosophy Quarterly* 14 (1997): 99–120.

Hausman, Alan. "Adhering to Inherence: A New Look at the Old Steps in Berkeley's March to Idealism." *Canadian Journal of Philosophy* 14 (1984): 421–43.

Hay, W. H. "Berkeley's Argument from Nominalism." *Revue internationale de philosophie* 7 (1953): 19–27.

Hestevold, H. S. "Berkeley's Theory of Time." *History of Philosophy Quarterly* 7 (1990): 179–92.

Immerwahr, John. "Berkeley's Causal Thesis." *New Scholasticism* 48 (1974): 153–70.

Jolley, S. Nicholas. "Berkeley, Malebranche, and Vision in God." *Journal of the History of Philosophy* 34 (1966): 535–48.

Laird, J. "Berkeley's Realism." *Mind* 25 (1916): 308–28.

Lennon, Thomas M. "Berkeley on the Act-Object Distinction." *Dialogue* 40 (2001): 651–67.

Leroy, André-Louis. "Was Berkeley an Idealist?" In W. Steinkraus (see II.G., *Collections of essays*).

Light, Marc A. "Why We Do Not See What We Feel." *Pacific Philosophical Quarterly* 83 (2002): 148–62.

Luce, A. A. "Berkeley's Existence in the Mind." *Mind* 50 (1941): 258–67.

Mabbott, J. D. "The Place of God in Berkeley's Philosophy." *Philosophy* 6 (1931): 18–29.

McCracken, Charles J. "Berkeley on the Relation of Ideas to the Mind." In *Minds, Ideas, and Objects: Essays on the Theory of Representation* in *Modern Philosophy*. ed. Phillip D. Cummins and Guenter Zoeller. Atascadero, CA: Ridgeview, 1992.

———. "What *Does* Berkeley's God See in the Quad?" *Archiv für Geschichte der Philosophie* 61 (1979): 280–92.

McKim, Robert. "Berkeley on Private Ideas and Public Objects." In *Minds, Ideas, and Objects: Essays on the Theory of Representation in Modern Philosophy*, ed. Phillip D. Cummins and Guenter Zoeller. Atascadero, CA: Ridgeview, 1992.

———. "Wenz on Abstract Ideas and Christian Neo-Platonism in Berkeley." *Journal of the History of Ideas* 43 (1982): 665–71.

———. "What *Is* God Doing in the Quad?" *Philosophy Research Archives* 13 (1987–88): 637–53.

Marc-Wogau, Konrad. "The Argument from Illusion and Berkeley's Idealism." *Theoria* 24 (1958): 94–106.

———. "Berkeley's Sensationalism and the *Esse Est Percipi* Principle." *Theoria* 23 (1957): 12–36.

Mates, Benson. "Berkeley Was Right." In S. C. Pepper et al., eds. (see II.G., *Collections of essays*).

Mill, John Stuart. "Berkeley's Life and Writings." In *The Collected Works of John Stuart Mill*, volume 11, ed. J. M. Robson. Toronto: University of Toronto Press, 1978.

Moore, G. E. "The Refutation of Idealism." In his *Philosophical Studies*. London: Routledge and Kegan Paul, 1922.

Nadler, Steven. "Berkeley's Ideas and the Primary/Secondary Quality Distinction." *Canadian Journal of Philosophy* 20 (1990): 47–61.

Oaklander, L. Nathan. "The Inherence Interpretation of Berkeley: A Critique." *Modern Schoolman* 54 (1977): 261–9.

Odegard, Douglas. "Berkeley and the Perception of Ideas." *Canadian Journal of Philosophy* 1 (1971): 155–71.

Ott, Walter, and Marc Light. "The New Berkeley." *Canadian Journal of Philosophy* 34 (2004): 1–24.

Pappas, George. "Adversary Metaphysics." *Philosophy Research Archives* 9 (1983): 571–85.

———. "Berkeley and Immediate Perception." In E. Sosa, ed. (see II.G., *Collections of essays*).

———. "Berkeley, Perception, and Common Sense." In C. M. Turbayne, ed. 1982 (see II.G., *Collections of essays*).

———. "Ideas, Minds and Berkeley." *American Philosophical Quarterly* 17 (1980): 181–94.

Park, Désirée. "Prior and Williams on Berkeley." *Philosophy* 56 (1981): 231–41.

Patey, Douglas. "Johnson's Refutation of Berkeley: Kicking the Stone Again." *Journal of the History of Ideas* 47 (1986): 139–45.

Peacocke, Christopher. "Imagination, Experience and Possibility: A Berkeleian View Defended." In J. Foster and H. Robinson, eds. (see II.G., *Collections of essays*).

Peirce, Charles S. Review of A. C. Fraser, *The Works of George Berkeley*. In *Writings of Charles S. Peirce*, volume 2, ed. Edward C. Moore. Bloomington: Indiana University Press, 1984.

Pitcher, George. "Berkeley and the Perception of Objects." *Journal of the History of Philosophy* 24 (1986): 99–105.

Popkin, Richard H. "Berkeley and Pyrrhonism." *Review of Metaphysics* 5 (1951–2): 223–46.

———. "The New Realism of Bishop Berkeley." In S. C. Pepper et al., eds. (see II.G., *Collections of essays*).

Preist, Graham. "The Limits of Conception." In his *Beyond the Limits of Thought*. 2nd edition. Oxford: Oxford University Press, 2002.

Prior, A. N. "Berkeley in Logical Form." *Theoria* 21 (1955): 117–22.

Raynor, David. "Berkeley's Ontology." *Dialogue* 26 (1987): 611–20.

Ritchie, A. D. *George Berkeley's* Siris: *The Philosophy of the Great Chain of Being and the Alchemical Theory*. London: British Academy, 1954.

Robles, José. "Berkeley: Scepticism, Matter and Infinite Divisibility." In *Scepticism in the History of Philosophy: A Pan-American Dialogue*, ed. Richard H. Popkin. Dordrecht: Kluwer, 1996.

Saporiti, Katia. "Berkeley's Perceptual Realism." In *Perception and Reality: From Descartes to the Present*, ed. Ralph Schumacher. Paderborn: Mentis, 2004.

Sellars, Wilfrid. "Berkeley and Descartes: Reflections on the Theory of Ideas." In *Studies in Perception*, ed. Peter K. Machamer and Robert G. Turnbull. Columbus: Ohio State University Press, 1977.

Silver, Bruce. "Boswell on Johnson's Refutation of Berkeley: Revisiting the Stone." *Journal of the History of Ideas* 54 (1993): 437–48.

Smith, A. D. "Berkeley's Central Argument Against Material Substance." In J. Foster and H. Robinson, eds. (see II.G., *Collections of essays*).

Stewart, Dugald. "On the Idealism of Berkeley." In his *Philosophical Essays*, ed. Sir William Hamilton. *The Collected Works of Dugald Stewart*, volume 5. Edinburgh: T. and T. Clark, 1877.

Stroud, Barry. "Berkeley *v.* Locke on Primary Qualities." *Philosophy* 55 (1980): 149–66.

Taylor, C. C. W. "Berkeley on Archetypes." *Archiv für Geschichte der Philosophie* 67 (1985): 65–79.

Thomas, George H. "Berkeley's God Does Not Perceive." *Journal of the History of Philosophy* 14 (1976): 163–8.

Thomson, James. "Berkeley." In *A Critical History of Western Philosophy*, ed. D. J. O'Connor. New York: Free Press, 1964.

Tipton, Ian. "Berkeley's Imagination." In E. Sosa, ed. (see II.G., *Collections of essays*).

———. "Descartes' Demon and Berkeley's World." *Philosophical Investigations* 15 (1992): 111–30.

———. "'Ideas' in Berkeley and Arnauld." *History of European Ideas* 7 (1986): 575–84.

Turbayne, Colin M. "Lending a Hand to Hylas: The Berkeley, Plato, Aristotle Connection." In C. M. Turbayne, ed. 1982 (see II.G., *Collections of essays*).

Van Iten, Richard J. "Berkeley's Alleged Solipsism." *Revue internationale de philosophie* 16 (1962): 447–52.

Watson, Richard. "Berkeley in a Cartesian Context." *Revue internationale de philosophie* 17 (1963): 381–94.

Wenz, Peter. "Berkeley's Christian Neo-Platonism." *Journal of the History of Ideas* 37 (1976): 537–46.

———. "Berkeley's Two Concepts of Impossibility: A Reply to McKim." *Journal of the History of Ideas* 43 (1982): 673–80.

Williams, Bernard. "Imagination and the Self." In his *Problems of the Self*. Cambridge: Cambridge University Press, 1973.

Wilson, Fred. "Berkeley's Metaphysics and Ramist Logic." In *Logic and the Workings of the Mind*, ed. Patricia A. Easton. Atascadero, CA: Ridgeview, 1997.

Wilson, Margaret Dauler. "Berkeley on the Mind-Dependence of Colors." *Pacific Philosophical Quarterly* 68 (1987): 249–64.

———. "Did Berkeley Completely Misunderstand the Basis of the Primary-Secondary Quality Distinction in Locke?" In C. M. Turbayne, ed. 1982 (see II.G., *Collections of essays*).

Winkler, Kenneth P. "Berkeley, Pyrrhonism, and the *Theaetetus*." In *Pyrrhonian Skepticism*, ed. Walter Sinnott-Armstrong. New York: Oxford University Press, 2004.

———. "Ideas, Sentiments, and Qualities." In *Minds, Ideas, and Objects: Essays on the Theory of Representation in Modern Philosophy*, ed. Phillip D. Cummins and Guenter Zoeller. Atascadero, CA: Ridgeview, 1992.

Yandell, David. "Berkeley on Common Sense and the Privacy of Ideas." *History of Philosophy Quarterly* 12 (1995): 411–23.

I. Studies of selected topics

1. Berkeley's notebooks

Aaron, Richard I. "Locke and Berkeley's Commonplace Book." *Mind* 40 (1931): 439–59.

Belfrage, Bertil. "The Order and Dating of Berkeley's *Notebooks*." *Revue Internationale de Philosophie* 154 (1985): 196–214.

———. "A New Appoach to Berkeley's *Philosophical Notebooks*." In E. Sosa, ed. (see II.G., *Collections of essays*).

———. "The Clash on Semantics in Berkeley's Notebook A." *Hermathena* 139 (1985): 117–26.

———. "A Response to M. A. Stewart's 'Berkeley's Introduction Draft'." *Berkeley Newsletter* 12 (1991–92): 1–10.

Luce, A. A. "Another Look at Berkeley's Notebooks." *Hermathena* 110 (1970): 5–23.

———. "Development within Berkeley's Commonplace Book." *Mind* 49 (1940): 42–51.

McKim, Robert. "The Entries in Berkeley's Notebooks: A Reply to Bertil Belfrage." *Hermathena* 139 (1985): 156–61.

Stewart, M. A. "Add. MS 39305." *Berkeley Newsletter* 9 (1986): 6–11.

———. "Berkeley's Introduction Draft." *Berkeley Newsletter* 11 (1989–90): 1–10.

2. Theory of vision

Abbott, Thomas. *Sight and Touch: An Attempt to Disprove the Received (or Berkeleian) Theory of Vision*. London: Longman, Roberts and Green, 1864.

Armstrong, D. M. "Discussion: Berkeley's New Theory of Vision." *Journal of the History of Ideas* 17 (1956): 127–9.

———. *Berkeley's Theory of Vision: A Critical Examination of Bishop Berkeley's Essay Towards a New Theory of Vision.* Parkeville: Melbourne University Press, 1960. Reprinted, New York: Garland, 1988.

Arsić, Branka. *The Passive Eye: Gaze and Subjectivity in Berkeley (via Beckett)*. Stanford: Stanford University Press, 2003.

Atherton, Margaret. *Berkeley's Revolution in Vision*. Ithaca: Cornell University Press, 1990.

Bailey, Samuel. *A Review of Berkeley's Theory of Vision, Designed to Show the Unsoundness of That Celebrated Speculation*. London: James Ridgway, 1842.

Belfrage, Bertil. "The Constructivism of Berkeley's *New Theory of Vision*." In *Minds, Ideas and Objects*, ed. Philip D. Cummins and Guenter Zoeller. Atascadero, CA: Ridgeview, 1992.

Berchielli, Laura. "Color, Space, and Figure in Locke: An Interpretation of the Molyneux Problem." *Journal of the History of Philosophy* 40 (2002): 47–65.

Berman, David. "Berkeley and the Moon Illusions." *Revue internationale de philosophie* 154 (1985): 215–22.

Brandt, Reinhard. "Historical Obervations on the Genesis of the Three-Dimensional Optical Picture." *Ratio* 17 (1975): 176–90.

Brook, Richard J. "Berkeley's Theory of Vision: Transparency and Signification." *British Journal for the History of Philosophy* 11 (2003): 691–9.

Condillac, Etienne Bonnot de. *Essay on the Origin of Human Knowledge*. Translated by Hans Aarsleff. Cambridge: Cambridge University Press, 2001.

Cummins, Phillip D. "On the Status of Visuals in Berkeley's *New Theory of Vision*." In C. M. Turbayne, ed. 1982 (see II.G., *Collections of essays*).

Davis, John W. "The Molyneux Problem." *Journal of the History of Ideas* 21 (1960): 392–408.

Donagan, Alan. "Berkeley's Theory of the Immediate Objects of Vision." In *Studies in Perception*, ed. Peter Machamer and Robert Turnbull. Columbus: Ohio State University Press, 1978.

Falkenstein, Lorne. "Intuition and Construction in Berkeley's Account of Visual Space." *Journal of the History of Philosophy* 32 (1994): 63–84.

———. "Reid's Critique of Berkeley's Position on the Inverted Image." *Reid Studies* 4 (2000): 35–51.

Ferrier, James F. "Berkeley and Idealism." *Blackwood's Magazine* 51 (1842): 812–30.

Graham, Elsie C. *Optics and Vision: The Background of the Metaphysics of Berkeley*. New York: Columbia University Press, 1929.

Gregory, Richard L. "Blindness, Recovery from." In *The Oxford Companion to the Mind*, ed. Richard L. Gregory. Oxford: Oxford University Press, 1987.

Hara, Akira. "Depth and Distance in Berkeley's Theory of Vision." *History of Philosophy Quarterly* 21 (2004): 101–17

Mill, John Stuart. "Bailey on Berkeley's Theory of Vision." In *Collected Works of John Stuart Mill*, volume 11, ed. J. M. Robson. Toronto: University of Toronto Press, 1978.

Pappas, George. "Abstract Ideas and the New Theory of Vision." *British Journal for the History of Philosophy* 10 (2002): 55–70.

Pitcher, George, ed. *Berkeley on Vision: A Nineteenth-Century Debate*. New York: Garland, 1988.

Raynor, David. "'*Minima Sensibilia*' in Berkeley and Hume." *Dialogue* 19 (1980): 196–200.

Sacks, Oliver. "To See and Not See." In Oliver Sacks, *An Anthropologist on Mars: Seven Paradoxical Tales*. New York: Knopf, 1995.

Schwartz, Robert. *Vision: Variations on Some Berkeleian Themes*. Oxford: Blackwell, 1994.

Smith. A. D. "Space and Sight." *Mind* 109 (2000): 487–518.

Smith, Adam. "Of the External Senses." In *Essays on Philosophical Subjects*, ed. W. P. D. Wightman, J. C. Bryce, and I. S. Ross. Oxford: Clarendon Press, 1980. See the section entitled "Of the Sense of Seeing."

Thrane, Gary. "Berkeley's Proper Objects of Vision." *Journal of the History of Ideas* 37 (1977): 243–60.

Turbayne, Colin M. "Berkeley and Molyneux on Retinal Images." *Journal of the History of Ideas* 16 (1955): 339–55.

Vesey, G. N. A. "Berkeley and the Man Born Blind." *Proceedings of the Aristotelian Society* 61 (1960–1): 189–206.

Voltaire. *The Elements of Sir Isaac Newton's Philosophy.* London: S. Austen, 1738. Reprinted, London: Cass, 1967. See in particular chapters 5 and 6.

von Senden, Marius. *Space and Sight.* Translated by Peter Heath. Glencoe, IL: Free Press, 1960.

Wilson, Margaret Dauler. "The Issue of 'Common Sensibles' in Berkeley's *New Theory of Vision.*" In M. D. Wilson, *Ideas and Mechanism* (see II.E., *Other books relating to immaterialism*).

Yaffe, Gideon. "Berkeley and the 'Mighty Difficulty': The Idealist Lesson of the Inverted Retinal Image." *Philosophical Topics* 31 (2003): 485–510.

3. The doctrine of signs (including abstract ideas)

Armstrong, R. L. "Berkeley's Theory of Signification." *Journal of the History of Philosophy* 7 (1969): 163–76.

Atherton, Margaret. "Berkeley's Anti-Abstractionism." In E. Sosa, ed. (see II.G., *Collections of essays*).

Baxter, Donald L. M. "Abstraction, Inseparability, and Identity." *Philosophy and Phenomenological Research* 57 (1997): 307–30.

Beal, Melvin W. "Berkeley's Linguistic Criterion." *Personalist* 52 (1971): 499–514.

Beardsley, Monroe C. "Berkeley on 'Abstract Ideas.'" *Mind* 52 (1943): 157–70.

Benschop, Hans-Peter. "Berkeley, Lee and Abstract Ideas." *British Journal for the History of Philosophy* 5 (1997): 55–66.

Belfrage, Bertil. "Berkeley's Theory of Emotive Meaning (1708)." *History of European Ideas* 7 (1986): 643–9.

———. "Development of Berkeley's Early Theory of Meaning." *Revue philosophique de la France et de l'etranger* 176 (1986): 319–30.

Berman, David. "Berkeley's Semantic Revolution: 19 November 1707–11 January 1708." *History of European Ideas* 7 (1986): 603–7.

Bolton, Martha Brandt. "Berkeley's Objection to Abstract Ideas and Unconceived Objects." In E. Sosa, ed. (see II.G., *Collections of essays*).

Cornman, James W. "Theoretical Terms, Berkeleian Notions, and Minds." In C. M. Turbayne, ed. 1970 (see II.G., *Collections of essays*).

Craig, E. J. "Berkeley's Attack on Abstract Ideas." *Philosophical Review* 77 (1968): 425–37.

Doney, Willis. "Berkeley's Argument Against Abstract Ideas." *Midwest Studies in Philosophy* 8 (1983): 295–308.

———, ed. *Berkeley on Abstraction and Abstract Ideas*. New York: Garland, 1989.

Drebushenko, David. "Abstraction and a New Argument for the *Esse* is *Percipi* Thesis." *Hermathena* 167 (1999): 35–58.

Flage, Daniel E. *Berkeley's Doctrine of Notions: A Reconstruction Based on His Theory of Meaning*. London: Croom Helm, 1987.

———. "Relative Ideas and Notions." In *Minds, Ideas, and Objects: Essays on the Theory of Representation in Modern Philosophy*, ed. Phillip D. Cummins and Guenter Zoeller. Atascadero, CA: Ridgeview, 1992.

Flew, Antony. "Was Berkeley a Precursor of Wittgenstein?" In *Hume and the Enlightenment: Essays Presented to Ernest Campbell Mossner*, ed. W. B. Todd. Edinburgh: Edinburgh University Press, 1974.

Friedman, Lesley. "Pragmatism: The Unformulated Method of Bishop Berkeley." *Journal of the History of Philosophy* 41 (2003): 81–96.

Glouberman, Mark. "Berkeley's Anti-Abstractionism." *British Journal for the History of Philosophy* 2 (1994): 145–63.

Hacking, Ian. *Why Does Language Matter to Philosophy?* Cambridge: Cambridge University Press, 1975.

Jakapi, Roomet. "Emotive Meaning and Christian Mysteries in Berkeley's *Alciphron*." *British Journal for the History of Philosophy* 10 (2002): 401–11.

———. "Entry 720 of Berkeley's *Philosophical Commentaries* and 'Non-Cognitive' Propositions in Scripture." *Archiv für Geschichte der Philosophie* 85 (2003): 86–90.

Land, S. K. "Berkeleyan Linguistics." *Linguistics* 213 (1978): 5–28.

Lee, R. N. "What Berkeley's Notions Are." *Idealistic Studies* 20 (1990): 19–41.

Lennon, Thomas M. "Berkeley and the Ineffable." *Synthese* 75 (1988): 231–50.

McGowan, William. "Berkeley's Doctrine of Signs." In C. M. Turbayne, ed. 1982 (see II.G., *Collections of essays*).

McKim, Robert. "Abstraction and Immaterialism: Recent Interpretations." *Berkeley Newsletter* 15 (1997–98): 1–13.

Ott, Walter R. *Locke's Philosophy of Language*. Cambridge: Cambridge University Press, 2004.

Pappas, George. "Abstraction and Existence." *History of Philosophy Quarterly* 19 (2002): 43–63.

Taylor, C. C. W. "Berkeley's Theory of Abstract Ideas." *Philosophical Quarterly* 28 (1978): 97–115.

Turbayne, Colin M. "Berkeley's Metaphysical Grammar." In C. M. Turbayne, ed. 1970 (see II.G., *Collections of essays*).

———. *The Myth of Metaphor*. New Haven: Yale University Press, 1962. Revised edition. Columbia: University of South Carolina Press, 1970.

Van Steenburgh, E. W. "Berkeley Revisited." *Journal of Philosophy* 60 (1963): 85–9.

Weinberg, Julius. "The Nominalism of Berkeley and Hume." In his *Abstraction, Relation, and Induction*. Madison: University of Wisconsin Press, 1965.

Williford, Kenneth. "Berkeley's Theory of Operative Language in the *Manuscript Introduction*." *British Journal of the History of Philosophy* 11 (2003): 271–301.

Winkler, Kenneth P. "Berkeley on Abstract Ideas." *Archiv für Geschichte der Philosophie* 65 (1983): 63–80.

Woozley, A. D. "Berkeley's Doctrine of Notions and Theory of Meaning." *Journal of the History of Philosophy* 14 (1976): 427–34.

4. Philosophy of mind and agency

Adams, Robert. "Berkeley's 'Notion' of Spiritual Substance." *Archiv für Geschichte der Philosophie* 55 (1973): 47–69.

Atherton, Margaret. "The Coherence of Berkeley's Theory of Mind." *Philosophy and Phenomenological Research* 43 (1983): 389–99.

Ayers, M. R. "Perception and Action." In *Knowledge and Necessity*, ed. G. N. A. Vesey. London: Macmillan, 1970.

Baier, Annette C. "The Intentionality of Intentions." *Review of Metaphysics* 30 (1977): 389–414.

Beardsley, William. "Berkeley on Spirit and Its Unity." *History of Philosophy Quarterly* 18 (2001): 259–77.

Cummins, Phillip. "Hylas' Parity Argument." In C. M. Turbayne, ed. 1982 (see II.G., *Collections of essays*).

Davis. John W. "Berkeley's Doctrine of the Notion." *Review of Metaphysics* 12 (1959): 378–89.

Doney, Willis. "Is Berkeley's a Cartesian Mind?" In C. M. Turbayne, ed. 1982 (see II.G., *Collections of essays*).

Jolley, Nicholas. "Malebranche and Berkeley on Causality and Volition." In *Central Themes in Early Modern Philosophy: Essays Presented to Jonathan Bennett*, ed. J. A. Cover and Mark Kulstad. Indianapolis: Hackett, 1990.

Lloyd, A. C. "The Self in Berkeley's Philosophy." In J. Foster and H. Robinson, eds. (see II.G., *Collections of essays*).

McCracken, Charles J., "Berkeley's Notion of Spirit." *History of European Ideas* 7 (1986): 597–602.

———. "Berkeley's Cartesian Conception of Mind." *Monist* 71 (1988): 596–611.

McKim, Robert. "Berkeley's Active Mind." *Archiv für Geschichte der Philosophie* 71 (1989): 335–43.

———. "Berkeley on Human Agency." *History of Philosophy Quarterly* 2 (1984): 181–94.

Pitcher, George. "Berkeley on the Mind's Activity." *American Philosophical Quarterly* 18 (1981): 221–7.

Taylor, C. C. W. "Action and Inaction in Berkeley." In J. Foster and H. Robinson, eds. (see II.G., *Collections of essays*).

Tipton. Ian C. "Berkeley's View of Spirit." In W. Steinkraus, ed. (see II.G., *Collections of essays*).

Turbayne. Colin M. "Berkeley's Two Concepts of Mind." *Philosophy and Phenomenological Research* 20 (1959): 85–92.

Woozley, A. D. "Berkeley on Action." *Philosophy* 60 (1985): 293–307.

5. Philosophy of science

Ardley, Gavin W. R. *Berkeley's Philosophy of Nature*. Auckland: University of Auckland, 1962.

Asher, Warren O. "Berkeley on Absolute Motion." *History of Philosophy Quarterly* 4 (1987): 447–66.

Atherton, Margaret. "Corpuscles, Mechanism and Essentialism in Berkeley and Locke." *Journal of the History of Philosophy* 29 (1991): 47–67.

Brook, Richard J. "Berkeley, Causality, and Signification." *International Studies in Philosophy* 27 (1995): 15–31.

———. *Berkeley's Philosophy of Science*. The Hague: Martinus Nijhoff, 1973.

Buchdahl, Gerd. *Metaphysics and the Philosophy of Science. The Classical Origins: Descartes to Kant*. Cambridge, MA: MIT Press, 1969.

Davidson, Arnold I., and Norbert Hornstein. "The Primary/Secondary Quality Distinction: Berkeley, Locke, and the Foundations of Corpuscularian Science." *Dialogue* 23 (1984): 281–303.

Downing, Lisa. "Berkeley's Case Against Realism About Dynamics." In R. G. Muehlmann, ed. (see II.G., *Collections of essays*).

———. "*Siris* and the Scope of Berkeley's Instrumentalism." *British Journal for the History of Philosophy* 3 (1995): 279–300.

Garber, Daniel. "Locke, Berkeley, and Corpuscular Scepticism." In C. M. Turbayne, ed. 1982 (see II.G., *Collections of essays*).

Hinrichs, Gerard. "The Logical Positivism of Berkeley's *De Motu*." *Review of Metaphysics* 3 (1950): 491–505.

Hughes, M. "Newton, Hermes and Berkeley." *British Journal for the Philosophy of Science* 43 (1992): 1–19.

Jessop, T. E. "Berkeley and the Contemporary Physics." *Revue internationale de philosophie* 7 (1953): 101–33.

———. "Berkeley's Philosophy of Science." *Hermathena* 97 (1963): 23–35.

Maull, Nancy L. "Berkeley on the Limits of Mechanistic Explanation." In C. M. Turbayne, ed. 1982 (see II.G., *Collections of essays*).

Mirarchi, Lawrence A. "Force and Absolute Motion in Berkeley's Philosophy of Physics." *Journal of the History of Ideas* (1977): 705–13.

Moked, Gabriel. *Particles and Ideas: Bishop Berkeley's Corpuscularian Philosophy*. Oxford: Clarendon Press, 1988.

Myhill, John. "Berkeley's *De Motu* – An Anticipation of Mach." In S. C. Pepper, et al., eds. (see II.G., *Collections of essays*).

Newton-Smith, W. H. "Berkeley's Philosophy of Science." In J. Foster and H. Robinson, eds. (see II.G., *Collections of essays*).

Pappas, George S. "Science and Metaphysics in Berkeley." *International Studies in the Philosophy of Science* 2 (1987): 105–14.

Popper, Karl. "Berkeley as Precursor of Mach and Einstein." *British Journal for the Philosophy of Science* 4 (1953): 26–36.

Silver, Bruce. "Berkeley and the Principle of Inertia." *Journal of the History of Ideas* 34 (1973): 599–608.

Suchting, W. A. "Berkeley's Criticism of Newton on Space and Time." *Isis* 58 (1967): 186–97.

Tipton, Ian C. "The 'Philosopher by Fire' in Berkeley's *Alciphron*." In C. M. Turbayne, ed. 1982 (see II.G.,*Collections of essays*).

Urmson, J. O. "Berkeley's Philosophy of Science in the *Siris*." *History of European Ideas* 7 (1986): 563–6.

Wilson, Margaret. "Berkeley and the Essences of the Corpuscularians." In J. Foster and H. Robinson, eds. (see II.G., *Collections of essays*).

Whitrow, G. J. "Berkeley's Critique of the Newtonian Analysis of Motion." *Hermathena* 82 (1953): 90–112.

———. "Berkeley's Philosophy of Motion." *British Journal for the Philosophy of Science* 4 (1953): 37–45.

Winkler, Kenneth P. "Berkeley, Newton, and the Stars." *Studies in History and Philosophy of Science* 17 (1986): 23–42.

6. Philosophy of mathematics

Baum, Robert J. "The Instrumentalist and Formalist Elements of Berkeley's Philosophy of Mathematics." *Studies in History and Philosophy of Science* 3 (1972): 119–35.

Cajori, Florian. "Discussion of Fluxions from Berkeley to Woodhouse." *American Mathematical Monthly* 24 (1917): 145–54.

———. *A History of the Conceptions of Limits and Fluxions from Berkeley to Woodhouse*. Chicago and London: Open Court, 1919.

Cantor, Geoffrey. "Berkeley's *The Analyst* Revisited." *Isis* 75 (1984): 668–83.
Grattan-Guinness, I. "Berkeley's Criticism of the Calculus as a Study in the Theory of Limits." *Janus* 56 (1969): 215–27.
Jesseph, Douglas M. *Berkeley's Philosophy of Mathematics*. Chicago: University of Chicago Press, 1993.
Levy, David M. "Bishop Berkeley Exorcises the Infinite: Fuzzy Consequences of Strict Finitism." *Hume Studies* 18 (1992): 511–36.
Pycior, Helena. "Mathematics and Philosophy: Wallis, Hobbes, Barrow, and Berkeley." *Journal of the History of Ideas* 48 (1987): 265–86.
Reid, Jasper. "Faith, Fluxions and Impossible Numbers in Berkeley's Writings of the Early 1730s." *Modern Schoolman* 80 (2002): 1–22.
Sherry, David. "The Wake of Berkeley's *Analyst*: Rigor Mathematicae?" *Studies in History and Philosophy of Science* 18 (1987): 455–80.
———. "Don't Take Me Half the Way: Berkeley on Mathematical Reasoning." *Studies in History and Philosophy of Science* 24 (1993): 207–22.
Strong, Edward W. "Mathematical Reasoning and Its Objects." In S. C. Pepper, et al., eds. (see II.G., *Collections of essays*).
Szabo, Zoltan. "Berkeley's Triangle." *History of Philosophy Quarterly* 12 (1995): 41–63.
Wisdom, J. O. "The *Analyst* Controversy: Berkeley as Mathematician." *Hermathena* 59 (1942): 111–28.
———. "Berkeley's Criticism of the Infinitesimal." *British Journal for the Philosophy of Science* 4 (1953): 22–5.

7. Economics

Caffentzis, C. George. *Exciting the Industry of Mankind: George Berkeley's Philosophy of Money*. Dordrecht: Kluwer Academic Press, 2000.
———. "Querying the Querist." *Maine Scholar* 3 (1990): 287–307.
Clark, Stephen R. L., ed. *Money, Obedience, and Affection: Essays on Berkeley's Moral and Political Thought*. New York: Garland, 1989.
Hutchison, T. W. "Berkeley's *Querist* and Its Place in the Economic Thought of the Eighteenth Century." *British Journal of the Philosophy of Science* 4 (1953–4): 52–77.
Johnston, Joseph. "Berkeley's Influence as an Economist." *Hermathena* 82 (1953): 76–89.
Kelly, Patrick. "Berkeley and Ireland." *Études Irlandaises* 11 (1986): 7–26.
———. "Ireland and the Critique of Mercantilism in Berkeley's *Querist*." *Hermathena* 139 (1985): 101–16.
———. "'Industry and Virtue versus Luxury and Corruption': Berkeley, Walpole, and the South Sea Bubble Crisis." *Eighteenth-Century Ireland* 7 (1992): 57–74

Murray, Patrick. "Money, Wealth, and Berkeley's Doctrine of Signs: A Reply to Patrick Kelly." *Hermathena* 139 (1985): 152–5.

Rashid, Salim. "Berkeley's *Querist* and Its Influence." *Journal of the History of Economic Thought* 12 (1990): 38–60.

———. "The Irish School of Economic Development: 1720–1750." *Manchester School of Economic and Social Studies* 56 (1988): 345–69.

Vickers, Douglas. *Studies in the Theory of Money, 1690–1776*. London: Peter Owen, 1960.

Ward, Ian D. S. "George Berkeley: Precursor of Keynes or Moral Economist on Underdevelopment?" *Journal of Political Economy* 67 (1959): 31–40.

8. Moral and political philosophy

Berman, David. "The Jacobitism of Berkeley's *Passive Obedience*." *Journal of the History of Ideas* 47 (1986): 309–19.

Broad, C. D. "Berkeley's Theory of Morals." *Revue internationale de philosophie* 7 (1953): 72–86.

Clark, Stephen R. L. "God-appointed Berkeley and the General Good." In J. Foster and H. Robinson, eds. (see II.G., *Collections of essays*).

———, ed. *Money, Obedience, and Affection: Essays on Berkeley's Moral and Political Thought*. New York: Garland, 1989.

Conroy, Graham P. "George Berkeley on Moral Demonstration." *Journal of the History of Ideas* 22 (1961): 205–14.

Hayry, Matti, and Hetta Hayry. "Obedience to Rules and Berkeley's Theological Utilitarianism." *Utilitas* 6 (1994): 233–42.

Johnston, G. A. "The Development of Berkeley's Ethical Theory." *Philosophical Review* 24 (1915): 419–30.

Kupfer, Joseph. "Universalization in Berkeley's Rule-Utilitarianism." *Revue internationale de philosophie* 28 (1974): 511–31.

Olscamp, Paul S. "Does Berkeley Have an Ethical Theory?" In C. M. Turbayne, ed. 1970 (see II.G., *Collections of essays*).

———. *The Moral Philosophy of George Berkeley*. The Hague: Martinus Nijhoff, 1970.

Orange, Hugh W. "Berkeley as a Moral Philosopher." *Mind* 15 (1890): 514–23.

Rivers, Isabel. *Reason, Grace, and Sentiment: A Study of the Language of Religion and Ethics in England, 1660–1780*. Volume 2, *Shaftesbury to Hume*. Cambridge: Cambridge University Press, 2000.

Robbins, Caroline. *The Eighteenth-Century Commonwealthman*. Cambridge, MA: Harvard University Press, 1959. Reprinted, Indianapolis: Liberty Fund, 2004.

Tussman, Joseph. "Berkeley as a Political Philosopher." In S. C. Pepper, et al., eds. (see II.G., *Collections of essays*).

Warnock, G. J. "On Passive Obedience." *History of European Ideas* 7 (1986): 555–62.

9. Religion

Berman, David. "Cognitive Theology and Emotive Mysteries in Berkeley's *Alciphron*." *Proceedings of the Royal Irish Academy* 81 (1981): 219–29.
Bracken, Harry M. "Berkeley on the Immortality of the Soul." *Modern Schoolman* 37 (1960): 77–94, 197–212.
Byrne, P. A. "Berkeley, Scientific Realism, and Creation." *Religious Studies* 20 (1984): 453–64.
Cates, Lynn D. "Berkeley on the Work of the Six Days." *Faith and Philosophy* 14 (1997): 82–6.
Crain, Steven D. "Must a Classical Theist Be an Immaterialist?" *Religious Studies* 33 (1997): 81–92.
Everitt, Nicholas. "Quasi-Berkeleyan Idealism as Perspicuous Theism." *Faith and Philosophy* 14 (1997): 353–77.
Hooker, Michael. "Berkeley's Argument from Design." In C. M. Turbayne, ed. 1982 (see II.G., *Collections of essays*).
Hurlbutt, Robert H. "Berkeley's Theology." In S. C. Pepper, et al., eds. (see II.G., *Collections of essays*).
Jakapi, Roomet. "Faith, Truth, Revelation and Meaning in Berkeley's Defense of the Christian Religion (in *Alciphron*)." *Modern Schoolman* 80 (2002): 23–34.
Kline, A. David. "Berkeley's Divine Language Argument." In E. Sosa, ed. (see II.G., *Collections of essays*).
Oakes, Robert A. "God and Physical Objects." *International Journal of the Philosophy of Religion* 9 (1978): 16–29.
Pittion, Jean-Paul, and David Berman, with A. A. Luce. "A New Letter by Berkeley to Browne on Divine Analogy." *Mind* 78 (1969): 375–92.
Silem, Edward A. *George Berkeley and the Proofs for the Existence of God*. London: Longmans, Green, 1957.
Spiegel, James S. "The Theological Orthodoxy of Berkeley's Immaterialism." *Faith and Philosophy* 13 (1996): 216–35.
Ramsey, I. T. "Sermon Preached at Festival Service in the Chapel of Trinity College, Dublin." *Hermathena* 82 (1953): 113–27.

10. Berkeley's influence

Ayers, M. R. "Berkeley and Hume: A Question of Influence." In *Philosophy in History*, ed. Richard Rorty, J. B. Schneewind, and Quentin Skinner. Cambridge: Cambridge University Press, 1984.

Atherton, Margaret. "Mr. Abbott and Professor Fraser: A Nineteenth-Century Debate about Berkeley's Theory of Vision." *Archiv für Geschichte der Philosophie* 85 (2003): 21–50.

Berman, David. "Berkeley's Philosophical Reception after America." *Archiv für Geschichte der Philosophie* 62 (1980): 311–20.

Bracken, Harry M. *The Early Reception of Berkeley's Immaterialism, 1710–1733.* The Hague: Martinus Nijhoff, 1959. Revised edition, The Hague: Martinus Nijhoff, 1965.

Breidert, Wolfgang. "On the Early Reception of Berkeley in Germany." In E. Sosa, ed. (see II.G., *Collection of essays*). Based on the author's "Die Rezeption Berkeleys in Deutschland im 18. Jahrhundert." *Revue internationale de philosophie* 154 (1985): 223–41.

Charles, Sébastien. *Berkeley au siècle des Lumières. Immatérialisme et scepticisme au XVIIIe siècle.* Paris: Vrin, 2003.

Charles, S., J. C. Laursen, R. H. Popkin, and A. Zakatistovs, "Hume and Berkeley in the Prussian Academy: Louis Frédéric Ancillon's 'Dialogue between Berkeley and Hume' of 1796." *Hume Studies* 27 (2001): 85–97.

Leroy, André-Louis. "Influence de la philosophie berkeleyenne sur la pensée continentale." *Hermathena* 82 (1953): 27–48.

McCracken, C. J. and I. C. Tipton, eds. *Berkeley's* Principles *and* Dialogues: *Background Source Materials.* Cambridge: Cambridge University Press, 2000.

Morrisroe, Michael, Jr. "Did Hume Read Berkeley? A Conclusive Answer." *Philological Quarterly* 52 (1973): 310–15.

Popkin, Richard. "Berkeley's Influence on American Philosophy." *Hermathena* 82 (1953): 128–46.

———. "Did Hume Ever Read Berkeley?" *Journal of Philosophy* 56 (1959): 535–45.

———. "So, Hume Did Read Berkeley." *Journal of Philosophy* 61 (1964): 773–8.

Raynor David. "Hume and Berkeley's *Three Dialogues.*" In *Studies in the Philosophy of the Scottish Enlightenment*, ed. M. A. Stewart. Oxford Studies in Modern Philosophy, vol. 1. Oxford: Clarendon Press, 1990.

Rome, S. C. "The Scottish Refutation of Berkeley's Immaterialism." *Philosophy and Phenomenological Research* (1943): 313–25.

Stäbler, Eugen. *George Berkeley's Auffassung and Wirkung in der Deutschen Philosophie bis Hegel.* Zeulenroda: B. Sporn, 1935.

Stewart, M. A. "Berkeley and the Rankenian Club." *Hermathena* 139 (1985): 25–45.

Turbayne, Colin M. "Hume's Influence on Berkeley." *Revue internationale de philosophie* 154 (1985): 259–69.

Walker, Ralph C. S. *The Real in the Ideal: Berkeley's Relation to Kant.* New York: Garland, 1989.

INDEX OF PASSAGES DISCUSSED OR CITED

For an account of the abbreviations and schemes of reference used here, see "Note on references."

INDEX OF NAMES AND SUBJECTS